Kamisama Kiss

Story & Art by

Julietta Suzuki

CHARACTERS

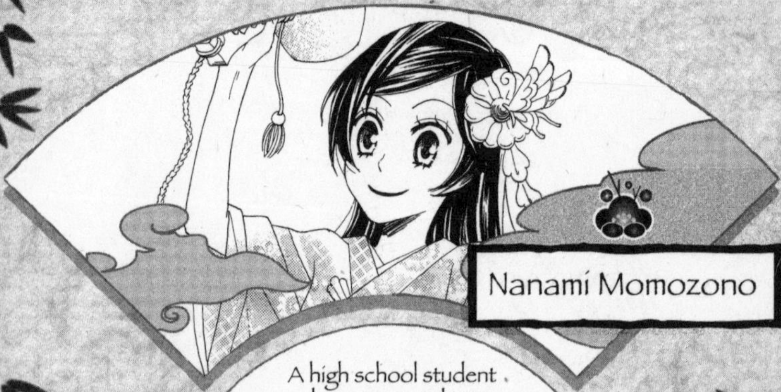

Nanami Momozono

A high school student who was turned into a kamisama by the tochigami Mikage.

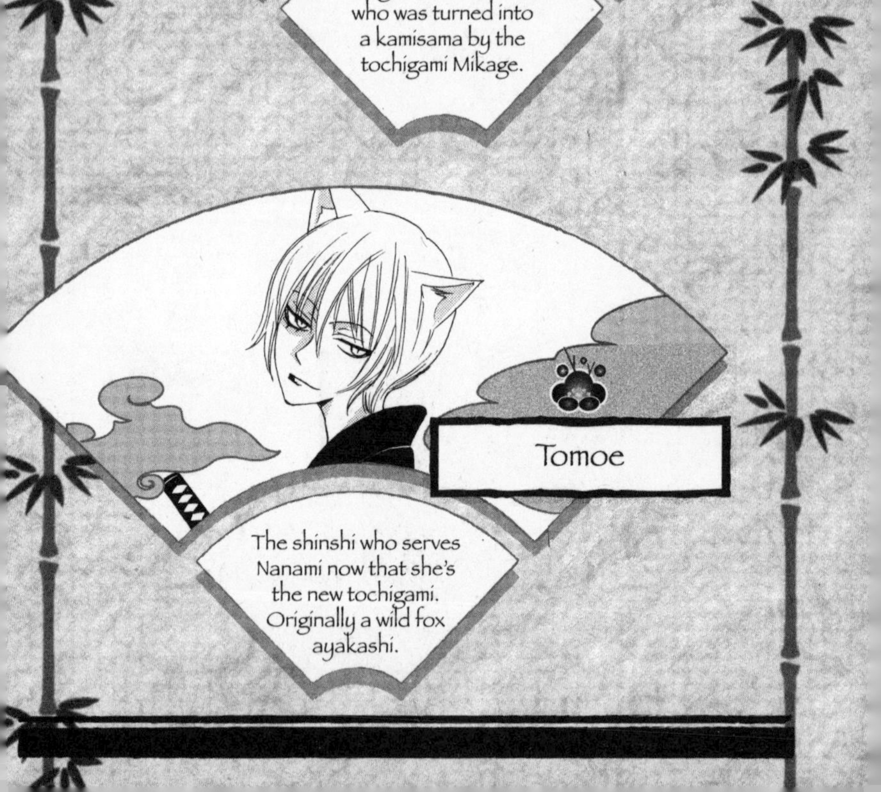

Tomoe

The shinshi who serves Nanami now that she's the new tochigami. Originally a wild fox ayakashi.

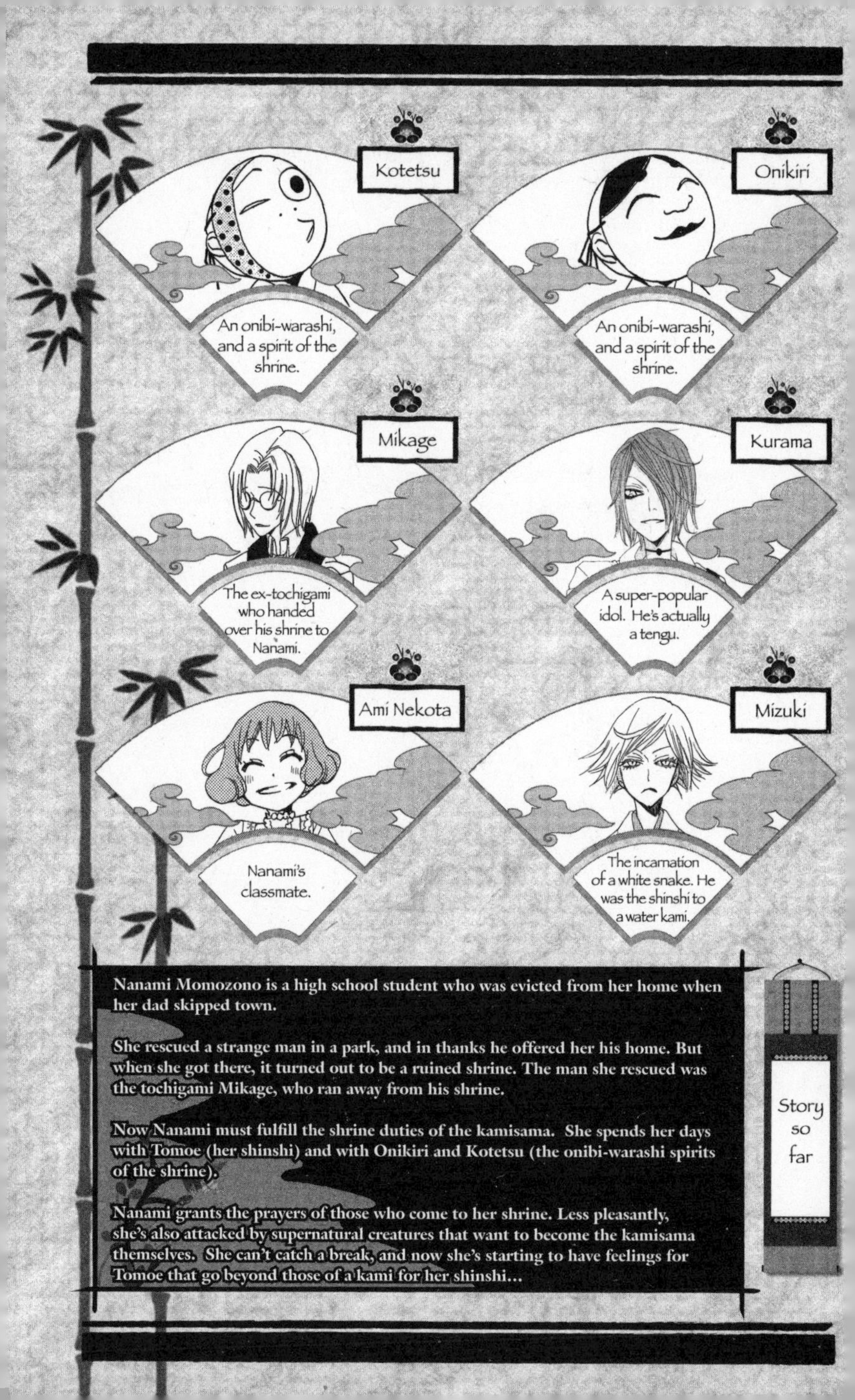
Kotetsu
An onibi-warashi, and a spirit of the shrine.
Onikiri
An onibi-warashi, and a spirit of the shrine.
Mikage
The ex-tochigami who handed over his shrine to Nanami.
Kurama
A super-popular idol. He's actually a tengu.
Ami Nekota
Nanami's classmate.
Mizuki
The incarnation of a white snake. He was the shinshi to a water kami.

Story so far

Nanami Momozono is a high school student who was evicted from her home when her dad skipped town.

She rescued a strange man in a park, and in thanks he offered her his home. But when she got there, it turned out to be a ruined shrine. The man she rescued was the tochigami Mikage, who ran away from his shrine.

Now Nanami must fulfill the shrine duties of the kamisama. She spends her days with Tomoe (her shinshi) and with Onikiri and Kotetsu (the onibi-warashi spirits of the shrine).

Nanami grants the prayers of those who come to her shrine. Less pleasantly, she's also attacked by supernatural creatures that want to become the kamisama themselves. She can't catch a break, and now she's starting to have feelings for Tomoe that go beyond those of a kami for her shinshi...

Kamisama Kiss

Volume 4
CONTENTS

Tomoe's Ennui Blog

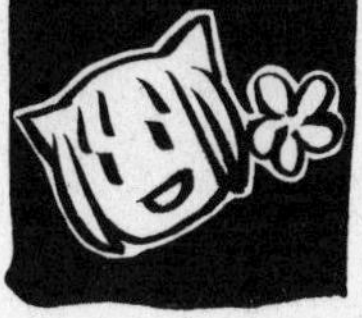

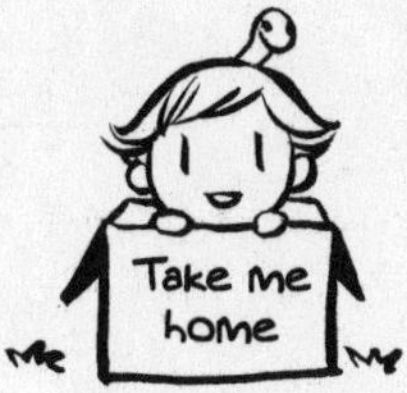
Take me home

I found a poor abandoned snake by the road.

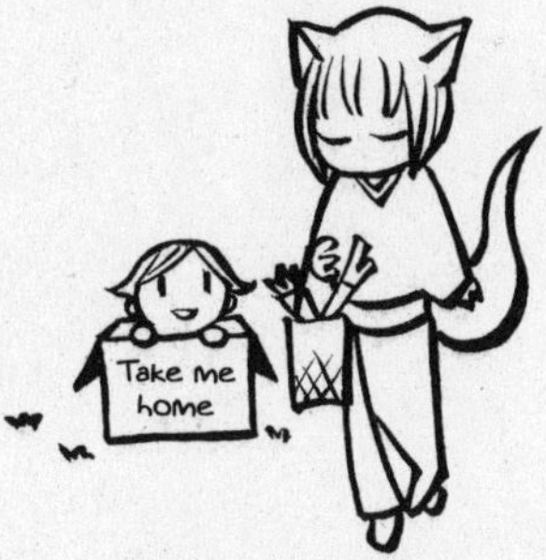
Take me home

I don't feel sorry for him, even though I may end up like him...

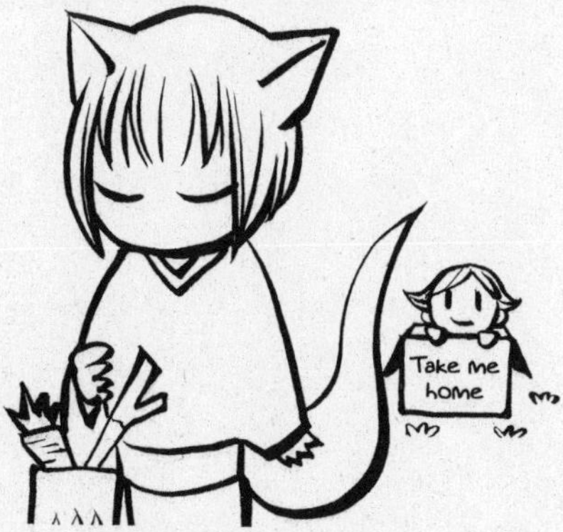
Take me home

I warn myself that it could happen to me tomorrow.
So I will work hard today.
I will make nikujaga for dinner.

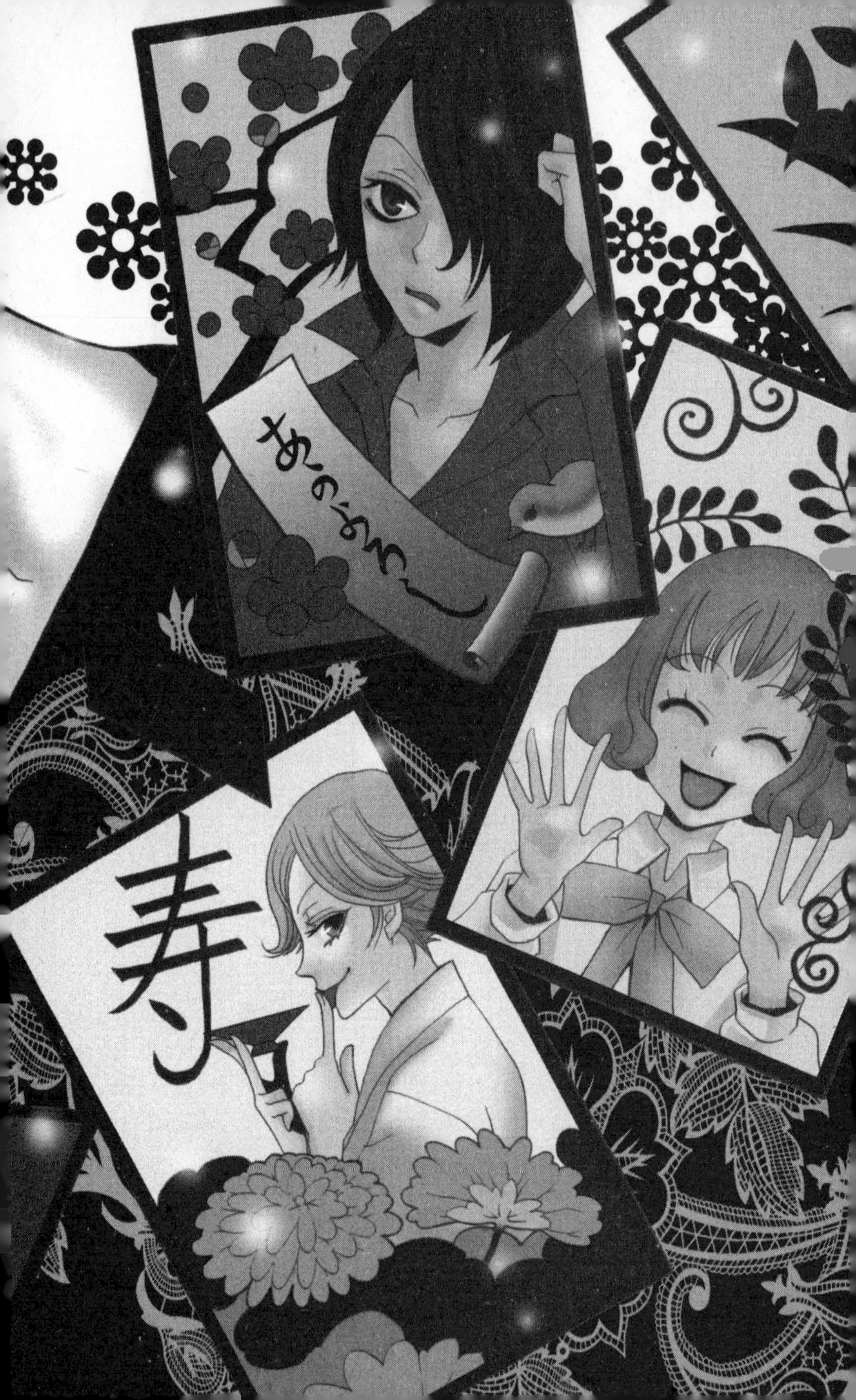
あのよろし
寿

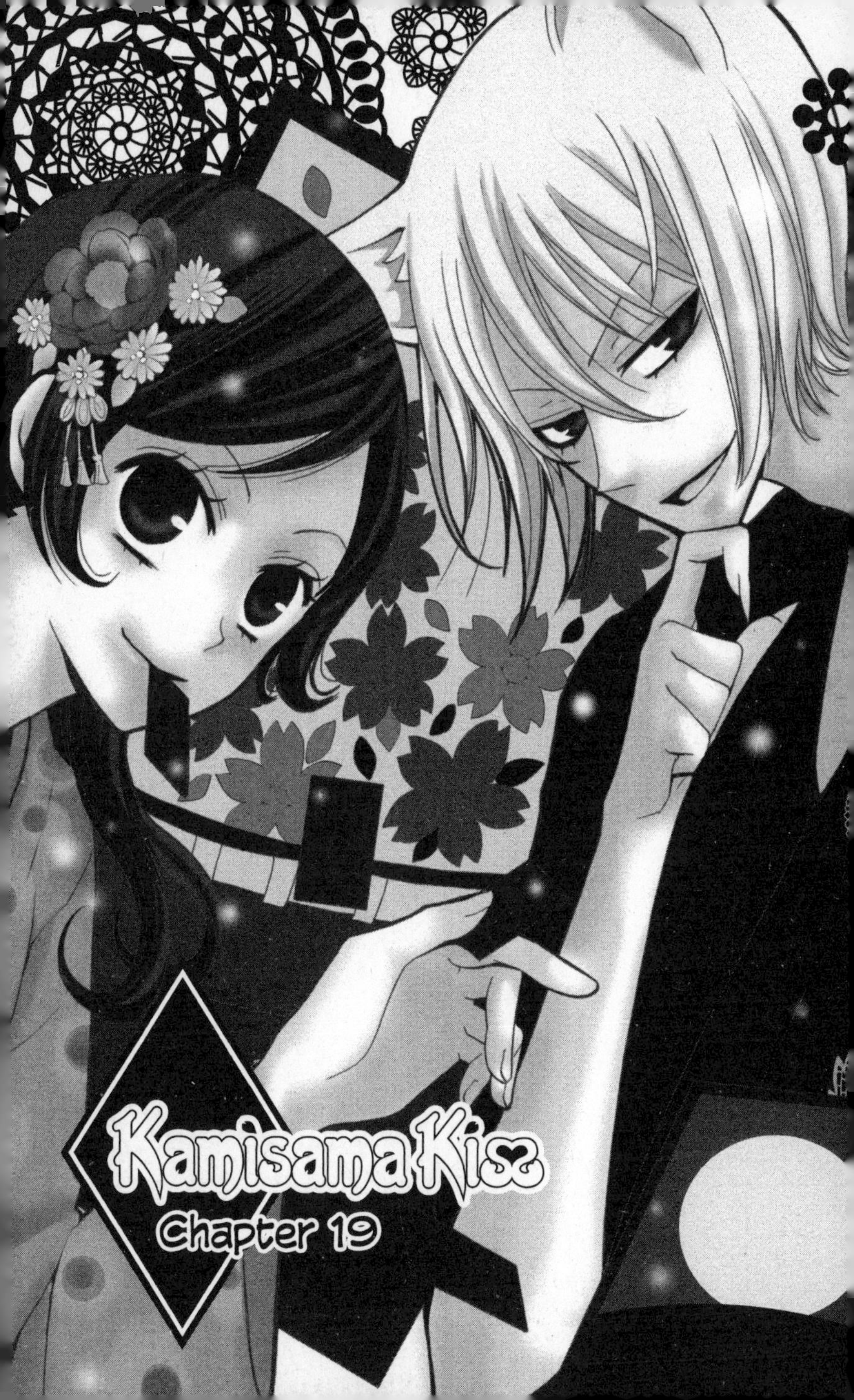
Kamisama Kiss
Chapter 19

TOMOE'S Ennui Blog

Take me home

Nanami brought the snake home.

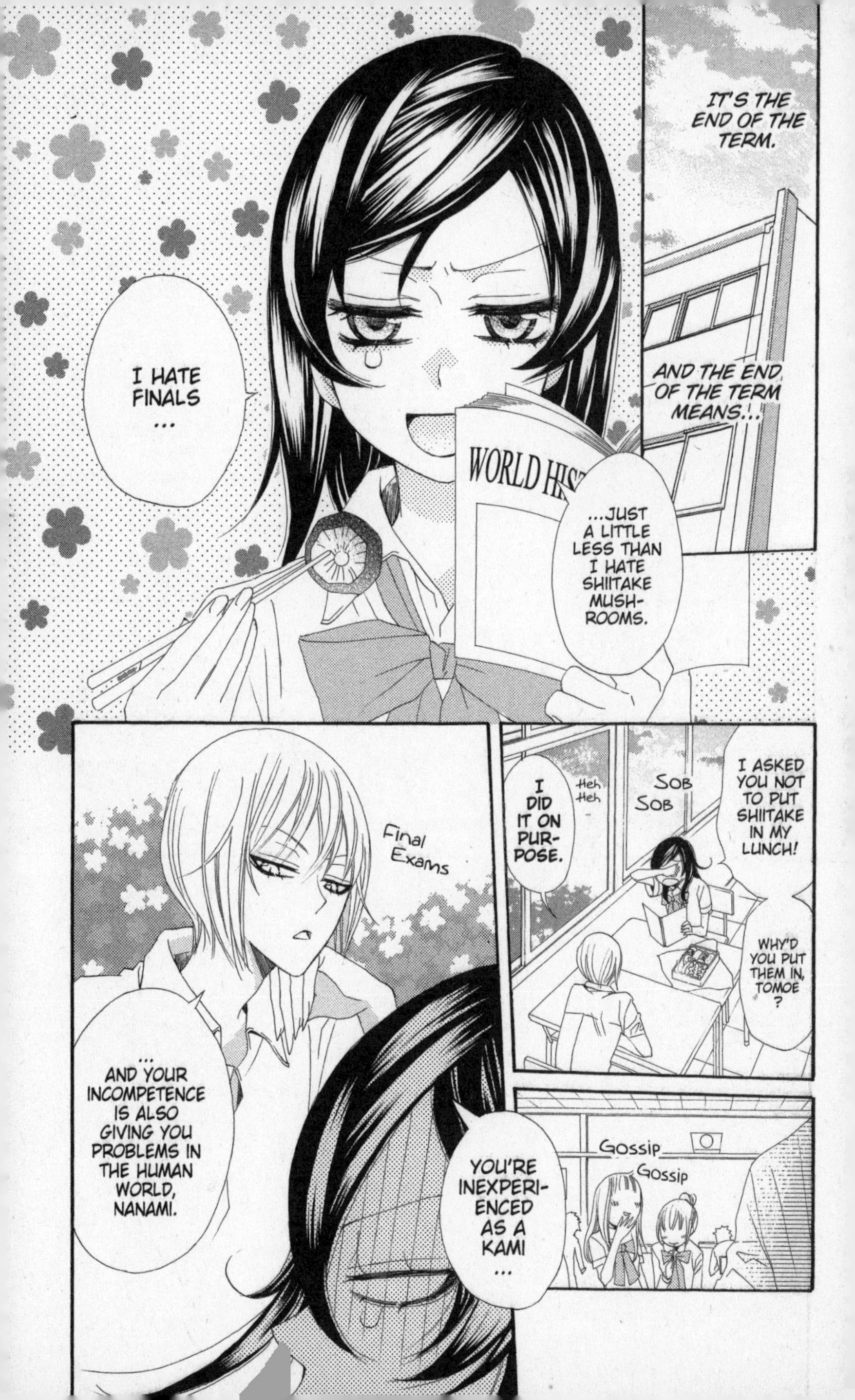
IT'S THE END OF THE TERM.
AND THE END OF THE TERM MEANS...
I HATE FINALS ...
...JUST A LITTLE LESS THAN I HATE SHIITAKE MUSH-ROOMS.
WORLD HIS
I ASKED YOU NOT TO PUT SHIITAKE IN MY LUNCH!
SOB SOB
WHY'D YOU PUT THEM IN, TOMOE?
Heh Heh
I DID IT ON PUR-POSE.
Gossip
Gossip
YOU'RE INEXPERI-ENCED AS A KAMI ...
Final Exams
... AND YOUR INCOMPETENCE IS ALSO GIVING YOU PROBLEMS IN THE HUMAN WORLD, NANAMI.

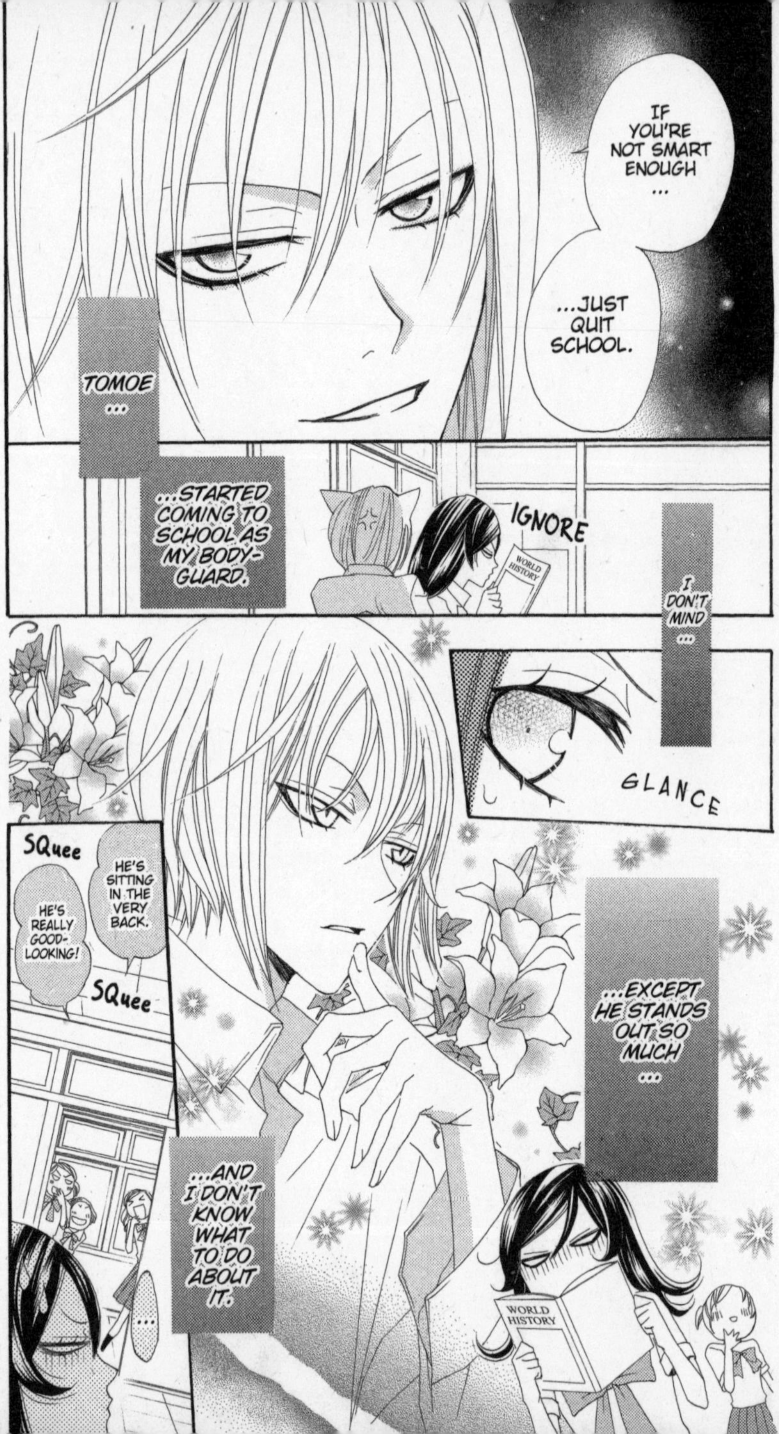

IF YOU'RE NOT SMART ENOUGH ...
...JUST QUIT SCHOOL.
TOMOE ...
...STARTED COMING TO SCHOOL AS MY BODY-GUARD.
IGNORE
WORLD HISTORY
I DON'T MIND ...
GLANCE
...EXCEPT HE STANDS OUT SO MUCH ...
...AND I DON'T KNOW WHAT TO DO ABOUT IT.
SQuee
HE'S SITTING IN THE VERY BACK.
HE'S REALLY GOOD-LOOKING!
SQuee
...
WORLD HISTORY

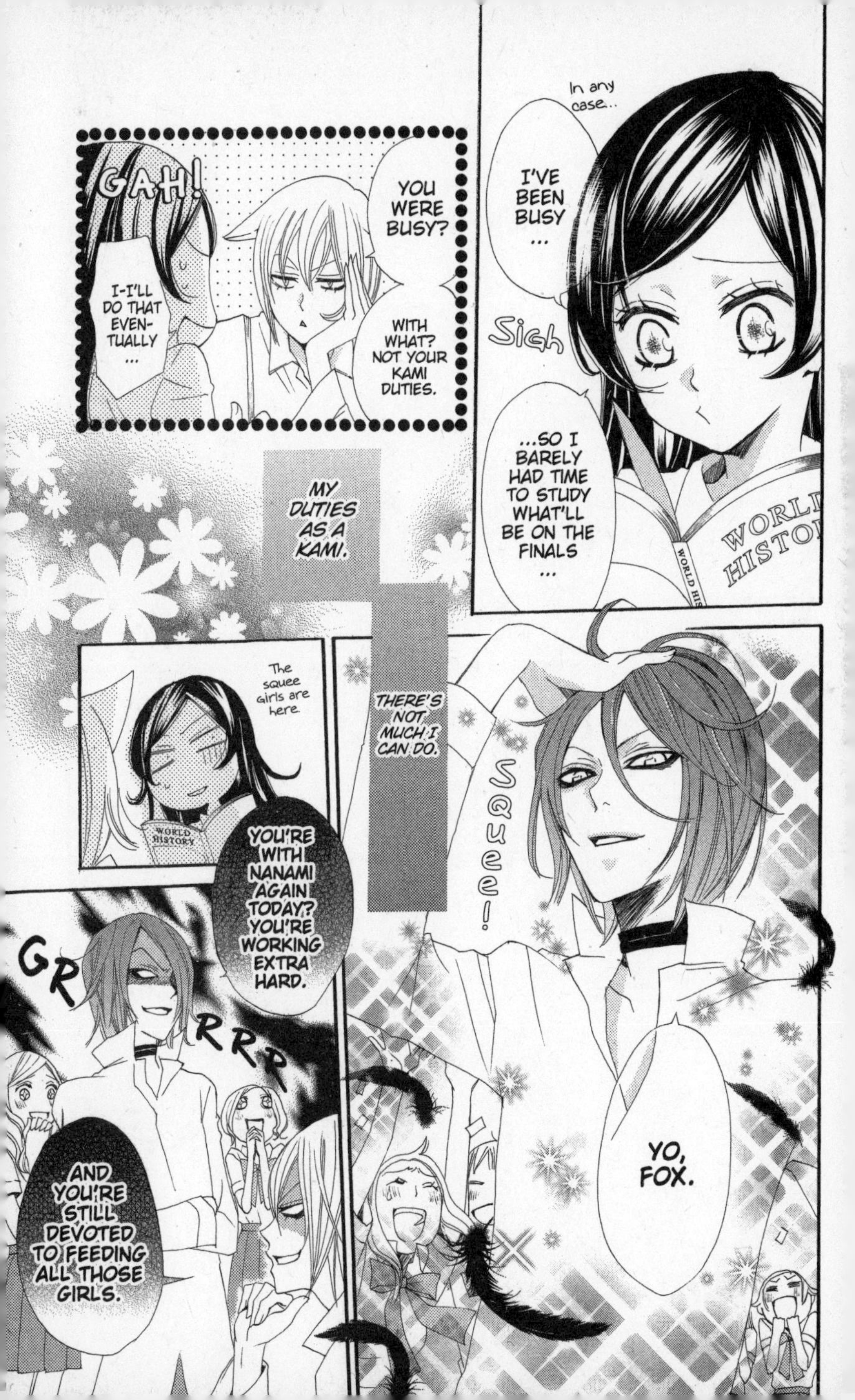
In any case...
I'VE BEEN BUSY ...
Sigh
...SO I BARELY HAD TIME TO STUDY WHAT'LL BE ON THE FINALS ...
WORLD HISTORY
YOU WERE BUSY?
WITH WHAT? NOT YOUR KAMI DUTIES.
GAH!
I-I'LL DO THAT EVEN-TUALLY ...
MY DUTIES AS A KAMI.
THERE'S NOT MUCH I CAN DO.
Squeee!
YO, FOX.
The squee girls are here.
WORLD HISTORY
YOU'RE WITH NANAMI AGAIN TODAY? YOU'RE WORKING EXTRA HARD.
GR RRR
AND YOU'RE STILL DEVOTED TO FEEDING ALL THOSE GIRLS.

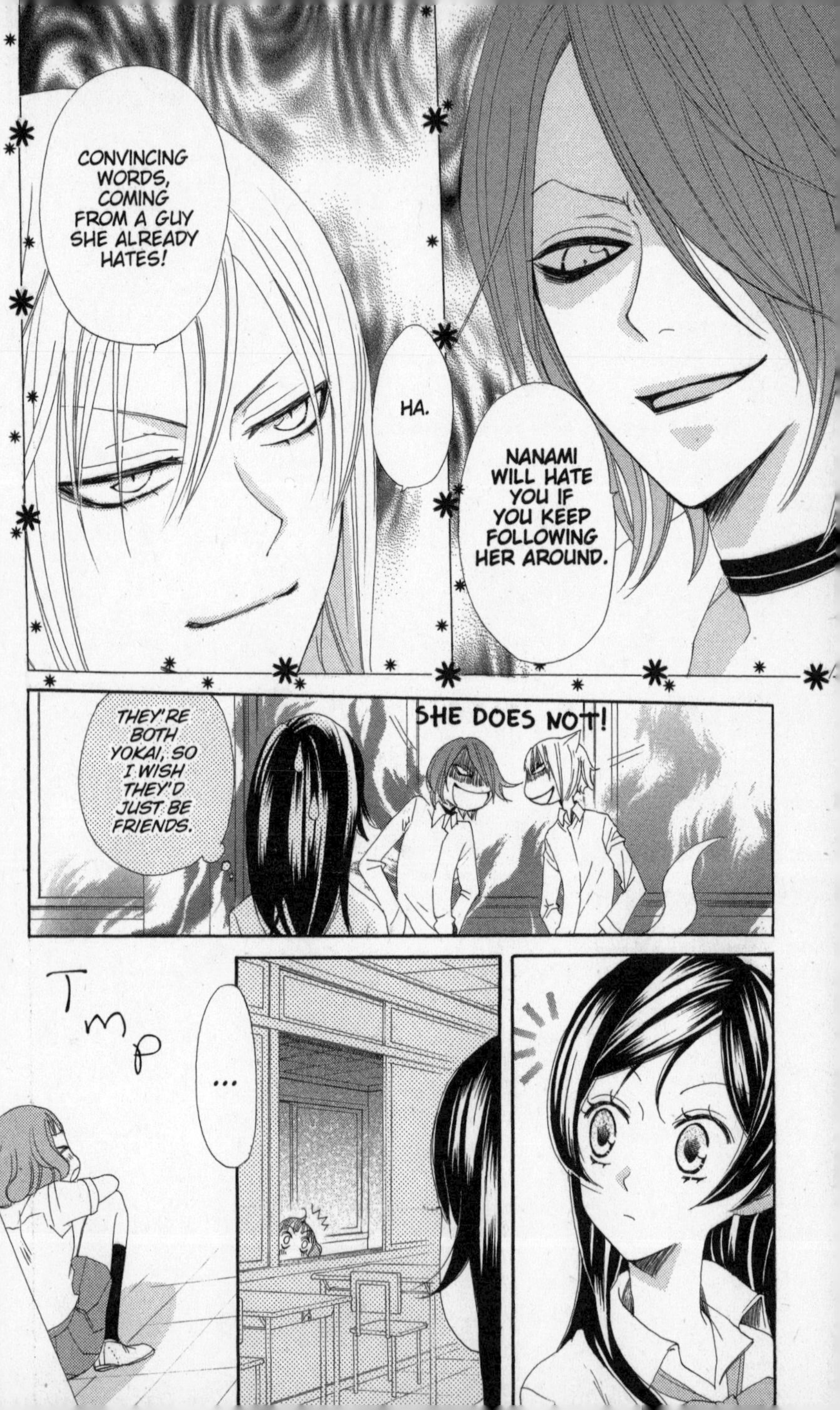
NANAMI WILL HATE YOU IF YOU KEEP FOLLOWING HER AROUND.
HA.
CONVINCING WORDS, COMING FROM A GUY SHE ALREADY HATES!
SHE DOES NOT!
THEY'RE BOTH YOKAI, SO I WISH THEY'D JUST BE FRIENDS.
...
Tmp

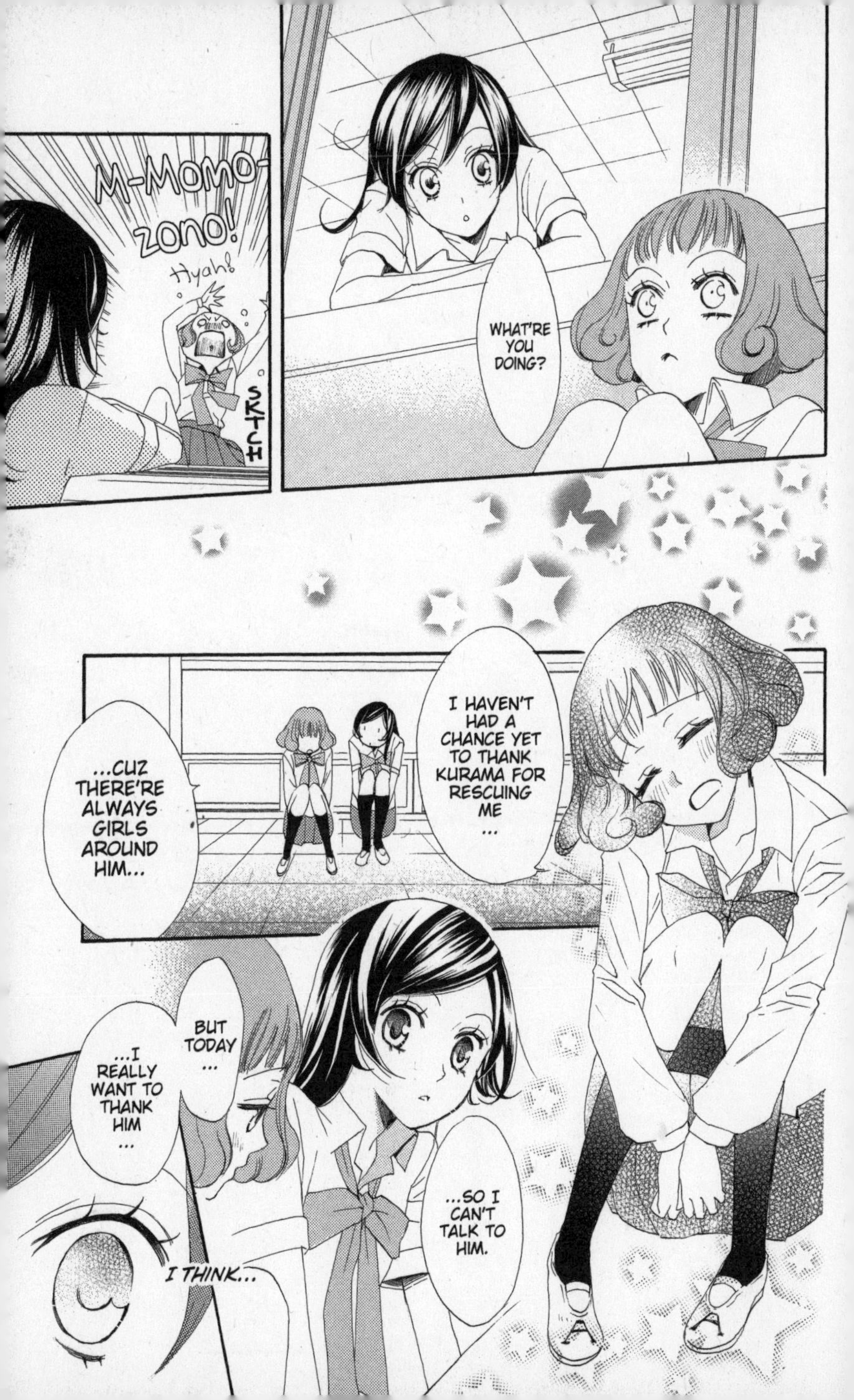
WHAT'RE YOU DOING?
M-MOMO-ZONO!
Hyah!
SKTCH
I HAVEN'T HAD A CHANCE YET TO THANK KURAMA FOR RESCUING ME ...
...CUZ THERE'RE ALWAYS GIRLS AROUND HIM...
...SO I CAN'T TALK TO HIM.
BUT TODAY ...
...I REALLY WANT TO THANK HIM ...
I THINK...

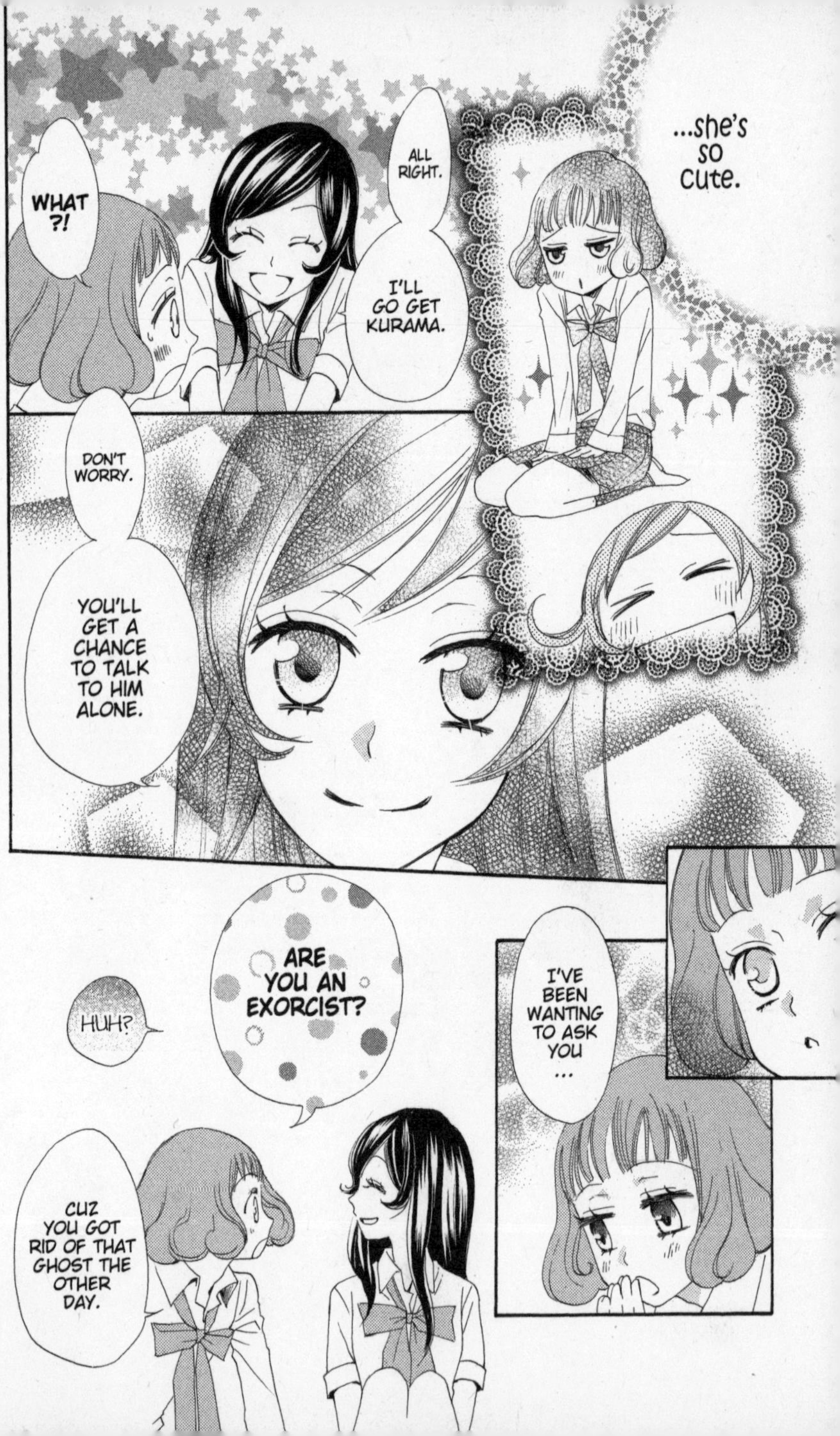
ALL RIGHT.
I'LL GO GET KURAMA.
WHAT?!
...she's so cute.
DON'T WORRY.
YOU'LL GET A CHANCE TO TALK TO HIM ALONE.
I'VE BEEN WANTING TO ASK YOU...
ARE YOU AN EXORCIST?
HUH?
CUZ YOU GOT RID OF THAT GHOST THE OTHER DAY.

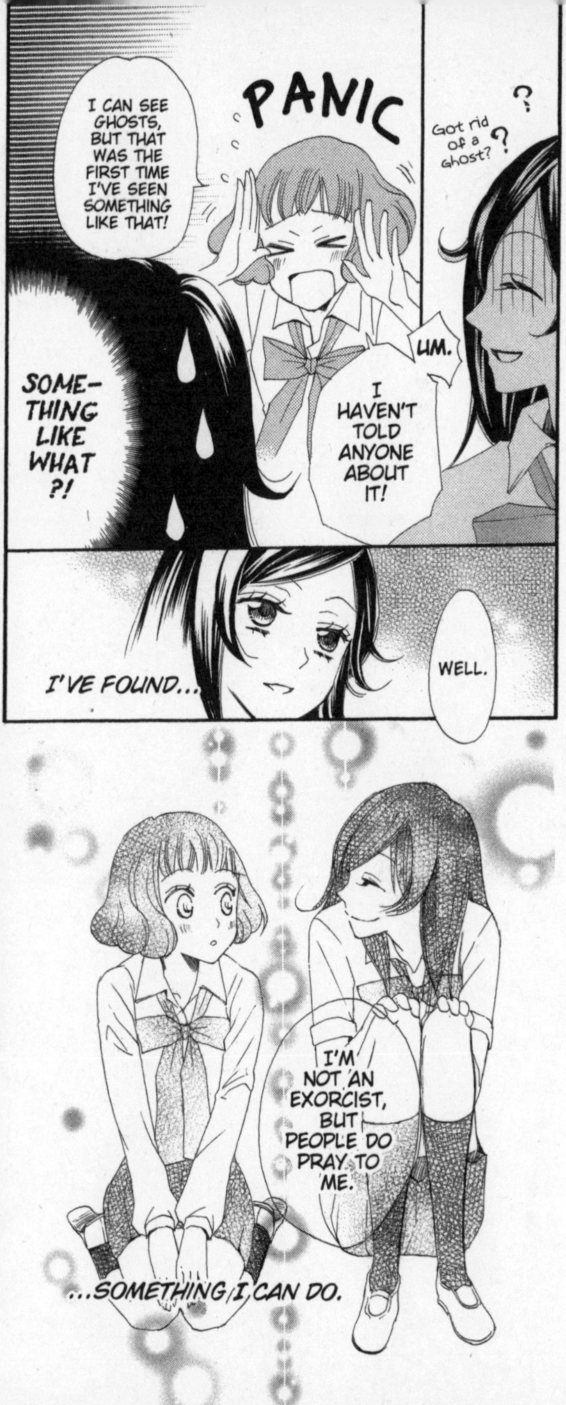
Got rid of a Ghost?
PANIC
I CAN SEE GHOSTS, BUT THAT WAS THE FIRST TIME I'VE SEEN SOMETHING LIKE THAT!
UM.
I HAVEN'T TOLD ANYONE ABOUT IT!
SOME-THING LIKE WHAT ?!
WELL.
I'VE FOUND...
I'M NOT AN EXORCIST, BUT PEOPLE DO PRAY TO ME.
...SOMETHING I CAN DO.

Thank you for reading Vol. 4 of Kamisama Kiss. ✿

I hope you enjoy reading it.
In the manga, it's summertime.
It's July or August. They go to the seaside because it's summer vacation.

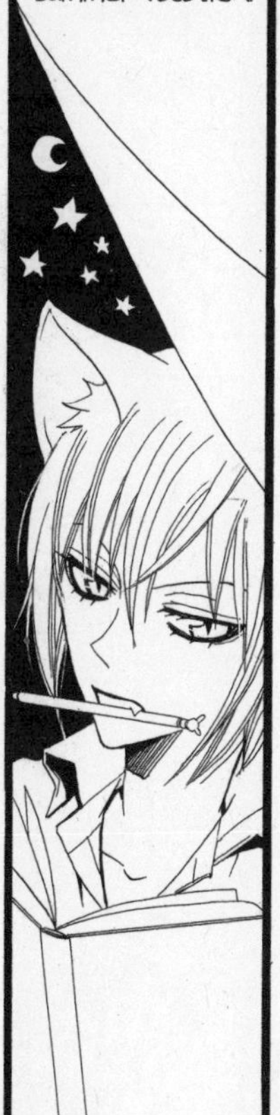

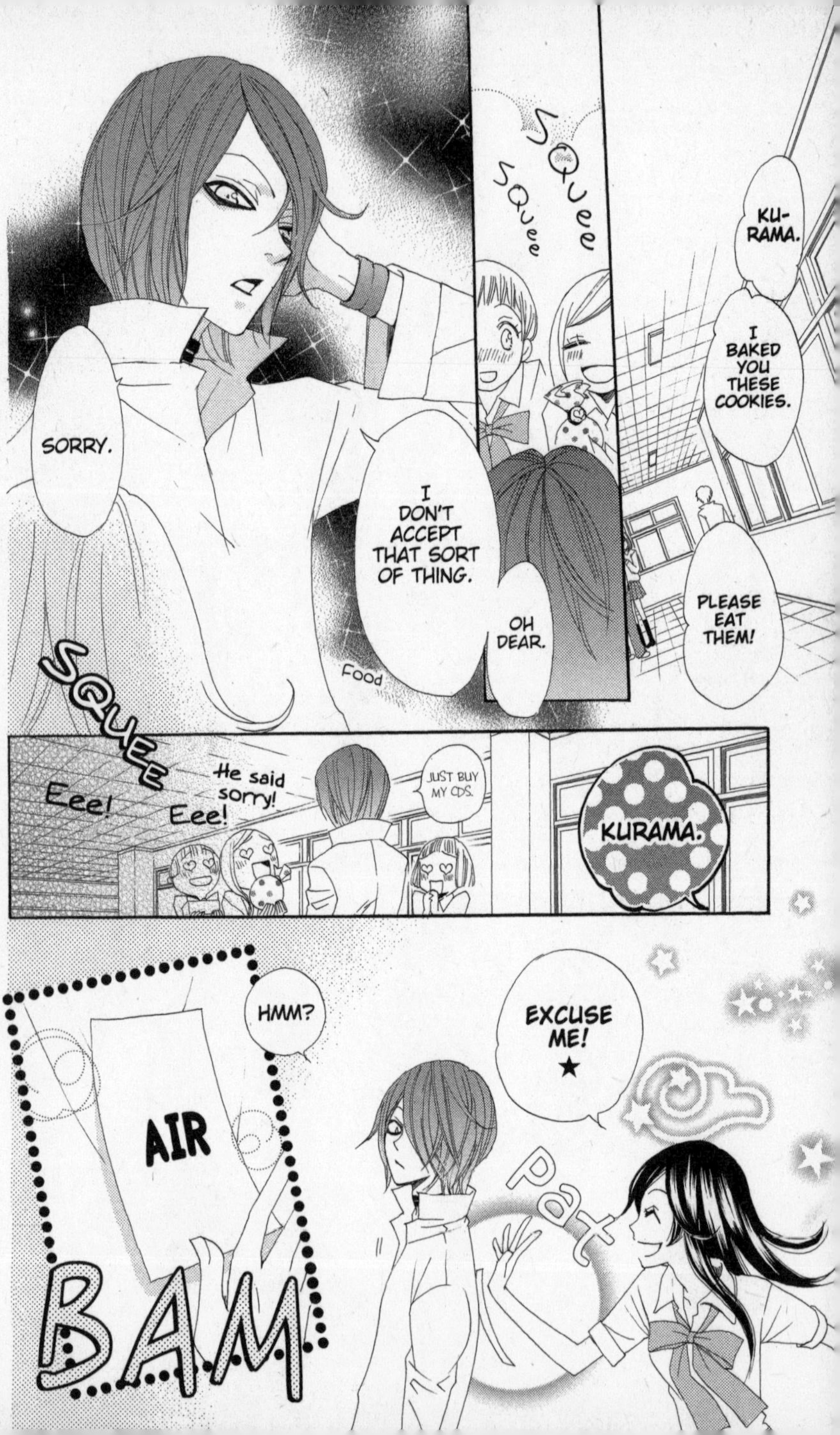
KU-RAMA.
I BAKED YOU THESE COOKIES.
PLEASE EAT THEM!
SQuee
SQuee
OH DEAR.
I DON'T ACCEPT THAT SORT OF THING.
SORRY.
Food
SQUEE
KURAMA.
JUST BUY MY CDS.
He said sorry!
Eee!
Eee!
EXCUSE ME! ★
Pat
HMM?
AIR
BAM

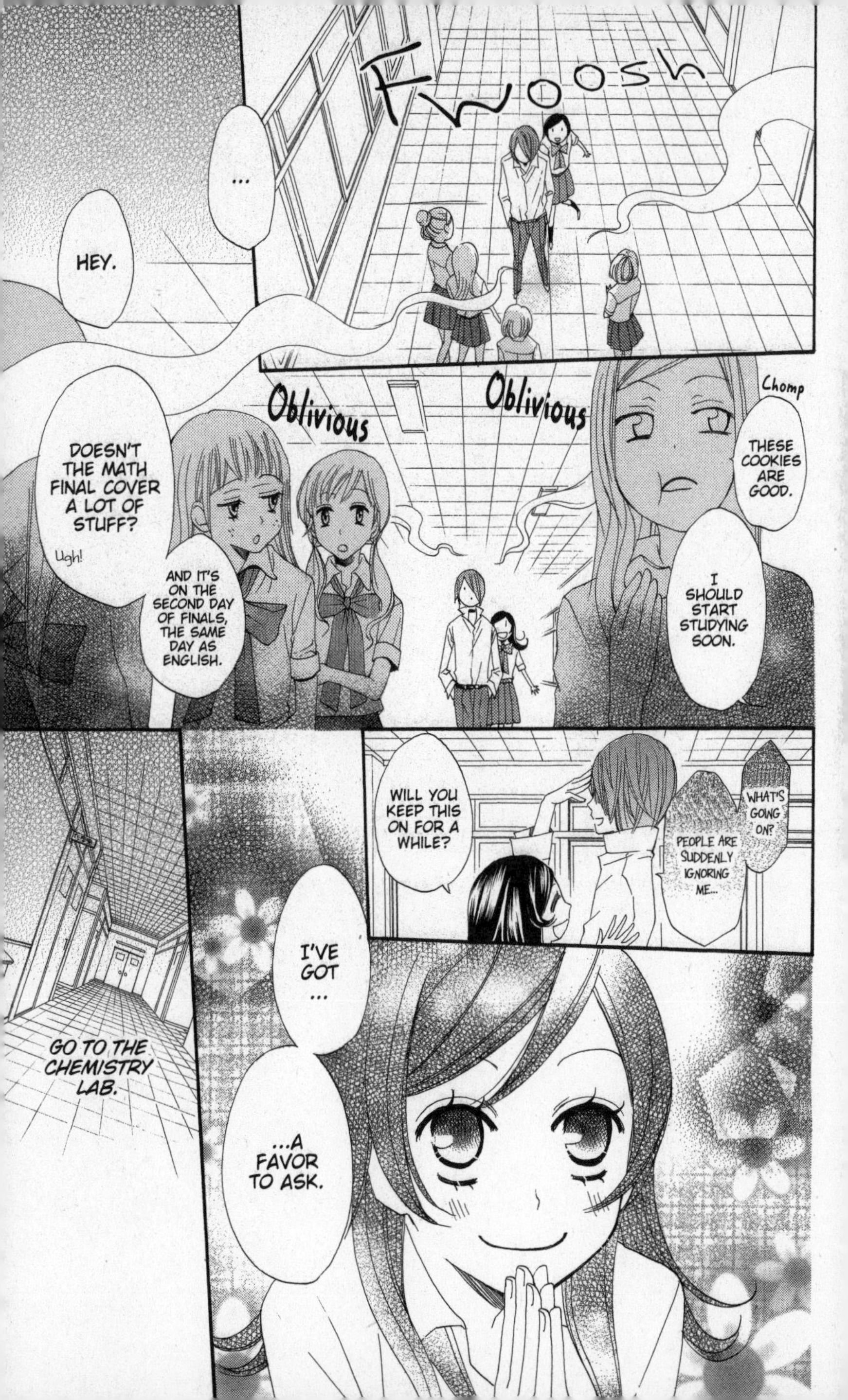
Fwoosh
...
HEY.
Chomp
THESE COOKIES ARE GOOD.
I SHOULD START STUDYING SOON.
Oblivious
Oblivious
DOESN'T THE MATH FINAL COVER A LOT OF STUFF?
Ugh!
AND IT'S ON THE SECOND DAY OF FINALS, THE SAME DAY AS ENGLISH.
WHAT'S GOING ON?
PEOPLE ARE SUDDENLY IGNORING ME...
WILL YOU KEEP THIS ON FOR A WHILE?
I'VE GOT ...
...A FAVOR TO ASK.
GO TO THE CHEMISTRY LAB.

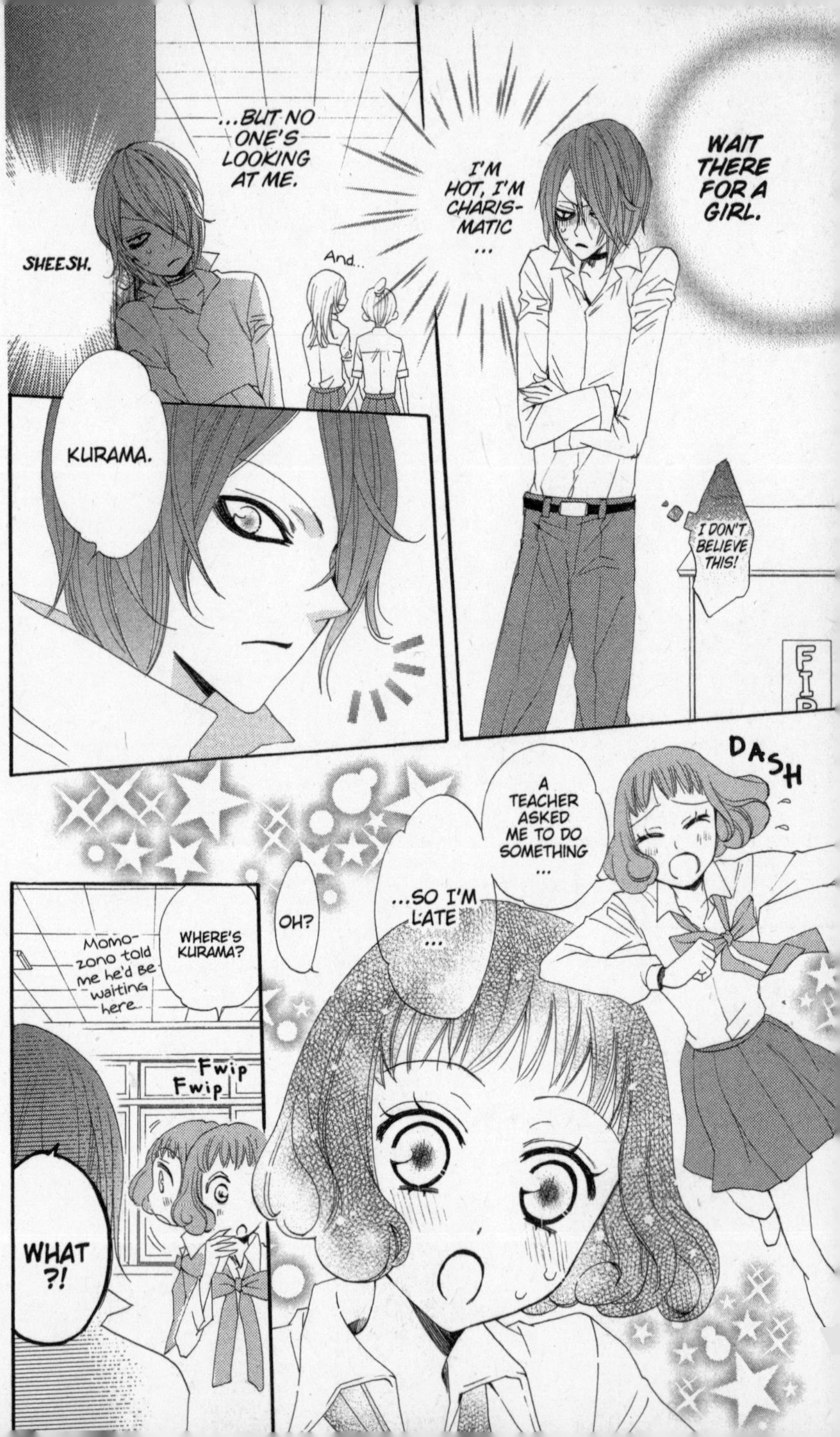
WAIT THERE FOR A GIRL.
I'M HOT, I'M CHARIS-MATIC ...
...BUT NO ONE'S LOOKING AT ME.
And...
SHEESH.
I DON'T BELIEVE THIS!
KURAMA.
DASH
A TEACHER ASKED ME TO DO SOMETHING ...
...SO I'M LATE ...
OH?
WHERE'S KURAMA?
Momo-zono told me he'd be waiting here..
Fwip Fwip
WHAT ?!

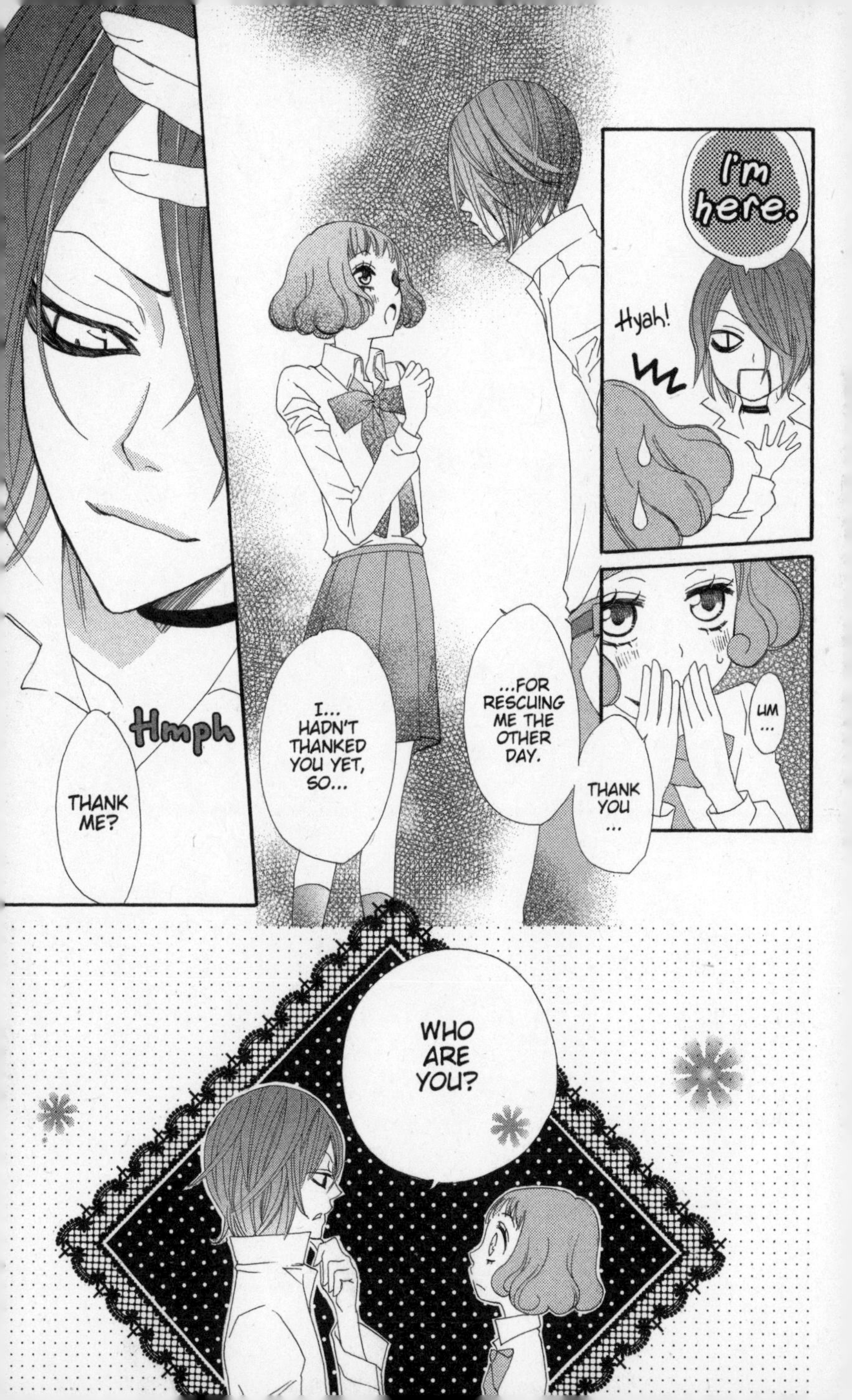
I'm here.
Hyah!
UM...
THANK YOU...
...FOR RESCUING ME THE OTHER DAY.
I... HADN'T THANKED YOU YET, SO...
Hmph
THANK ME?
WHO ARE YOU?

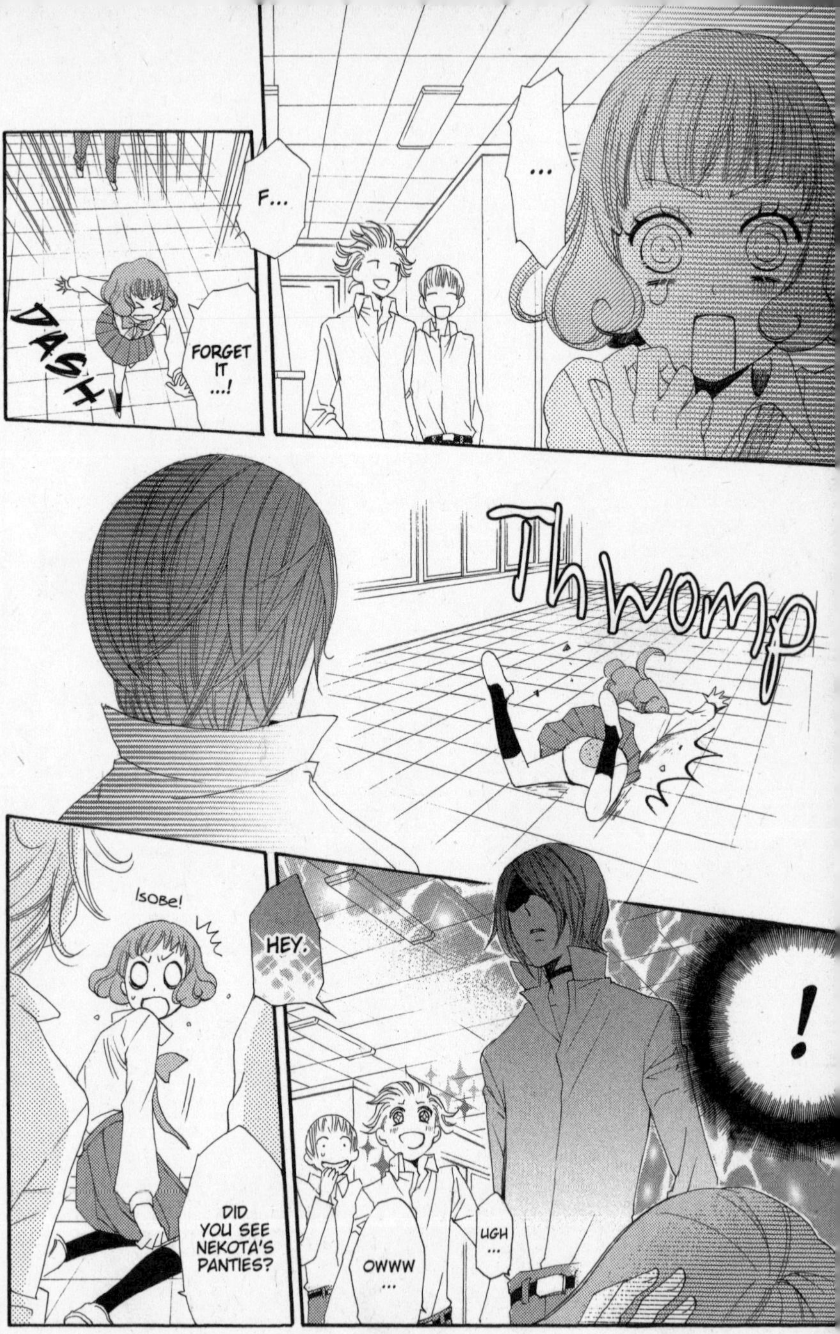
...
F...
DASH
FORGET IT ...!
Thwomp
!
HEY.
UGH ...
OWWW ...
Isobe!
DID YOU SEE NEKOTA'S PANTIES?

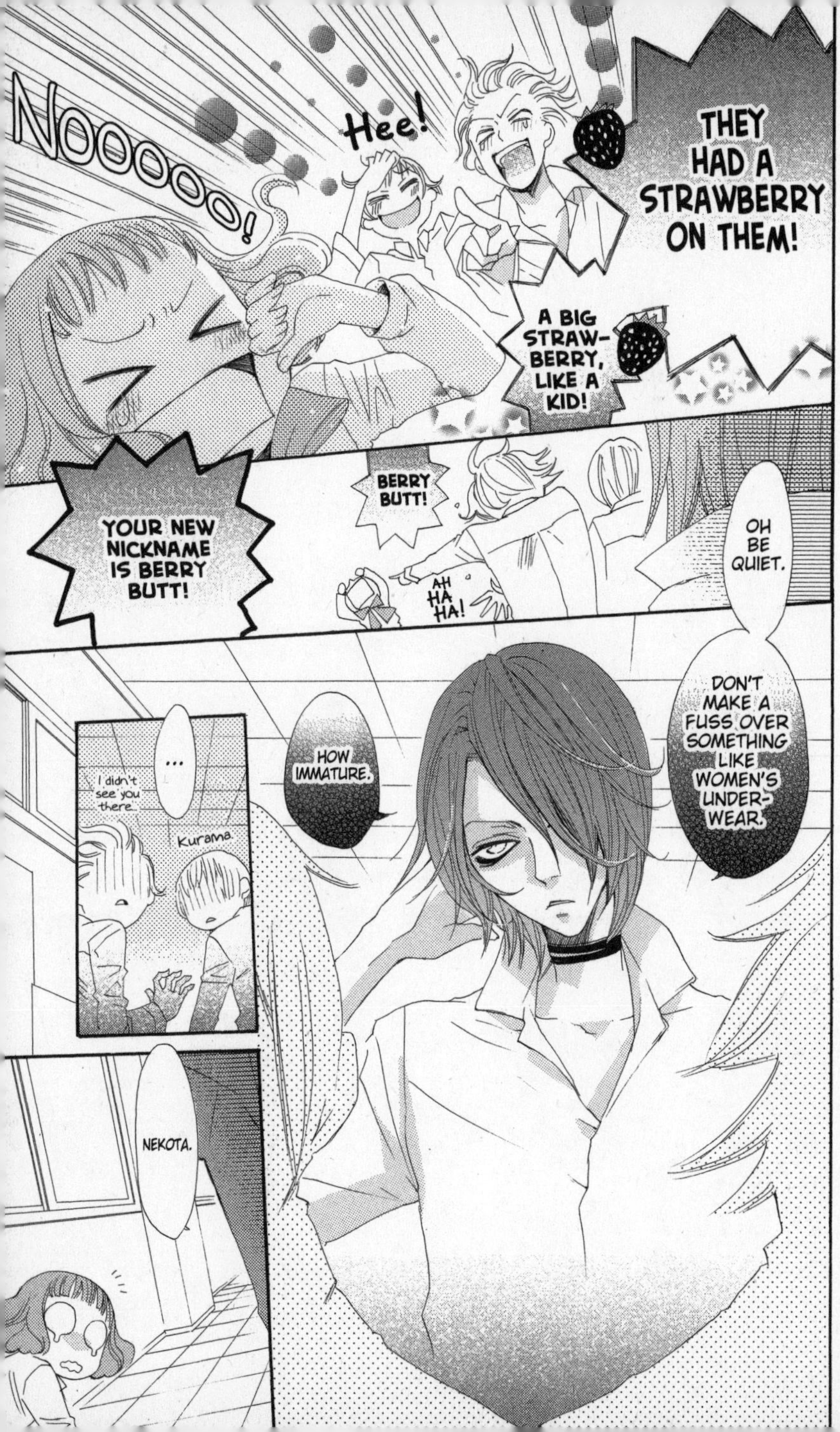
THEY HAD A STRAWBERRY ON THEM!
Hee!
A BIG STRAWBERRY, LIKE A KID!
Noooooo!
OH BE QUIET.
BERRY BUTT!
AH HA HA!
YOUR NEW NICKNAME IS BERRY BUTT!
DON'T MAKE A FUSS OVER SOMETHING LIKE WOMEN'S UNDERWEAR.
HOW IMMATURE.
...
Kurama.
I didn't see you there...
NEKOTA.

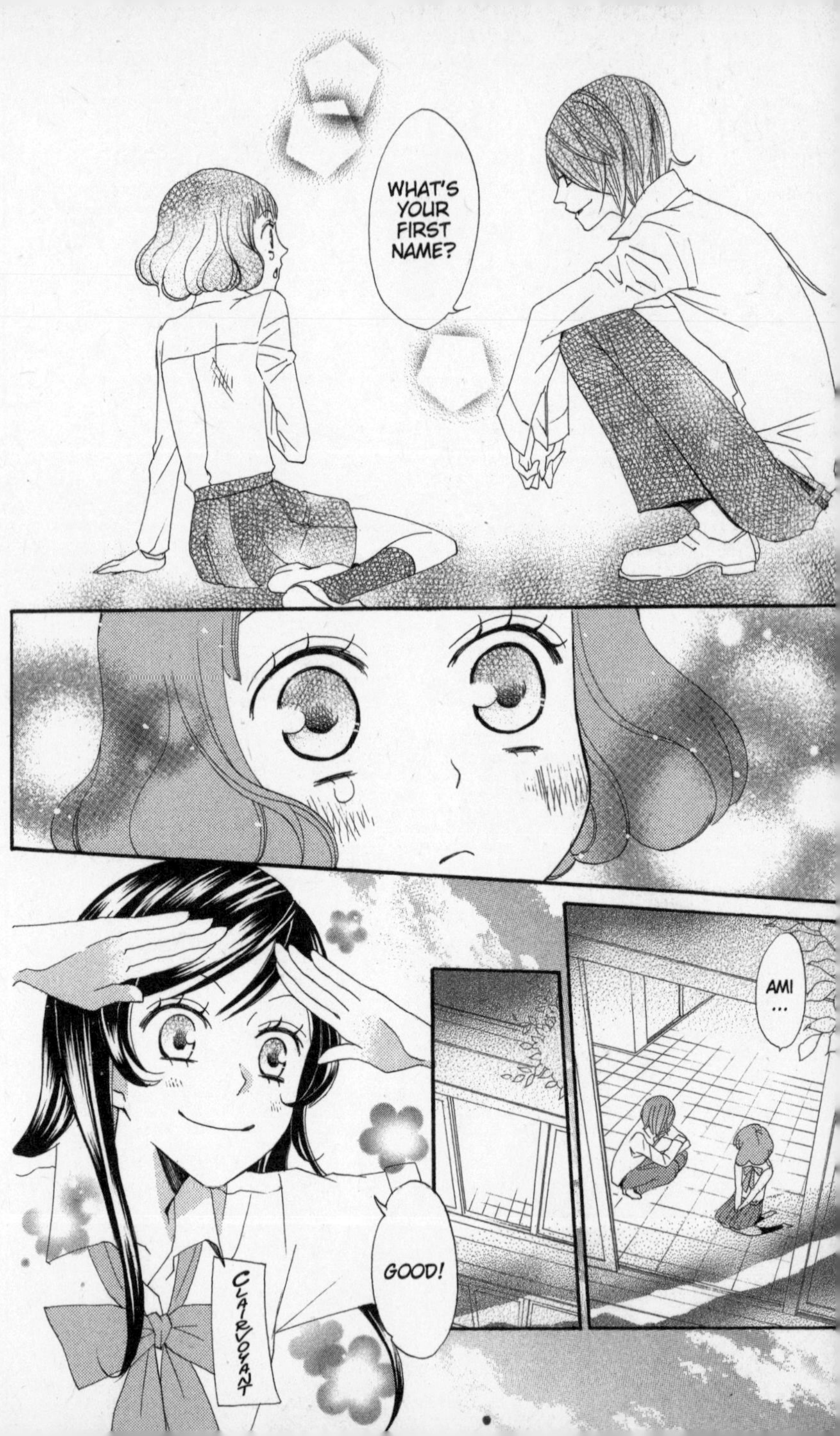
WHAT'S YOUR FIRST NAME?
AMI ...
GOOD!
CLAIRVOYANT

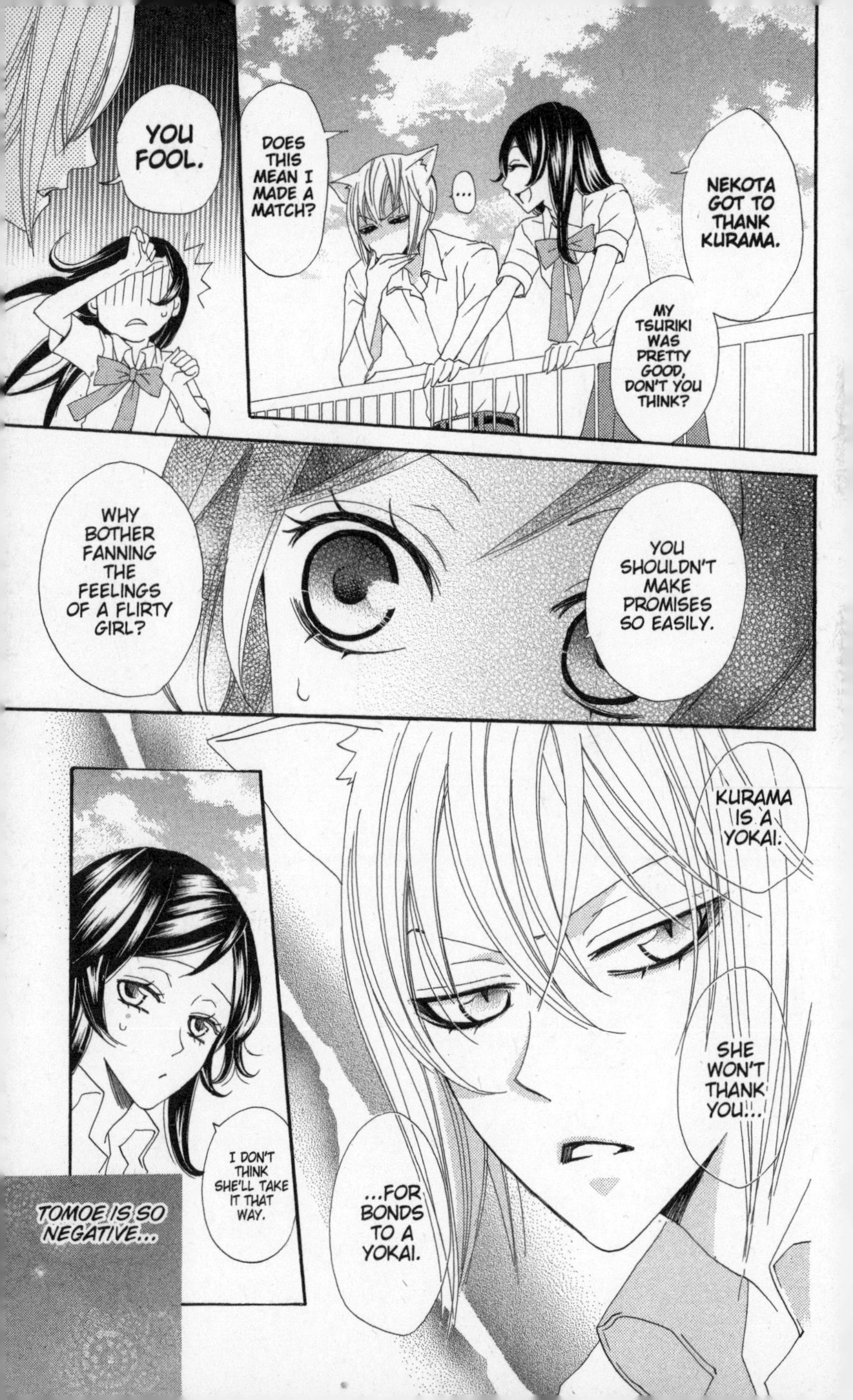
NEKOTA GOT TO THANK KURAMA.
MY TSURIKI WAS PRETTY GOOD, DON'T YOU THINK?
...
DOES THIS MEAN I MADE A MATCH?
YOU FOOL.
YOU SHOULDN'T MAKE PROMISES SO EASILY.
WHY BOTHER FANNING THE FEELINGS OF A FLIRTY GIRL?
KURAMA IS A YOKAI.
SHE WON'T THANK YOU...
...FOR BONDS TO A YOKAI.
I DON'T THINK SHE'LL TAKE IT THAT WAY.
TOMOE IS SO NEGATIVE...

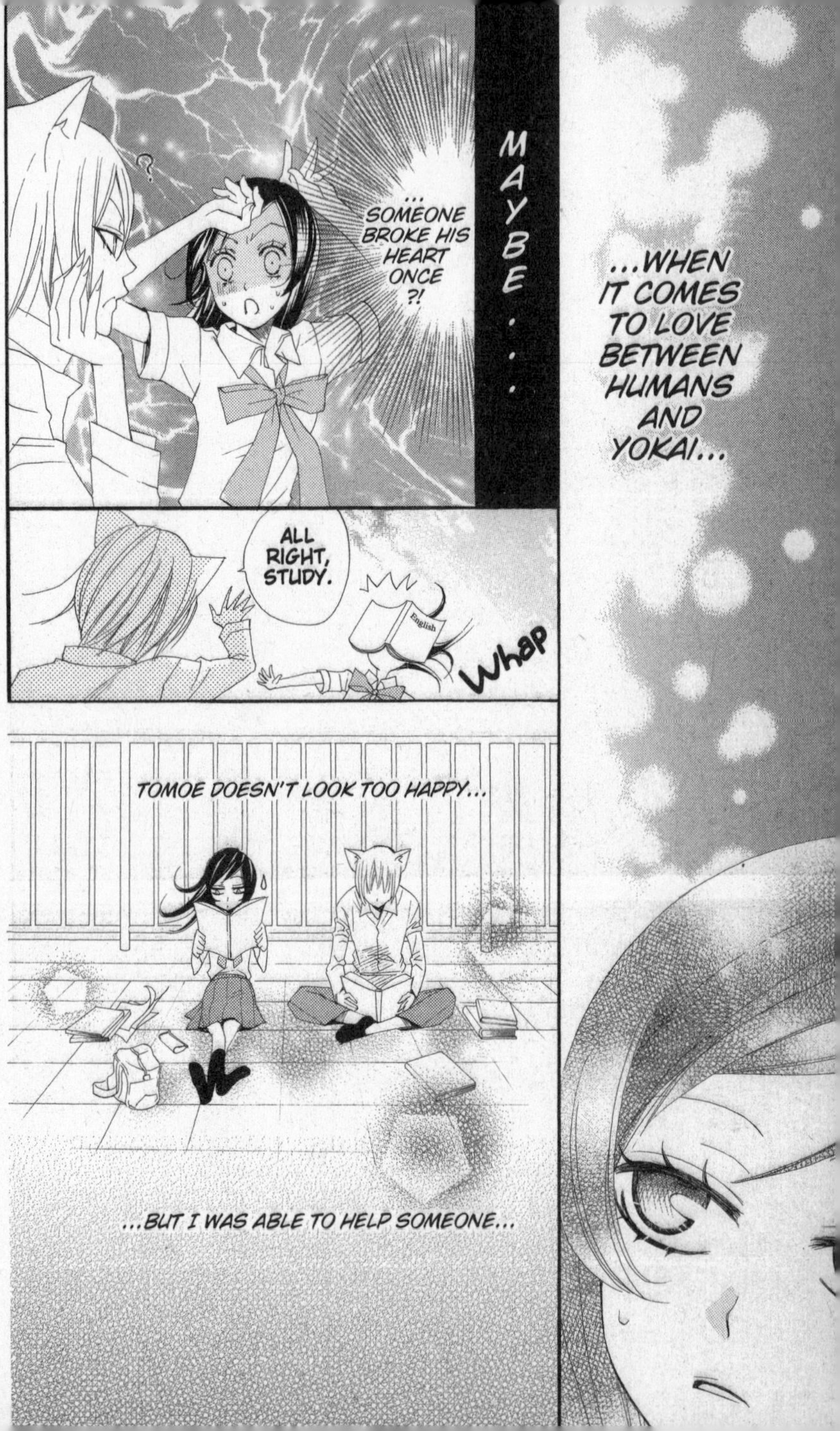
...WHEN IT COMES TO LOVE BETWEEN HUMANS AND YOKAI...
MAYBE...
...SOMEONE BROKE HIS HEART ONCE?!
ALL RIGHT, STUDY.
English
Whap
TOMOE DOESN'T LOOK TOO HAPPY...
...BUT I WAS ABLE TO HELP SOMEONE...

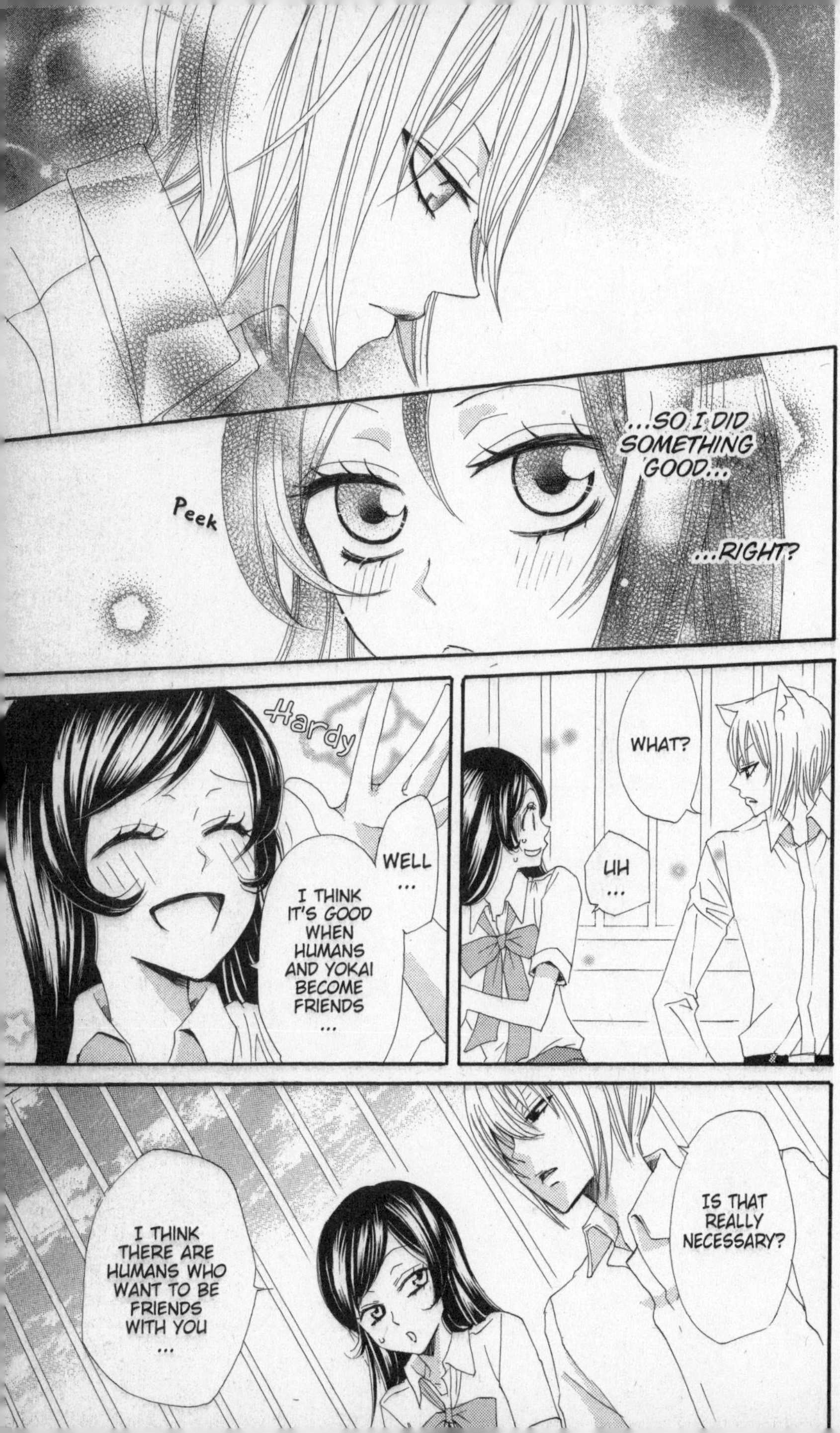

...SO I DID SOMETHING GOOD...
...RIGHT?
Peek
WHAT?
UH ...
Hardy
WELL ...
I THINK IT'S GOOD WHEN HUMANS AND YOKAI BECOME FRIENDS ...
IS THAT REALLY NECESSARY?
I THINK THERE ARE HUMANS WHO WANT TO BE FRIENDS WITH YOU ...

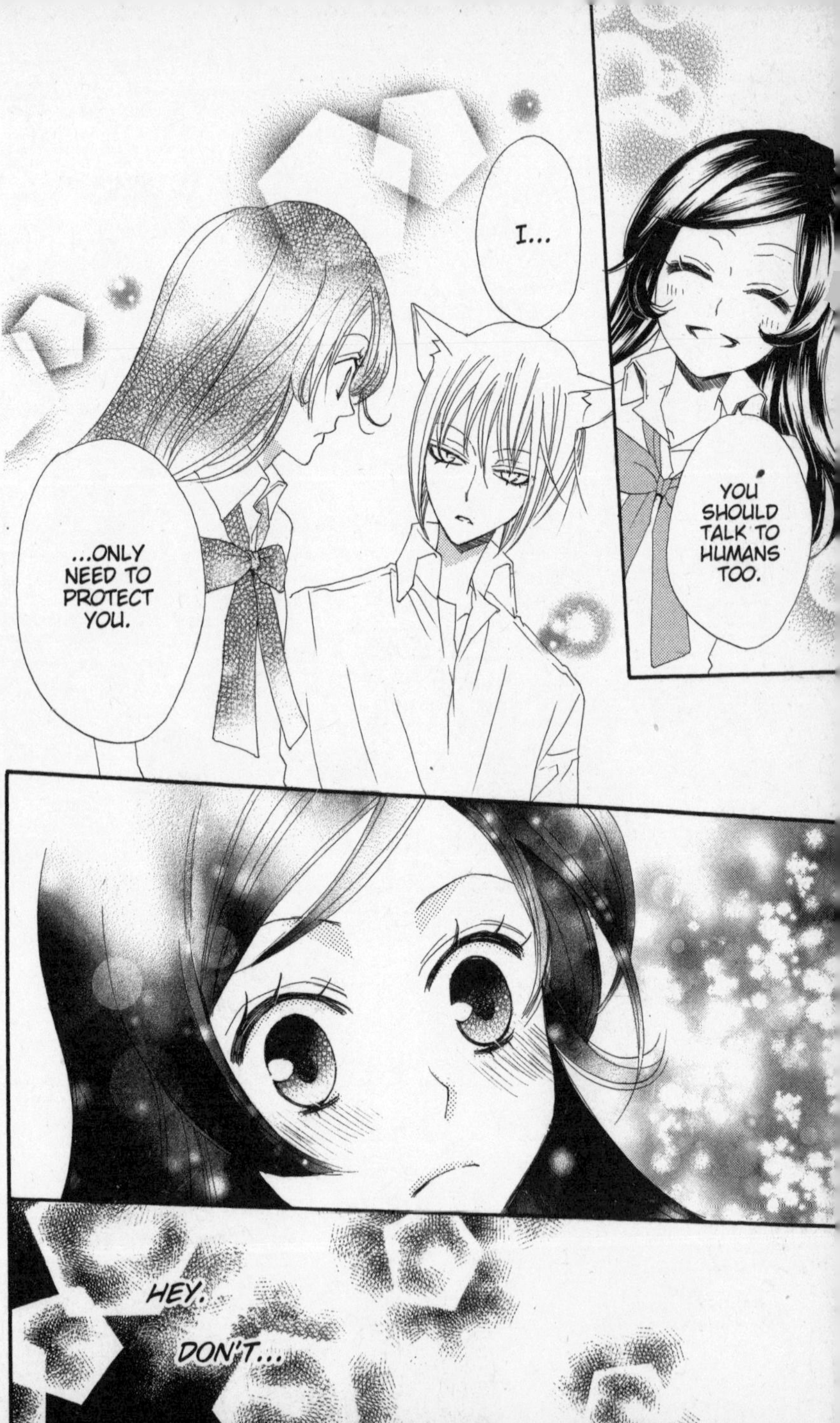
YOU SHOULD TALK TO HUMANS TOO.
I...
...ONLY NEED TO PROTECT YOU.
HEY.
DON'T...

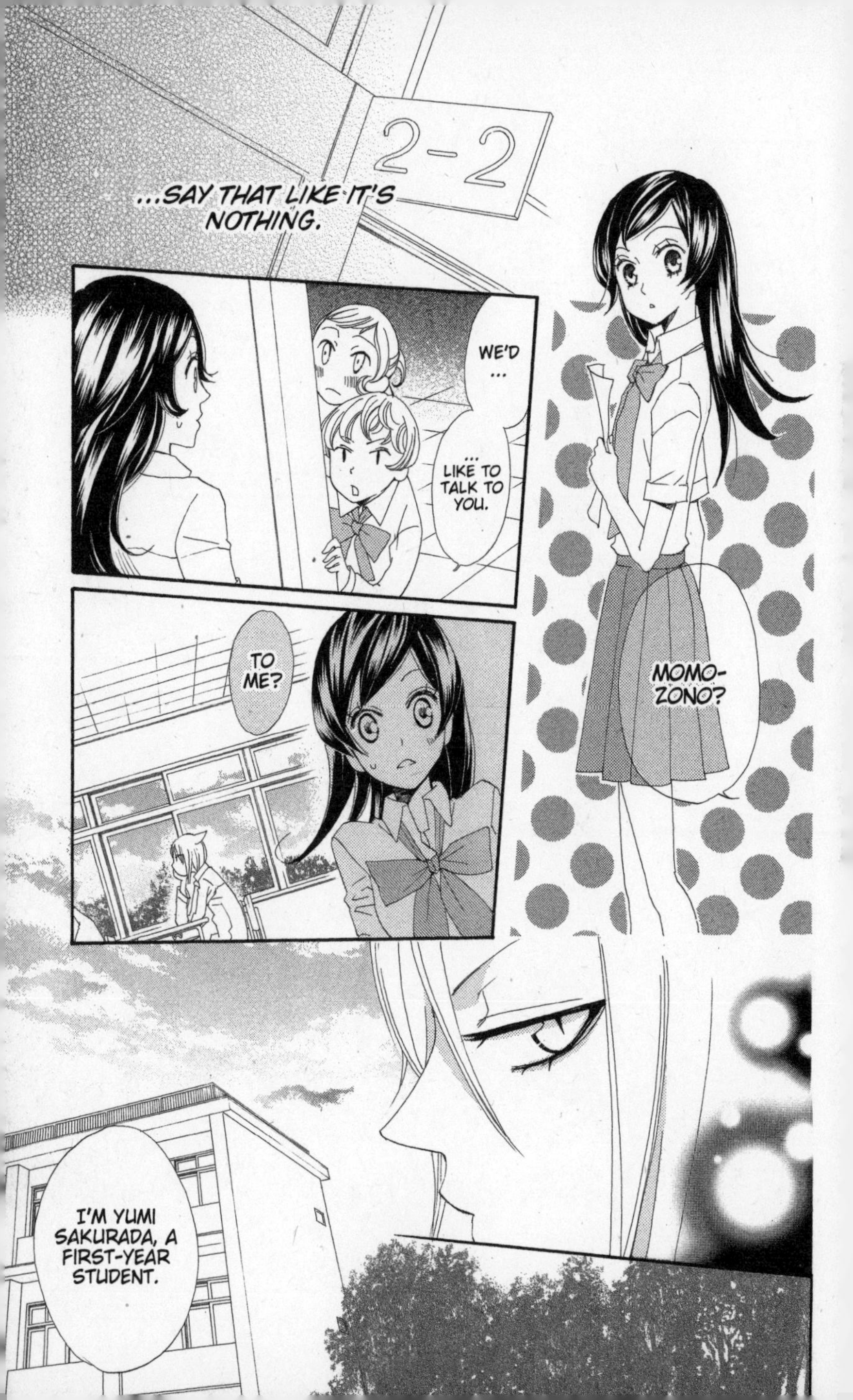
...SAY THAT LIKE IT'S NOTHING.
MOMO-ZONO?
WE'D ...
... LIKE TO TALK TO YOU.
TO ME?
I'M YUMI SAKURADA, A FIRST-YEAR STUDENT.

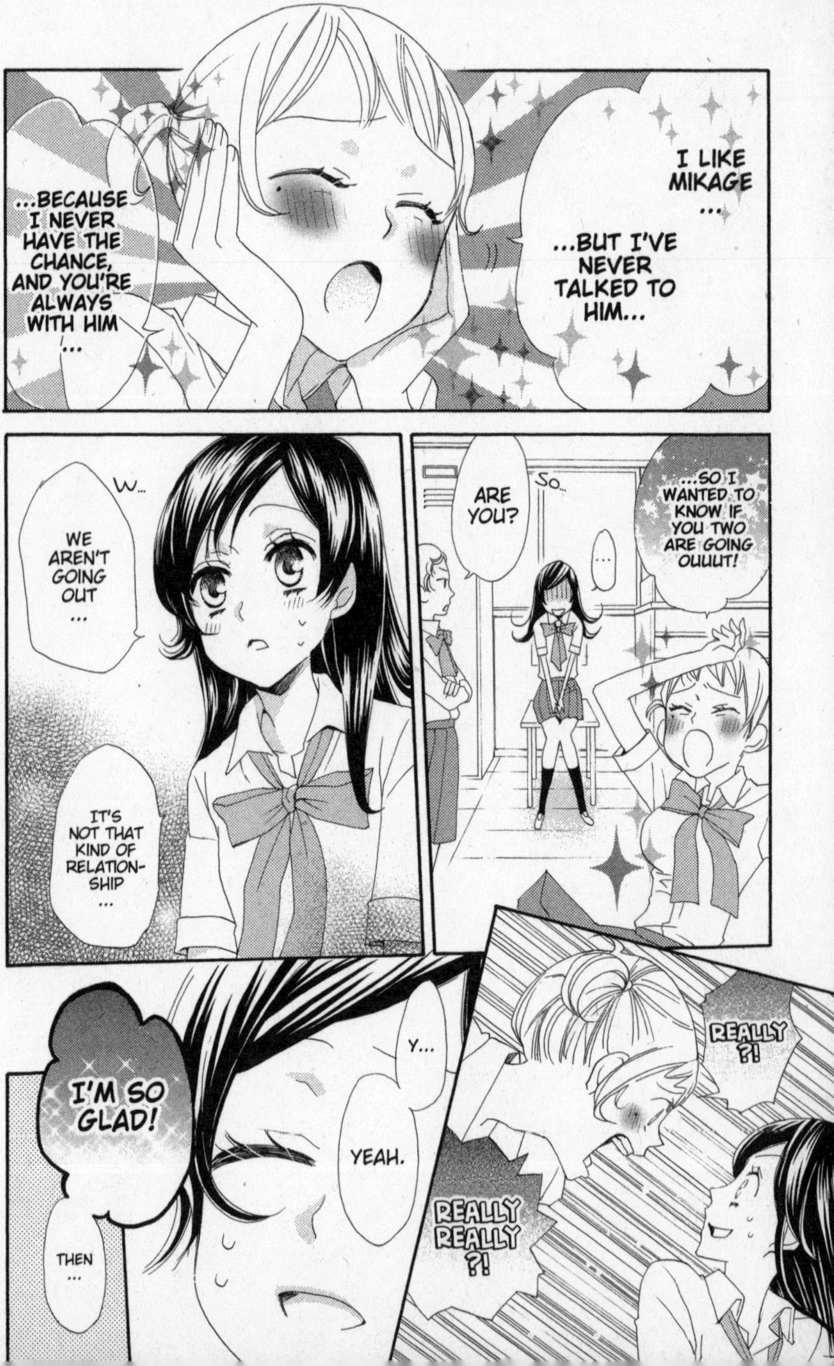
I LIKE MIKAGE ...
...BUT I'VE NEVER TALKED TO HIM...
...BECAUSE I NEVER HAVE THE CHANCE, AND YOU'RE ALWAYS WITH HIM ...
...SO I WANTED TO KNOW IF YOU TWO ARE GOING OUUUT!
...
So...
ARE YOU?
W...
WE AREN'T GOING OUT ...
IT'S NOT THAT KIND OF RELATION-SHIP ...
REALLY ?!
REALLY REALLY ?!
Y...
YEAH.
I'M SO GLAD!
THEN ...

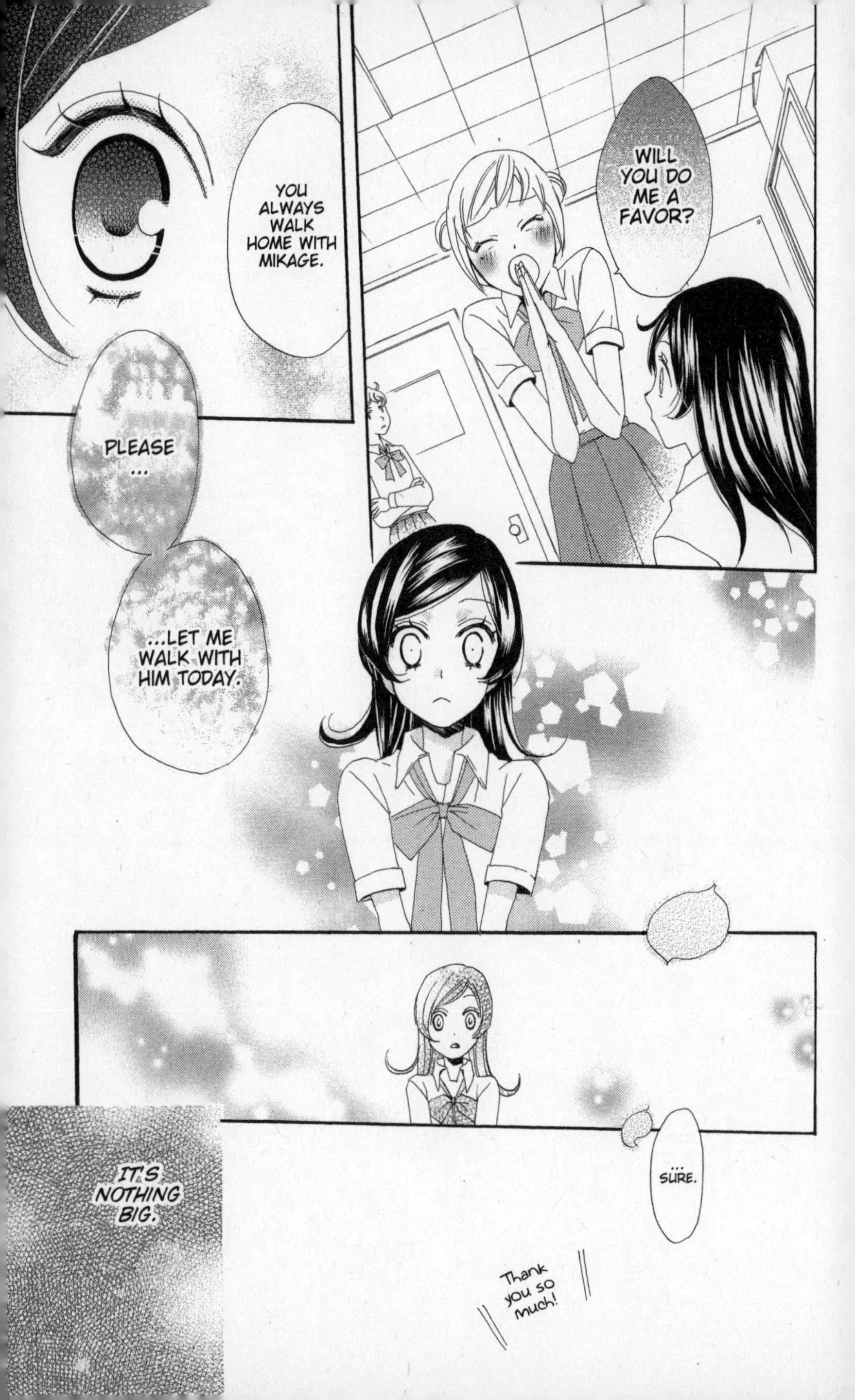
WILL YOU DO ME A FAVOR?
YOU ALWAYS WALK HOME WITH MIKAGE.
PLEASE...
...LET ME WALK WITH HIM TODAY.
...SURE.
Thank you so much!
IT'S NOTHING BIG.

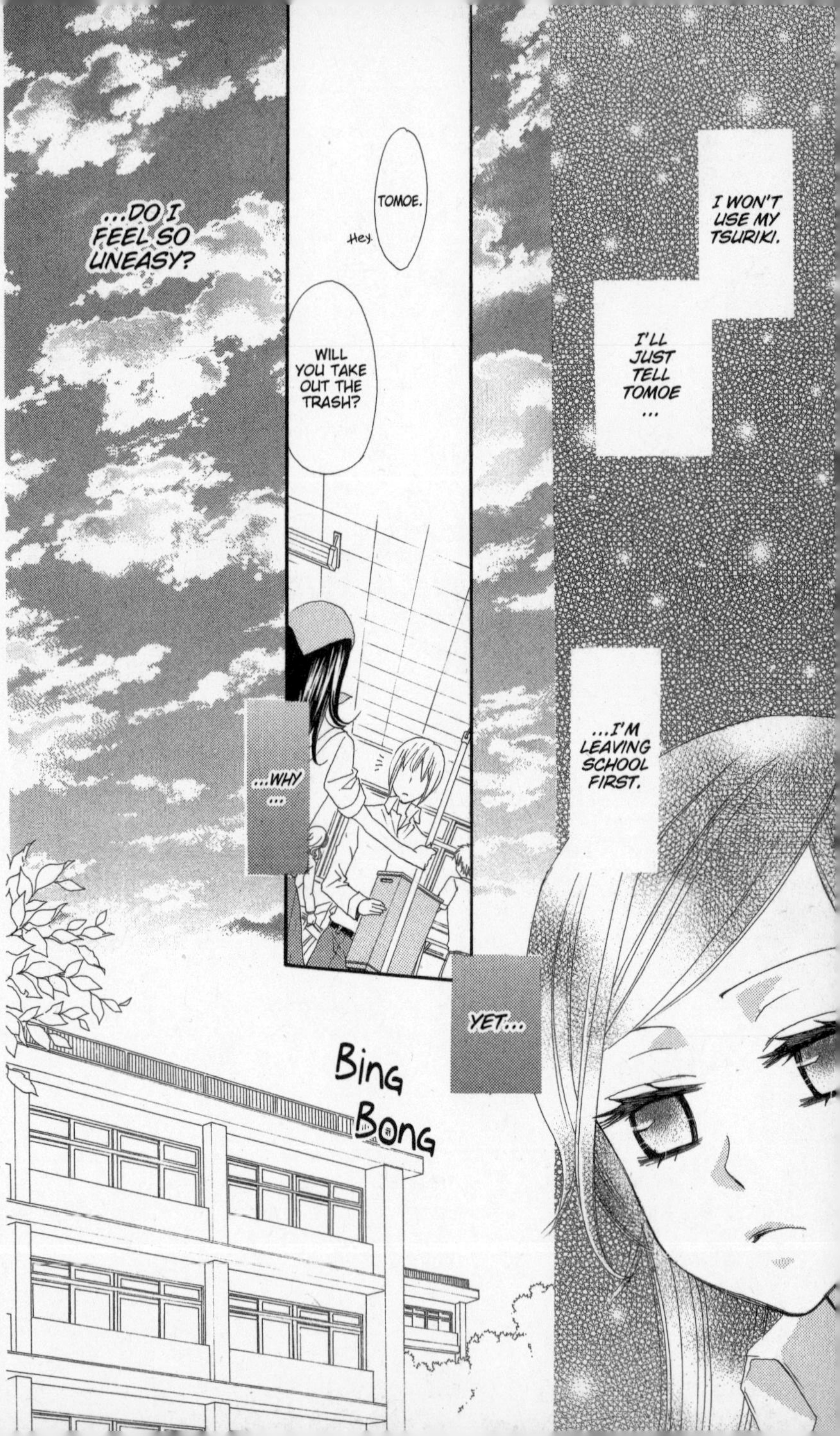
I WON'T USE MY TSURIKI.
I'LL JUST TELL TOMOE ...
...I'M LEAVING SCHOOL FIRST.
Hey.
TOMOE.
WILL YOU TAKE OUT THE TRASH?
YET...
...WHY ...
...DO I FEEL SO UNEASY?
Bing Bong

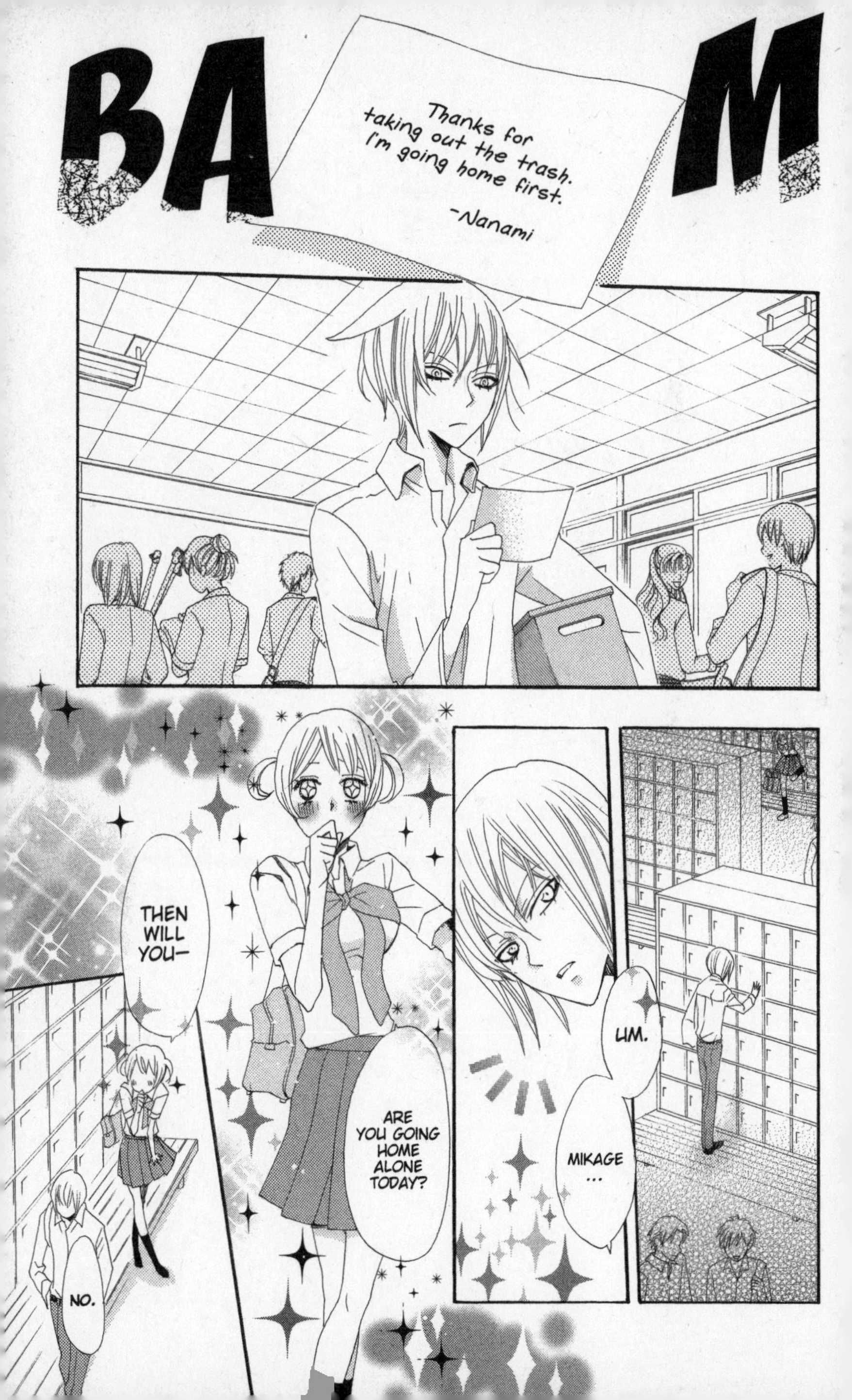
BAM
Thanks for taking out the trash. I'm going home first.
-Nanami
UM.
MIKAGE …
THEN WILL YOU—
ARE YOU GOING HOME ALONE TODAY?
NO.

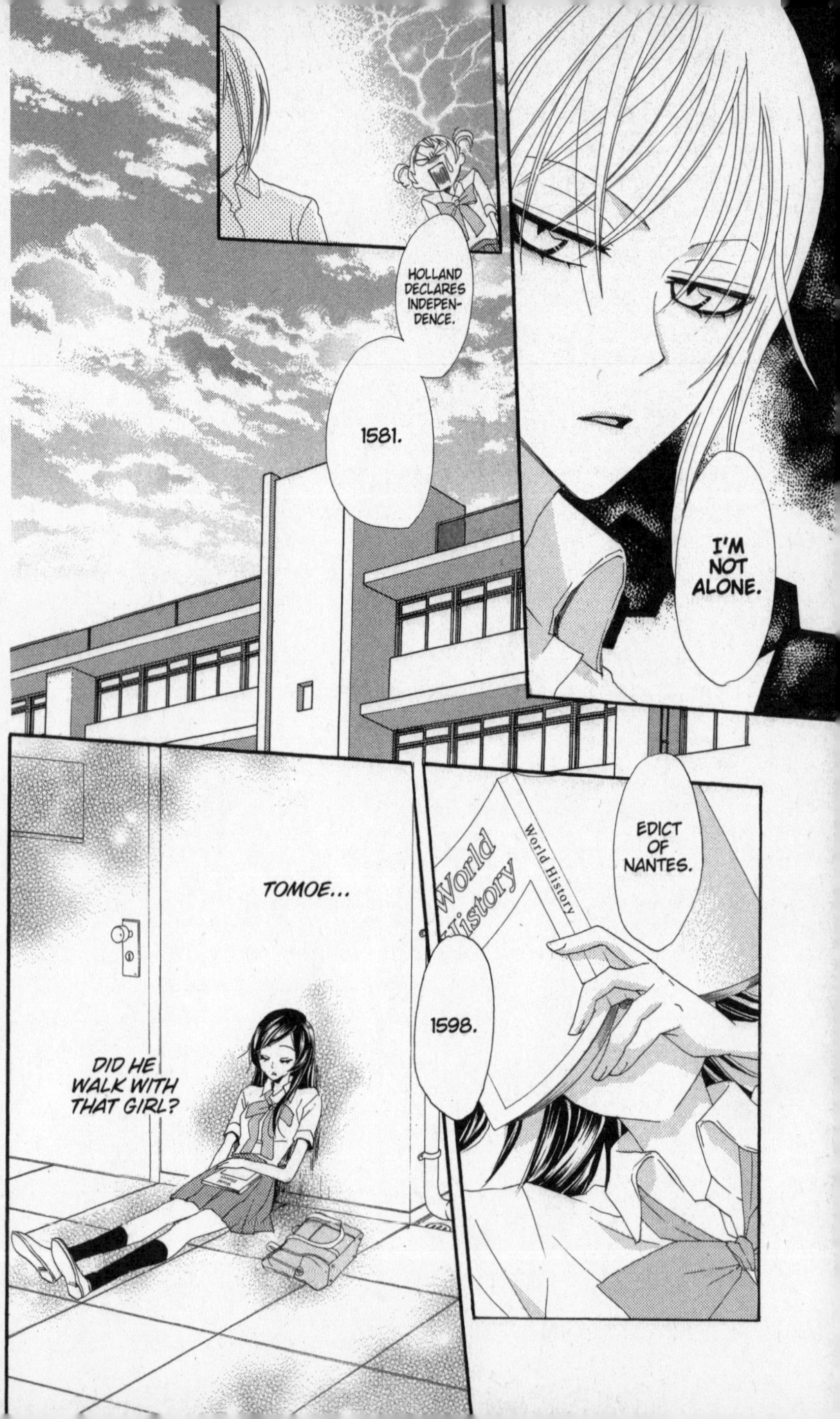
I'M NOT ALONE.
HOLLAND DECLARES INDEPENDENCE.
1581.
EDICT OF NANTES.
1598.
World History
World History
TOMOE...
DID HE WALK WITH THAT GIRL?

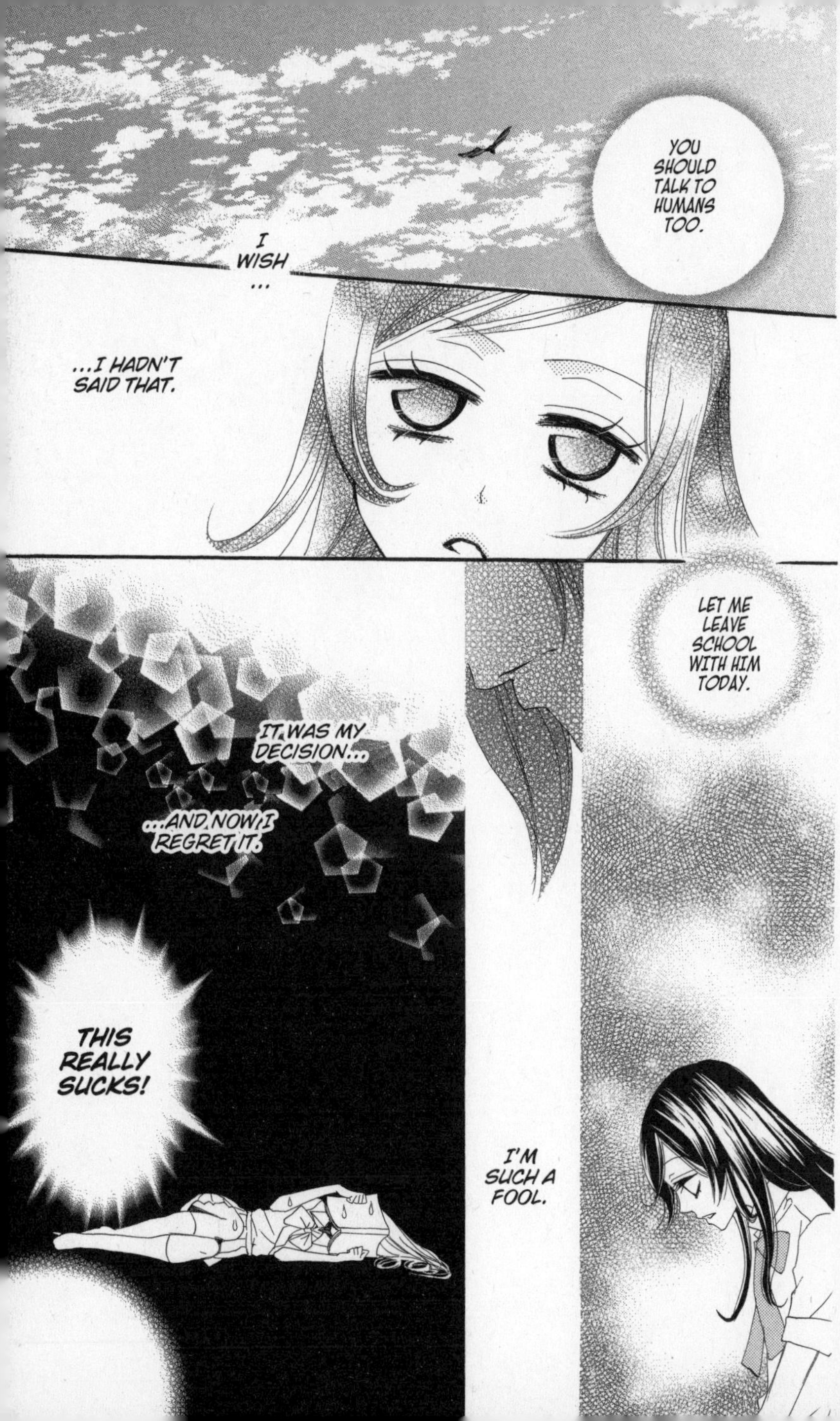
YOU SHOULD TALK TO HUMANS TOO.
I WISH ...
...I HADN'T SAID THAT.
LET ME LEAVE SCHOOL WITH HIM TODAY.
I'M SUCH A FOOL.
IT WAS MY DECISION...
...AND NOW I REGRET IT.
THIS REALLY SUCKS!

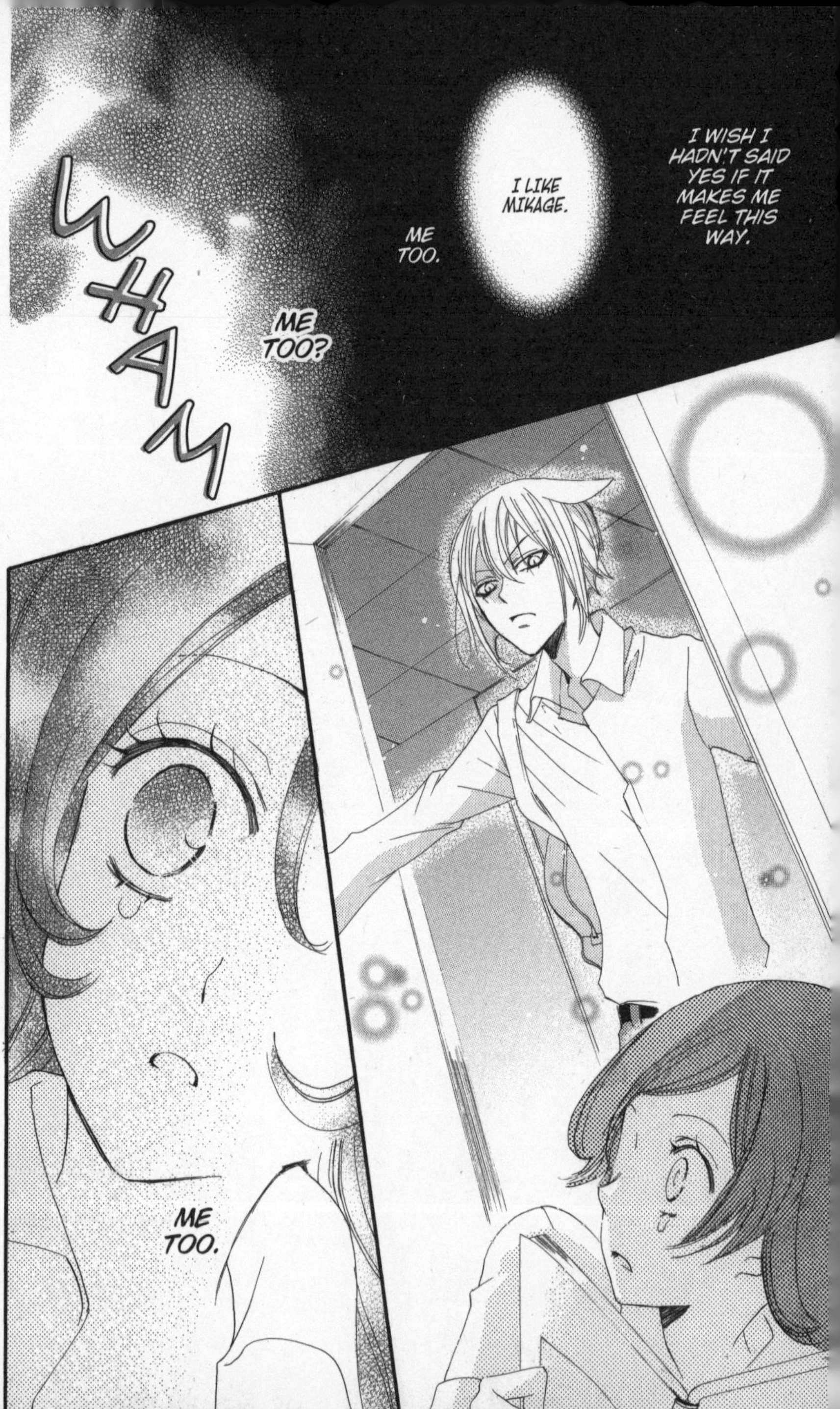
I WISH I HADN'T SAID YES IF IT MAKES ME FEEL THIS WAY.
I LIKE MIKAGE.
ME TOO.
ME TOO?
WHAM
ME TOO.

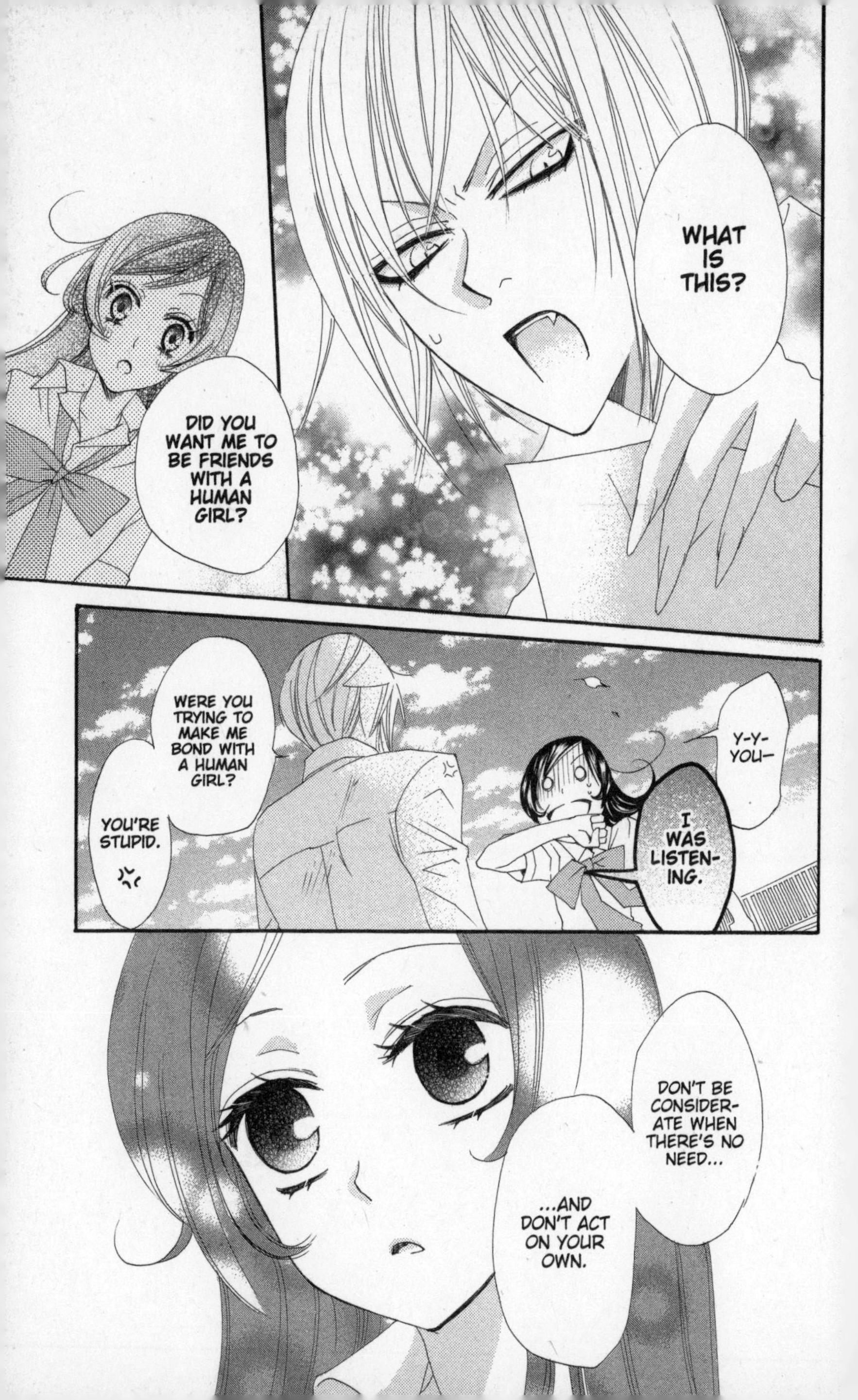
WHAT IS THIS?
DID YOU WANT ME TO BE FRIENDS WITH A HUMAN GIRL?
Y-Y-YOU—
I WAS LISTEN-ING.
WERE YOU TRYING TO MAKE ME BOND WITH A HUMAN GIRL?
YOU'RE STUPID.
DON'T BE CONSIDER-ATE WHEN THERE'S NO NEED...
...AND DON'T ACT ON YOUR OWN.

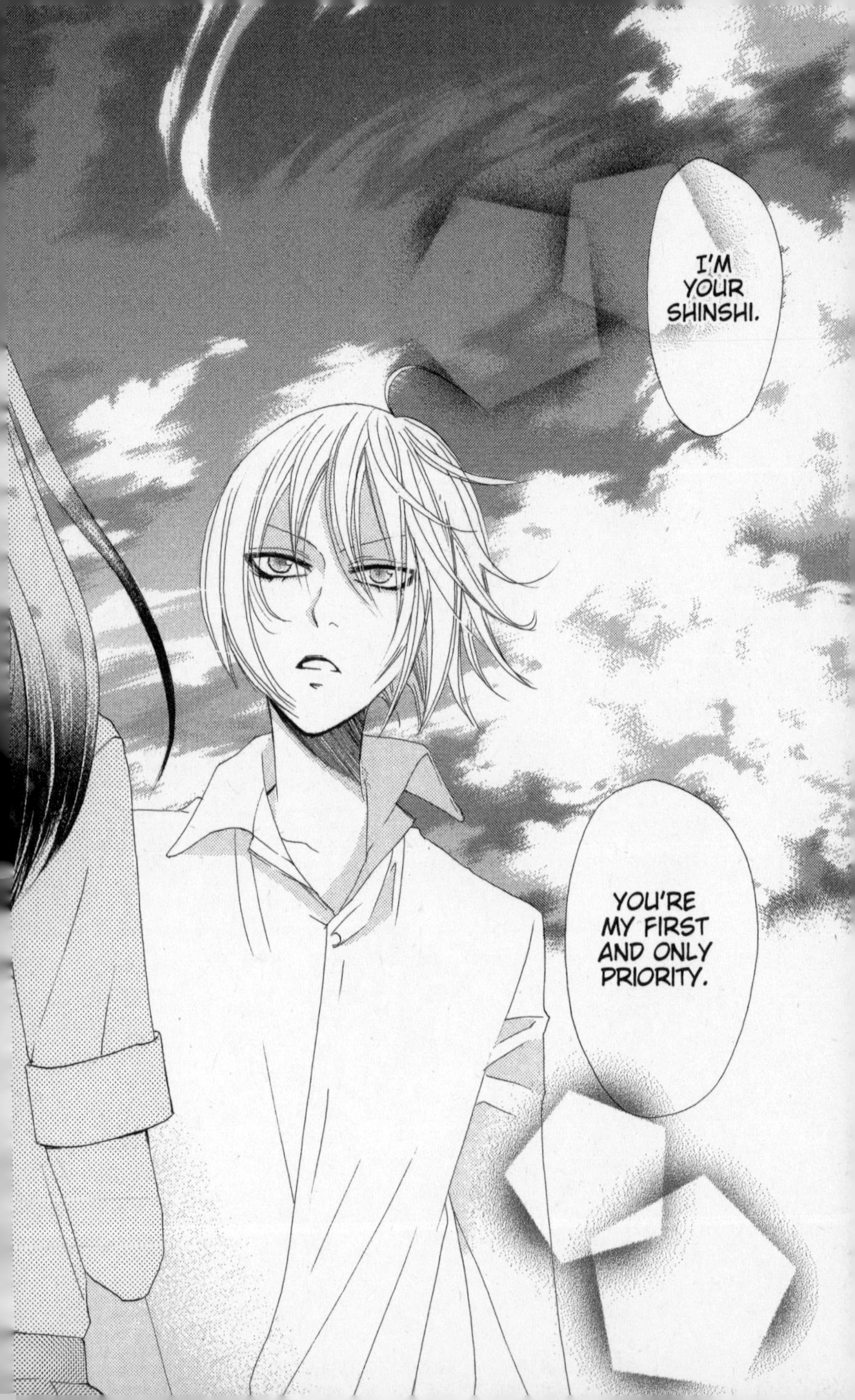
I'M YOUR SHINSHI.
YOU'RE MY FIRST AND ONLY PRIORITY.

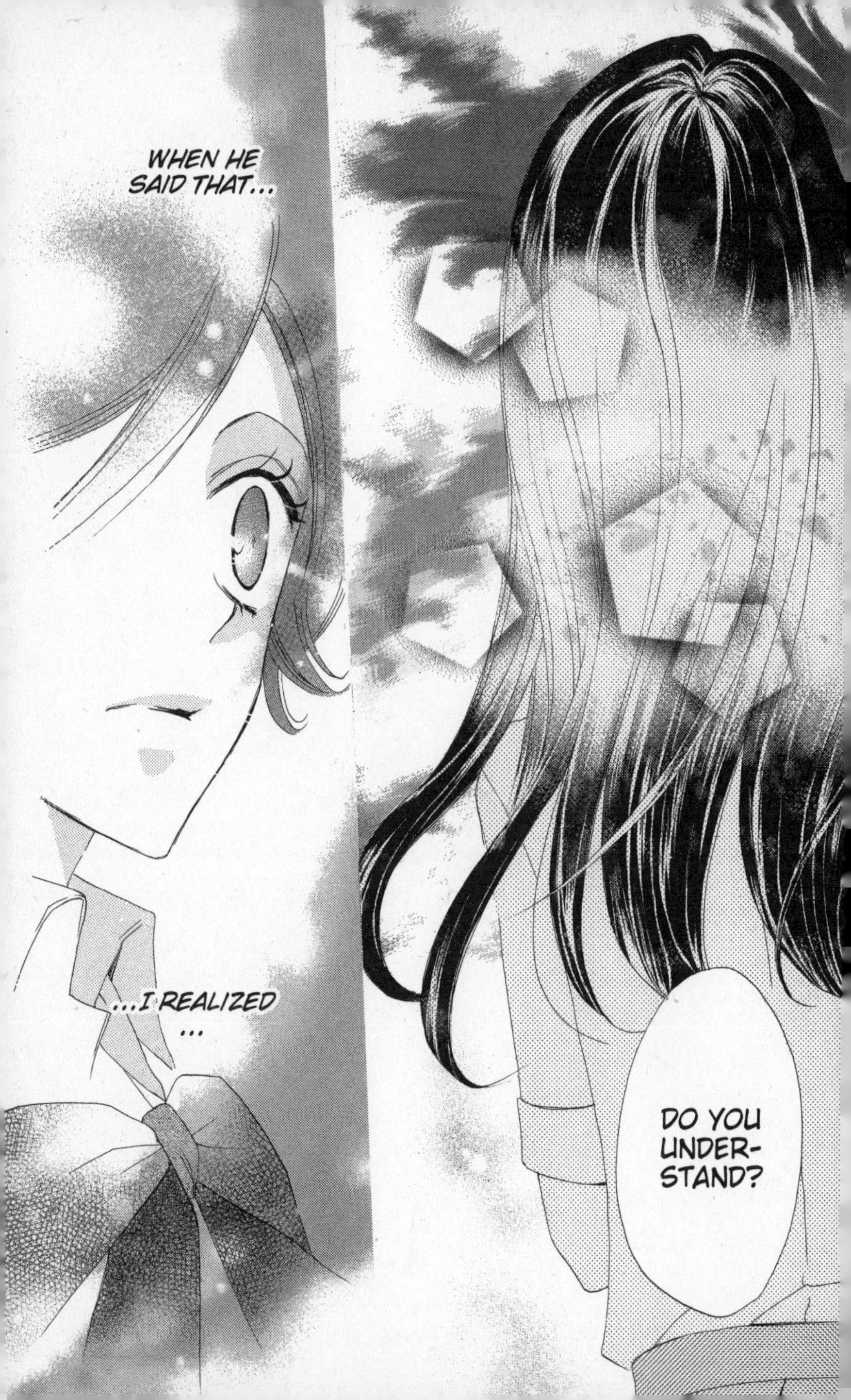
DO YOU UNDER-STAND?
WHEN HE SAID THAT...
...I REALIZED ...

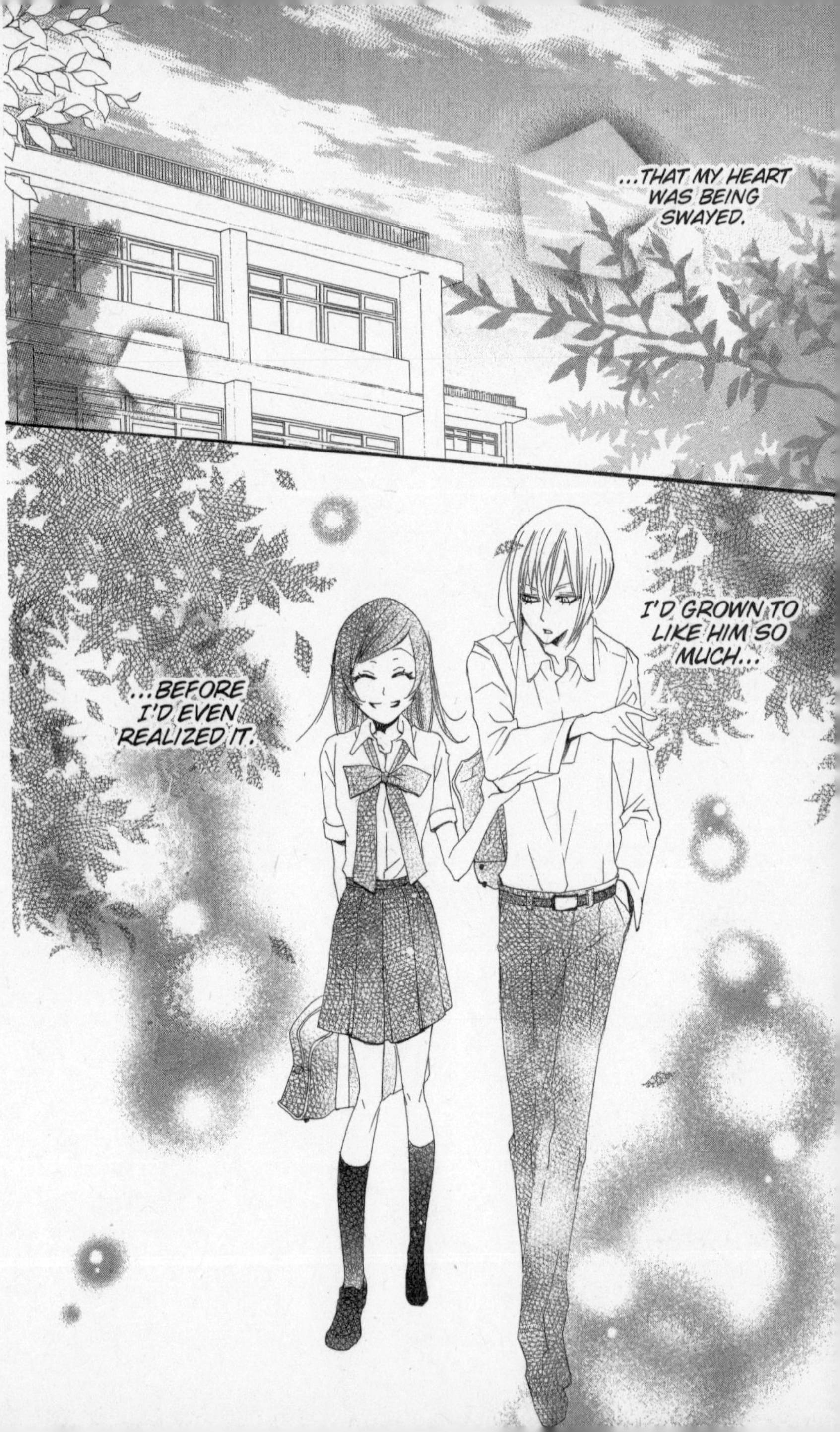
...THAT MY HEART WAS BEING SWAYED.
I'D GROWN TO LIKE HIM SO MUCH...
...BEFORE I'D EVEN REALIZED IT.

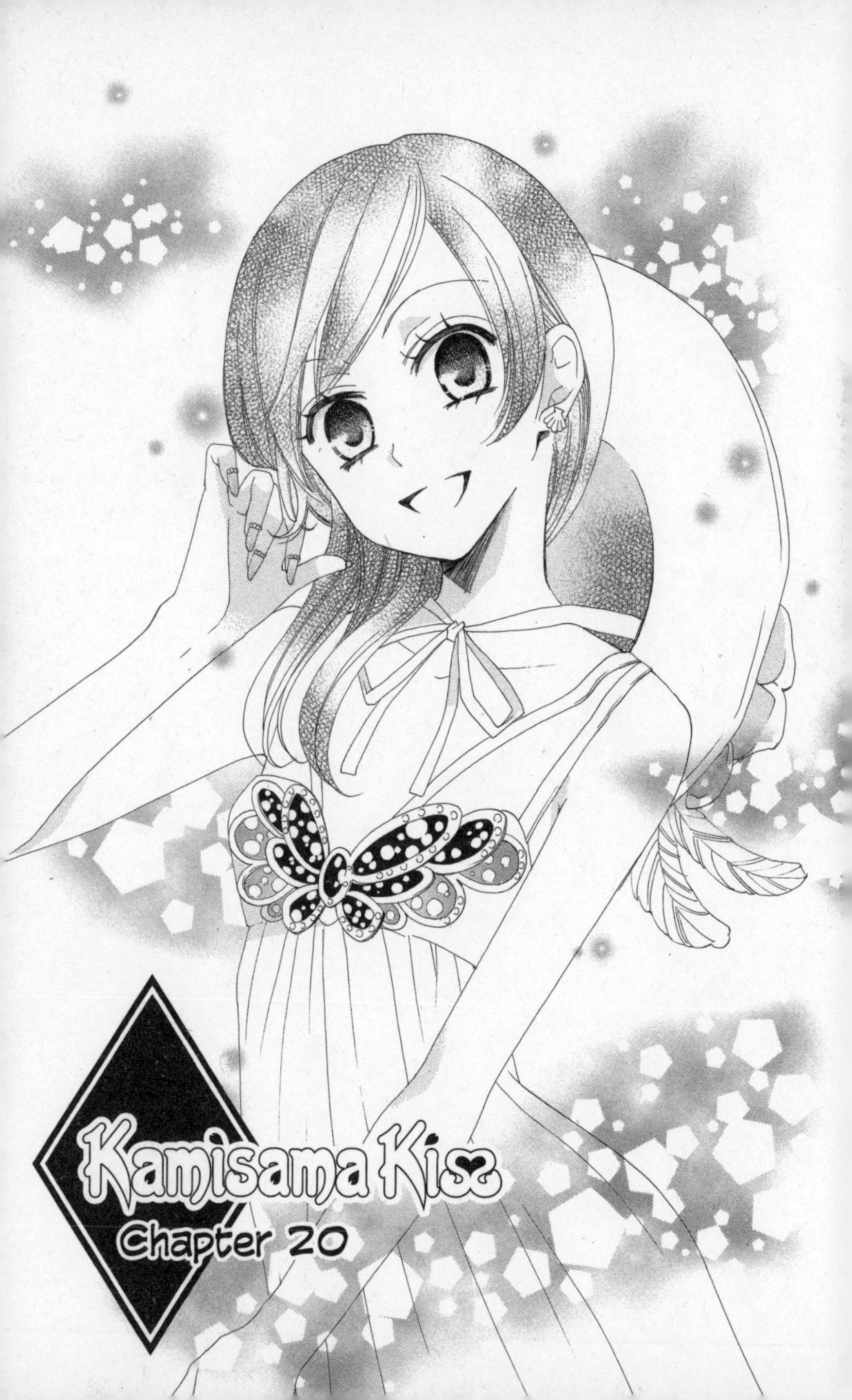
Kamisama Kiss
Chapter 20

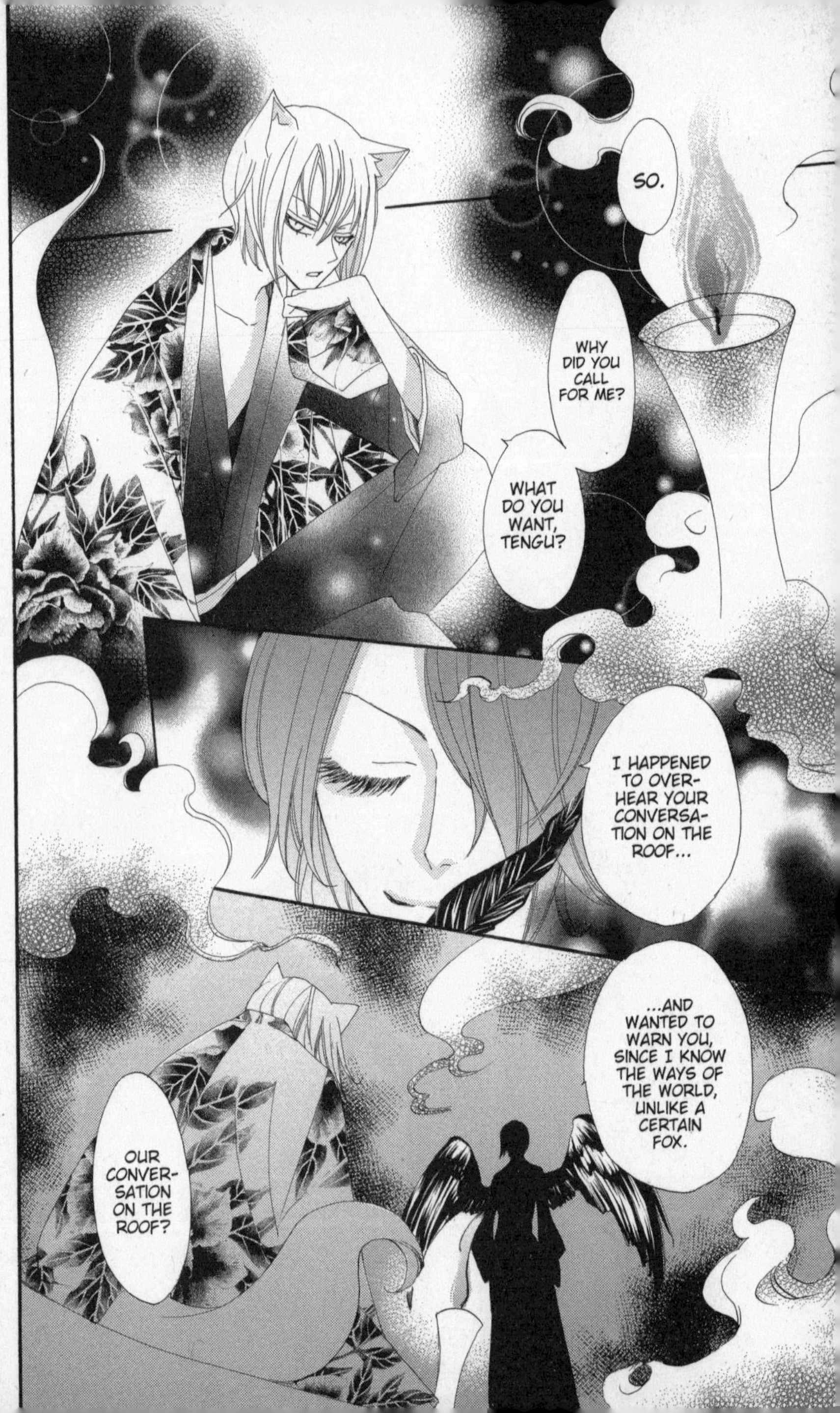
SO.
WHY DID YOU CALL FOR ME?
WHAT DO YOU WANT, TENGU?
I HAPPENED TO OVER-HEAR YOUR CONVERSA-TION ON THE ROOF...
...AND WANTED TO WARN YOU, SINCE I KNOW THE WAYS OF THE WORLD, UNLIKE A CERTAIN FOX.
OUR CONVER-SATION ON THE ROOF?

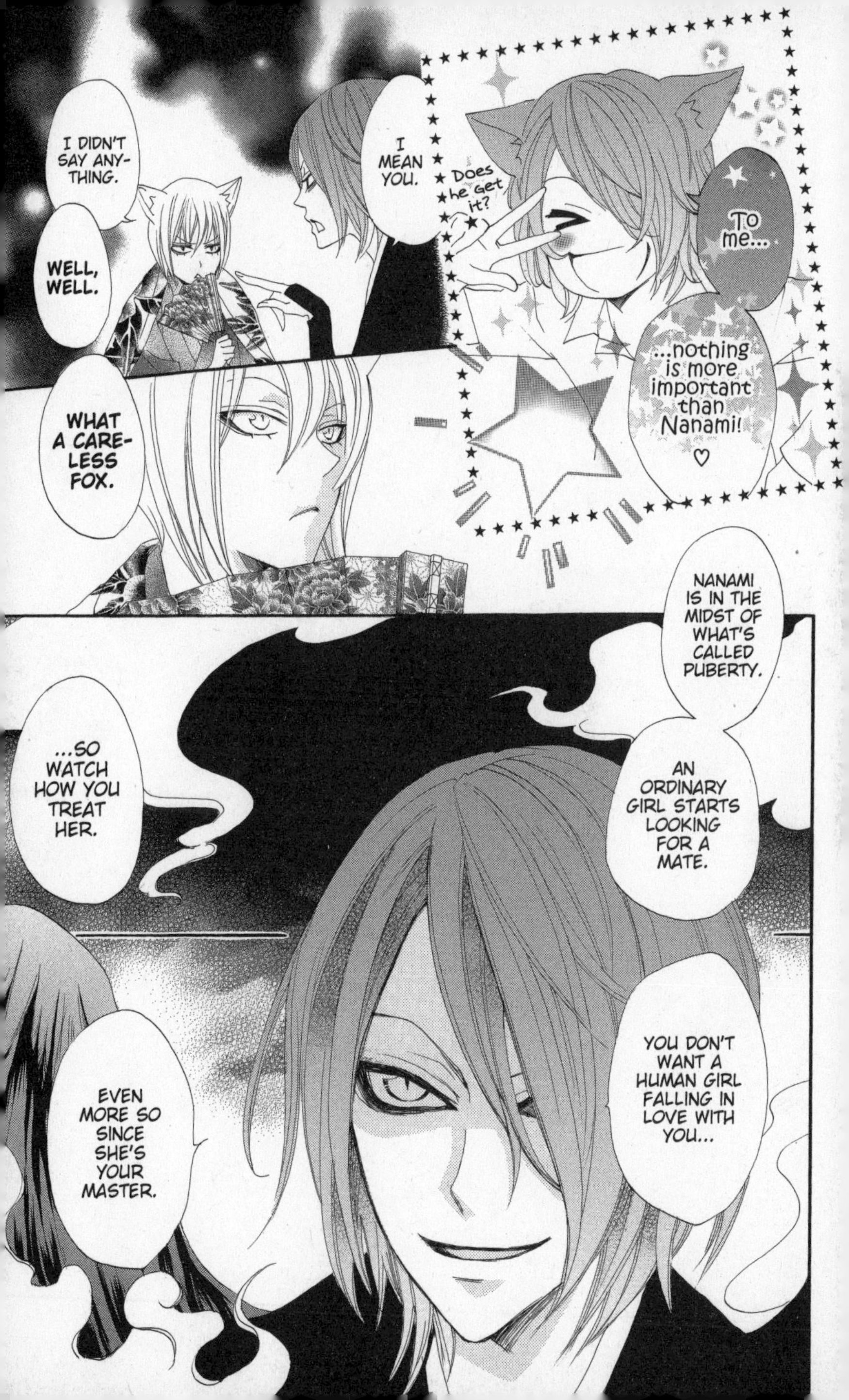
To me...
...nothing is more important than Nanami! ♡
Does he get it?
I MEAN YOU.
I DIDN'T SAY ANYTHING.
WELL, WELL.
WHAT A CARELESS FOX.
NANAMI IS IN THE MIDST OF WHAT'S CALLED PUBERTY.
AN ORDINARY GIRL STARTS LOOKING FOR A MATE.
...SO WATCH HOW YOU TREAT HER.
YOU DON'T WANT A HUMAN GIRL FALLING IN LOVE WITH YOU...
EVEN MORE SO SINCE SHE'S YOUR MASTER.

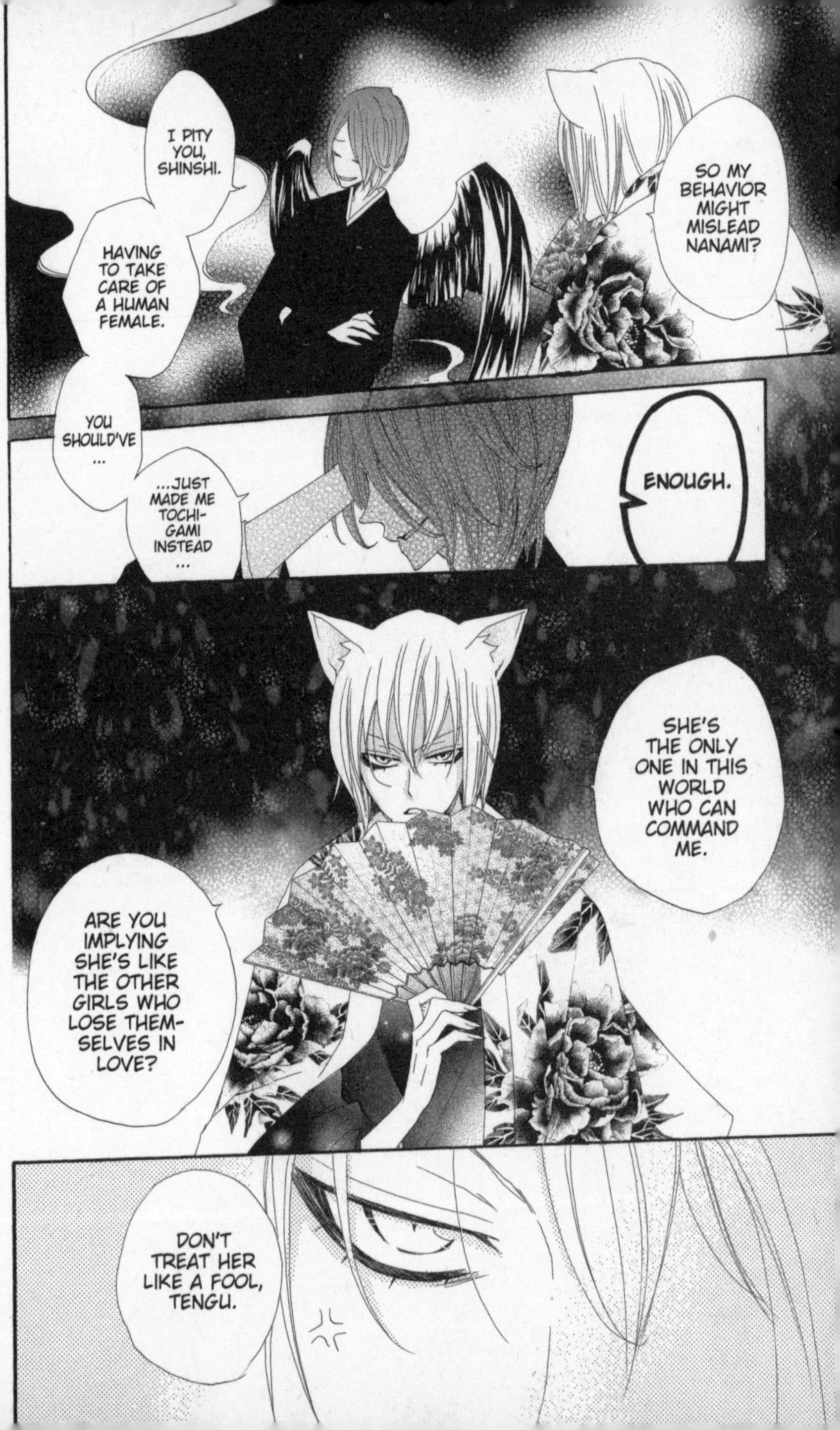
SO MY BEHAVIOR MIGHT MISLEAD NANAMI?
I PITY YOU, SHINSHI.
HAVING TO TAKE CARE OF A HUMAN FEMALE.
ENOUGH.
YOU SHOULD'VE ...
...JUST MADE ME TOCHIGAMI INSTEAD ...
SHE'S THE ONLY ONE IN THIS WORLD WHO CAN COMMAND ME.
ARE YOU IMPLYING SHE'S LIKE THE OTHER GIRLS WHO LOSE THEMSELVES IN LOVE?
DON'T TREAT HER LIKE A FOOL, TENGU.

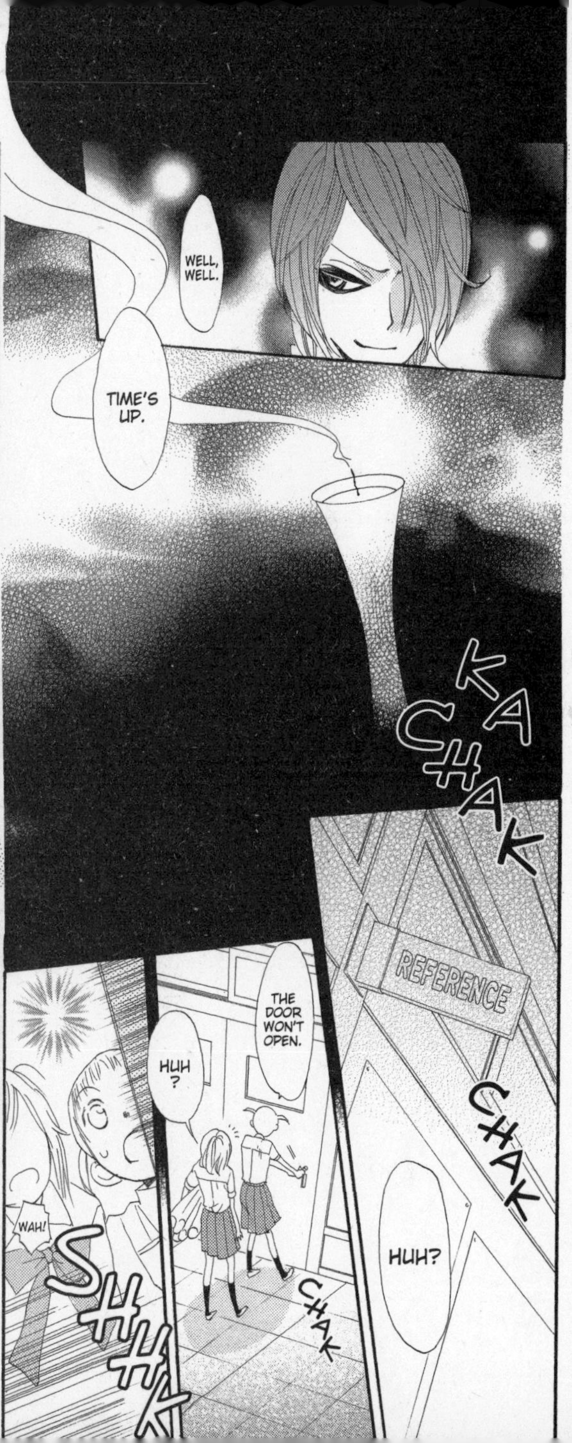
WELL, WELL.
TIME'S UP.
KA CHAK
REFERENCE
CHAK
HUH?
THE DOOR WON'T OPEN.
HUH?
CHAK
WAH!
SHHK

The other day, spirits appeared at my place. ✿

Someone came out of an empty bathroom, and the doorknob on the front door made sounds. W-o-w. It must be a zashiki-warashi. When there was one at my big sister's place, she was lucky at lotteries. I'll go buy some Lotto 6 tickets!

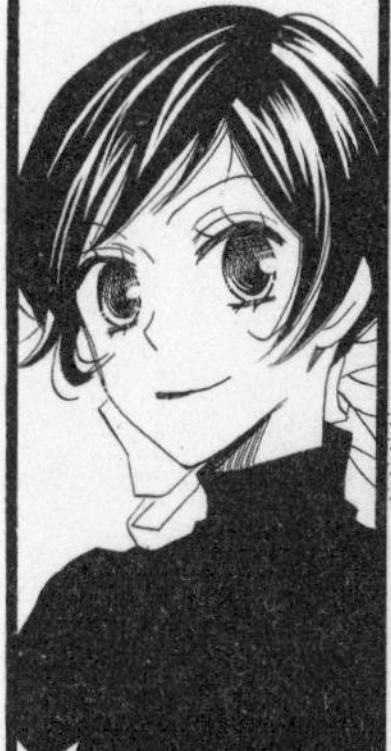

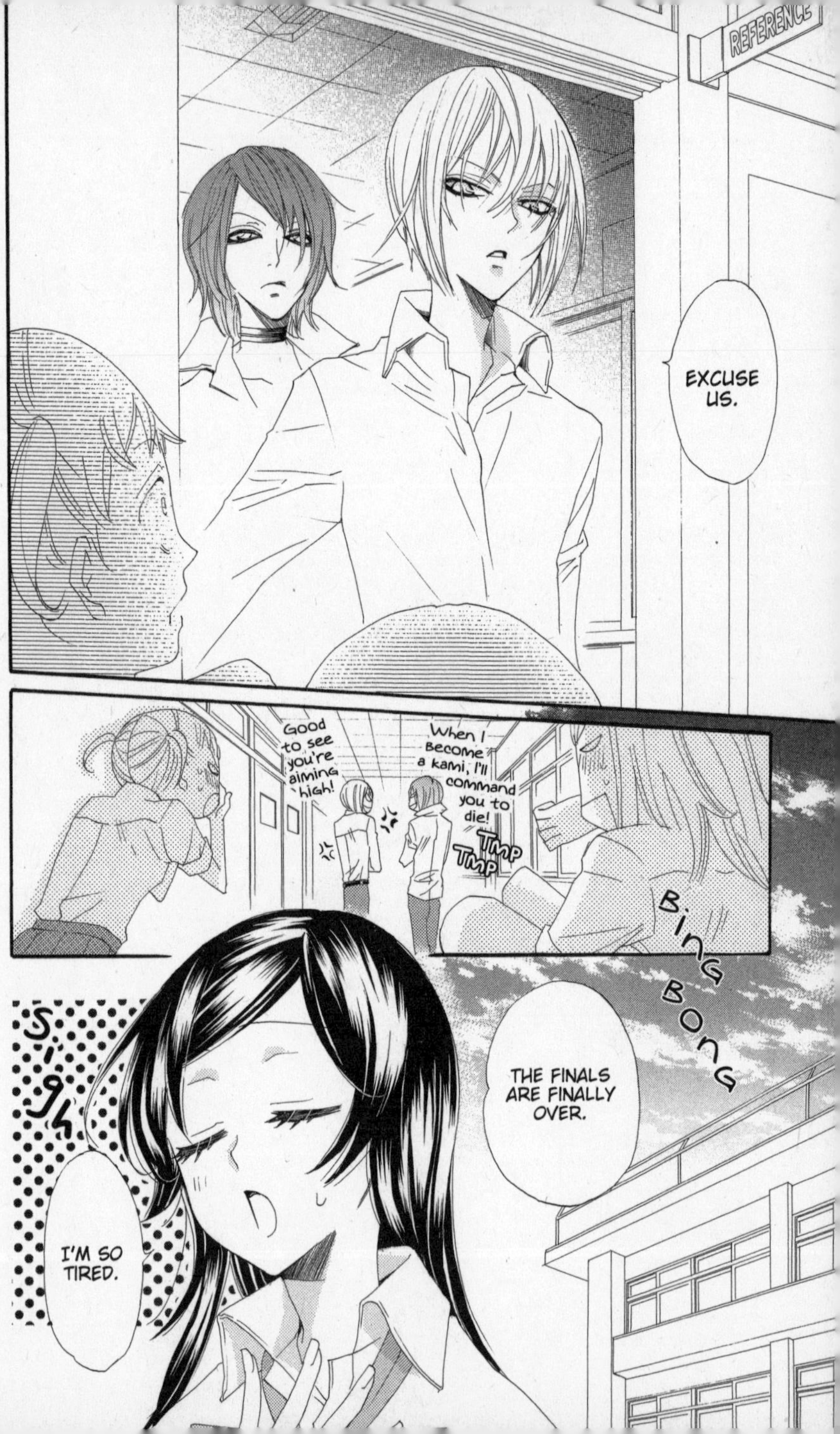
REFERENCE
EXCUSE US.
When I become a kami, I'll command you to die!
Good to see you're aiming high!
TMP TMP
BING BONG
THE FINALS ARE FINALLY OVER.
Sigh
I'M SO TIRED.

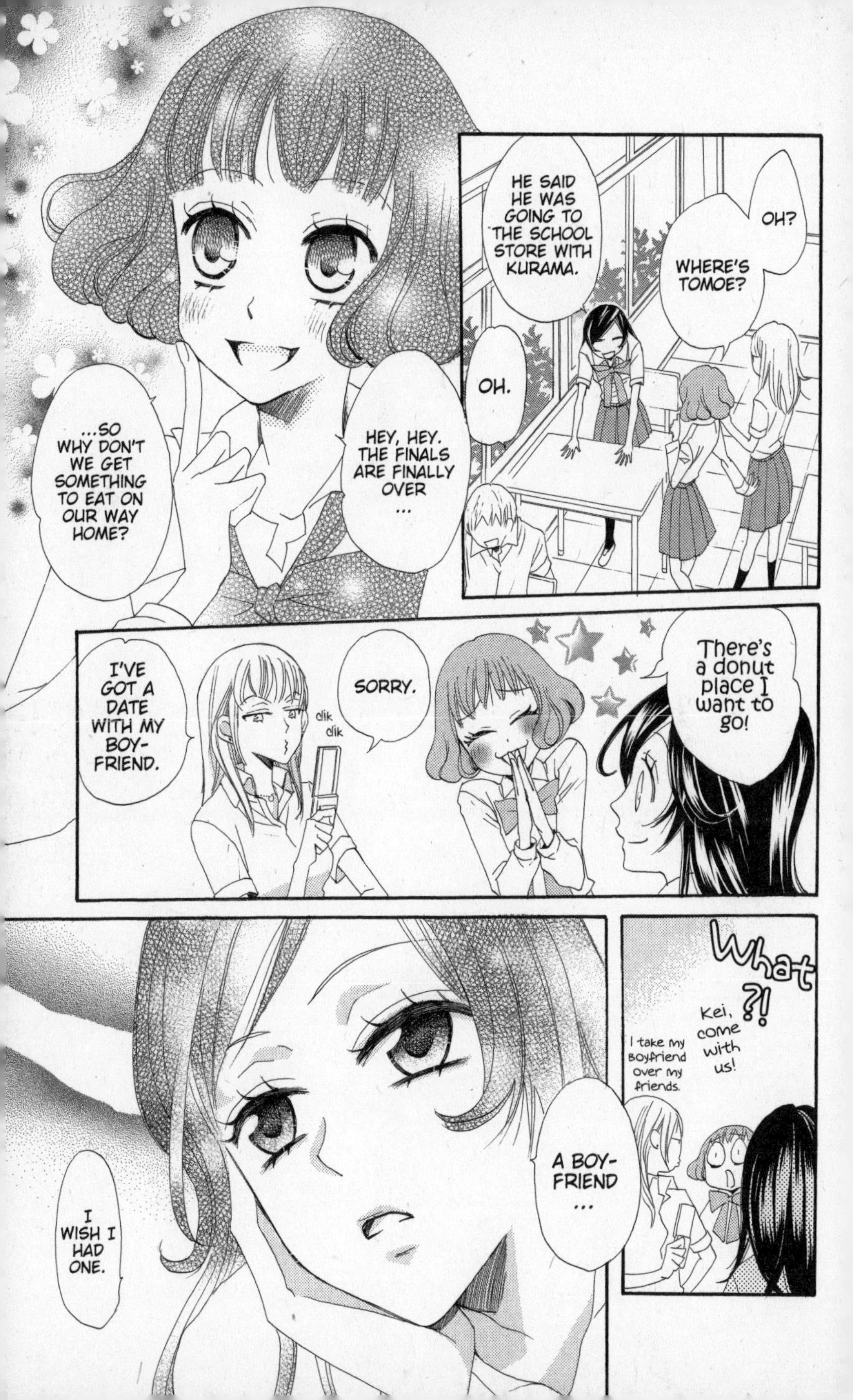
OH?
WHERE'S TOMOE?
HE SAID HE WAS GOING TO THE SCHOOL STORE WITH KURAMA.
OH.
HEY, HEY. THE FINALS ARE FINALLY OVER ...
...SO WHY DON'T WE GET SOMETHING TO EAT ON OUR WAY HOME?
There's a donut place I want to go!
SORRY.
clik clik
I'VE GOT A DATE WITH MY BOY-FRIEND.
What ?!
Kei, come with us!
I take my boyfriend over my friends.
A BOY-FRIEND ...
I WISH I HAD ONE.

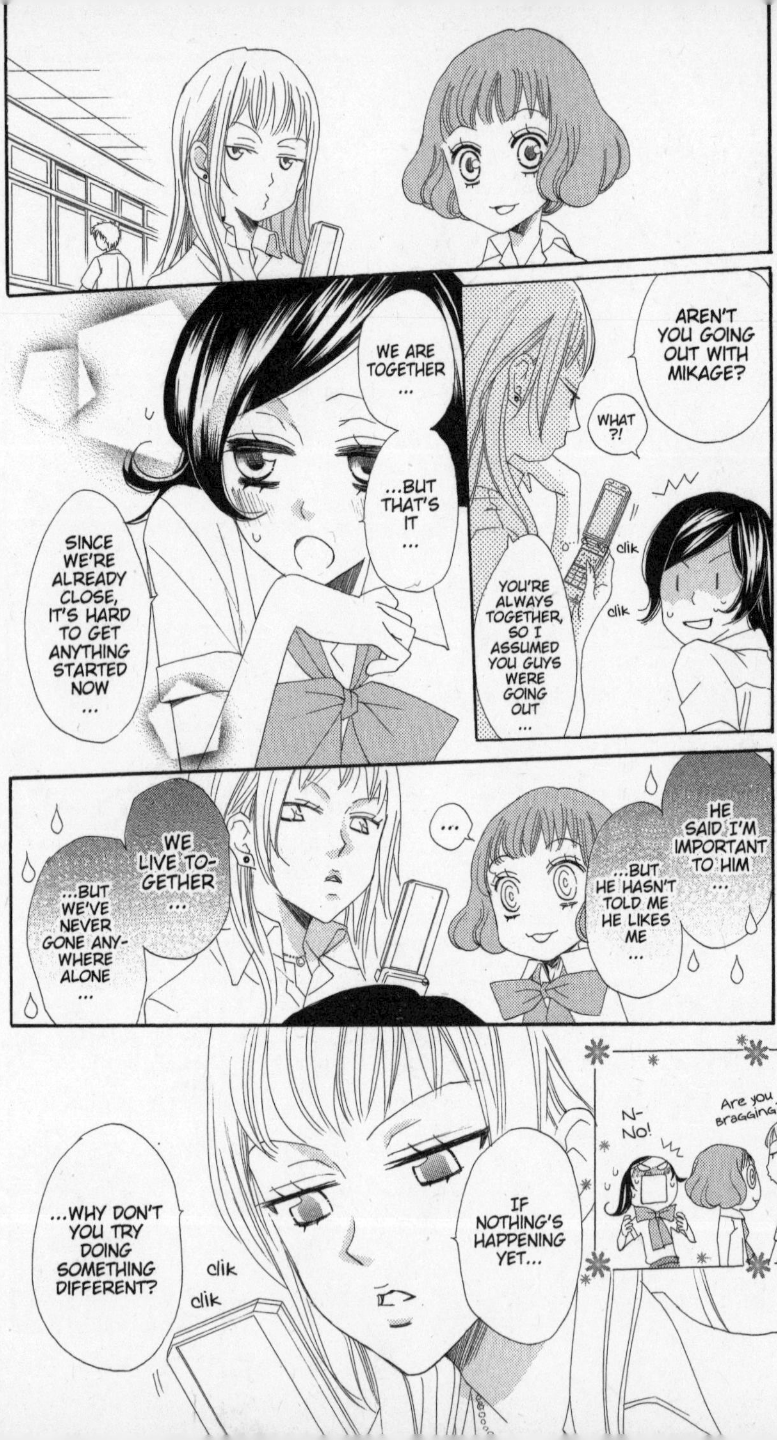
AREN'T YOU GOING OUT WITH MIKAGE?
WHAT?!
clik
clik
YOU'RE ALWAYS TOGETHER, SO I ASSUMED YOU GUYS WERE GOING OUT...
WE ARE TOGETHER...
...BUT THAT'S IT...
SINCE WE'RE ALREADY CLOSE, IT'S HARD TO GET ANYTHING STARTED NOW...
HE SAID I'M IMPORTANT TO HIM...
...BUT HE HASN'T TOLD ME HE LIKES ME...
...
WE LIVE TO-GETHER...
...BUT WE'VE NEVER GONE ANY-WHERE ALONE...
Are you bragging?
N-No!
IF NOTHING'S HAPPENING YET...
clik
clik
...WHY DON'T YOU TRY DOING SOMETHING DIFFERENT?

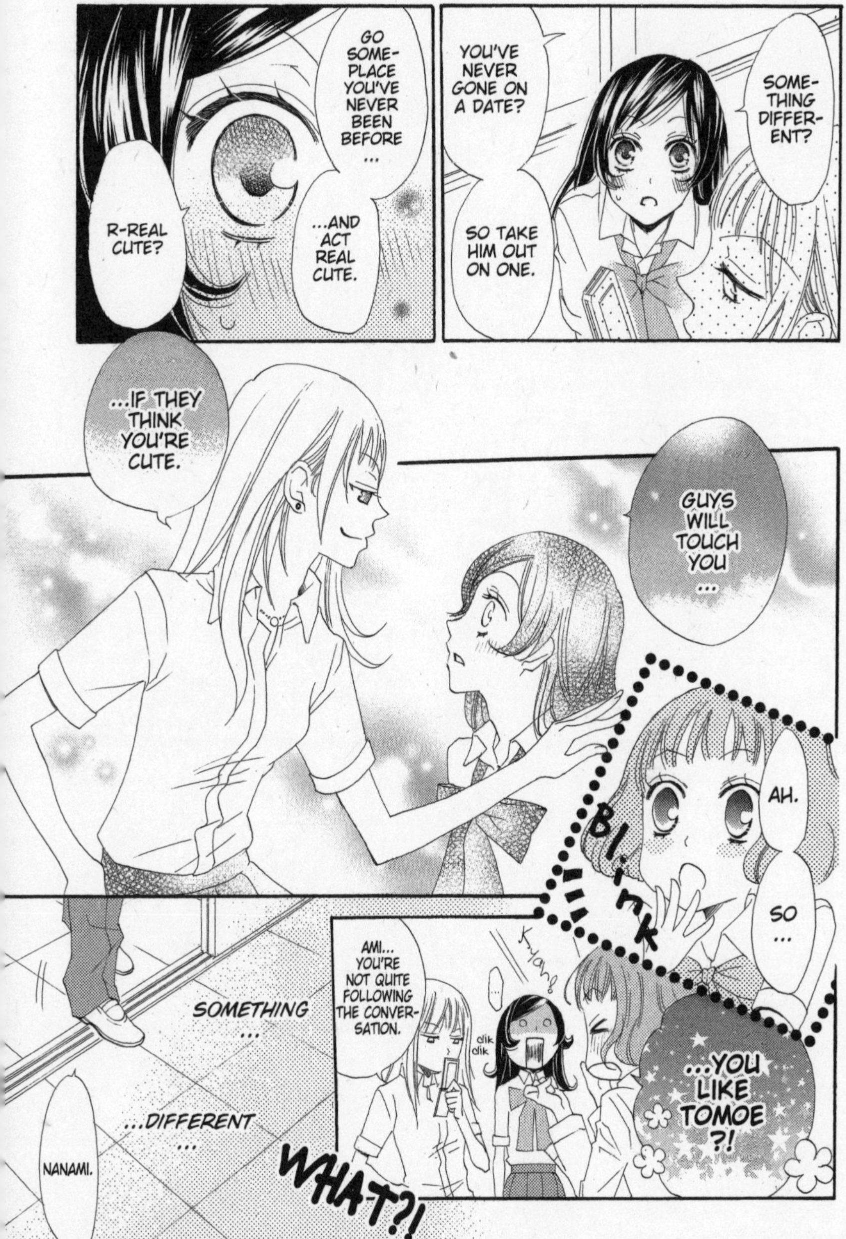
SOMETHING DIFFERENT?
YOU'VE NEVER GONE ON A DATE?
SO TAKE HIM OUT ON ONE.
GO SOMEPLACE YOU'VE NEVER BEEN BEFORE...
...AND ACT REAL CUTE.
R-REAL CUTE?
GUYS WILL TOUCH YOU...
...IF THEY THINK YOU'RE CUTE.
Blink
AH.
SO...
...YOU LIKE TOMOE?!
AMI... YOU'RE NOT QUITE FOLLOWING THE CONVERSATION.
...
Kyan!
clik clik
WHAT?!
SOMETHING...
...DIFFERENT...
NANAMI.

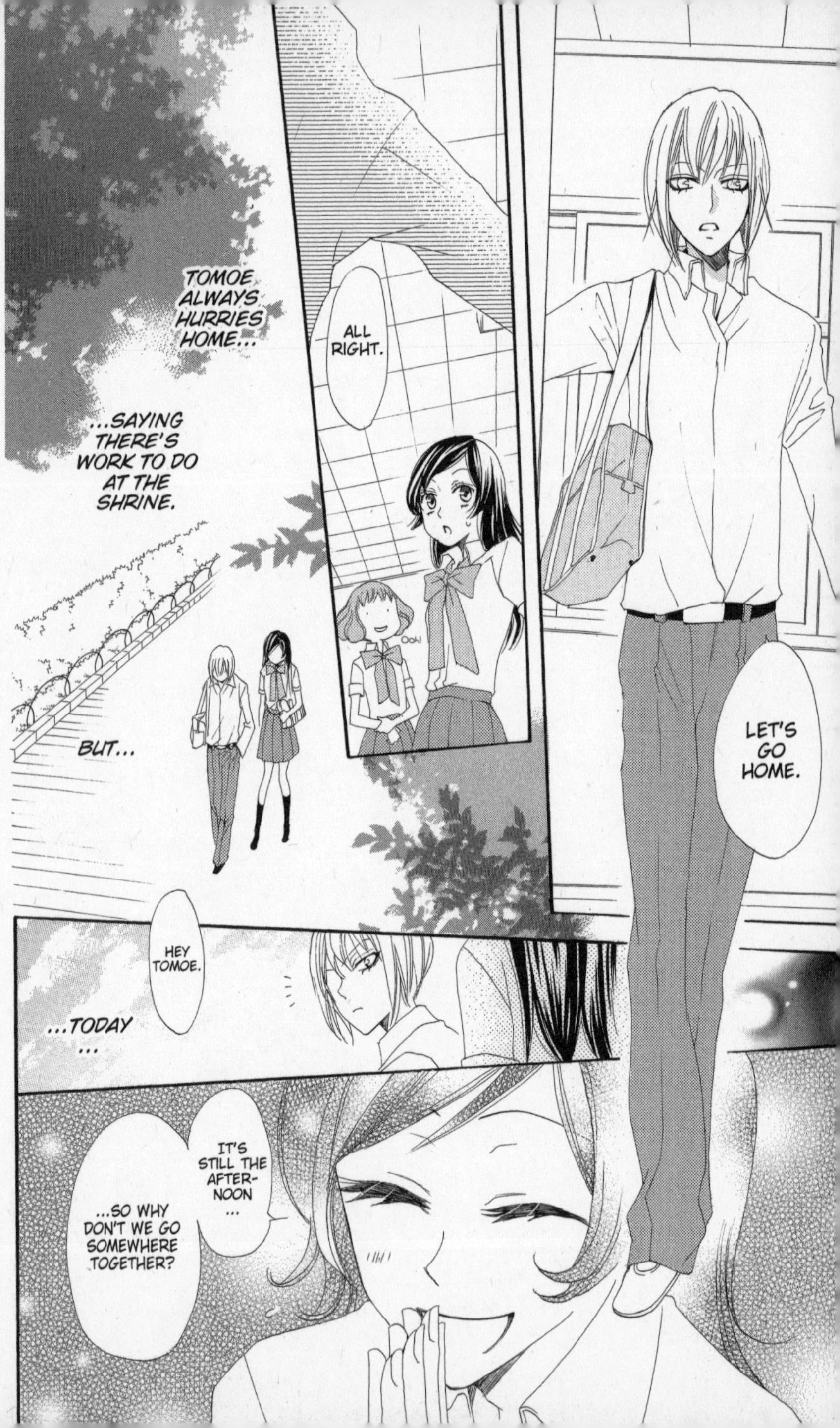
LET'S GO HOME.
ALL RIGHT.
Ooh!
TOMOE ALWAYS HURRIES HOME...
...SAYING THERE'S WORK TO DO AT THE SHRINE.
BUT...
HEY TOMOE.
...TODAY ...
IT'S STILL THE AFTER-NOON ...
...SO WHY DON'T WE GO SOMEWHERE TOGETHER?

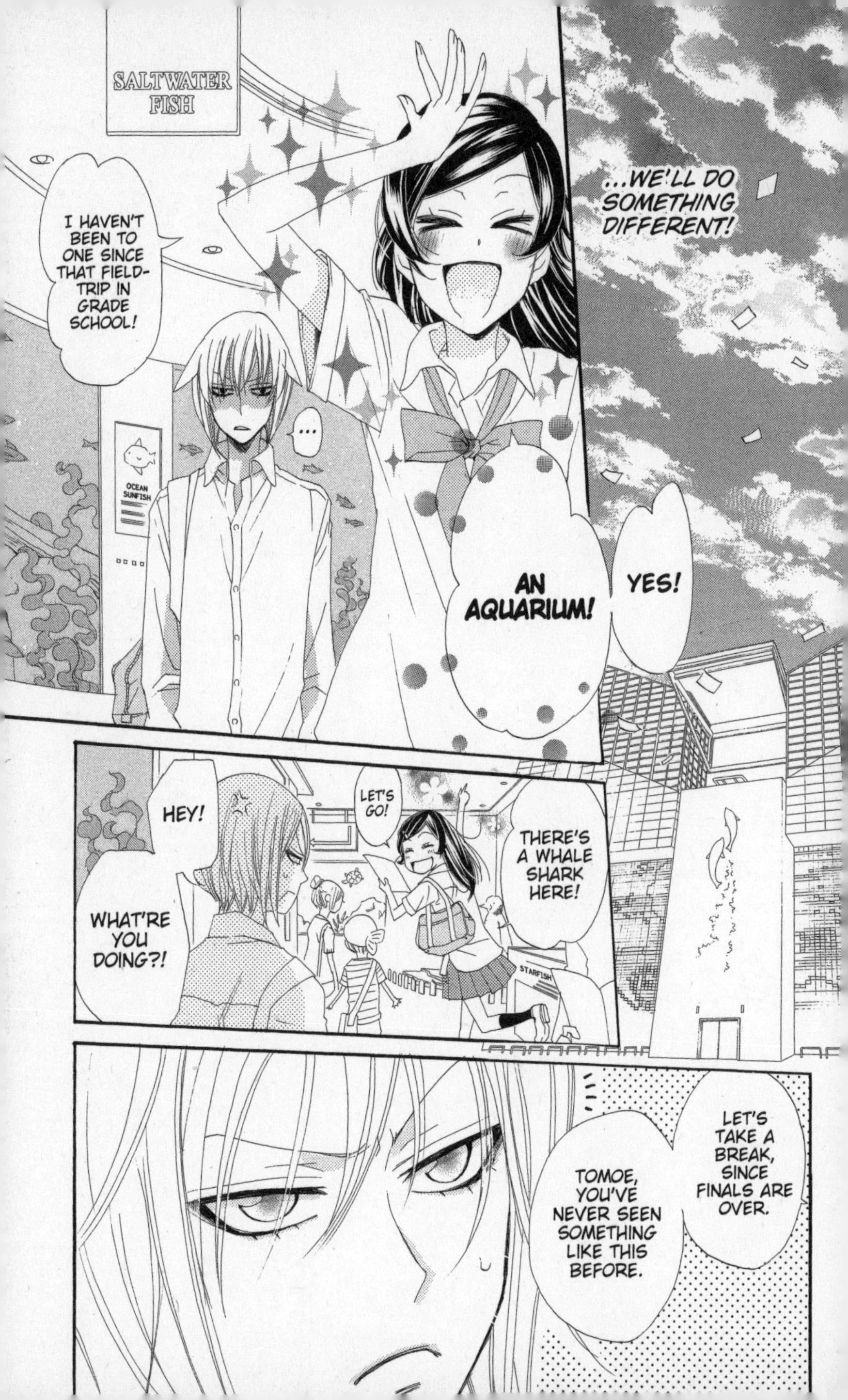
...WE'LL DO SOMETHING DIFFERENT!
YES!
AN AQUARIUM!
SALTWATER FISH
I HAVEN'T BEEN TO ONE SINCE THAT FIELD-TRIP IN GRADE SCHOOL!
...
OCEAN SUNFISH
THERE'S A WHALE SHARK HERE!
LET'S GO!
STARFISH
HEY!
WHAT'RE YOU DOING?!
LET'S TAKE A BREAK, SINCE FINALS ARE OVER.
TOMOE, YOU'VE NEVER SEEN SOMETHING LIKE THIS BEFORE.

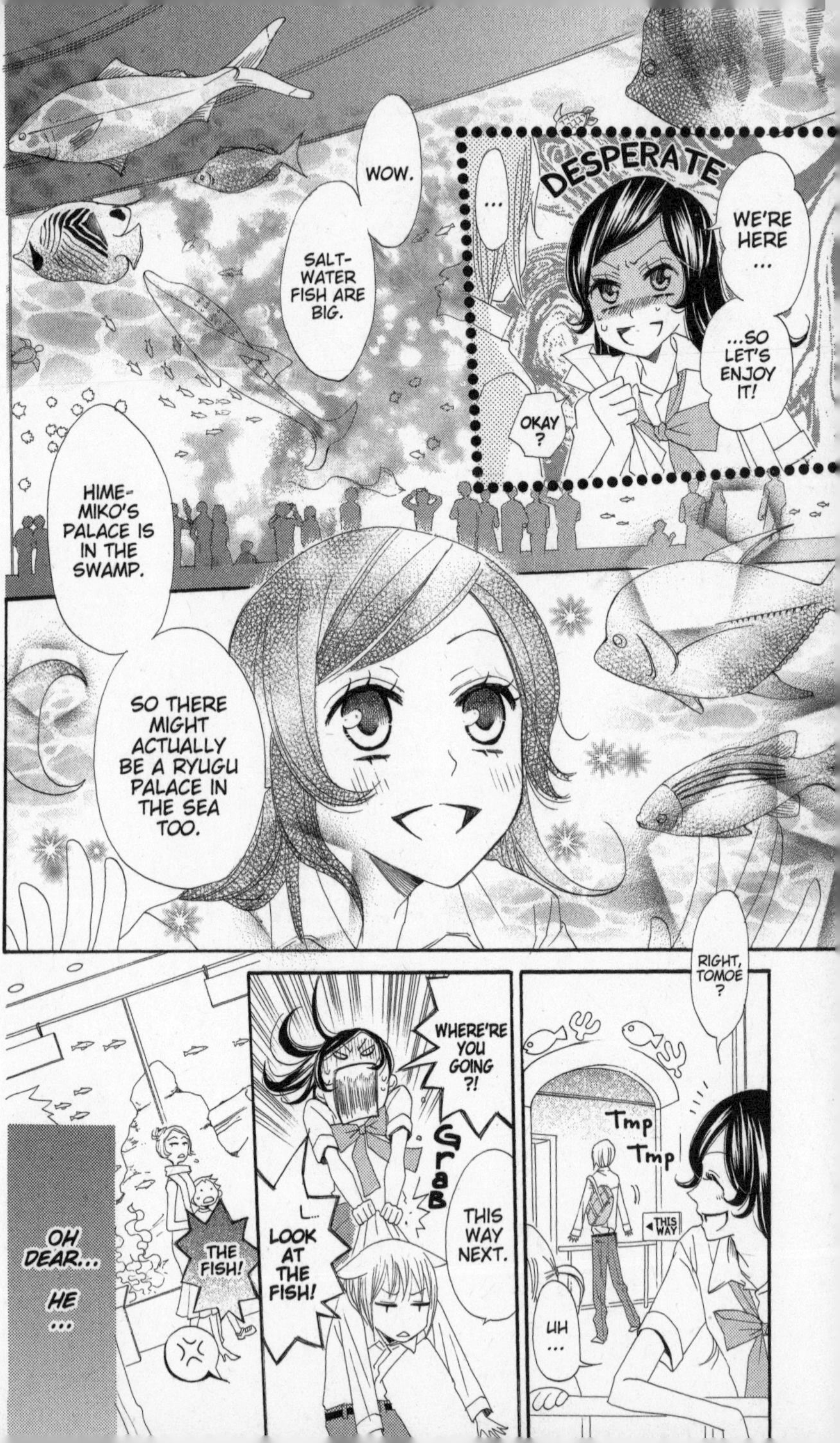
WOW.
SALT-WATER FISH ARE BIG.
DESPERATE
...
WE'RE HERE ...
...SO LET'S ENJOY IT!
OKAY?
HIME-MIKO'S PALACE IS IN THE SWAMP.
SO THERE MIGHT ACTUALLY BE A RYUGU PALACE IN THE SEA TOO.
RIGHT, TOMOE?
Tmp Tmp
THIS WAY
UH ...
WHERE'RE YOU GOING?!
GRAB
THIS WAY NEXT.
L... LOOK AT THE FISH!
THE FISH!
OH DEAR... HE ...

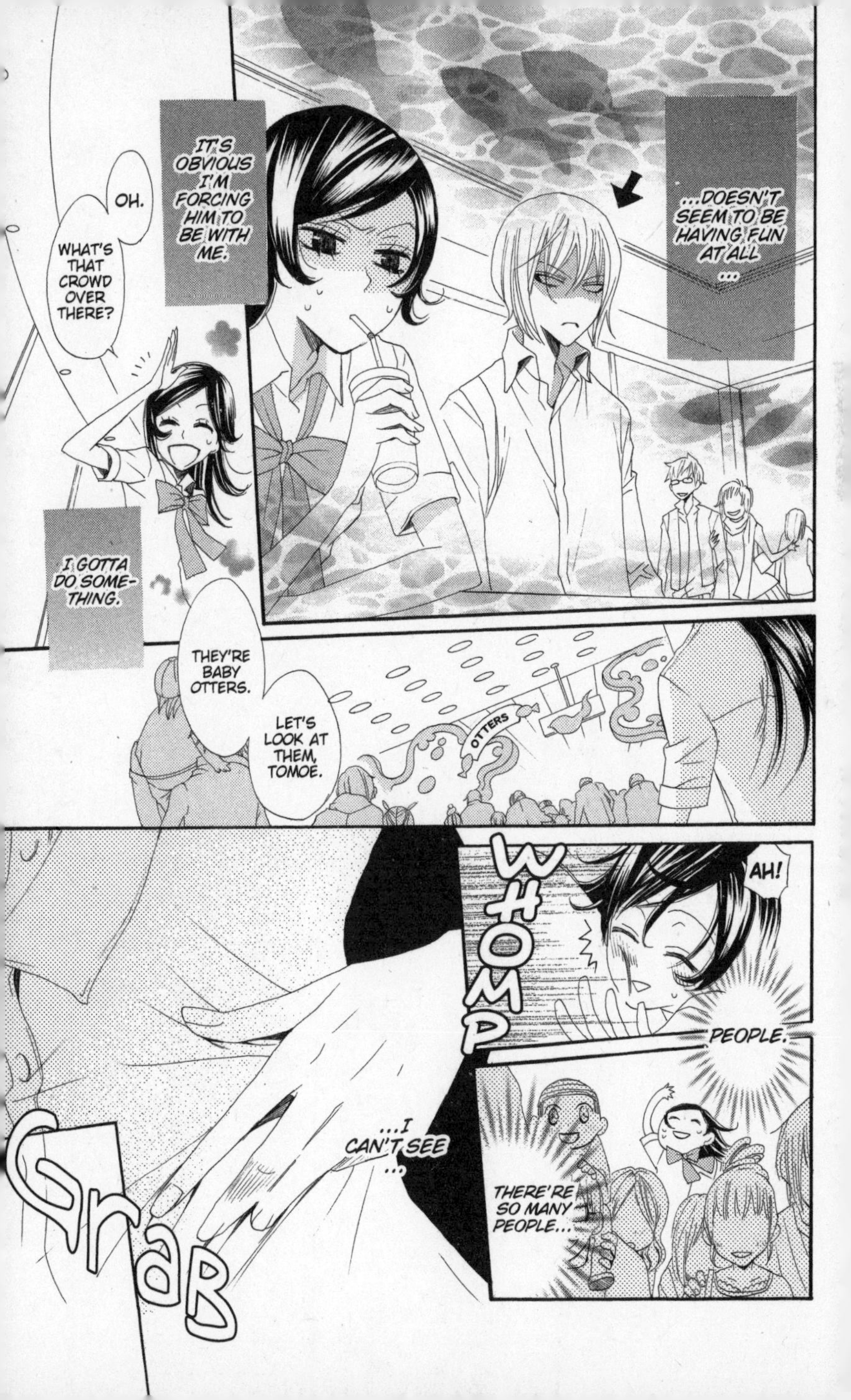
...DOESN'T SEEM TO BE HAVING FUN AT ALL ...
IT'S OBVIOUS I'M FORCING HIM TO BE WITH ME.
OH.
WHAT'S THAT CROWD OVER THERE?
I GOTTA DO SOMETHING.
THEY'RE BABY OTTERS.
LET'S LOOK AT THEM, TOMOE.
OTTERS
AH!
WHOMP
PEOPLE.
THERE'RE SO MANY PEOPLE...
...I CAN'T SEE ...
GRAB

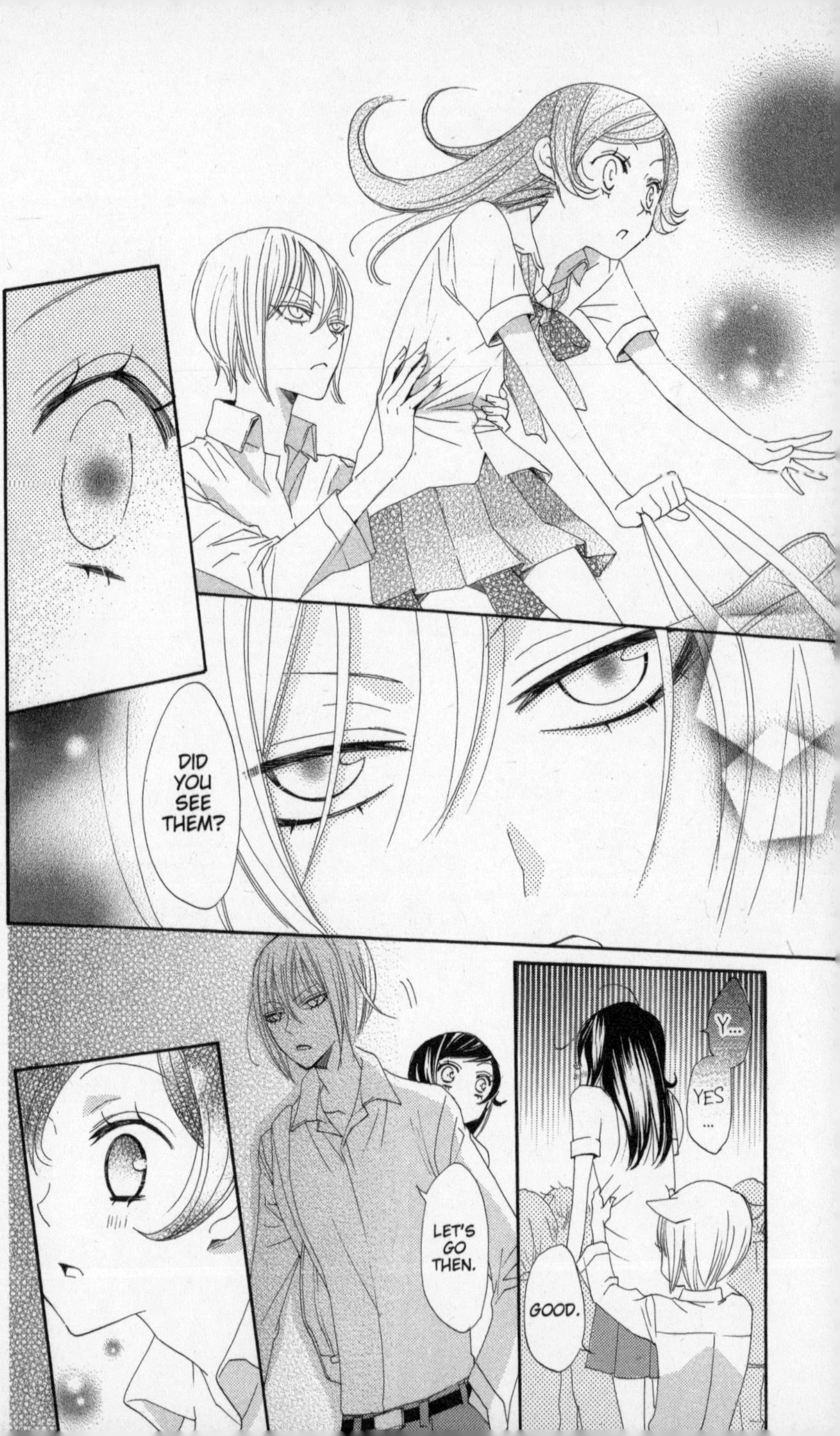
DID YOU SEE THEM?
Y...
YES...
GOOD.
LET'S GO THEN.

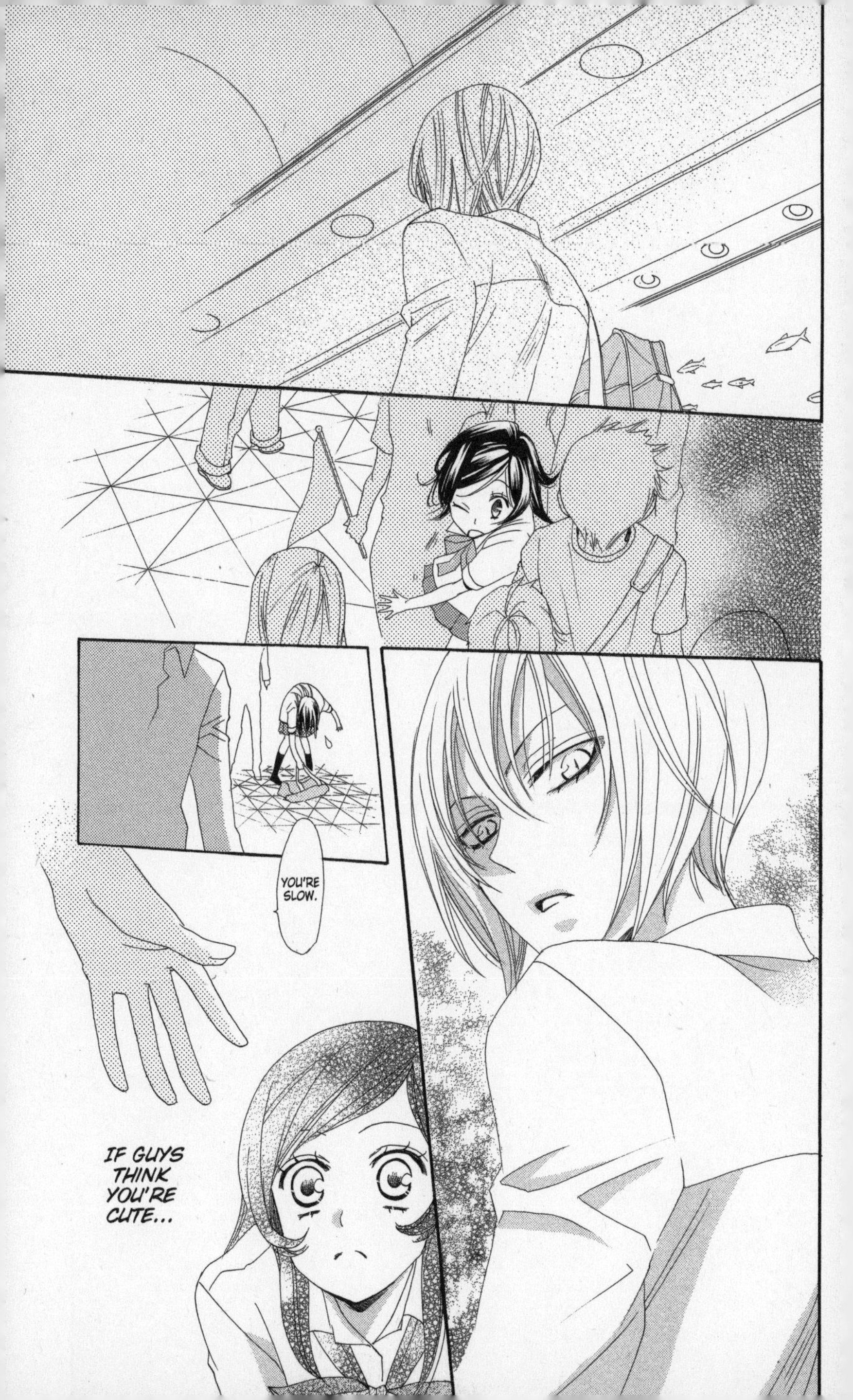
YOU'RE SLOW.
IF GUYS THINK YOU'RE CUTE...

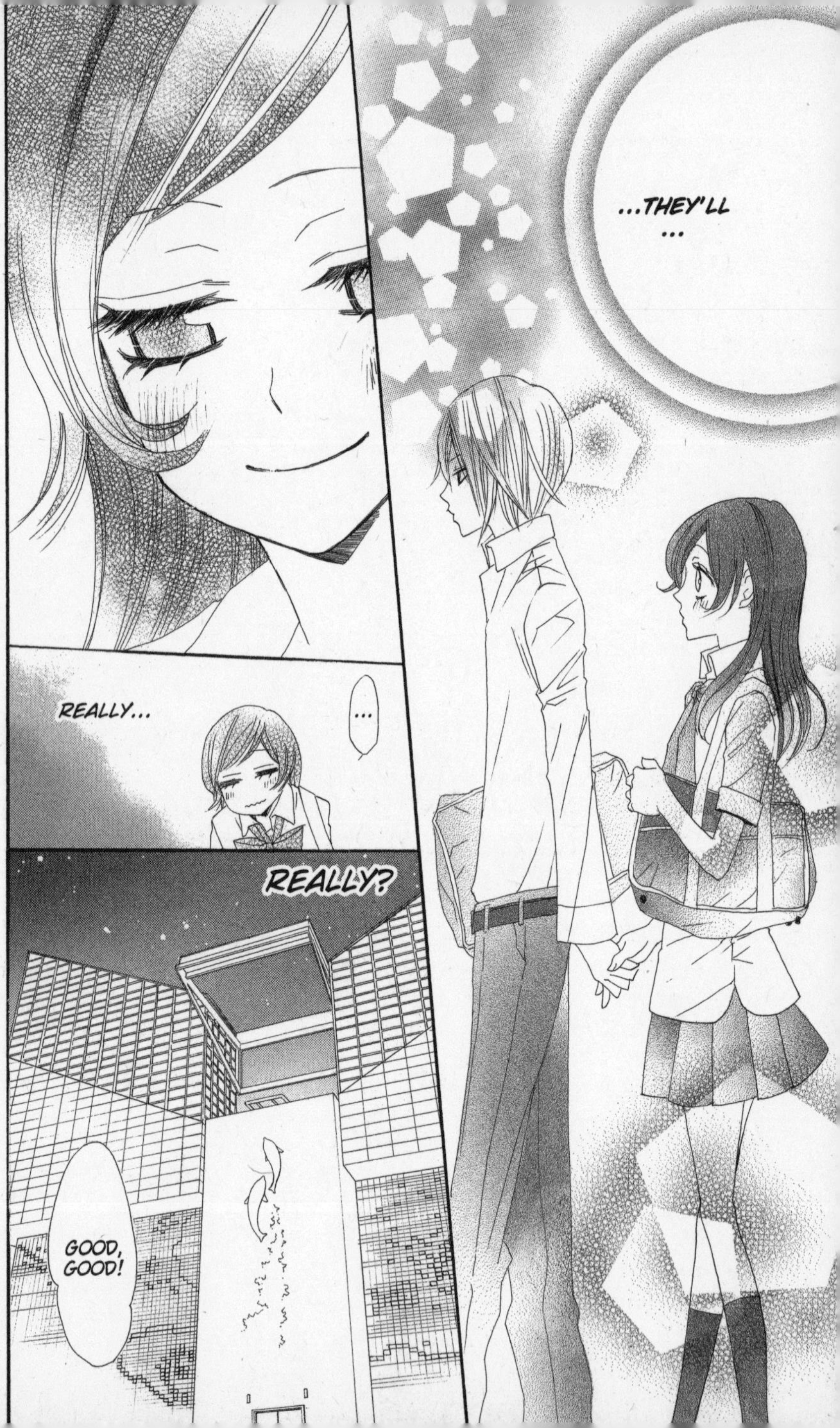
...THEY'LL ...
...
REALLY...
REALLY?
GOOD, GOOD!

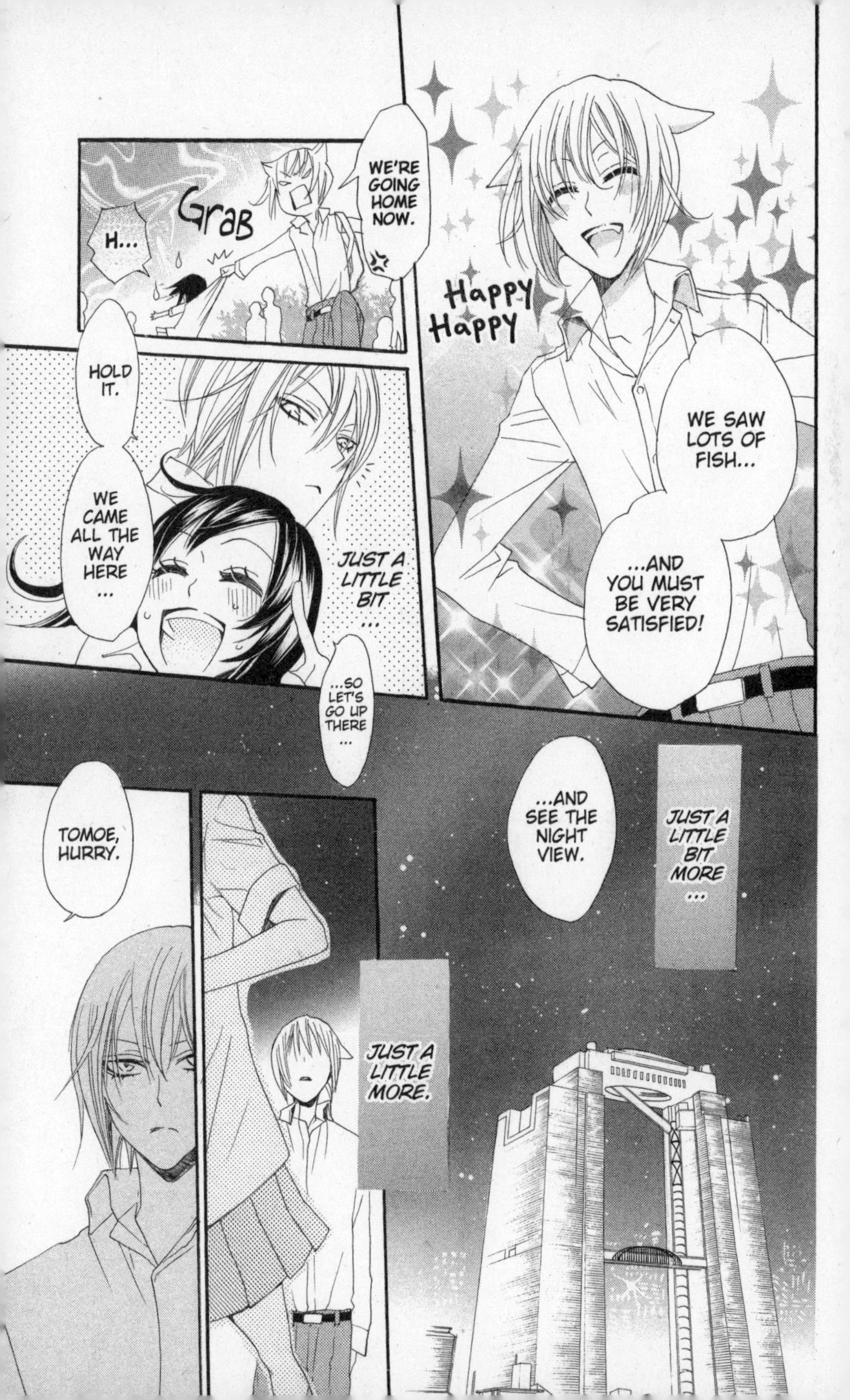
Happy Happy
WE SAW LOTS OF FISH...
...AND YOU MUST BE VERY SATISFIED!
WE'RE GOING HOME NOW.
Grab
H...
HOLD IT.
WE CAME ALL THE WAY HERE ...
JUST A LITTLE BIT ...
...SO LET'S GO UP THERE ...
...AND SEE THE NIGHT VIEW.
JUST A LITTLE BIT MORE ...
JUST A LITTLE MORE.
TOMOE, HURRY.

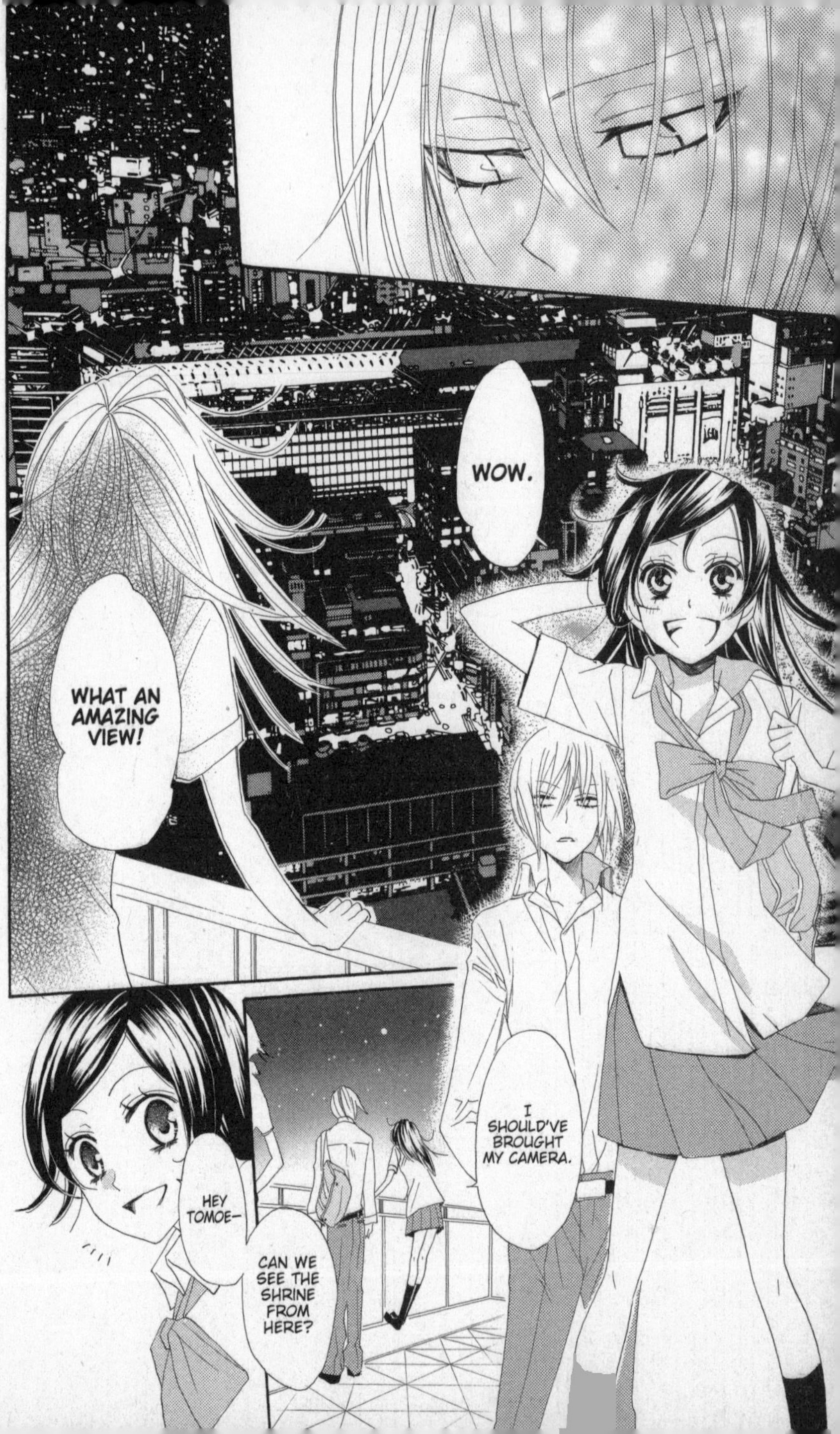
WOW.
WHAT AN AMAZING VIEW!
I SHOULD'VE BROUGHT MY CAMERA.
HEY TOMOE—
CAN WE SEE THE SHRINE FROM HERE?

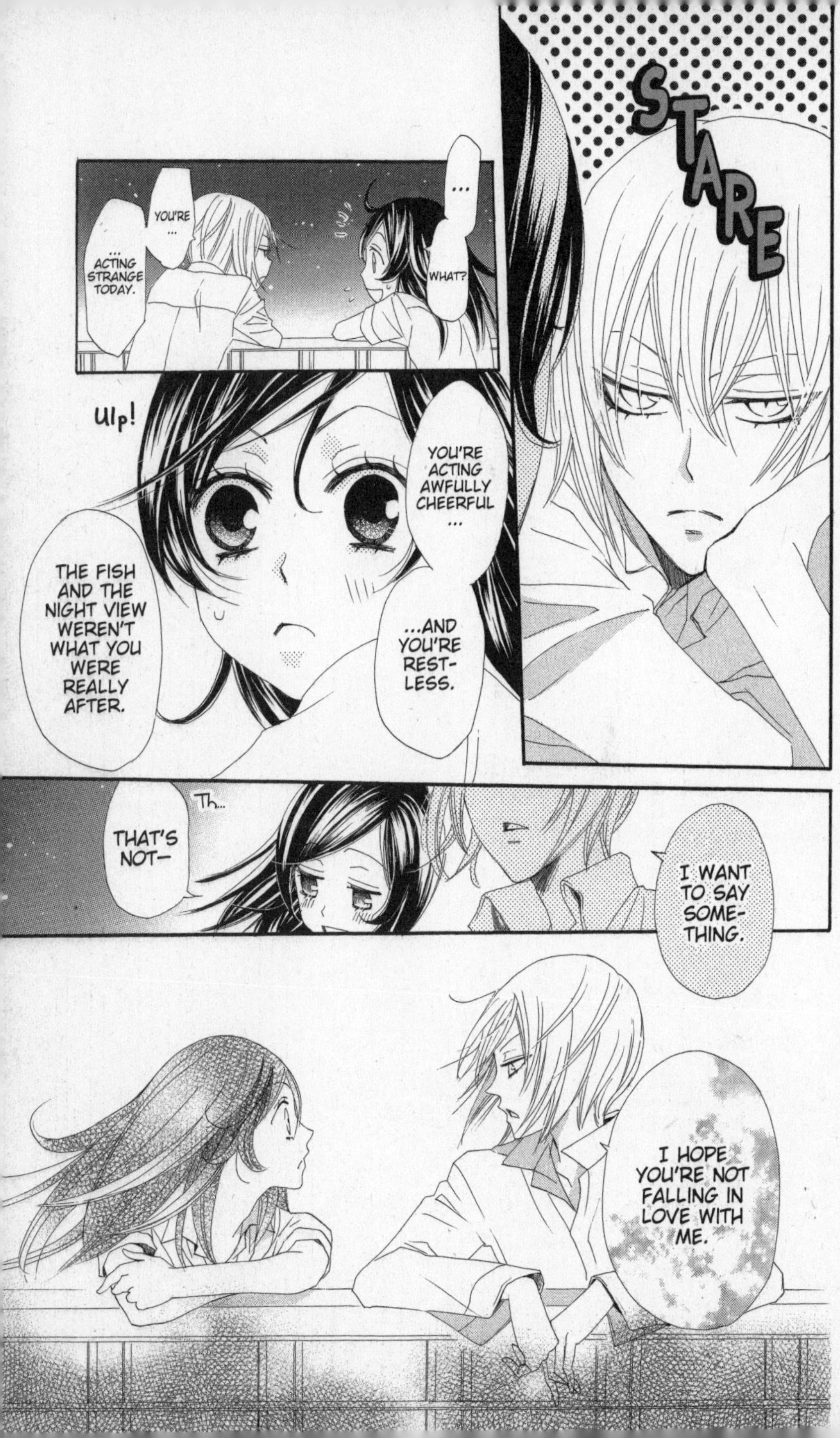
STARE
...
WHAT?
YOU'RE ...
... ACTING STRANGE TODAY.
YOU'RE ACTING AWFULLY CHEERFUL ...
...AND YOU'RE RESTLESS.
Ulp!
THE FISH AND THE NIGHT VIEW WEREN'T WHAT YOU WERE REALLY AFTER.
Th...
THAT'S NOT—
I WANT TO SAY SOMETHING.
I HOPE YOU'RE NOT FALLING IN LOVE WITH ME.

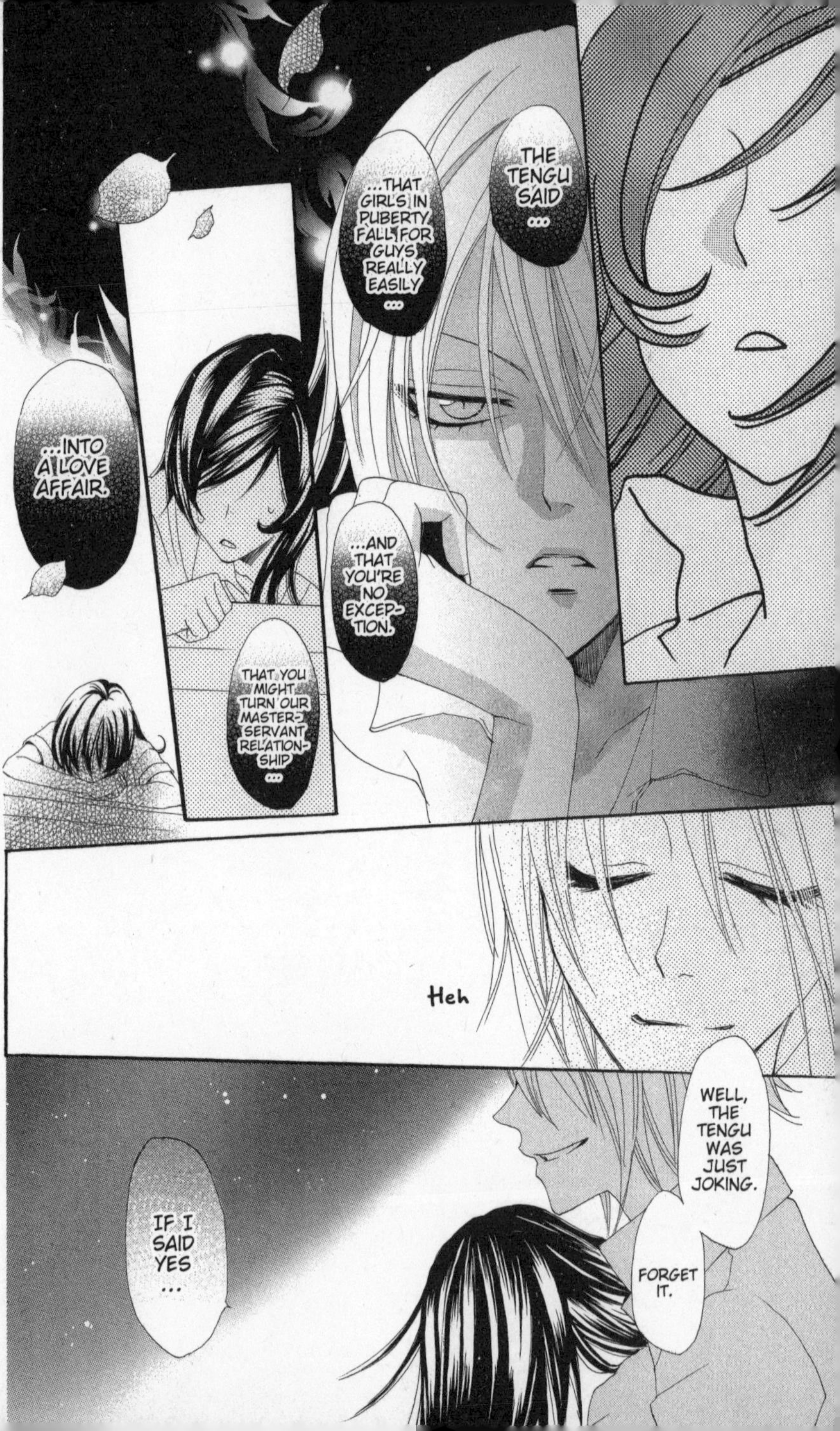

THE TENGU SAID ...
...THAT GIRLS IN PUBERTY FALL FOR GUYS REALLY EASILY ...
...AND THAT YOU'RE NO EXCEPTION.
THAT YOU MIGHT TURN OUR MASTER-SERVANT RELATIONSHIP ...
...INTO A LOVE AFFAIR.
Heh
WELL, THE TENGU WAS JUST JOKING.
FORGET IT.
IF I SAID YES ...

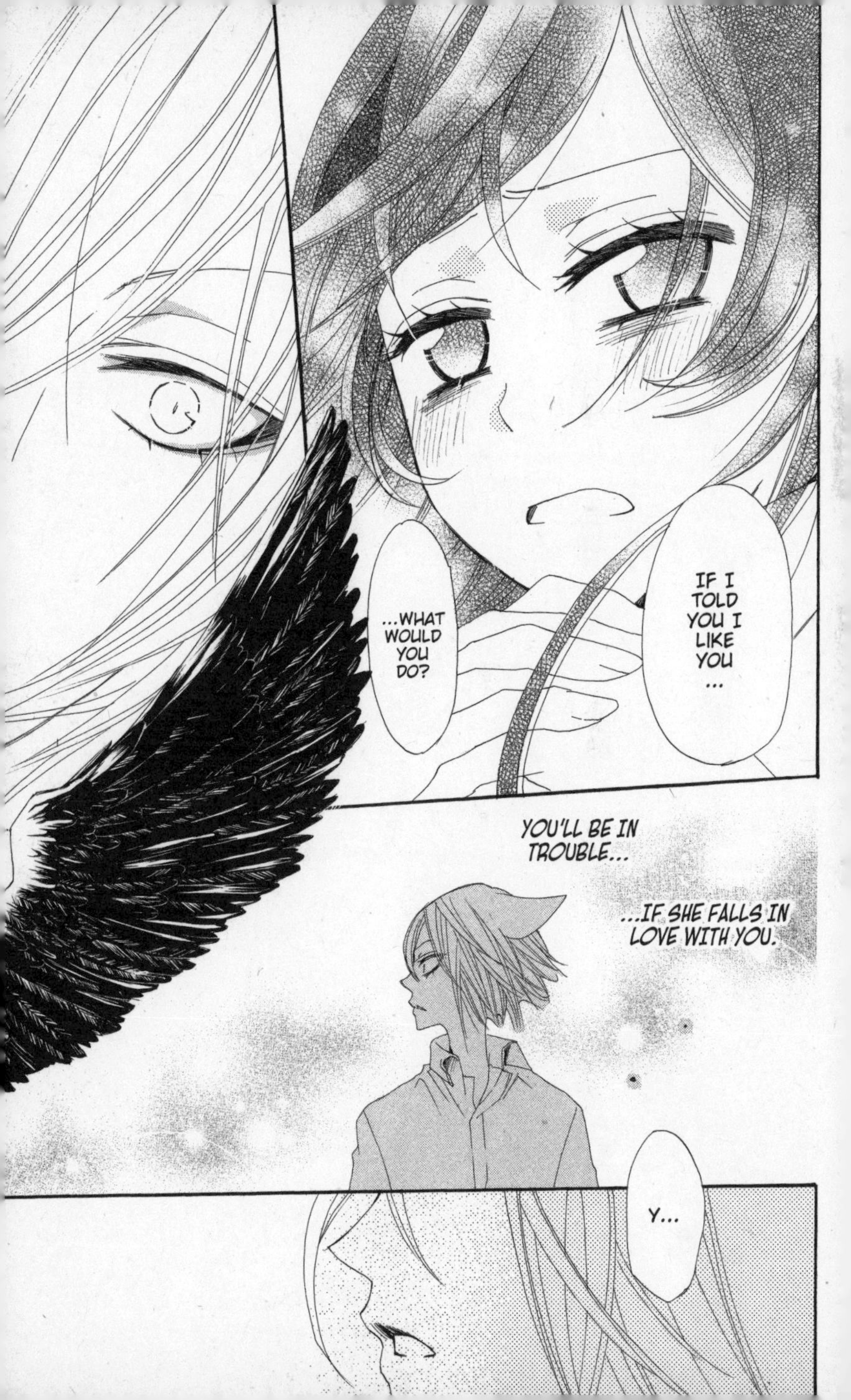
IF I TOLD YOU I LIKE YOU...
...WHAT WOULD YOU DO?
YOU'LL BE IN TROUBLE...
...IF SHE FALLS IN LOVE WITH YOU.
Y...

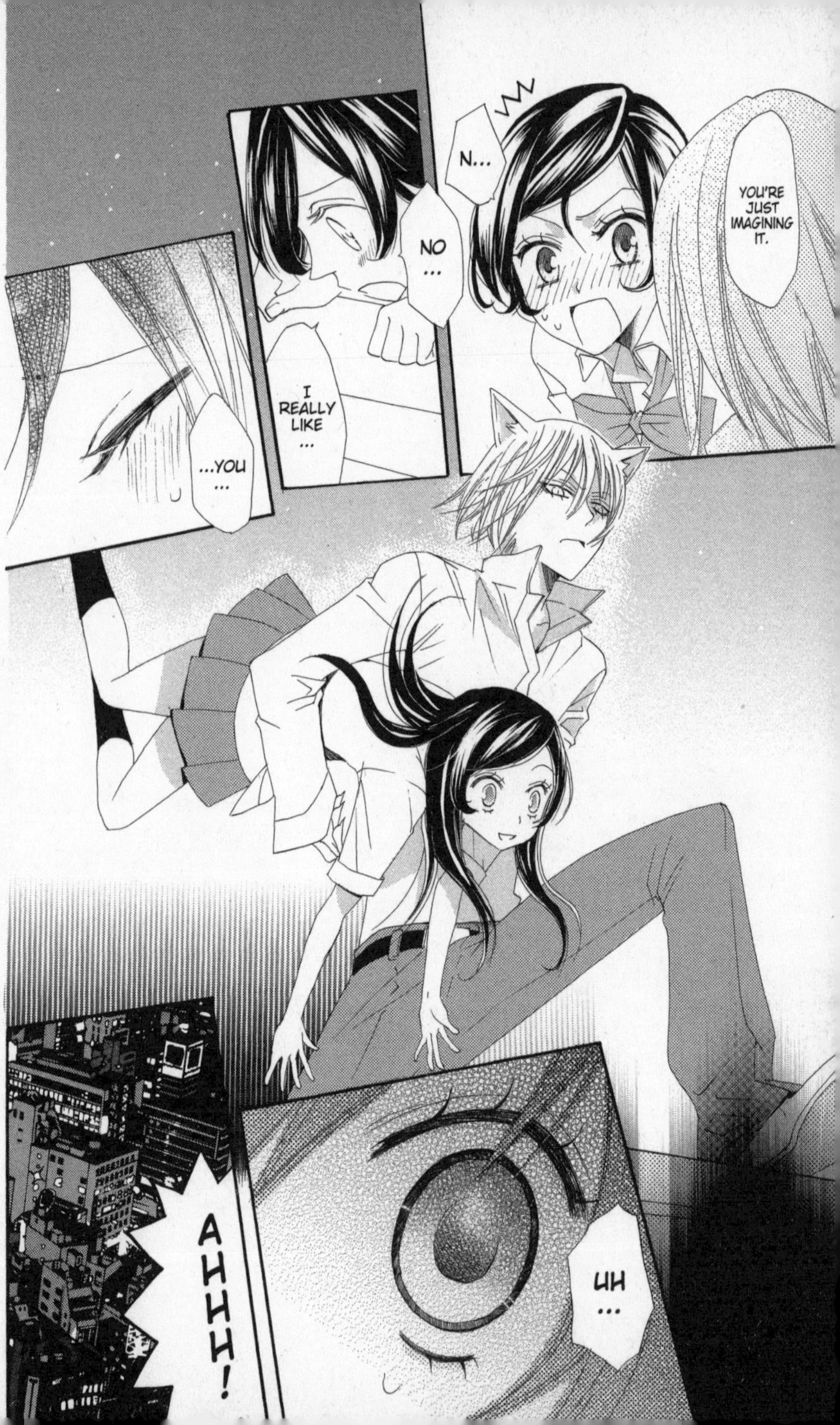

YOU'RE JUST IMAGINING IT.
N...
NO ...
I REALLY LIKE ...
...YOU ...
UH ...
AHHH!

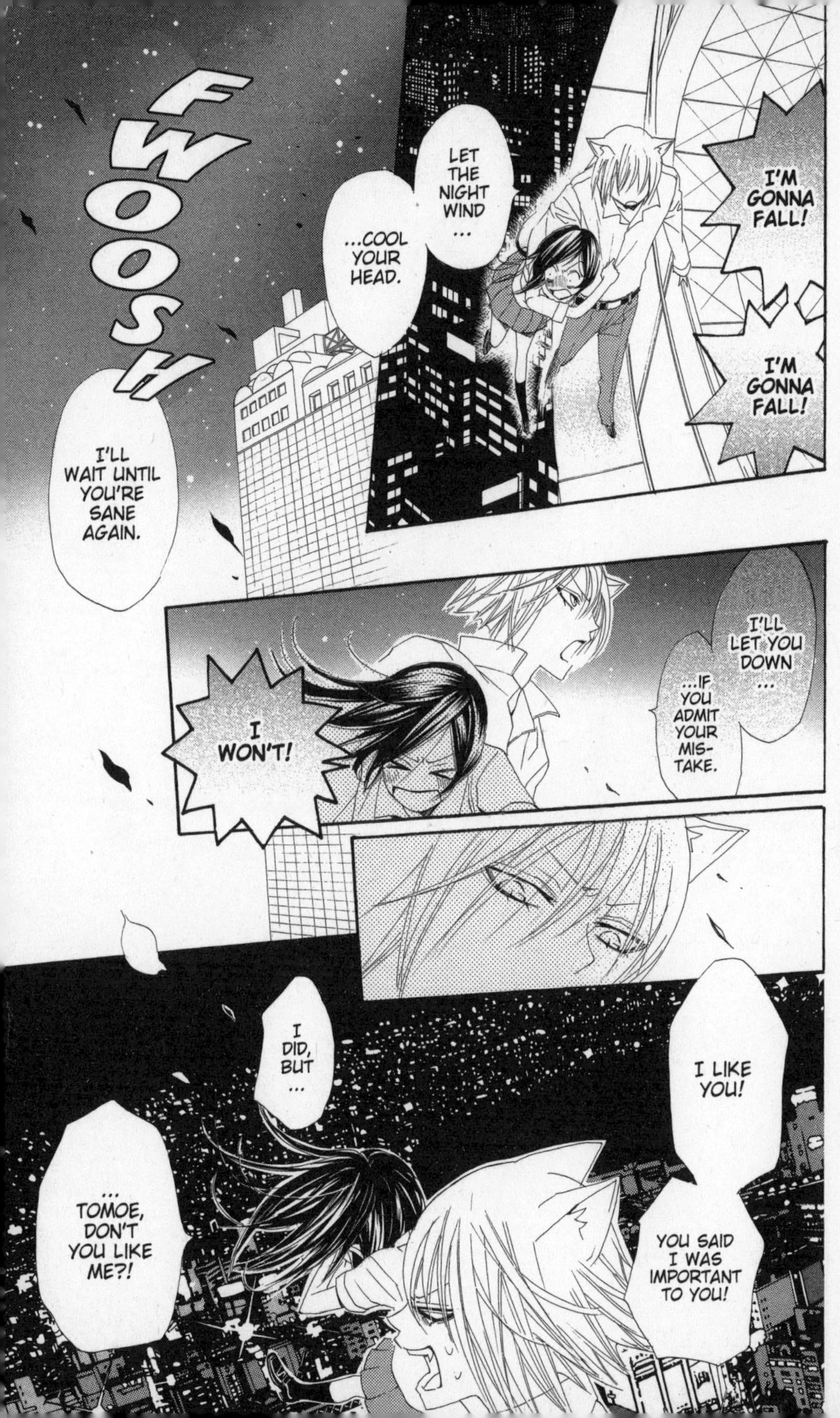
I'M GONNA FALL!
I'M GONNA FALL!
LET THE NIGHT WIND...
...COOL YOUR HEAD.
FWOOSH
I'LL WAIT UNTIL YOU'RE SANE AGAIN.
I'LL LET YOU DOWN...
...IF YOU ADMIT YOUR MIS-TAKE.
I WON'T!
I LIKE YOU!
YOU SAID I WAS IMPORTANT TO YOU!
I DID, BUT...
...TOMOE, DON'T YOU LIKE ME?!

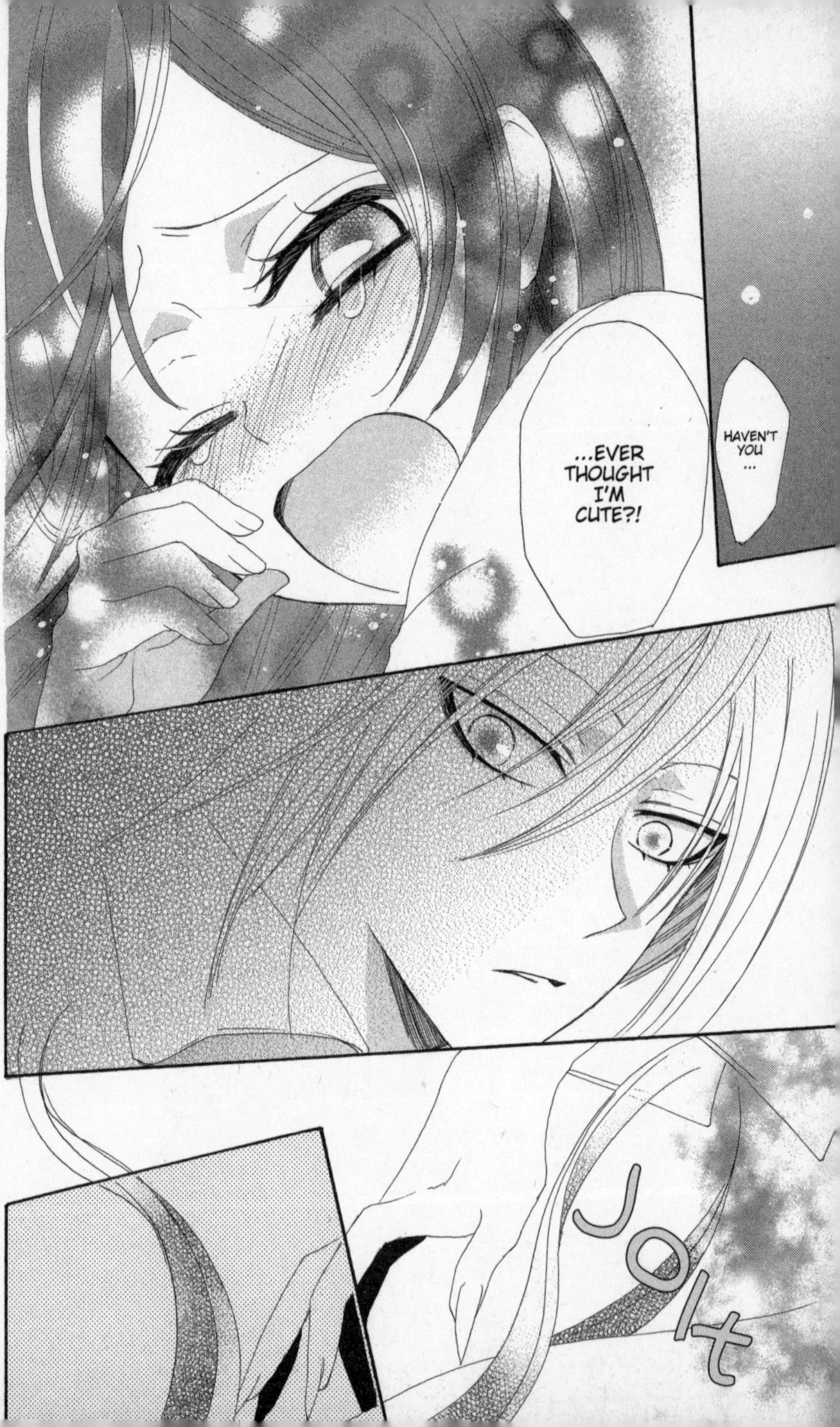
HAVEN'T YOU ...
...EVER THOUGHT I'M CUTE?!
Jolt

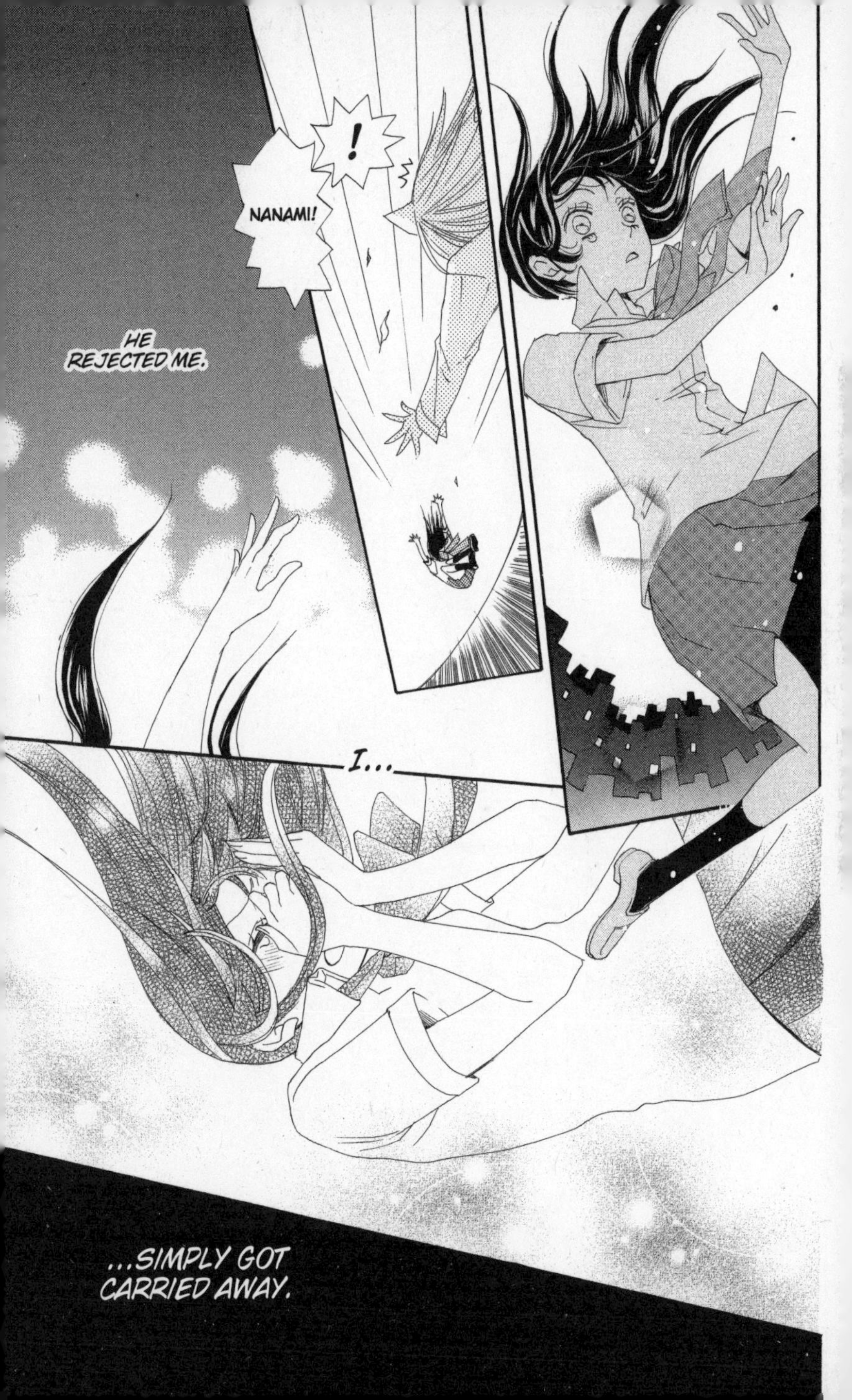
!
NANAMI!
HE REJECTED ME.
I...
...SIMPLY GOT CARRIED AWAY.

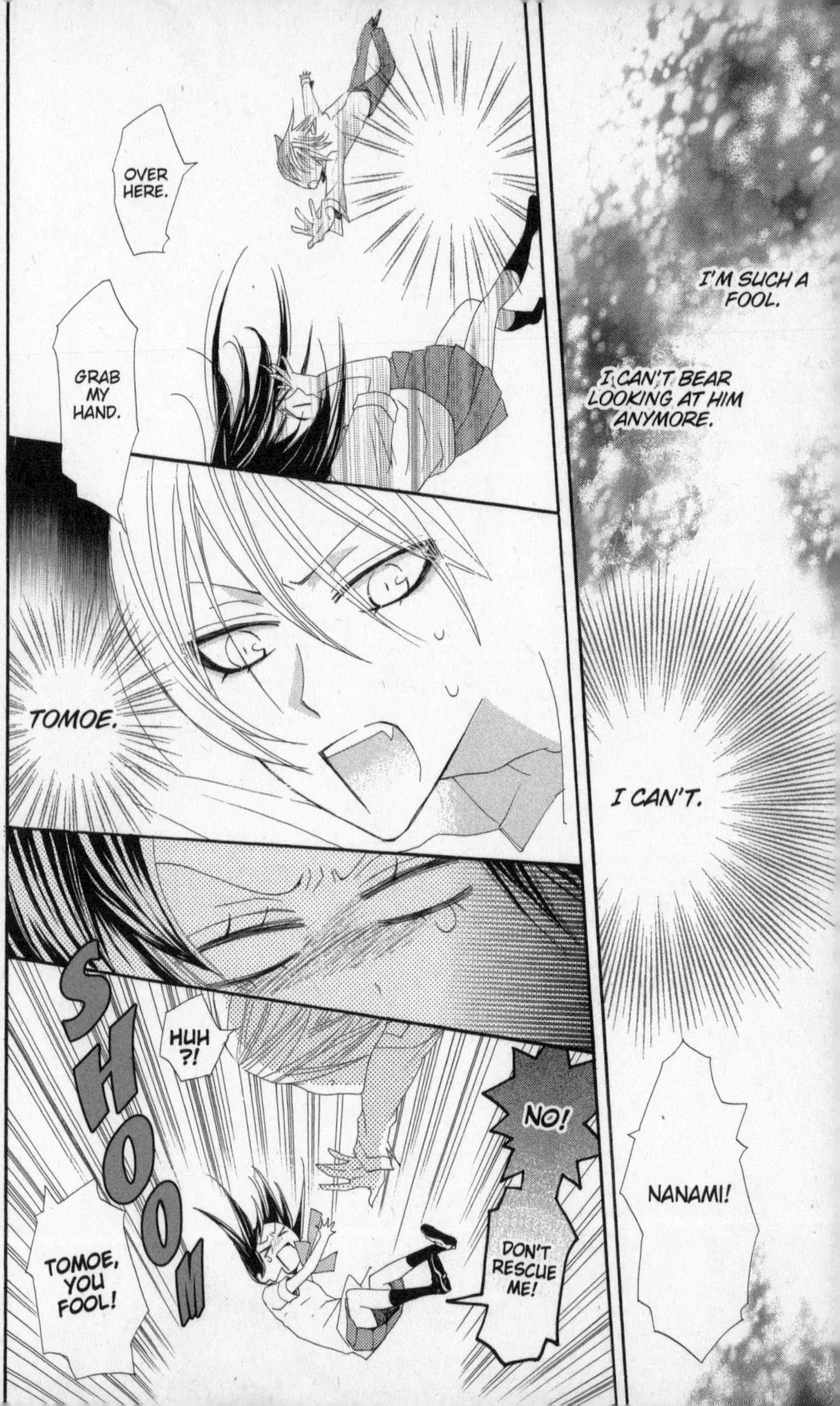
I'M SUCH A FOOL.
I CAN'T BEAR LOOKING AT HIM ANYMORE.
I CAN'T.
NANAMI!
OVER HERE.
GRAB MY HAND.
TOMOE.
HUH ?!
SHOOOOM
NO!
DON'T RESCUE ME!
TOMOE, YOU FOOL!

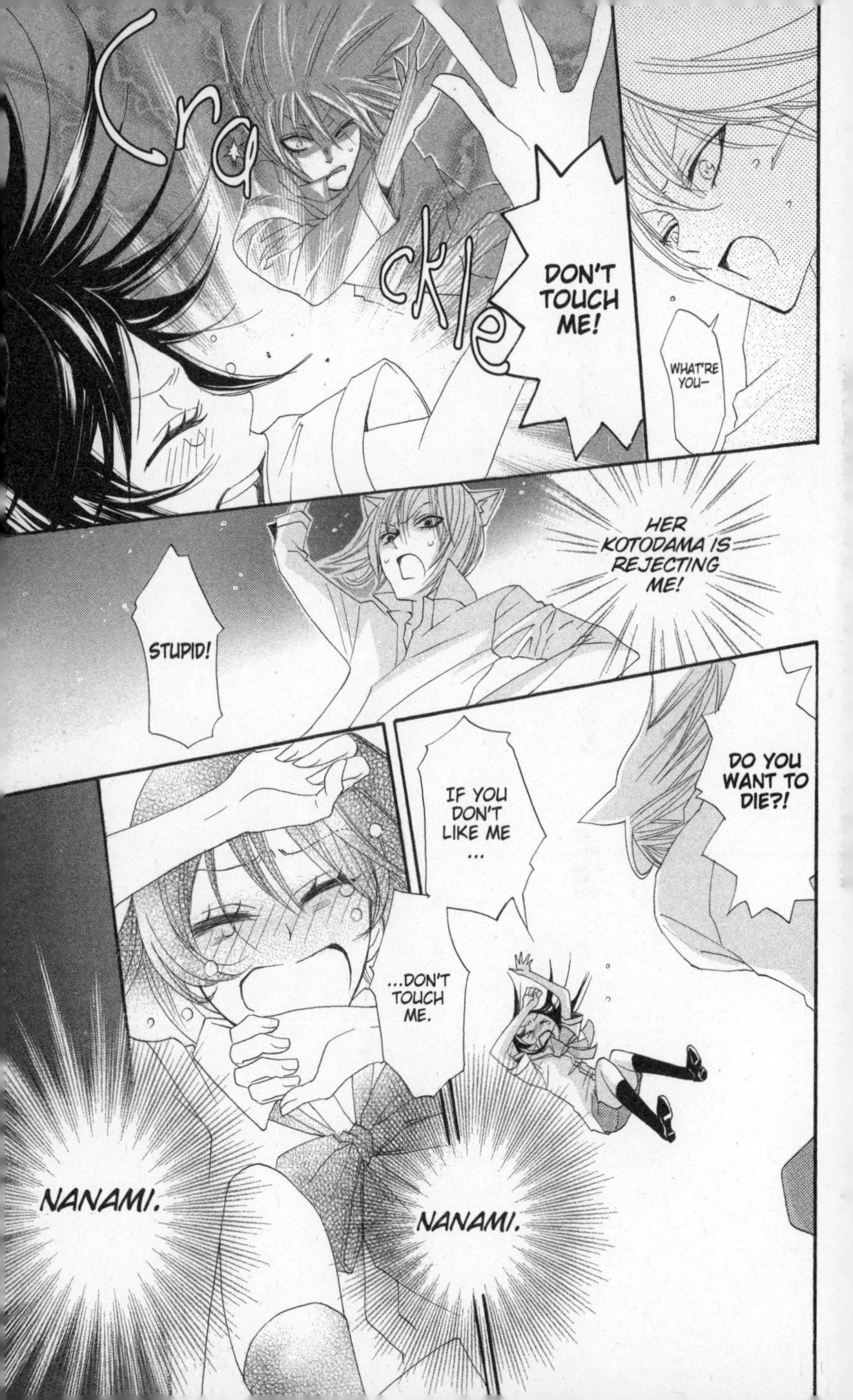

WHAT'RE YOU—
Crackle
DON'T TOUCH ME!
HER KOTODAMA IS REJECTING ME!
STUPID!
DO YOU WANT TO DIE?!
IF YOU DON'T LIKE ME ...
...DON'T TOUCH ME.
NANAMI.
NANAMI.

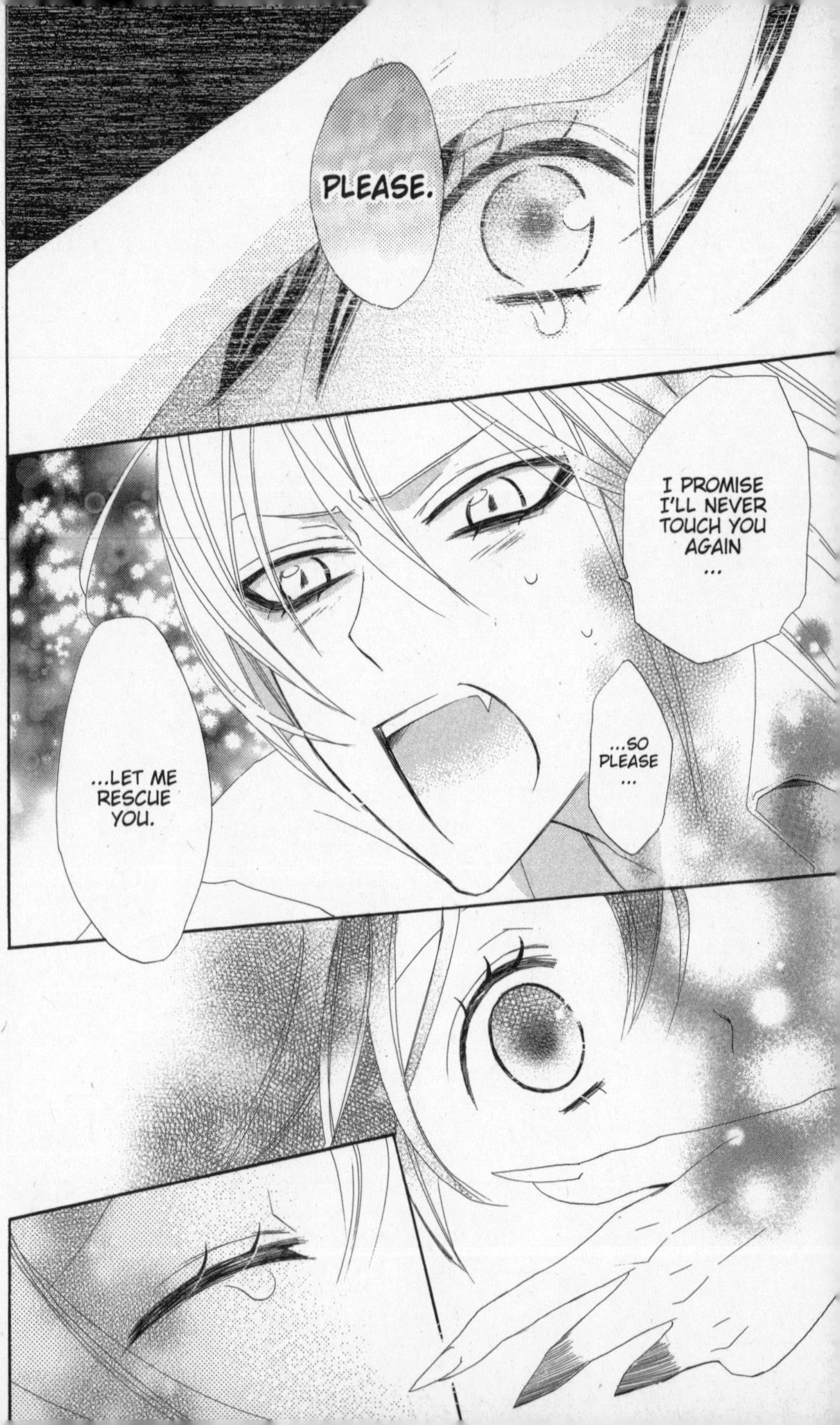
PLEASE.
I PROMISE I'LL NEVER TOUCH YOU AGAIN ...
...SO PLEASE ...
...LET ME RESCUE YOU.

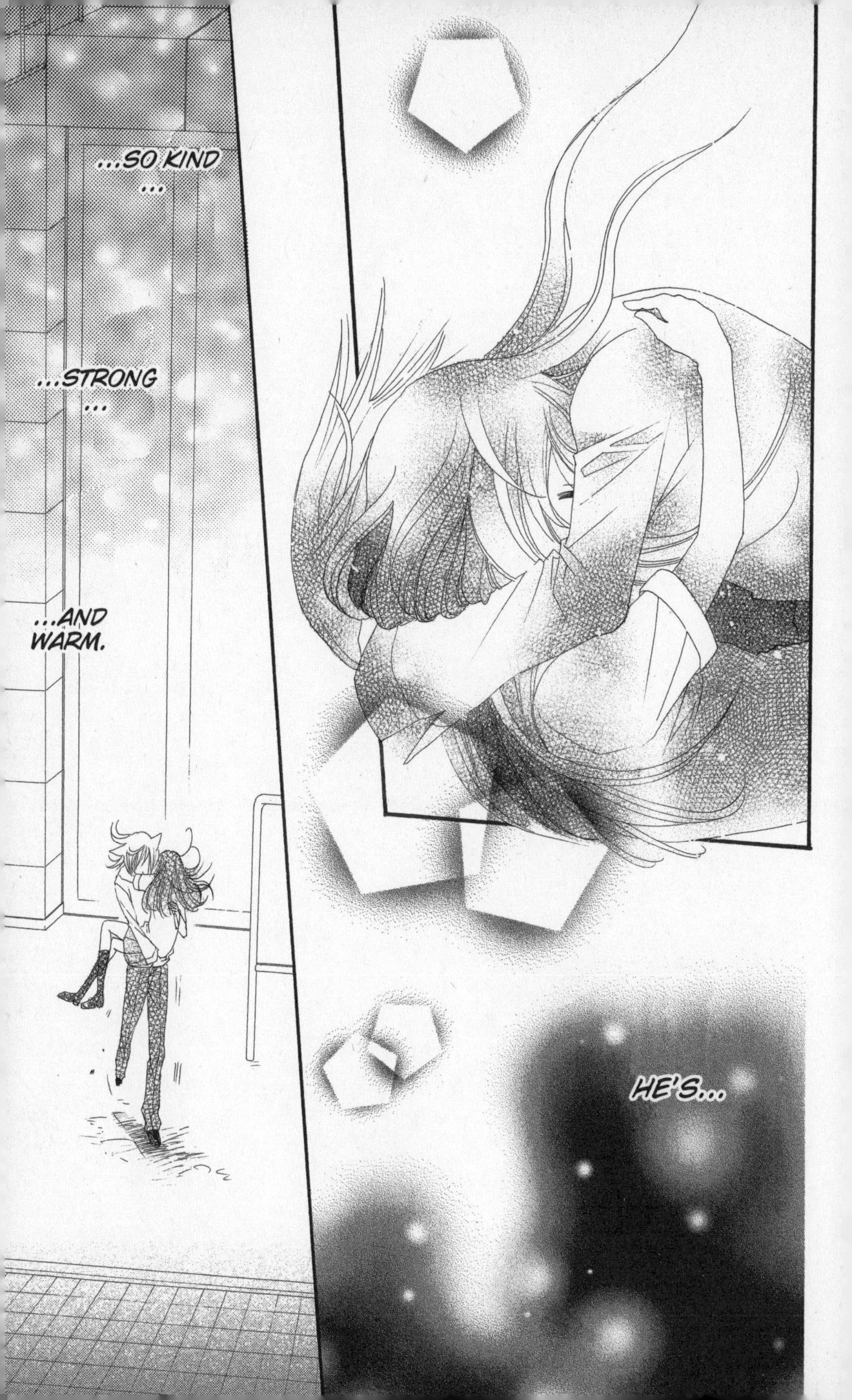
HE'S...
...SO KIND
...
...STRONG
...
...AND WARM.

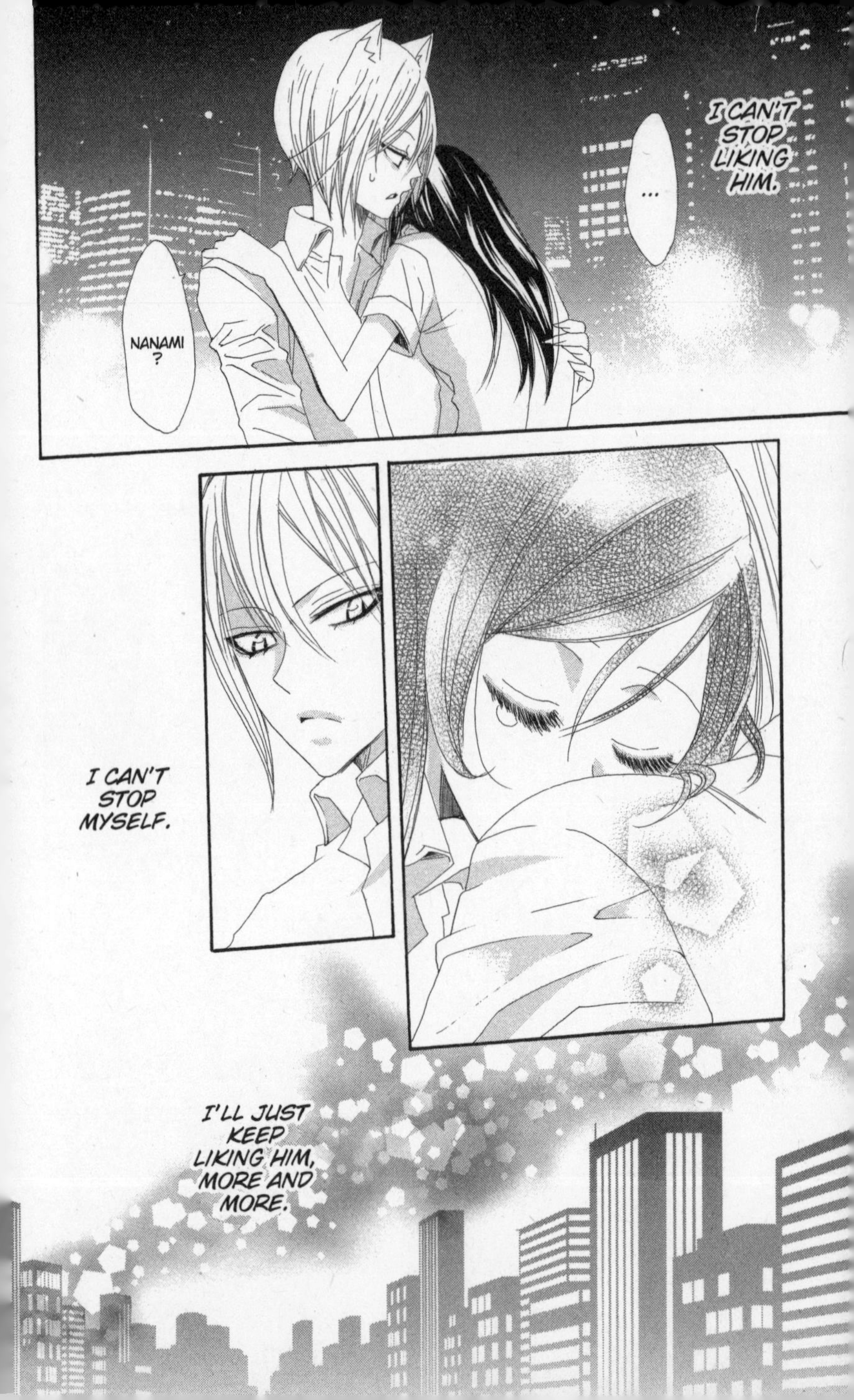
I CAN'T STOP LIKING HIM.
...
NANAMI?
I CAN'T STOP MYSELF.
I'LL JUST KEEP LIKING HIM, MORE AND MORE.

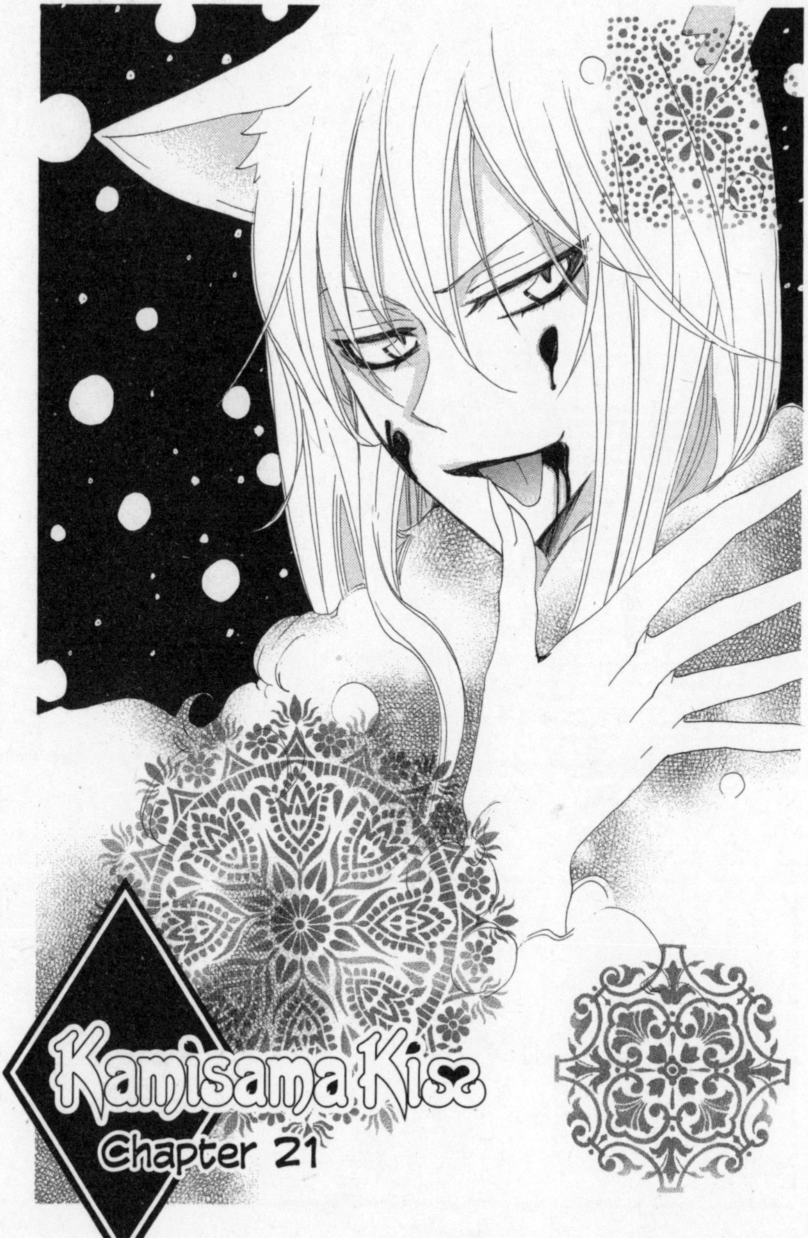
Kamisama Kiss
Chapter 21

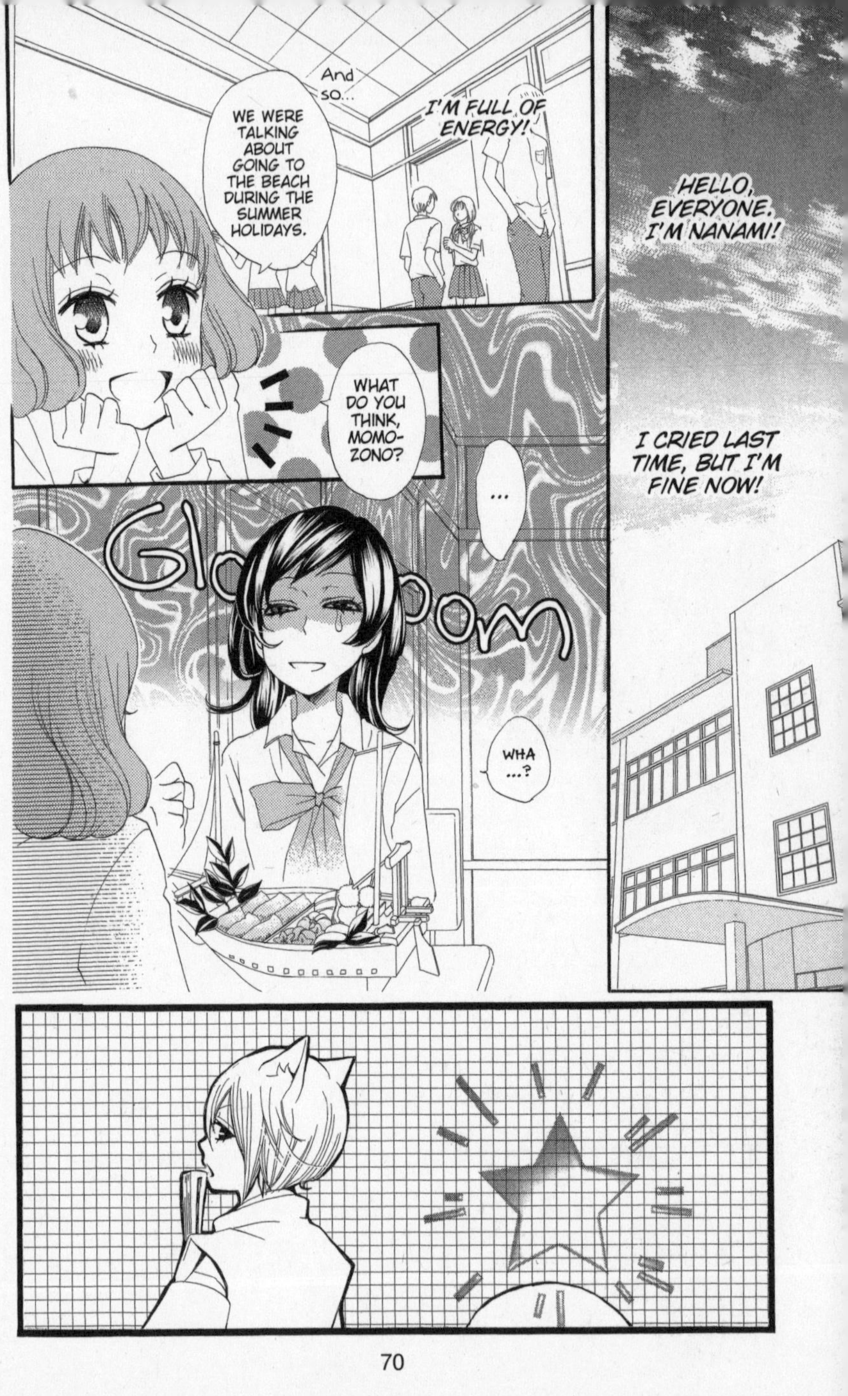
HELLO, EVERYONE. I'M NANAMI!
I CRIED LAST TIME, BUT I'M FINE NOW!
I'M FULL OF ENERGY!
And so...
WE WERE TALKING ABOUT GOING TO THE BEACH DURING THE SUMMER HOLIDAYS.
WHAT DO YOU THINK, MOMO-ZONO?
...
Gloom
WHA ...?

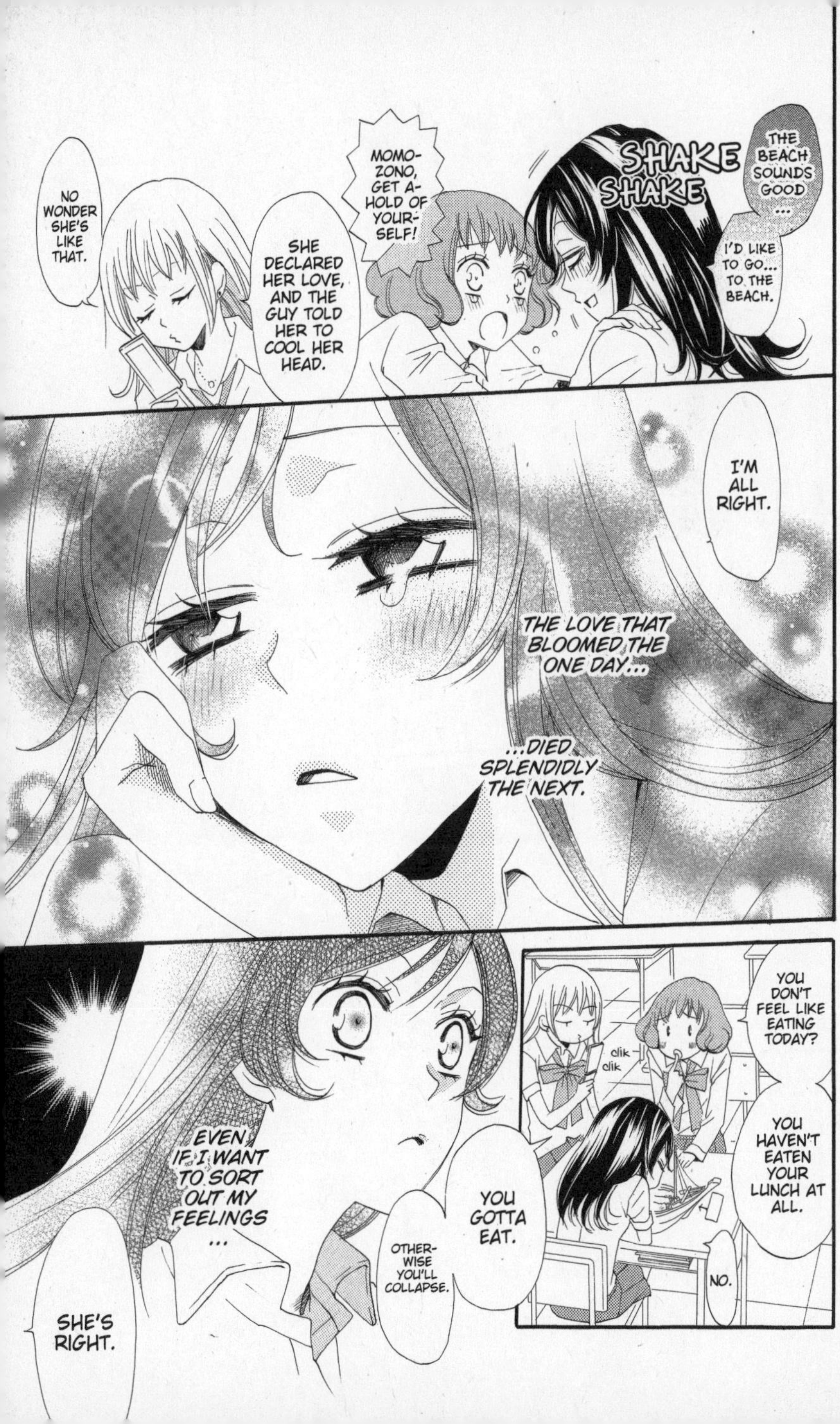
THE BEACH SOUNDS GOOD...
SHAKE SHAKE
I'D LIKE TO GO... TO THE BEACH.
MOMO-ZONO, GET A-HOLD OF YOUR-SELF!
SHE DECLARED HER LOVE, AND THE GUY TOLD HER TO COOL HER HEAD.
NO WONDER SHE'S LIKE THAT.
I'M ALL RIGHT.
THE LOVE THAT BLOOMED THE ONE DAY...
...DIED SPLENDIDLY THE NEXT.
YOU DON'T FEEL LIKE EATING TODAY?
clik clik
YOU HAVEN'T EATEN YOUR LUNCH AT ALL.
NO.
YOU GOTTA EAT.
OTHER-WISE YOU'LL COLLAPSE.
EVEN IF I WANT TO SORT OUT MY FEELINGS...
SHE'S RIGHT.

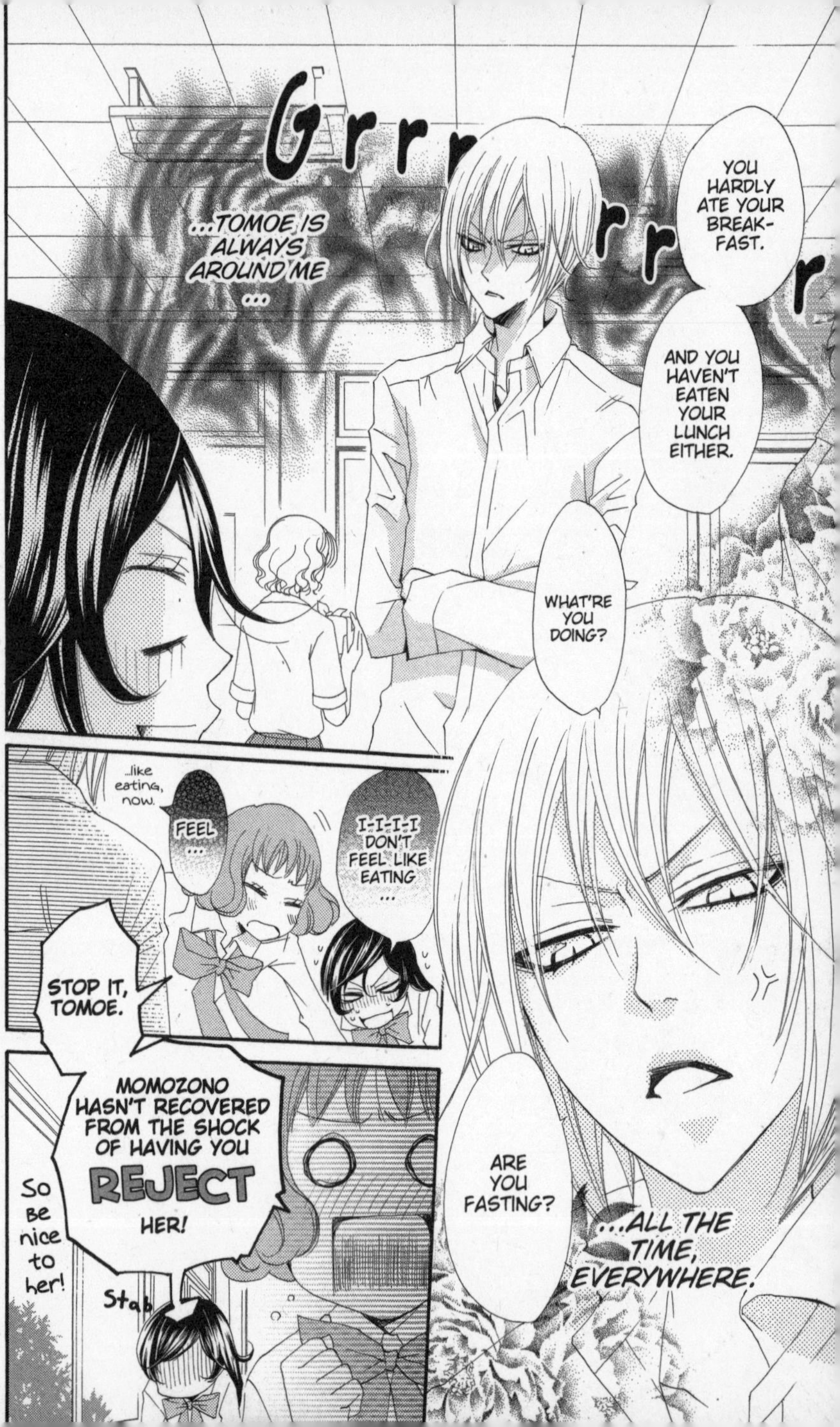

YOU HARDLY ATE YOUR BREAK-FAST.
AND YOU HAVEN'T EATEN YOUR LUNCH EITHER.
Grrrrrr
...TOMOE IS ALWAYS AROUND ME...
WHAT'RE YOU DOING?
ARE YOU FASTING?
...ALL THE TIME, EVERYWHERE.
I-I-I-I DON'T FEEL LIKE EATING...
FEEL...
...like eating, now.
STOP IT, TOMOE.
MOMOZONO HASN'T RECOVERED FROM THE SHOCK OF HAVING YOU REJECT HER!
So be nice to her!
Stab

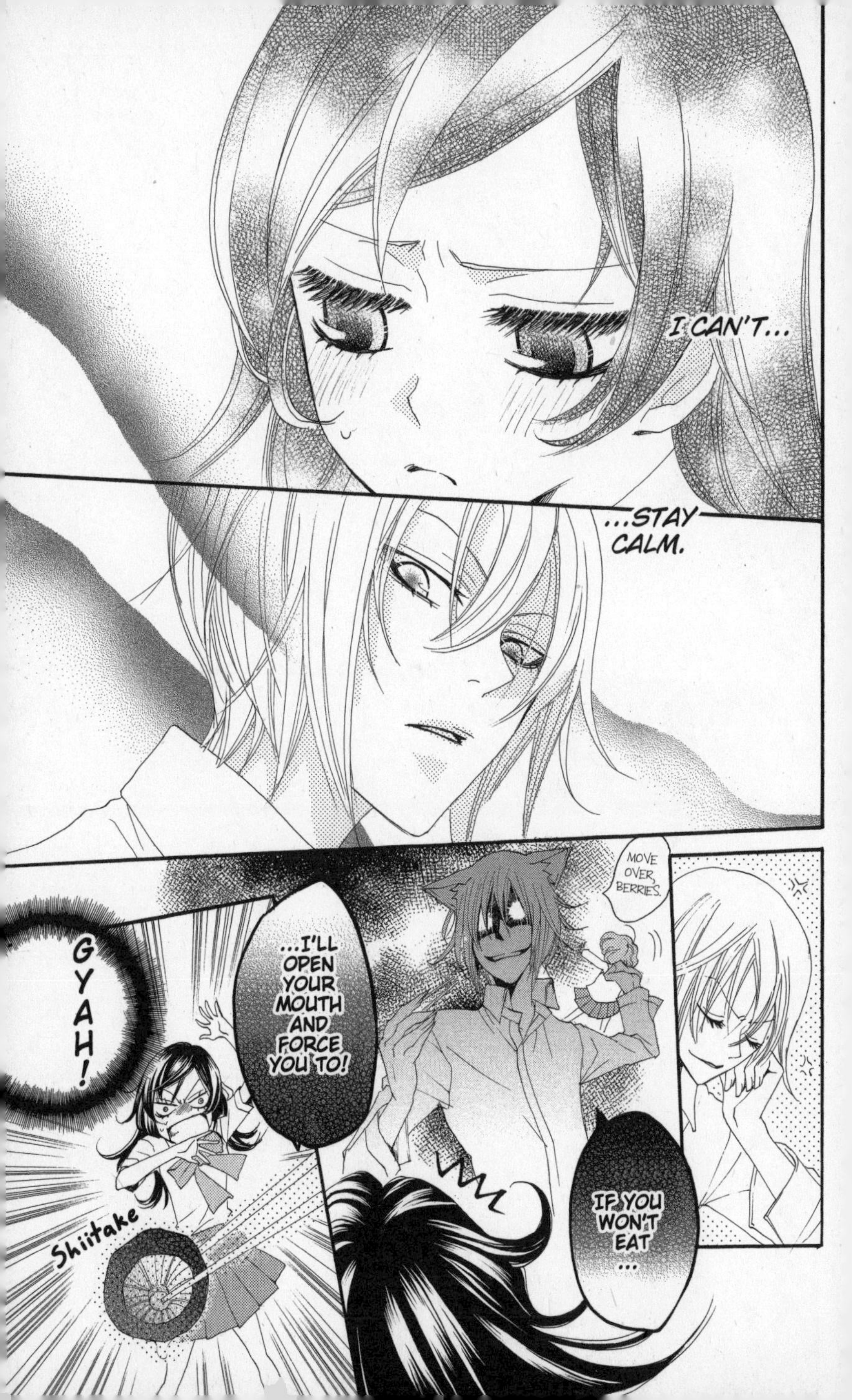
I CAN'T...
...STAY CALM.
MOVE OVER, BERRIES.
IF YOU WON'T EAT ...
...I'LL OPEN YOUR MOUTH AND FORCE YOU TO!
GYAH!
Shiitake

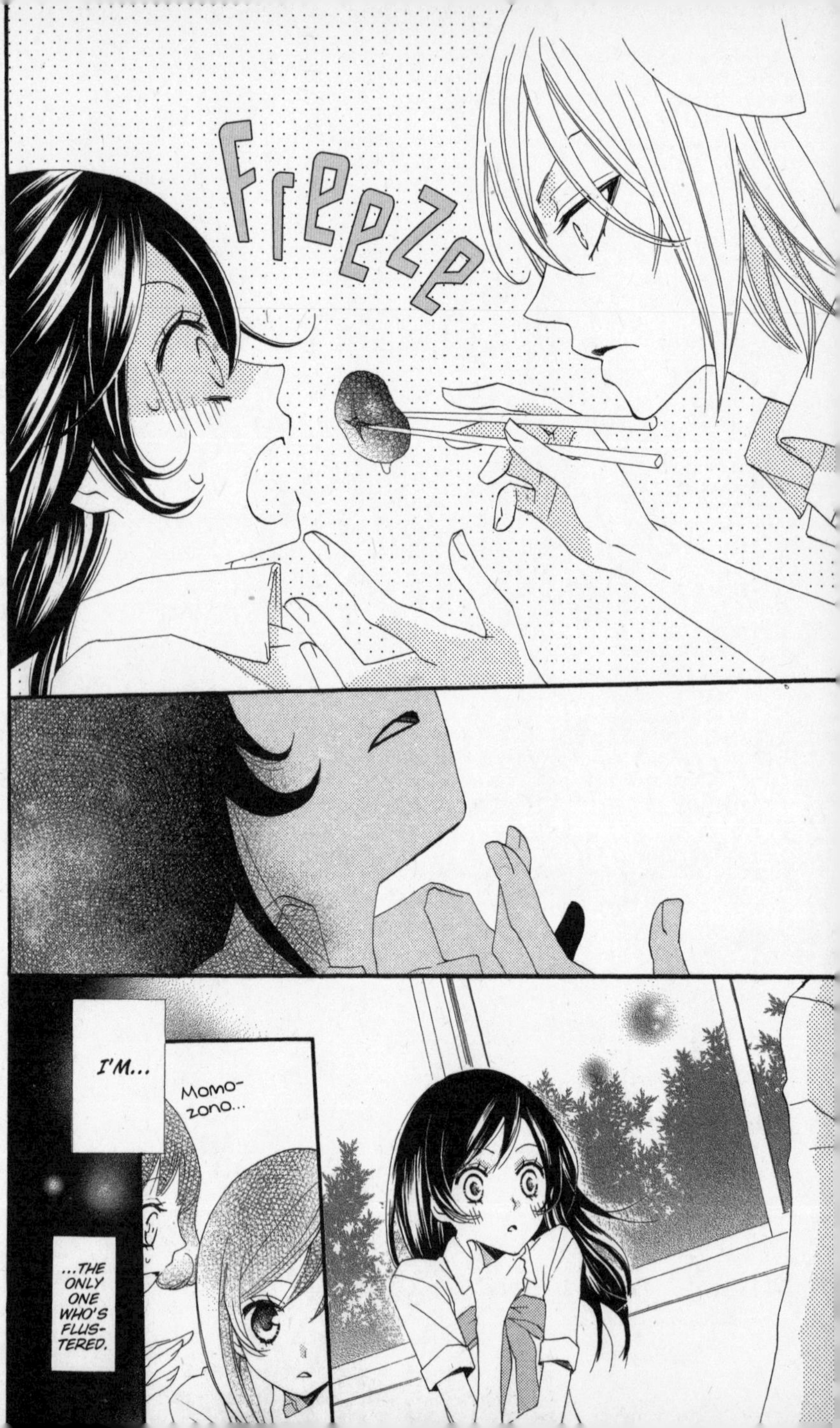
FREEZE
Momo-zono...
I'M...
...THE ONLY ONE WHO'S FLUS-TERED.

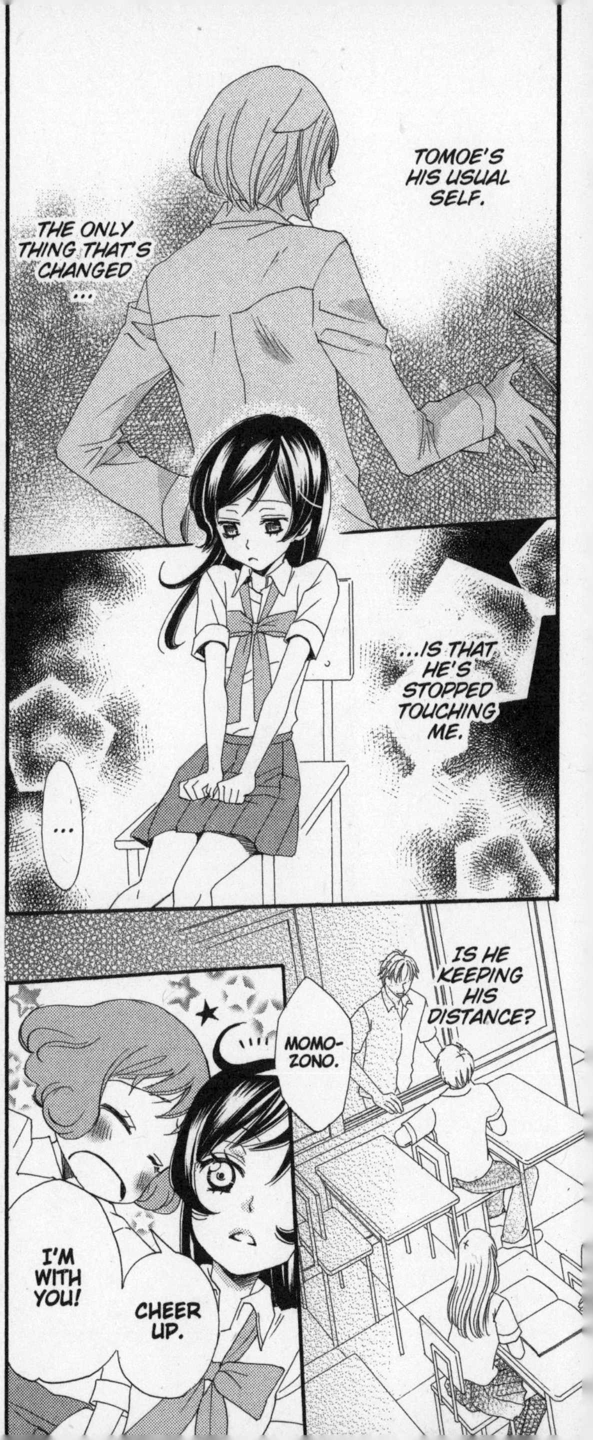
TOMOE'S HIS USUAL SELF.
THE ONLY THING THAT'S CHANGED ...
...IS THAT HE'S STOPPED TOUCHING ME.
...
IS HE KEEPING HIS DISTANCE?
MOMO-ZONO.
CHEER UP.
I'M WITH YOU!

I bought Wizardry Empire III for the PSP. I'd only played Wizardry on the Famicom, so I was surprised at how much the new Wiz has evolved. The spells are different, there're lots of dungeons, and you can choose from lots of species and occupations! Amazing! It's a game you can play for a long time, so I'm looking forward to it.

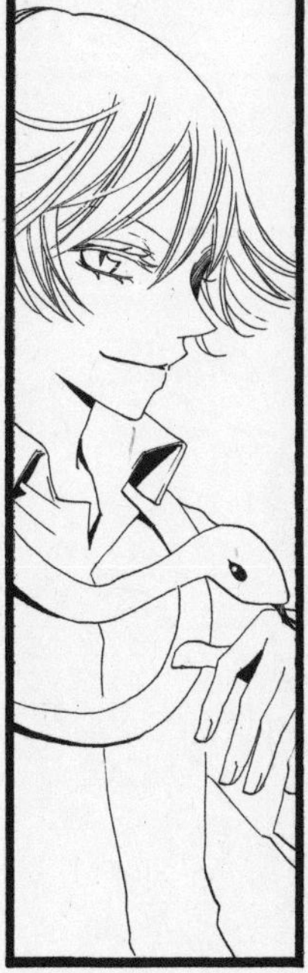

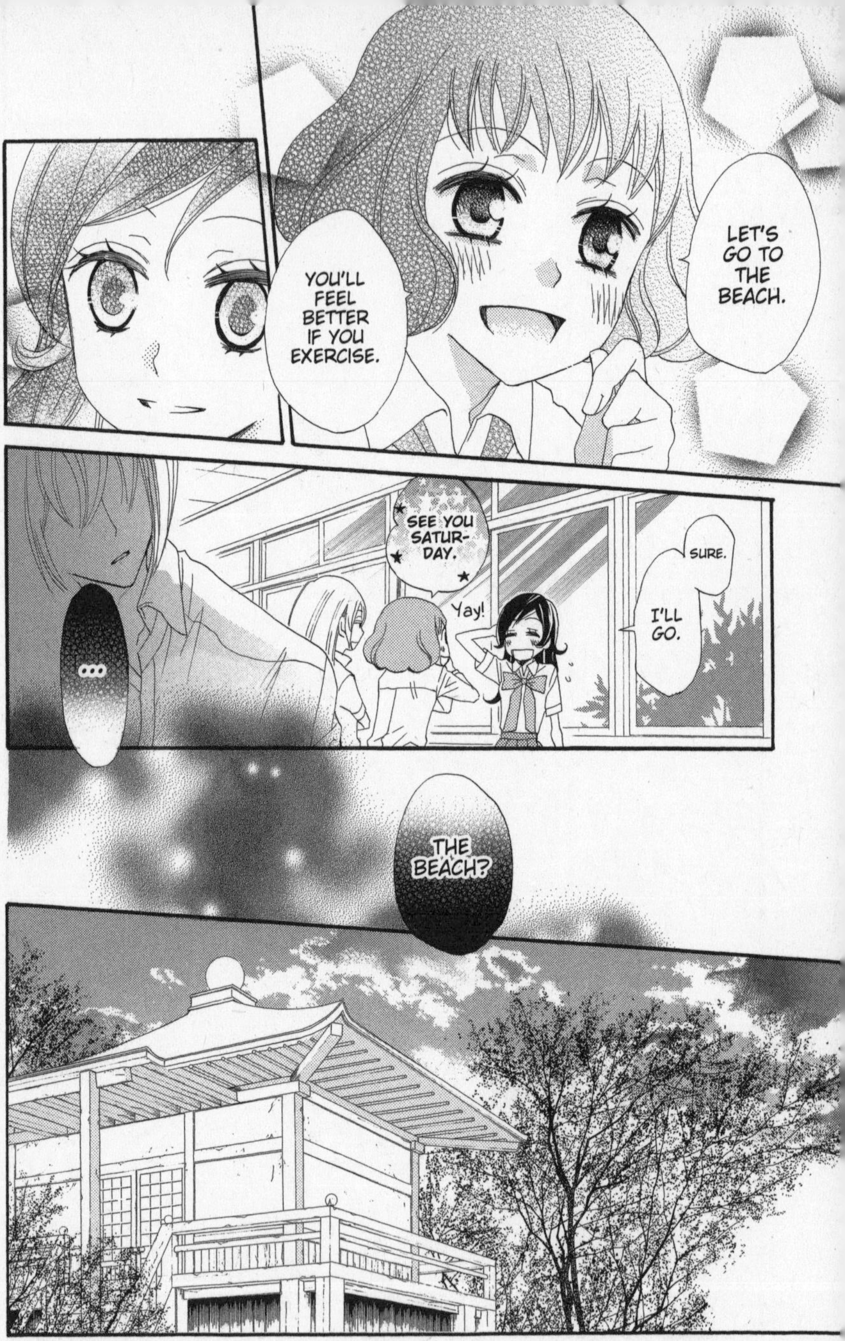
LET'S GO TO THE BEACH.
YOU'LL FEEL BETTER IF YOU EXERCISE.
SURE.
I'LL GO.
SEE YOU SATUR-DAY.
Yay!
...
THE BEACH?

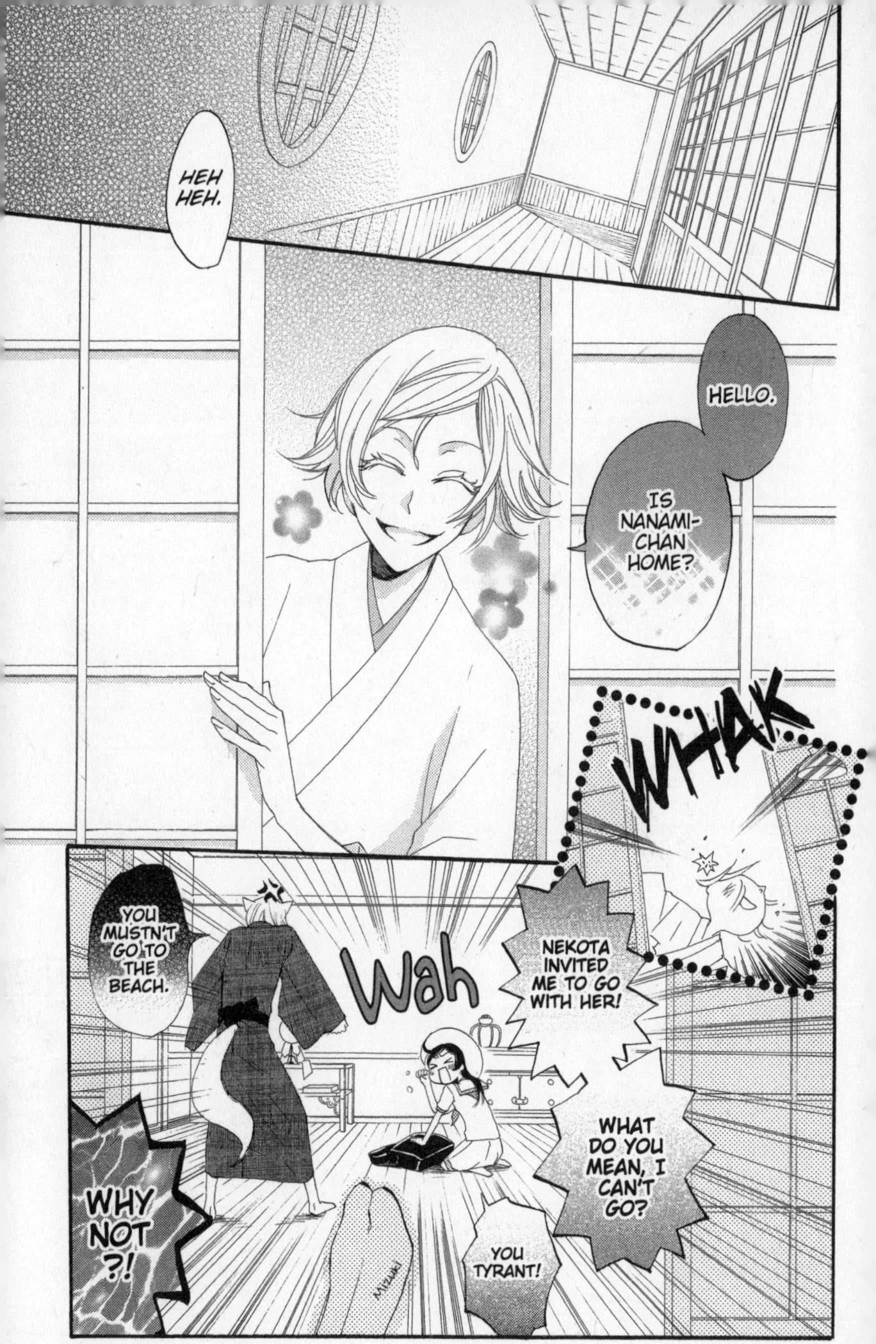
HEH HEH.
HELLO.
IS NANAMI-CHAN HOME?
WHAK
NEKOTA INVITED ME TO GO WITH HER!
Wah
YOU MUSTN'T GO TO THE BEACH.
WHAT DO YOU MEAN, I CAN'T GO?
YOU TYRANT!
MIZUKI
WHY NOT ?!

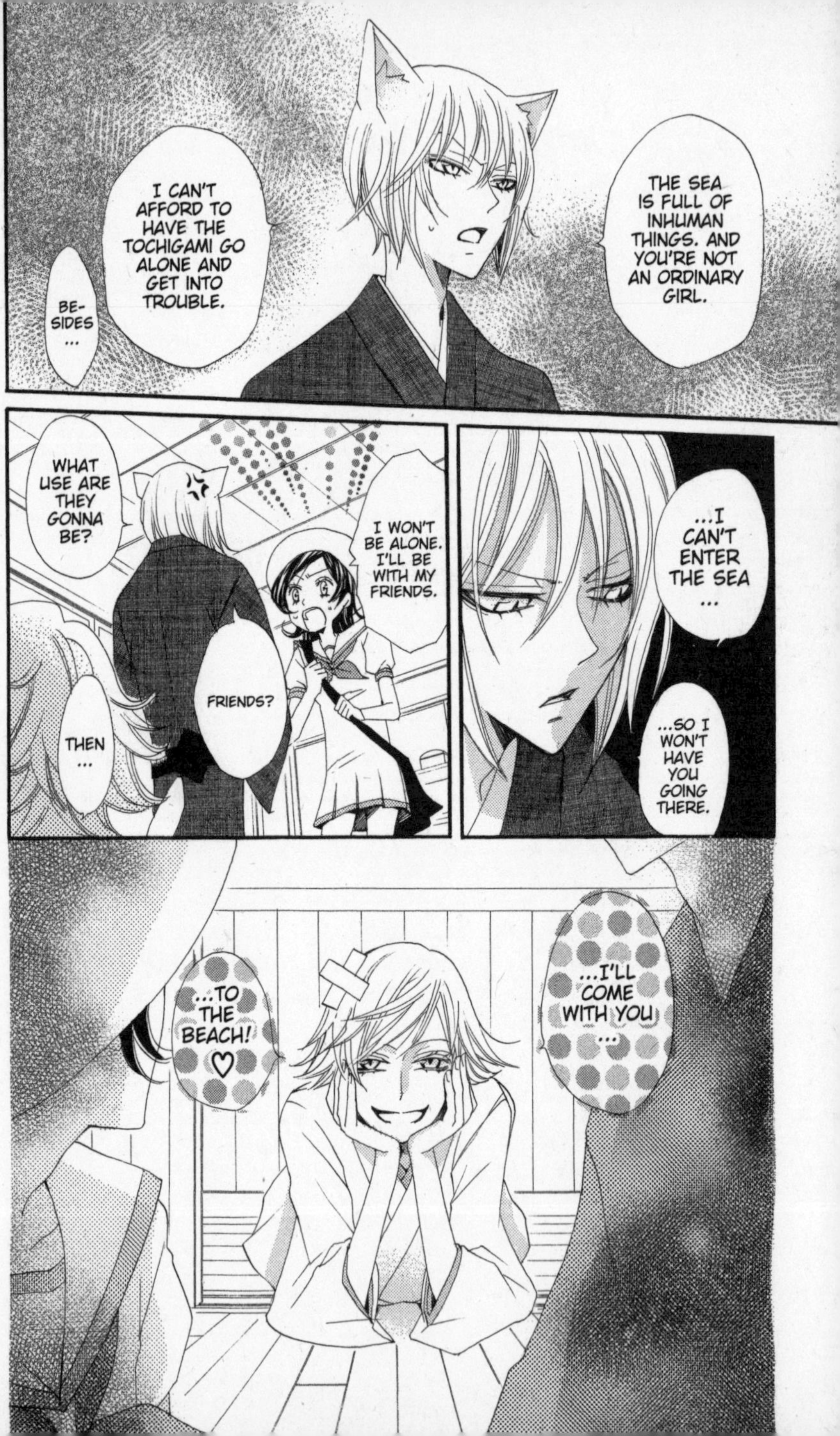

THE SEA IS FULL OF INHUMAN THINGS. AND YOU'RE NOT AN ORDINARY GIRL.
I CAN'T AFFORD TO HAVE THE TOCHIGAMI GO ALONE AND GET INTO TROUBLE.
BE-SIDES ...
...I CAN'T ENTER THE SEA ...
...SO I WON'T HAVE YOU GOING THERE.
I WON'T BE ALONE. I'LL BE WITH MY FRIENDS.
WHAT USE ARE THEY GONNA BE?
FRIENDS?
THEN ...
...I'LL COME WITH YOU ...
...TO THE BEACH! ♡

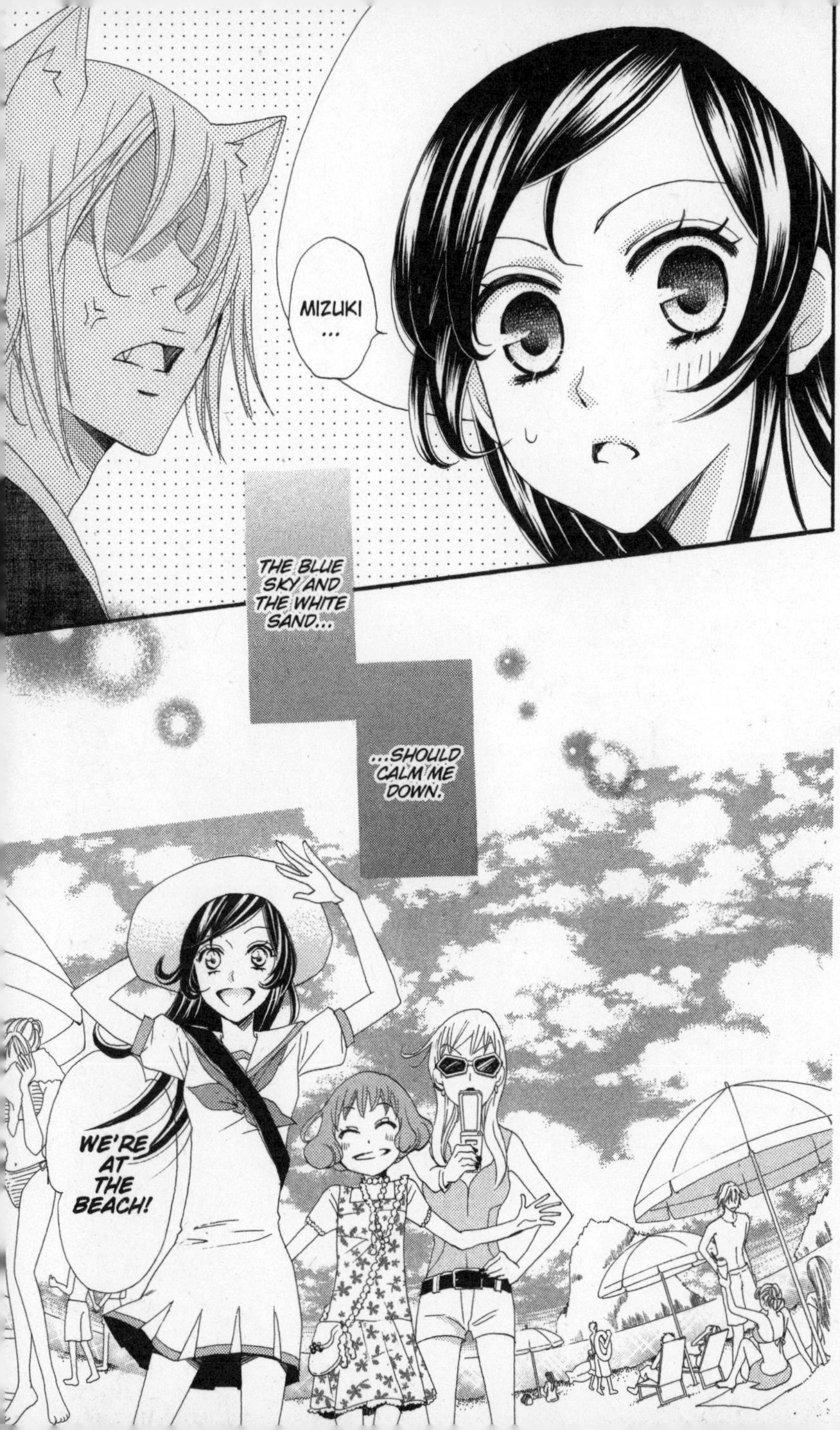
MIZUKI ...
THE BLUE SKY AND THE WHITE SAND...
...SHOULD CALM ME DOWN.
WE'RE AT THE BEACH!

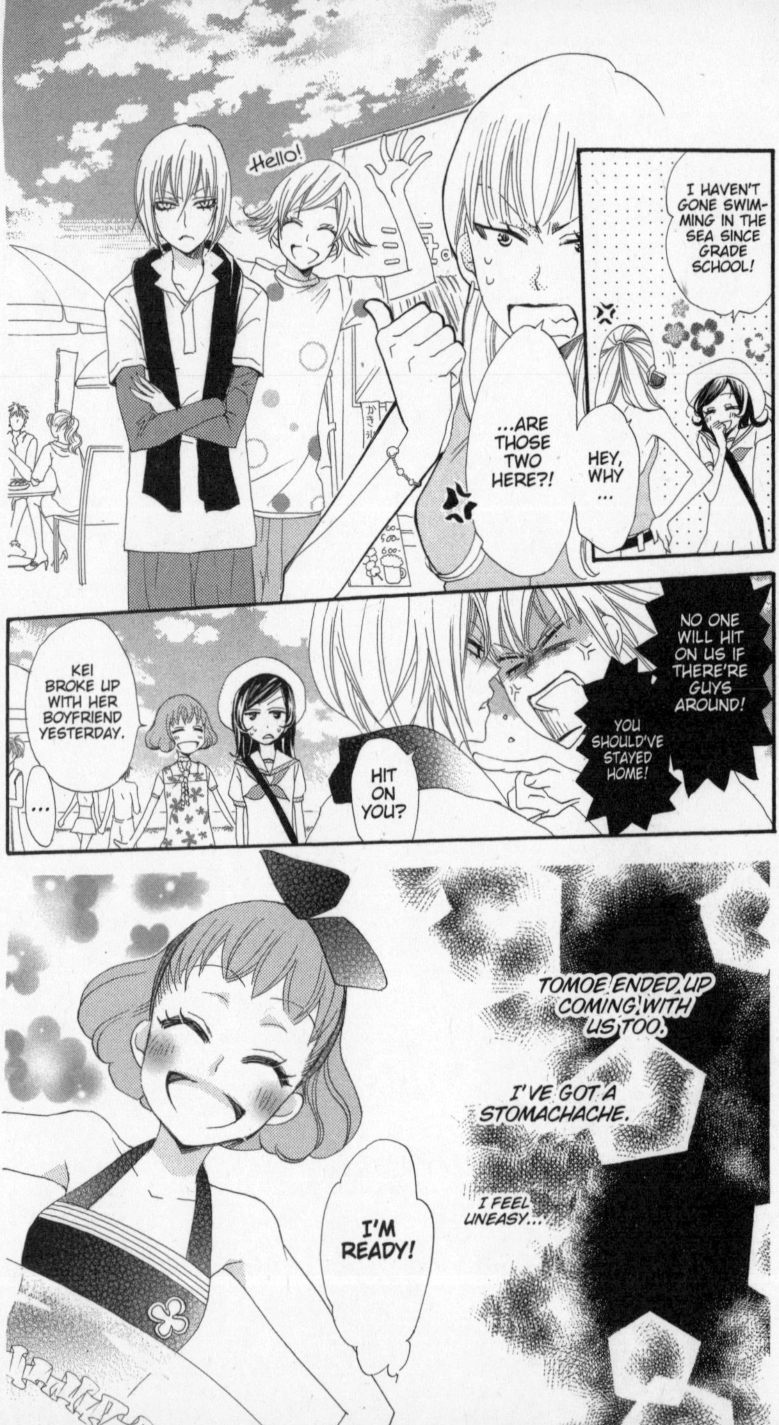
I HAVEN'T GONE SWIMMING IN THE SEA SINCE GRADE SCHOOL!
HEY, WHY ...
...ARE THOSE TWO HERE?!
Hello!
NO ONE WILL HIT ON US IF THERE'RE GUYS AROUND!
YOU SHOULD'VE STAYED HOME!
HIT ON YOU?
KEI BROKE UP WITH HER BOYFRIEND YESTERDAY.
...
TOMOE ENDED UP COMING WITH US TOO.
I'VE GOT A STOMACHACHE.
I FEEL UNEASY...
I'M READY!

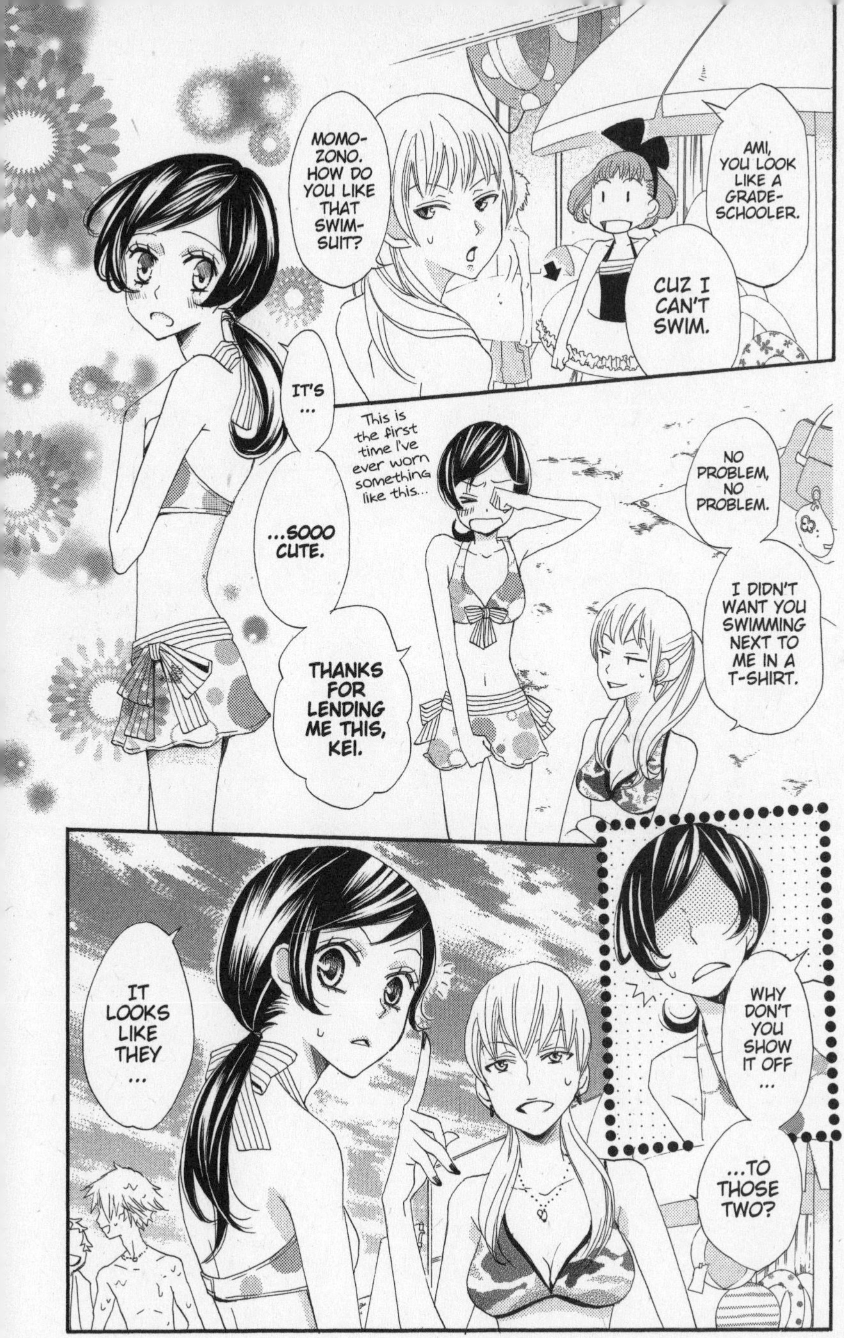
AMI, YOU LOOK LIKE A GRADE-SCHOOLER.
CUZ I CAN'T SWIM.
MOMO-ZONO. HOW DO YOU LIKE THAT SWIM-SUIT?
IT'S...
...SOOO CUTE.
This is the first time I've ever worn something like this...
THANKS FOR LENDING ME THIS, KEI.
NO PROBLEM, NO PROBLEM.
I DIDN'T WANT YOU SWIMMING NEXT TO ME IN A T-SHIRT.
WHY DON'T YOU SHOW IT OFF...
...TO THOSE TWO?
IT LOOKS LIKE THEY...

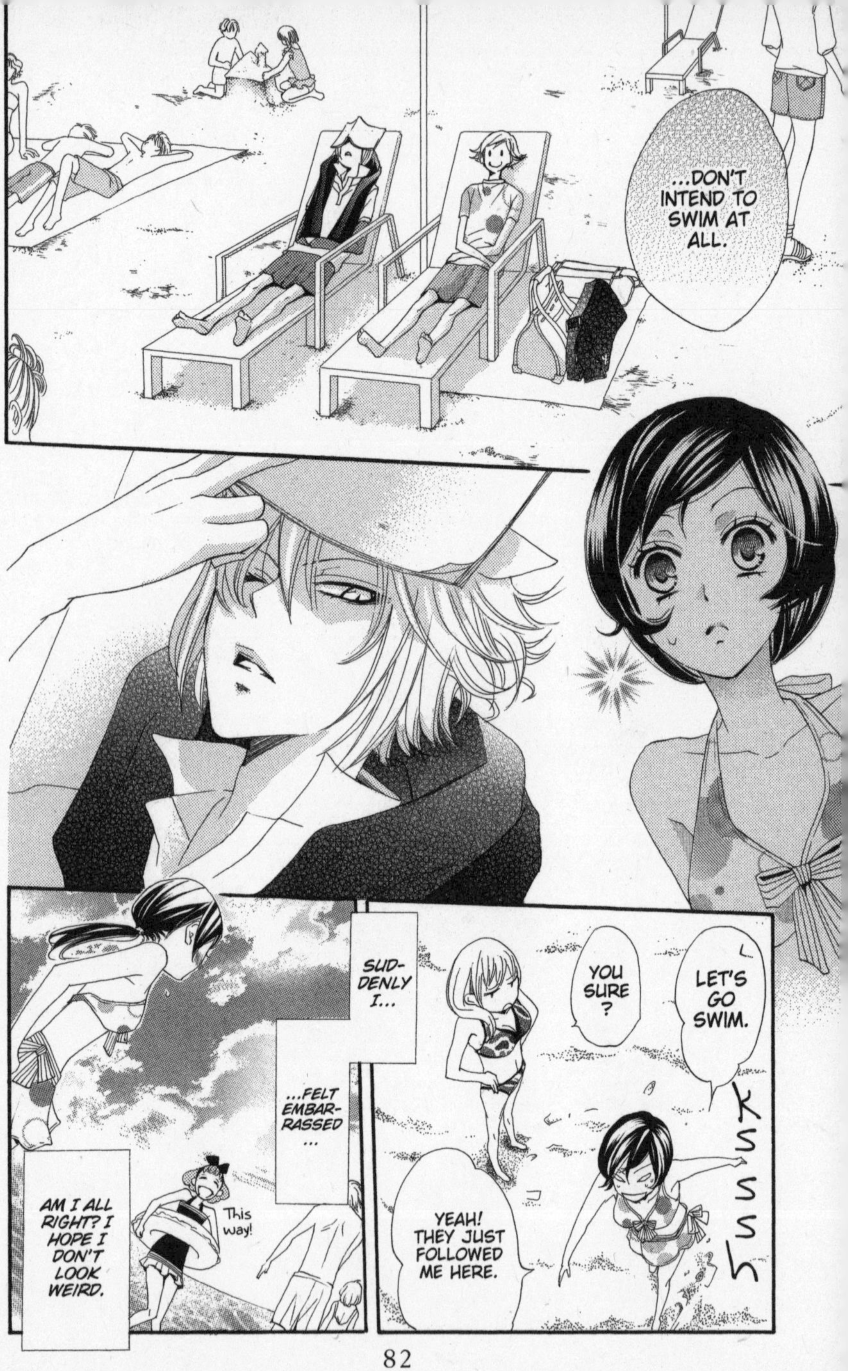
...DON'T INTEND TO SWIM AT ALL.
LET'S GO SWIM.
YOU SURE?
YEAH! THEY JUST FOLLOWED ME HERE.
KSSSH
SUD-DENLY I...
...FELT EMBAR-RASSED...
AM I ALL RIGHT? I HOPE I DON'T LOOK WEIRD.
This way!

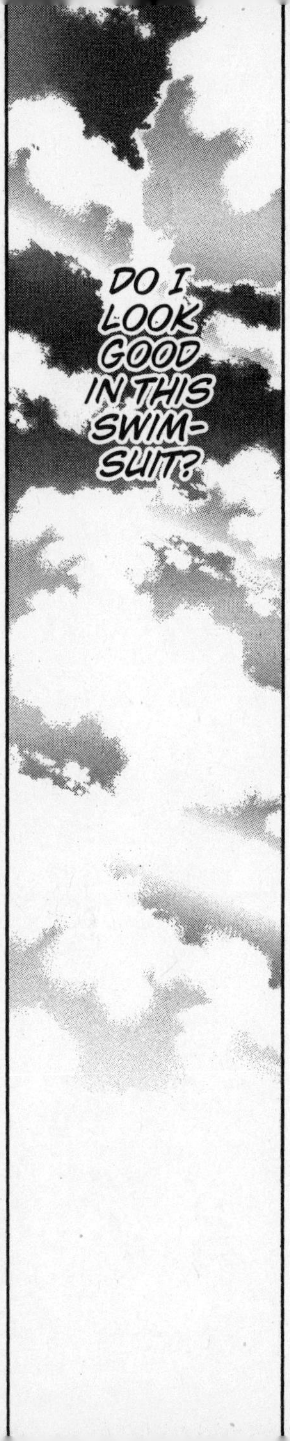
DO I LOOK GOOD IN THIS SWIM-SUIT?

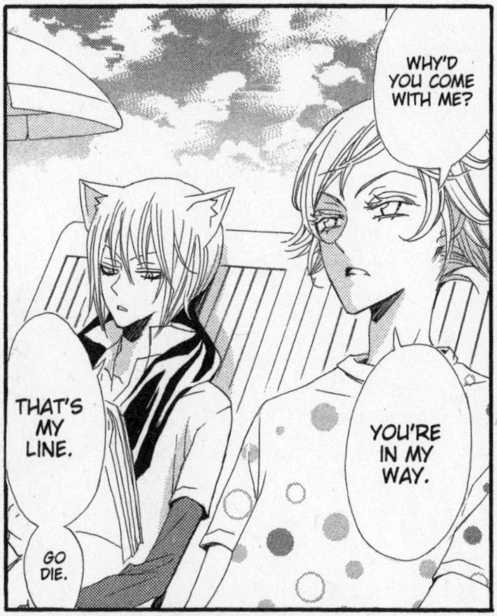
WHY'D YOU COME WITH ME?
YOU'RE IN MY WAY.
THAT'S MY LINE.
GO DIE.

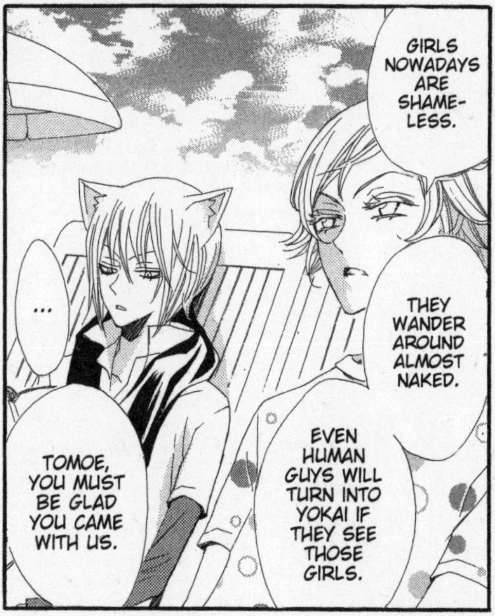
GIRLS NOWADAYS ARE SHAME-LESS.
THEY WANDER AROUND ALMOST NAKED.
...
EVEN HUMAN GUYS WILL TURN INTO YOKAI IF THEY SEE THOSE GIRLS.
TOMOE, YOU MUST BE GLAD YOU CAME WITH US.

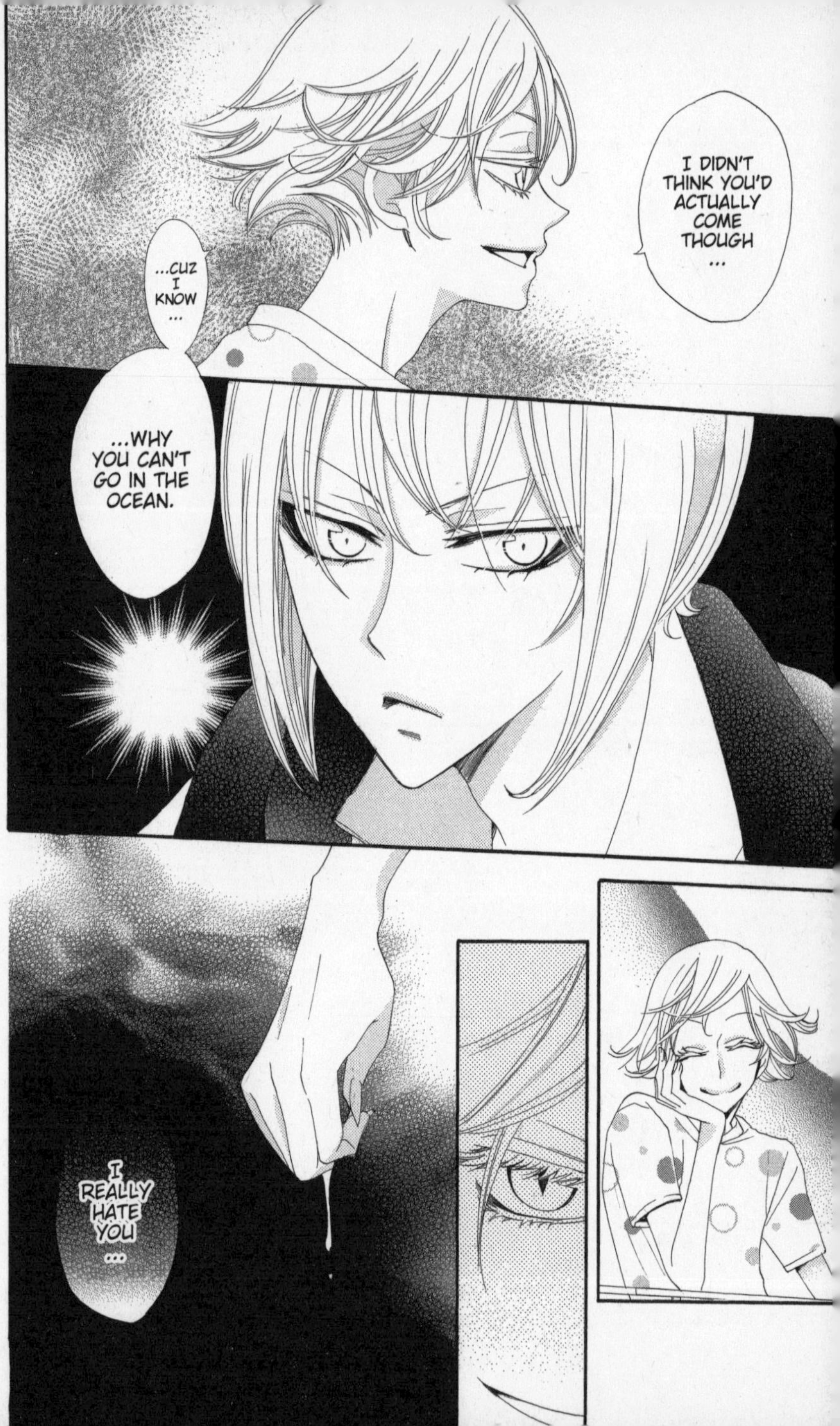
I DIDN'T THINK YOU'D ACTUALLY COME THOUGH ...
...CUZ I KNOW ...
...WHY YOU CAN'T GO IN THE OCEAN.
I REALLY HATE YOU ...

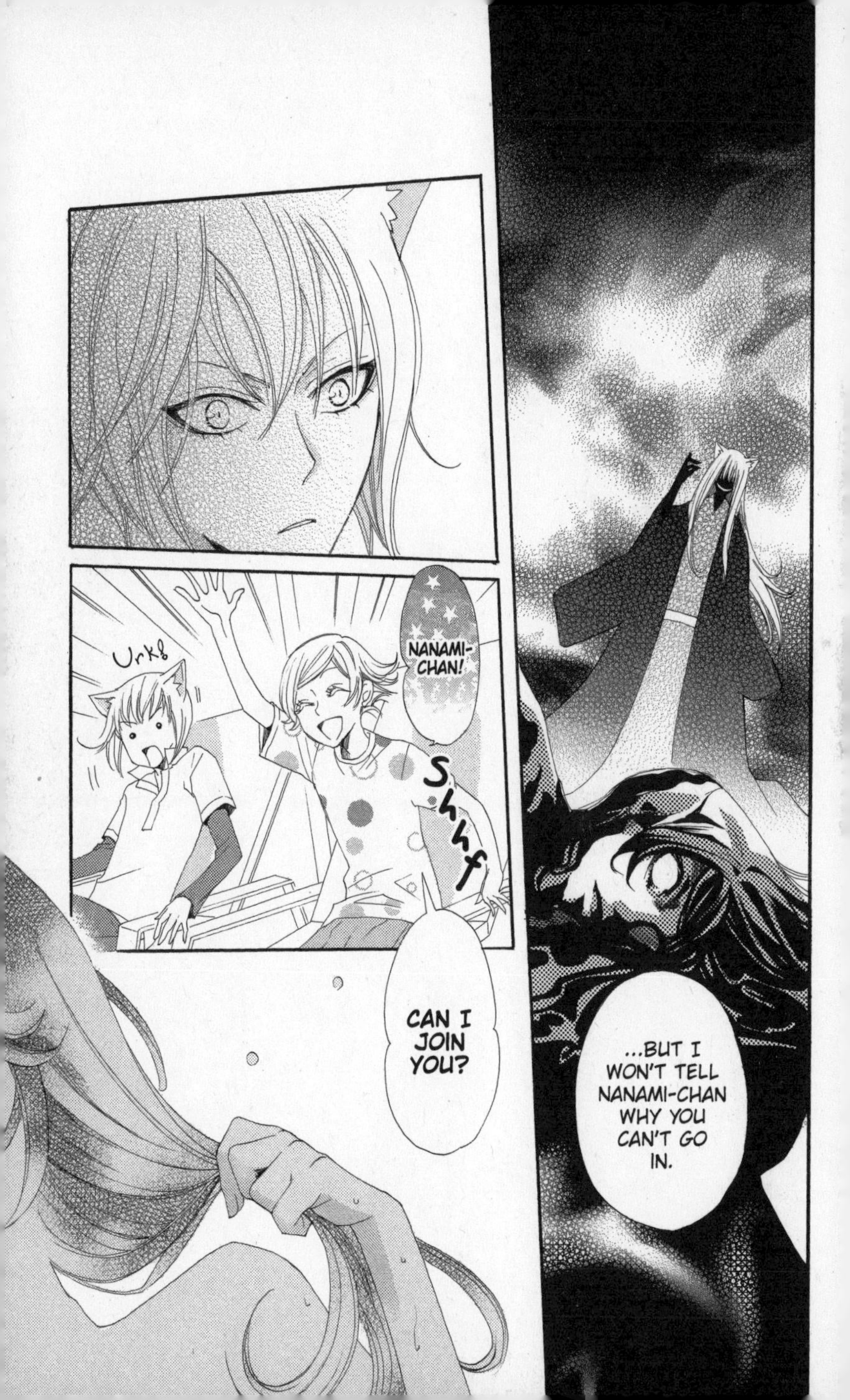
...BUT I WON'T TELL NANAMI-CHAN WHY YOU CAN'T GO IN.
NANAMI-CHAN!
Urk!
Shuf
CAN I JOIN YOU?

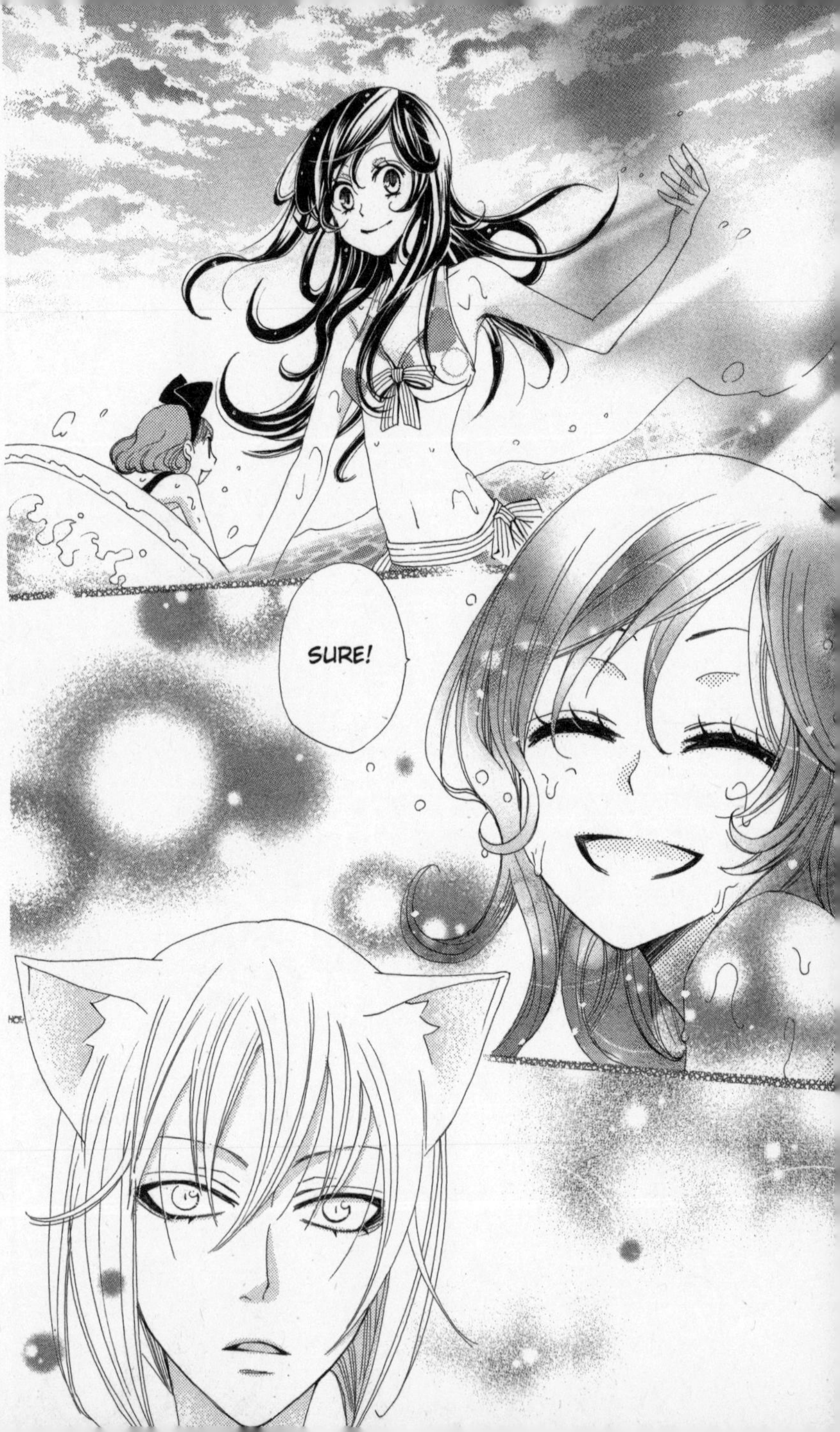
SURE!

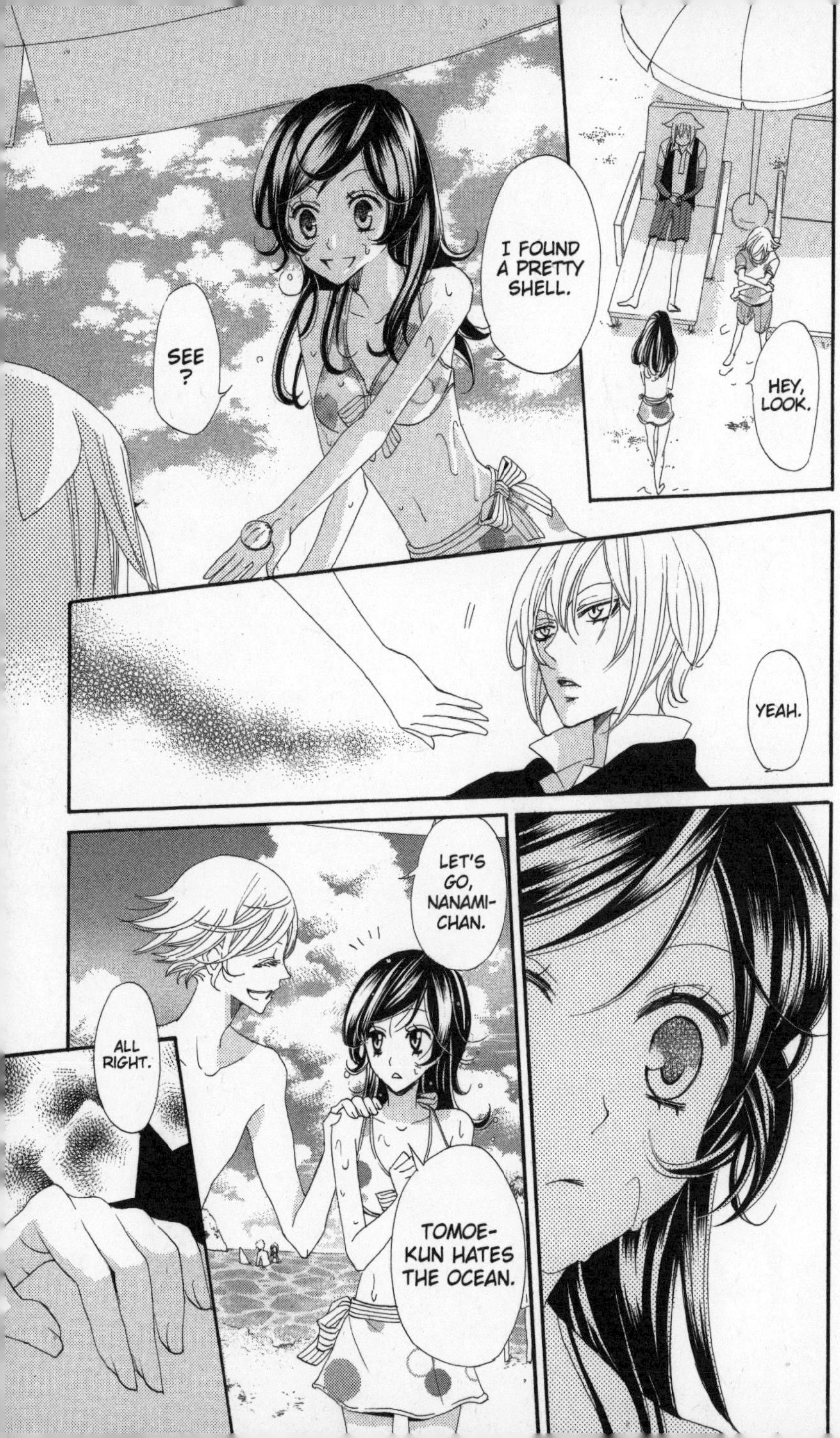
HEY, LOOK.
I FOUND A PRETTY SHELL.
SEE?
YEAH.
LET'S GO, NANAMI-CHAN.
ALL RIGHT.
TOMOE-KUN HATES THE OCEAN.

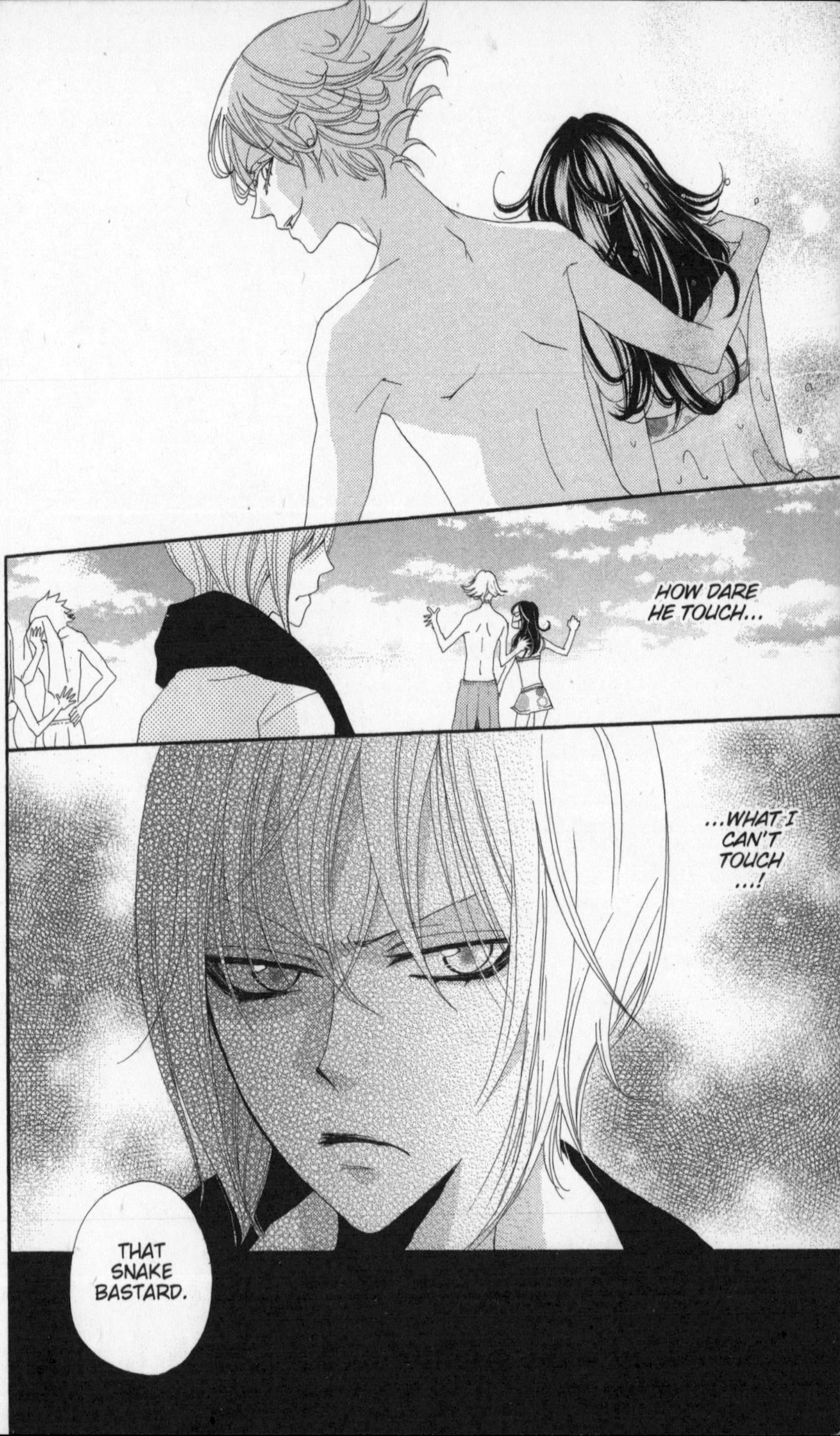
HOW DARE HE TOUCH...
...WHAT I CAN'T TOUCH ...!
THAT SNAKE BASTARD.

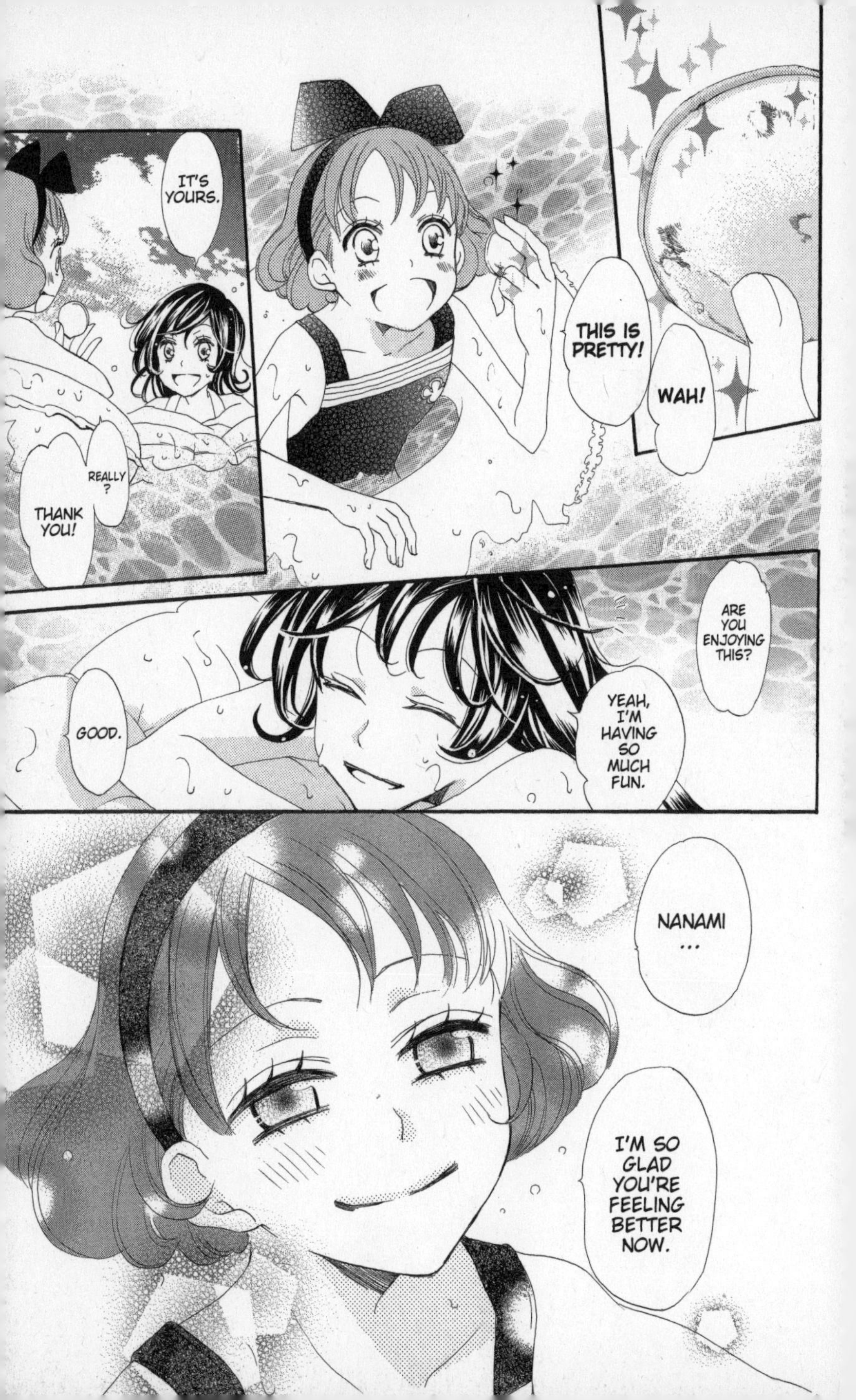
WAH!
THIS IS PRETTY!
IT'S YOURS.
REALLY?
THANK YOU!
ARE YOU ENJOYING THIS?
YEAH, I'M HAVING SO MUCH FUN.
GOOD.
NANAMI...
I'M SO GLAD YOU'RE FEELING BETTER NOW.

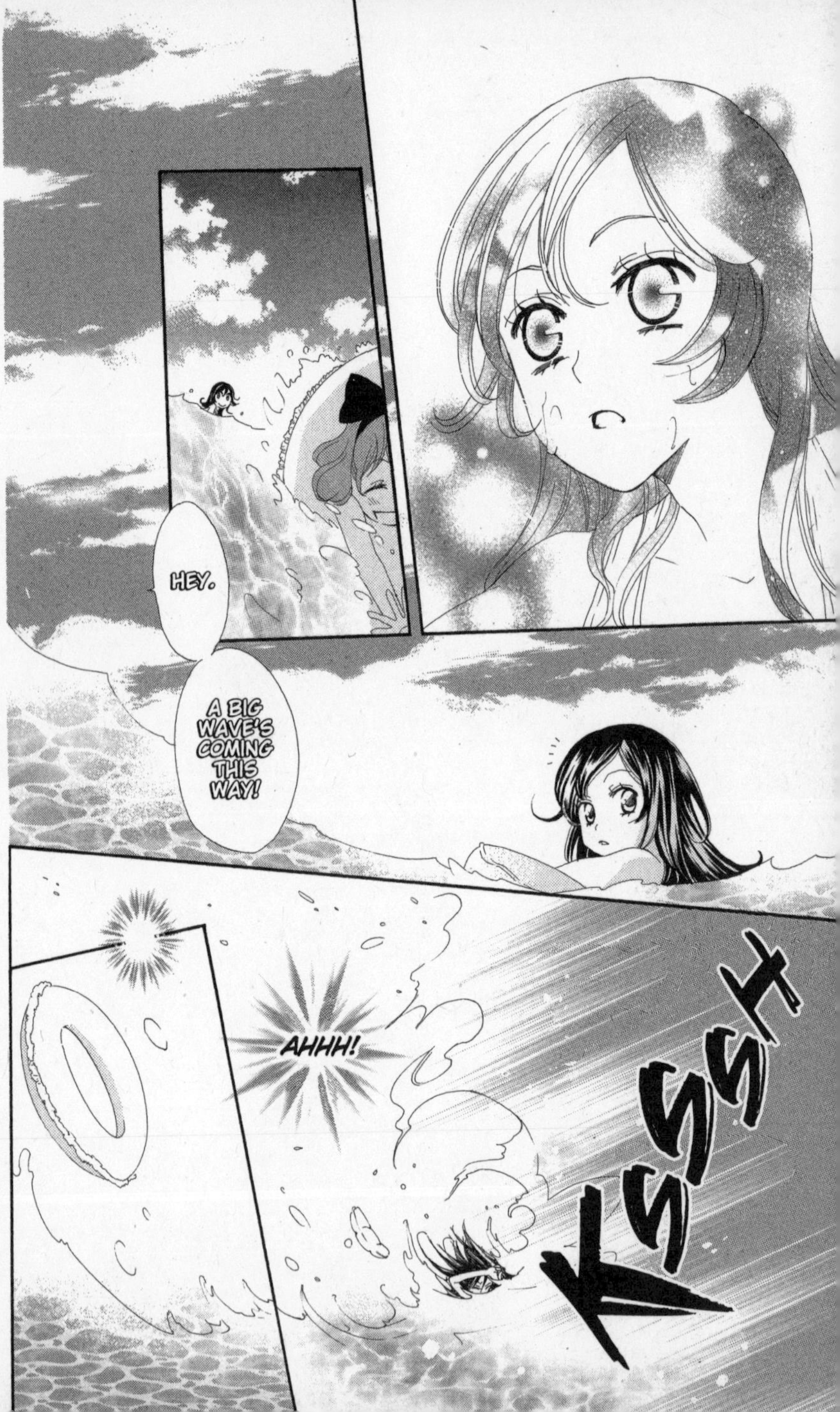
HEY.
A BIG WAVE'S COMING THIS WAY!
AHHH!
KSSSH

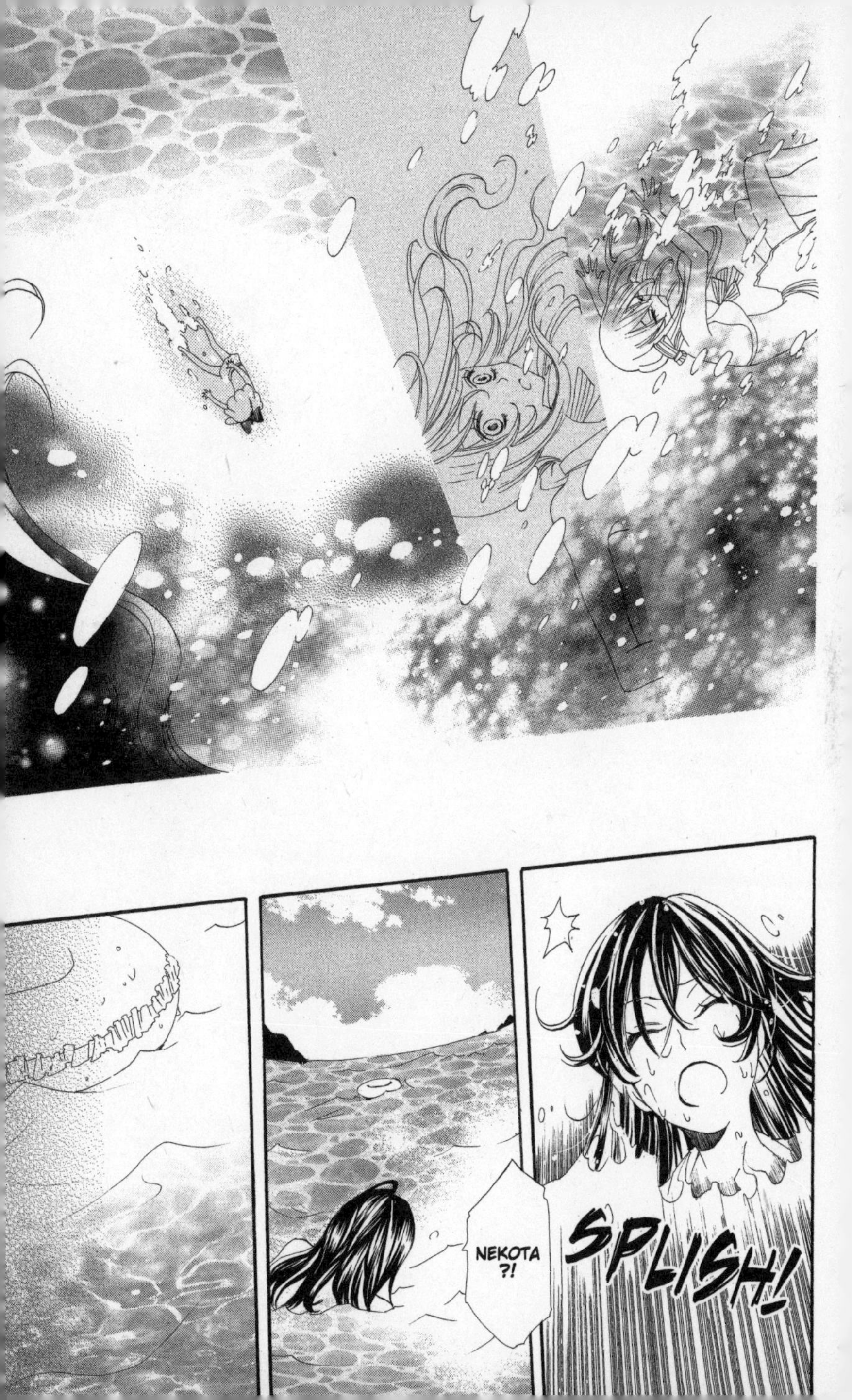
SPLISH!
NEKOTA ?!

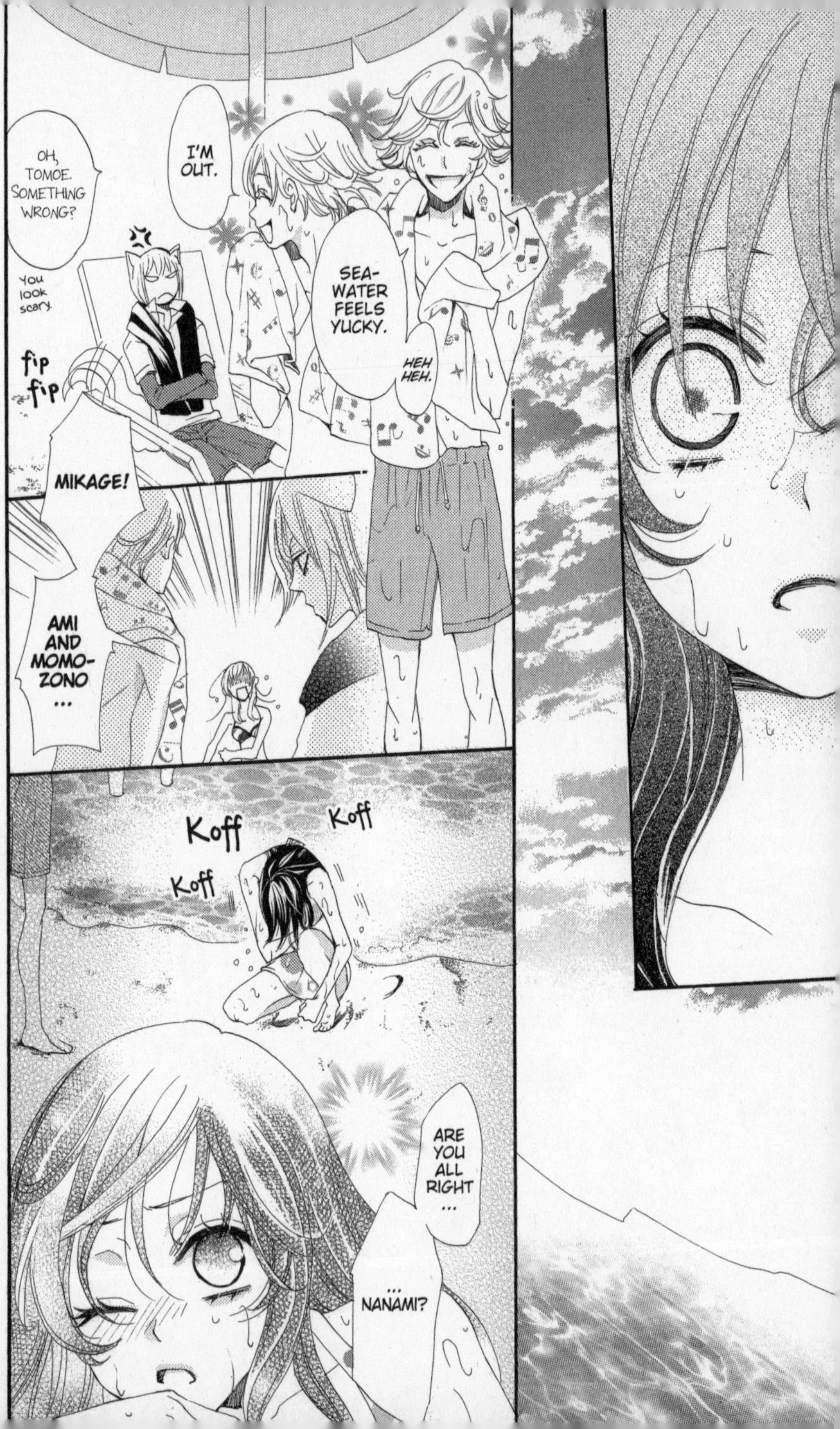
I'M OUT.
SEA-WATER FEELS YUCKY.
HEH HEH.
OH, TOMOE. SOMETHING WRONG?
You look scary.
fip fip
MIKAGE!
AMI AND MOMO-ZONO...
Koff
Koff
Koff
ARE YOU ALL RIGHT...
...NANAMI?

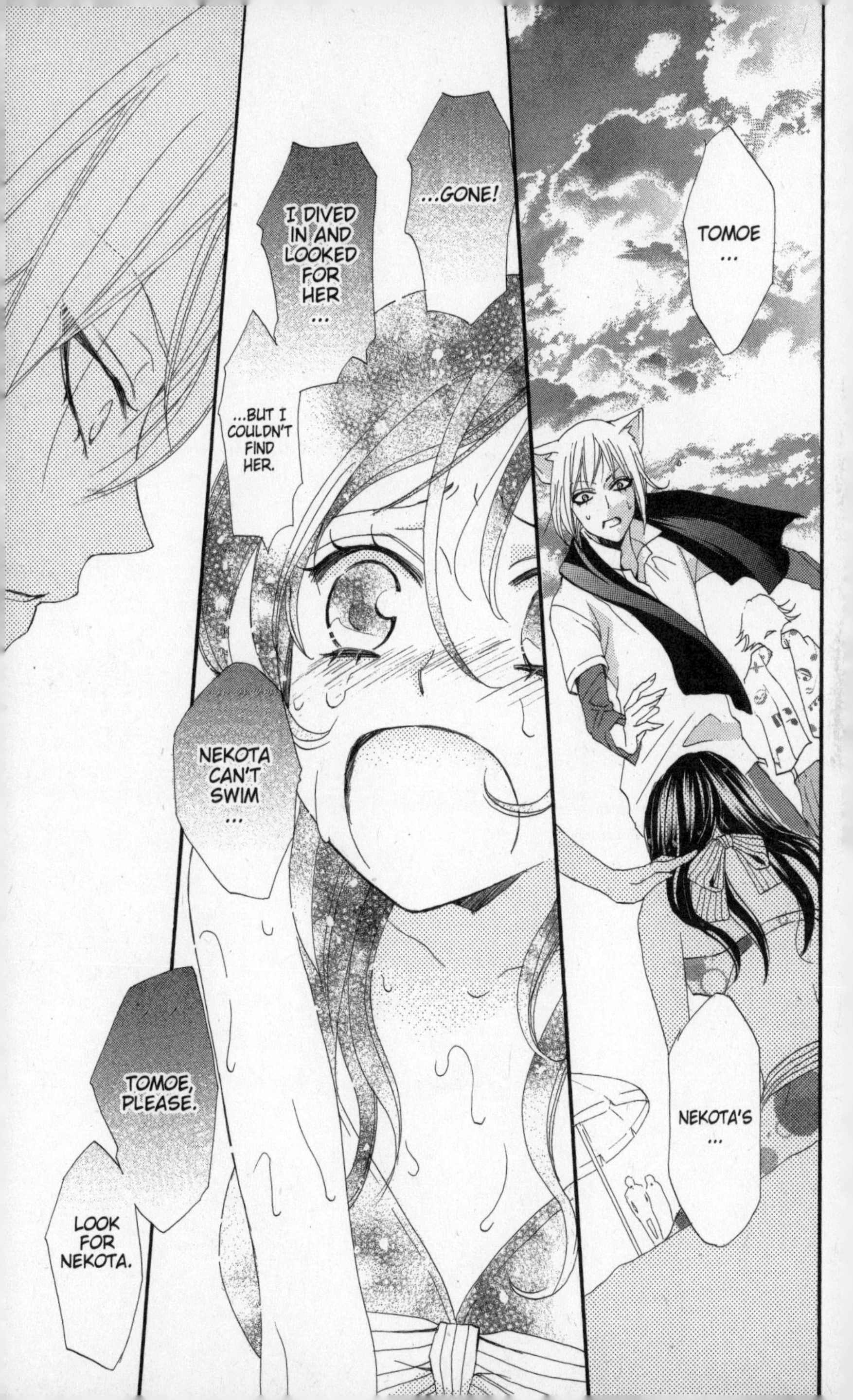
TOMOE ...
NEKOTA'S ...
...GONE!
I DIVED IN AND LOOKED FOR HER ...
...BUT I COULDN'T FIND HER.
NEKOTA CAN'T SWIM ...
TOMOE, PLEASE.
LOOK FOR NEKOTA.

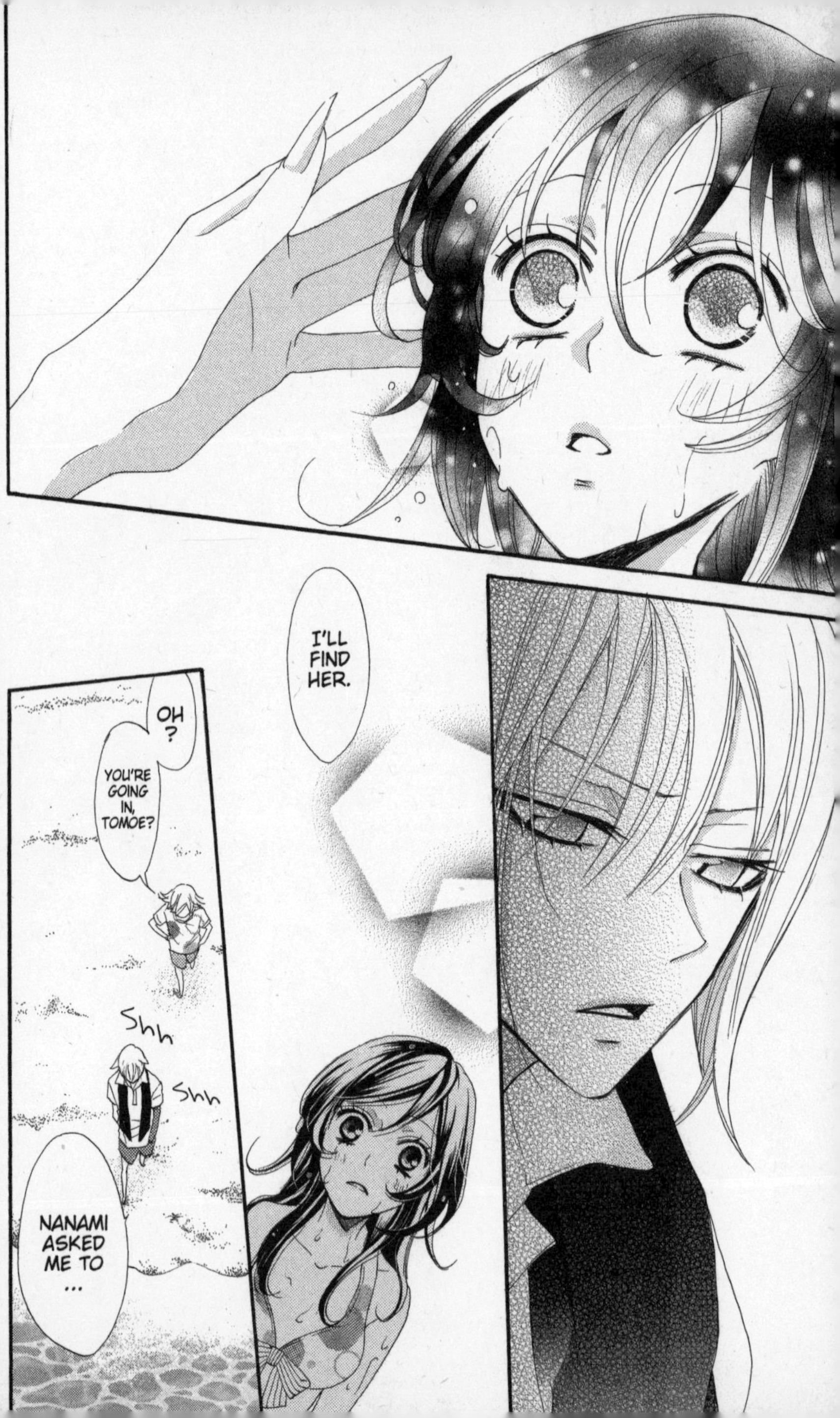
I'LL FIND HER.
OH?
YOU'RE GOING IN, TOMOE?
Shh
Shh
NANAMI ASKED ME TO ...

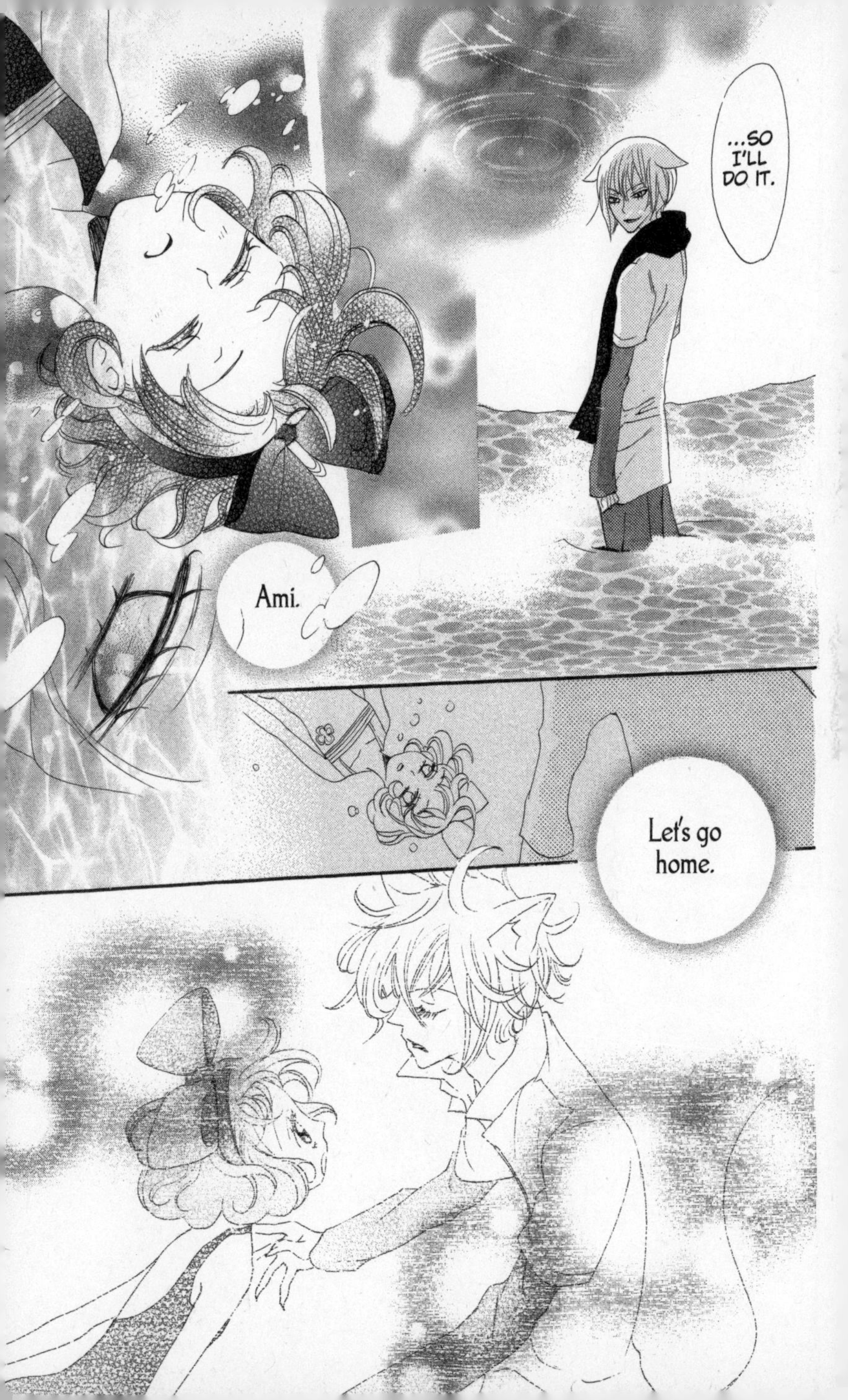
...SO I'LL DO IT.
Ami.
Let's go home.

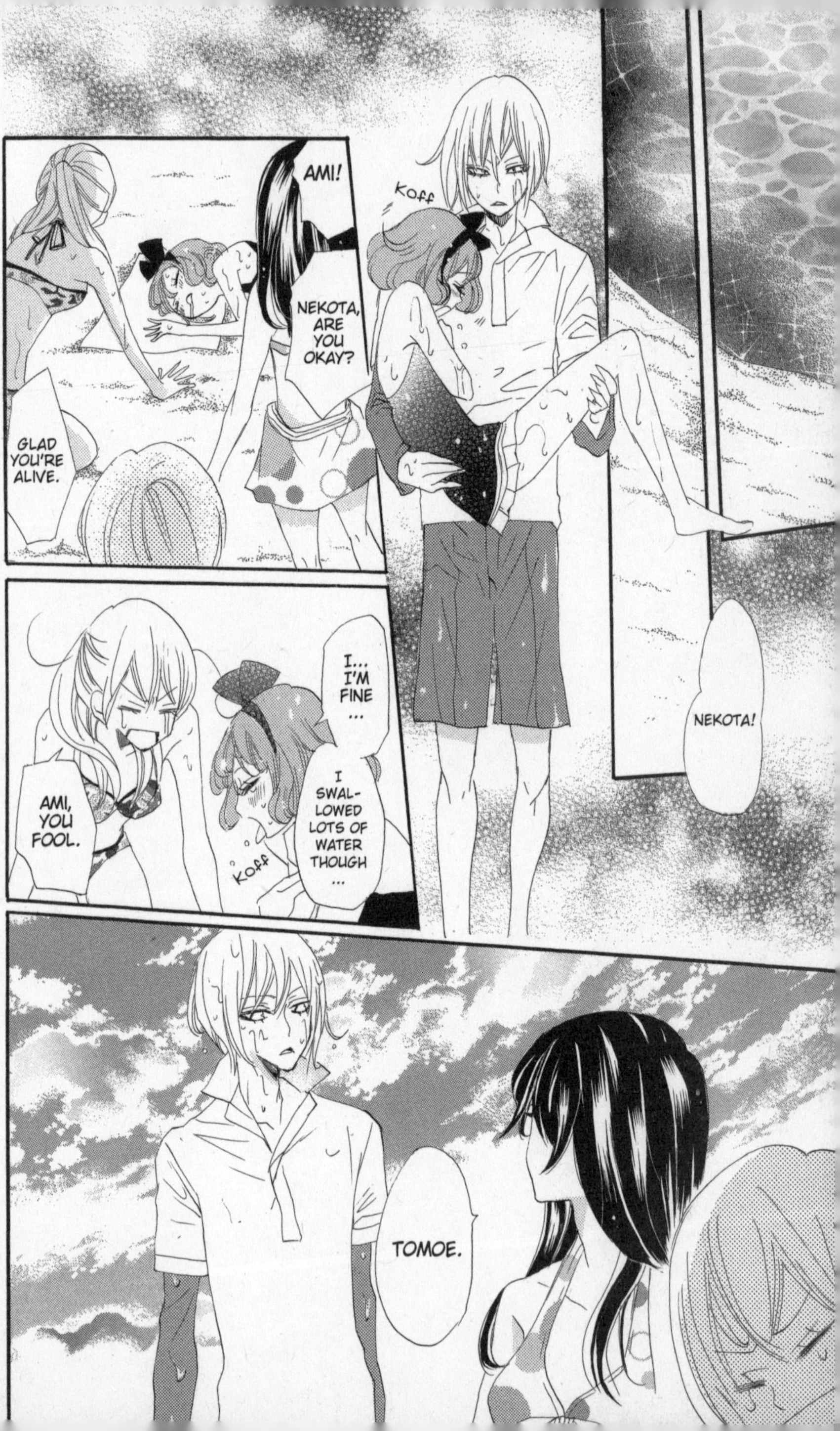
KOFF
NEKOTA!
AMI!
NEKOTA, ARE YOU OKAY?
GLAD YOU'RE ALIVE.
I... I'M FINE...
I SWAL-LOWED LOTS OF WATER THOUGH...
KOFF
AMI, YOU FOOL.
TOMOE.

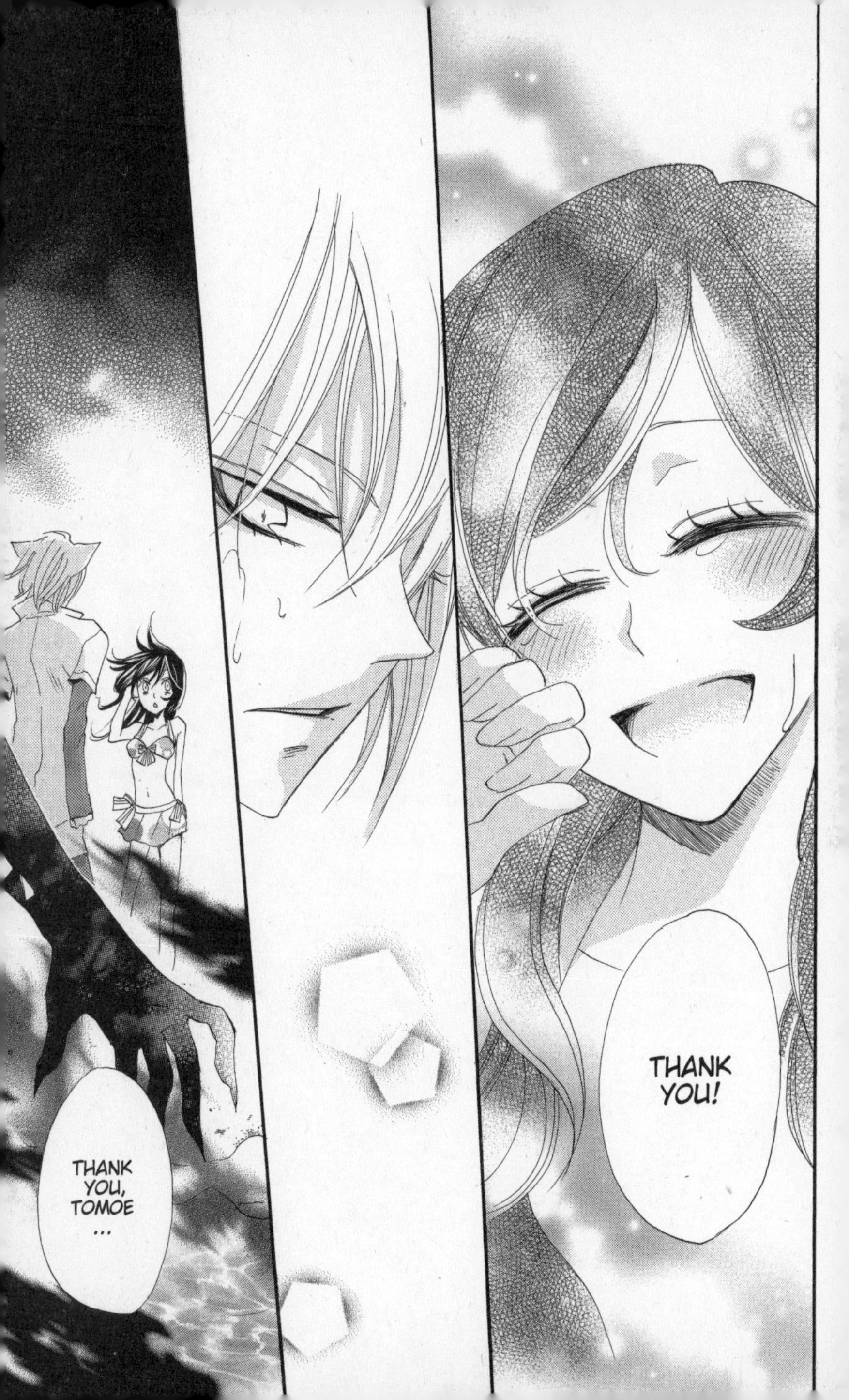
THANK YOU!
THANK YOU, TOMOE ...

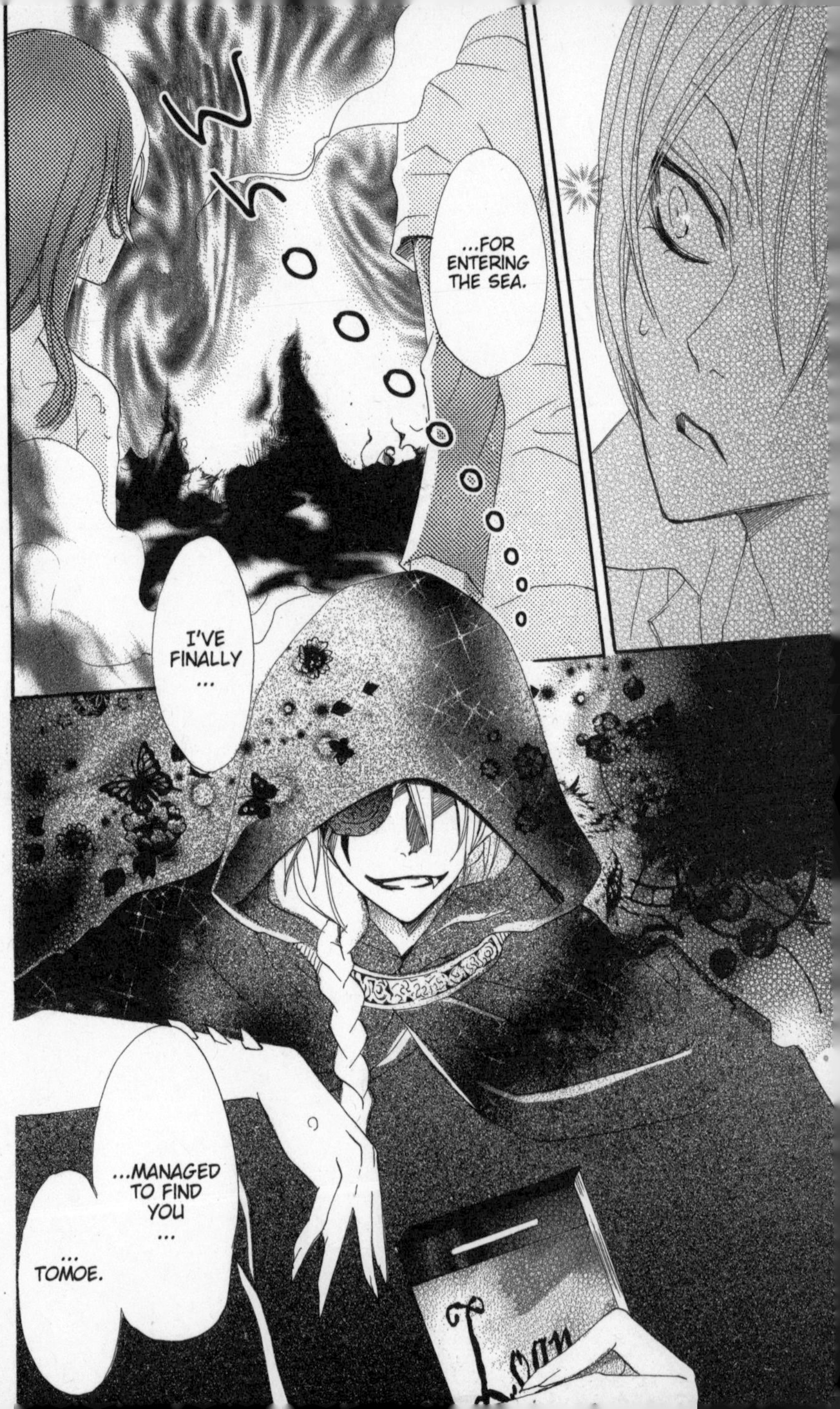
...FOR ENTERING THE SEA.
I'VE FINALLY ...
...MANAGED TO FIND YOU ...
... TOMOE.

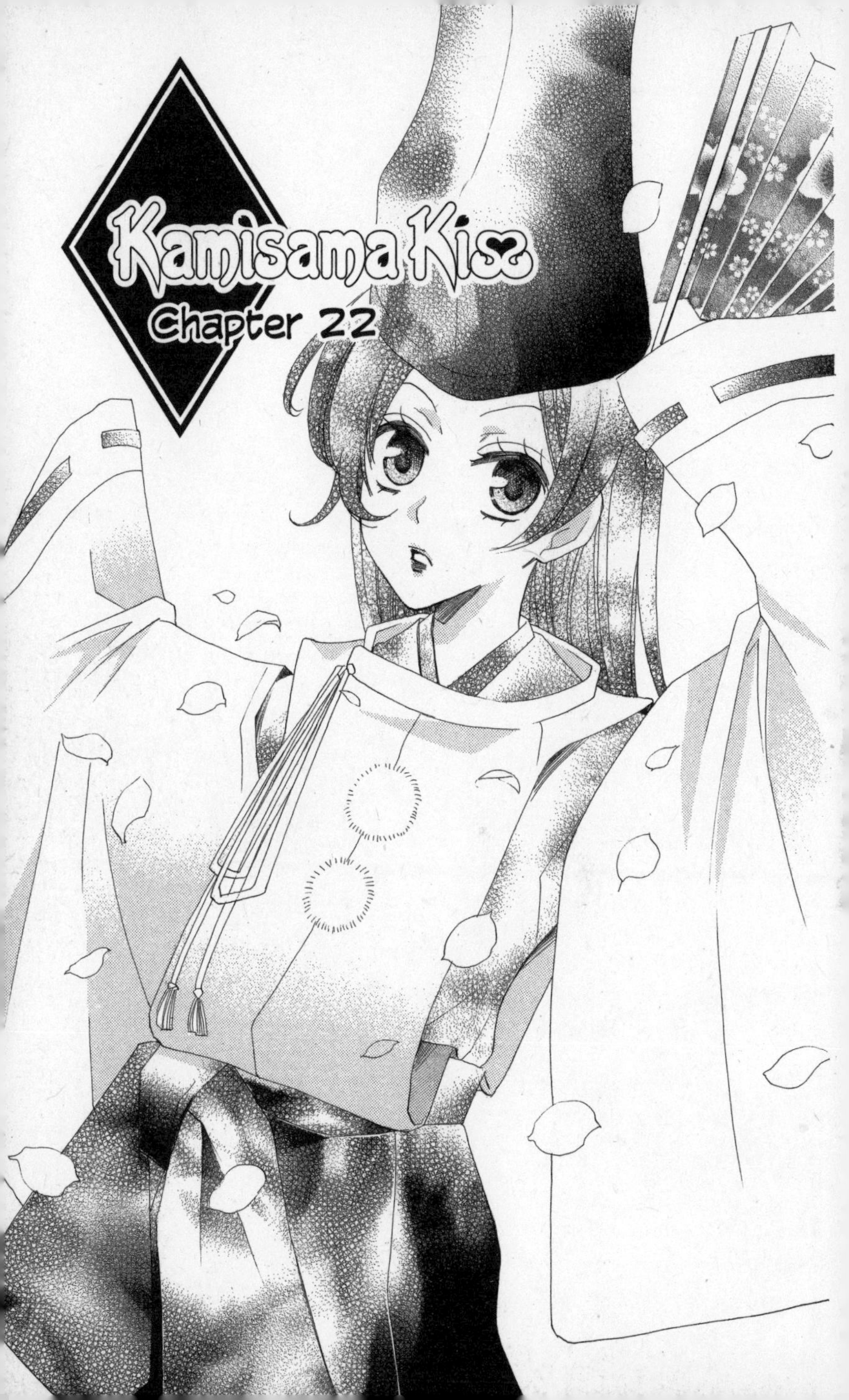
Kamisama Kiss
Chapter 22

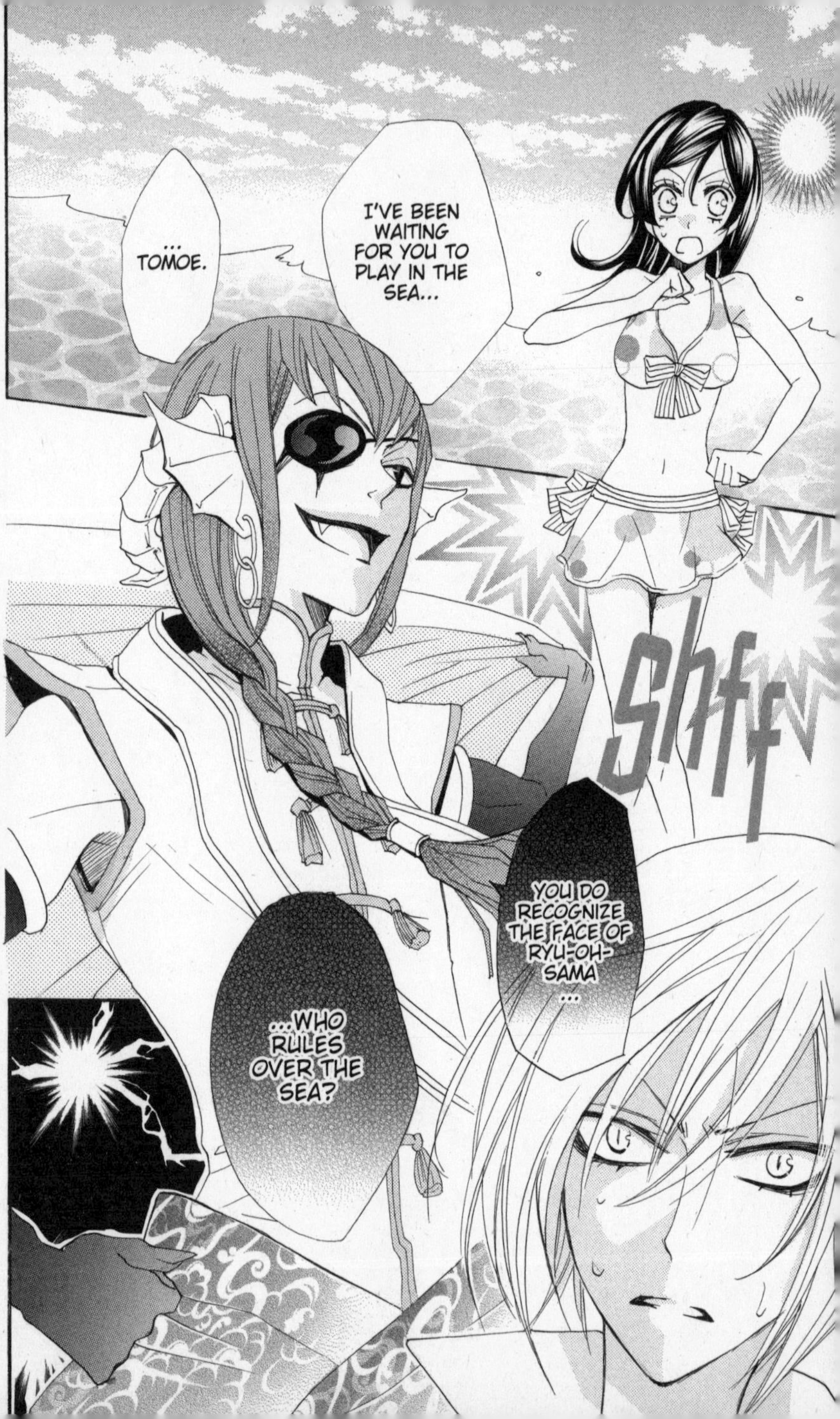
I'VE BEEN WAITING FOR YOU TO PLAY IN THE SEA...
... TOMOE.
Shff
YOU DO RECOGNIZE THE FACE OF RYU-OH-SAMA ...
...WHO RULES OVER THE SEA?

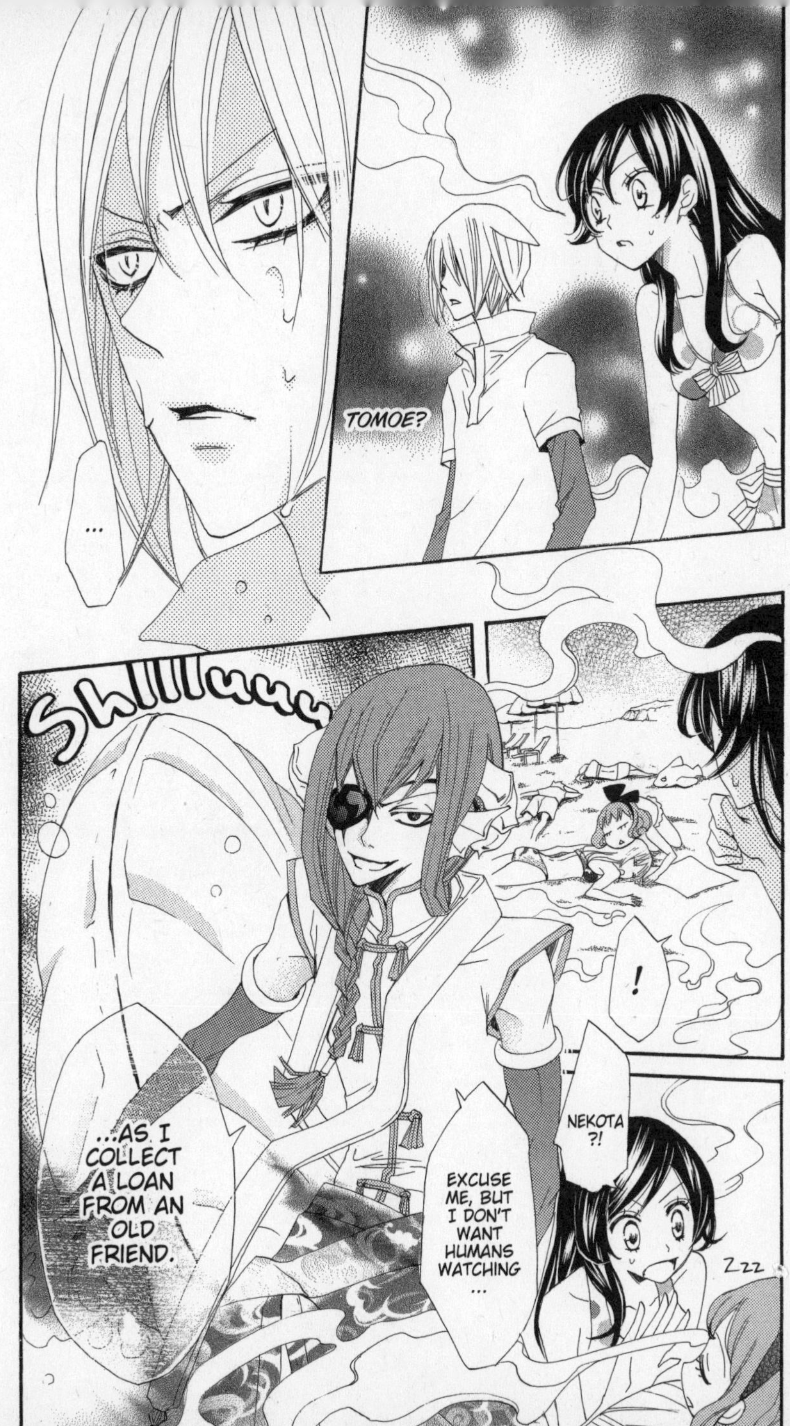
TOMOE?
...
!
NEKOTA ?!
Zzz
Shlllluuu
EXCUSE ME, BUT I DON'T WANT HUMANS WATCHING ...
...AS I COLLECT A LOAN FROM AN OLD FRIEND.

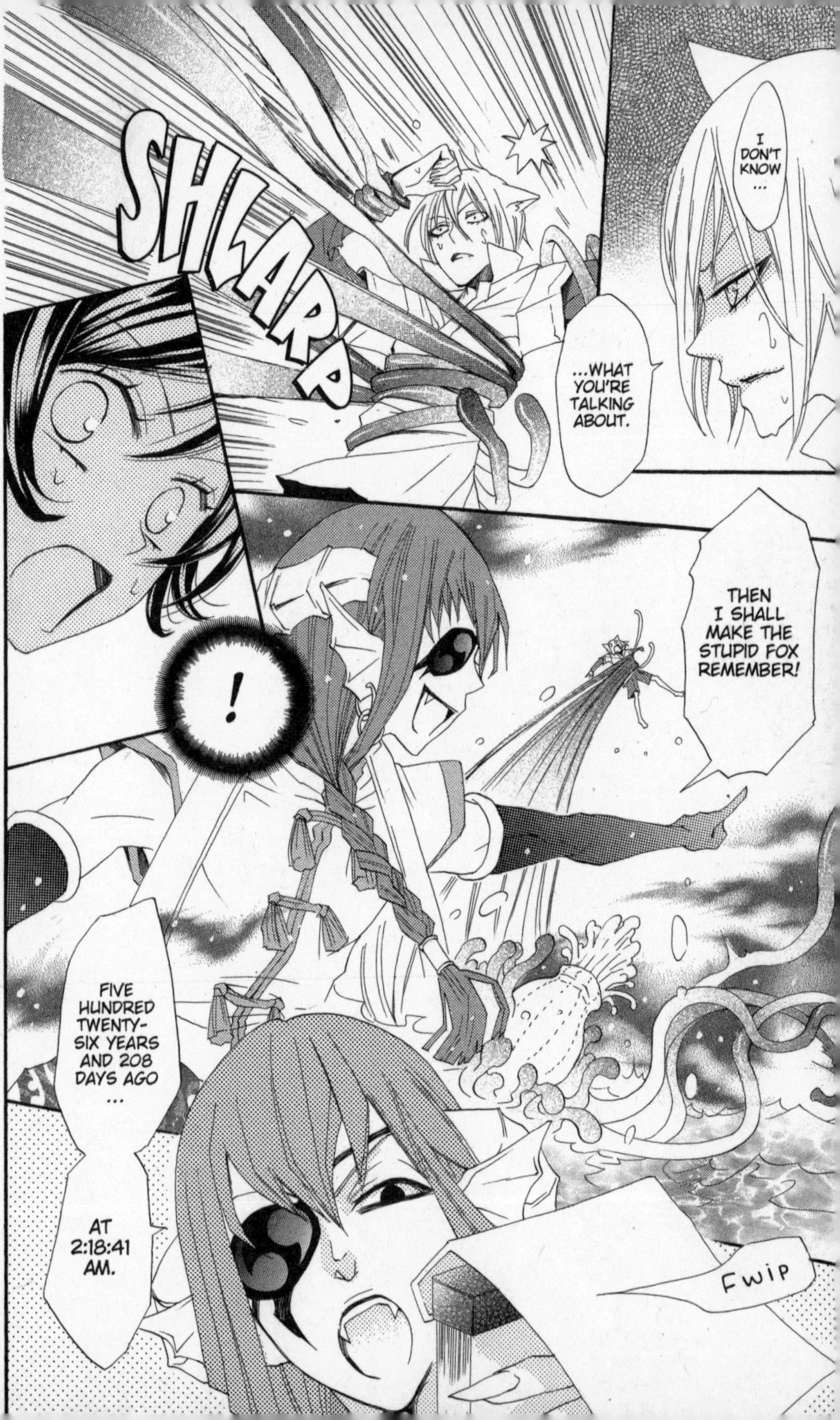
I DON'T KNOW ...
...WHAT YOU'RE TALKING ABOUT.
SHWARP
!
THEN I SHALL MAKE THE STUPID FOX REMEMBER!
FIVE HUNDRED TWENTY-SIX YEARS AND 208 DAYS AGO ...
AT 2:18:41 AM.
Fwip

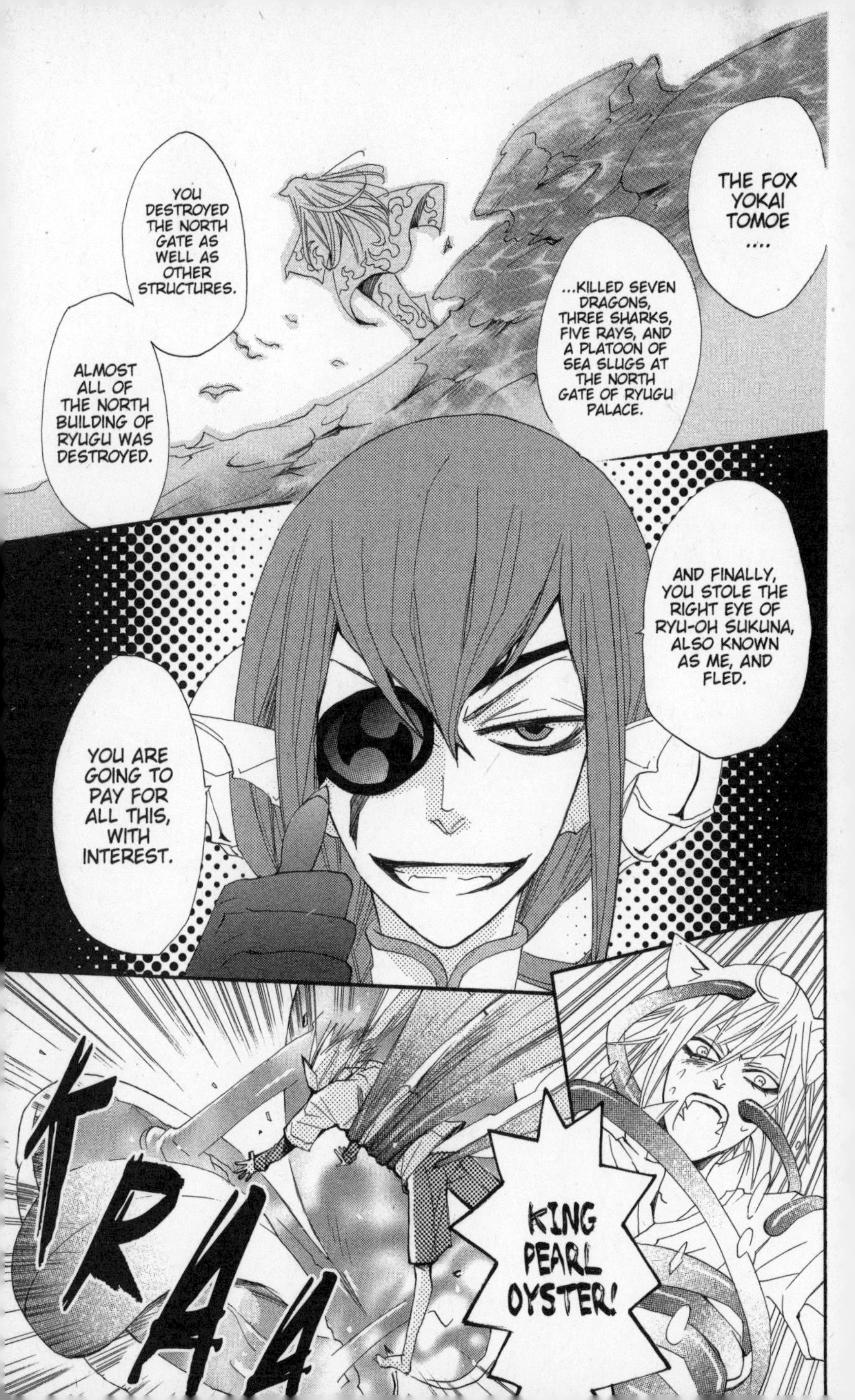
THE FOX YOKAI TOMOE ....
...KILLED SEVEN DRAGONS, THREE SHARKS, FIVE RAYS, AND A PLATOON OF SEA SLUGS AT THE NORTH GATE OF RYUGU PALACE.
YOU DESTROYED THE NORTH GATE AS WELL AS OTHER STRUCTURES.
ALMOST ALL OF THE NORTH BUILDING OF RYUGU WAS DESTROYED.
AND FINALLY, YOU STOLE THE RIGHT EYE OF RYU-OH SUKUNA, ALSO KNOWN AS ME, AND FLED.
YOU ARE GOING TO PAY FOR ALL THIS, WITH INTEREST.
KING PEARL OYSTER!
KRAA

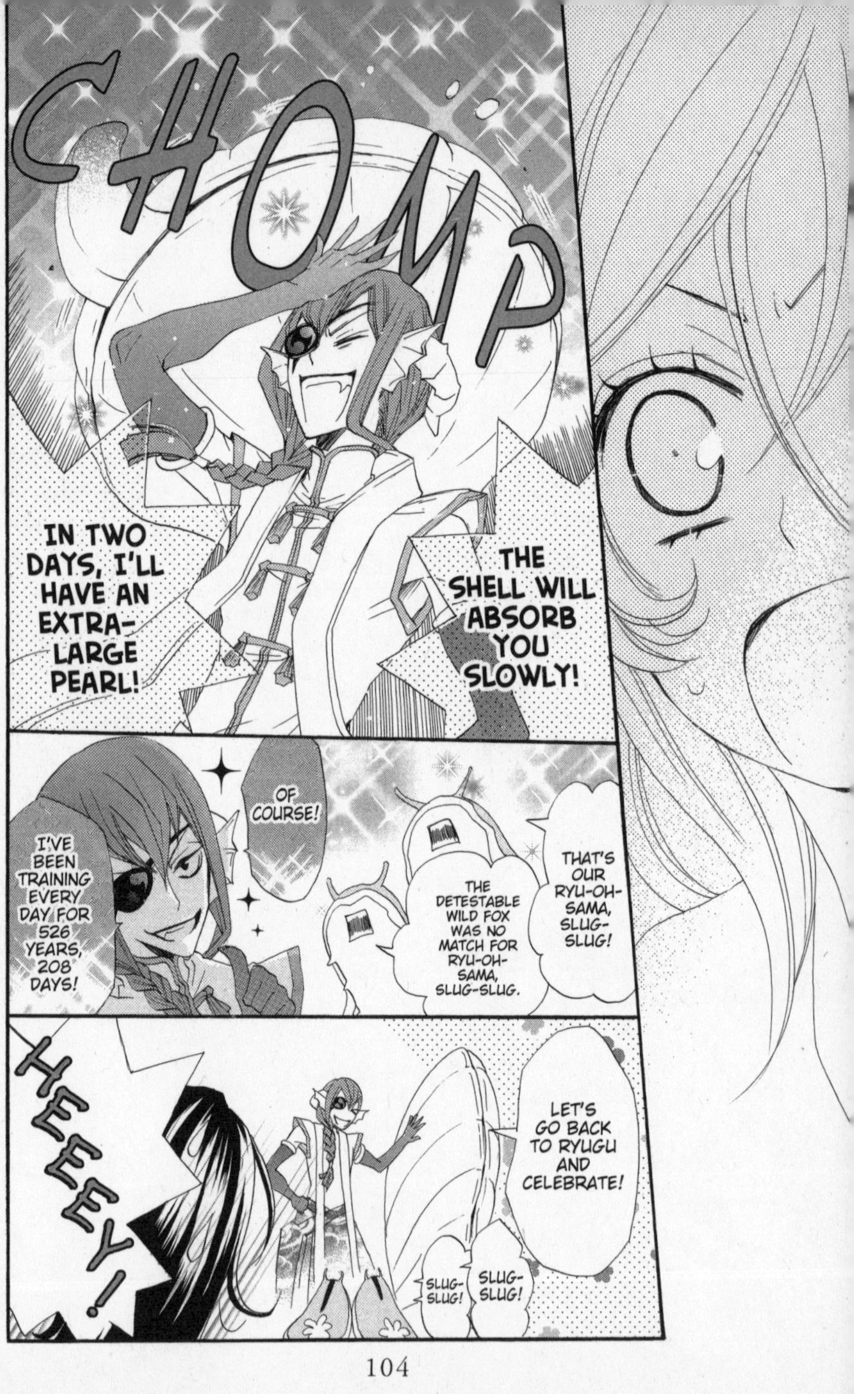
CHOMP
THE SHELL WILL ABSORB YOU SLOWLY!
IN TWO DAYS, I'LL HAVE AN EXTRA-LARGE PEARL!
THAT'S OUR RYU-OH-SAMA, SLUG-SLUG!
THE DETESTABLE WILD FOX WAS NO MATCH FOR RYU-OH-SAMA, SLUG-SLUG.
OF COURSE!
I'VE BEEN TRAINING EVERY DAY FOR 526 YEARS, 208 DAYS!
LET'S GO BACK TO RYUGU AND CELEBRATE!
SLUG-SLUG!
SLUG-SLUG!
HEEEY!

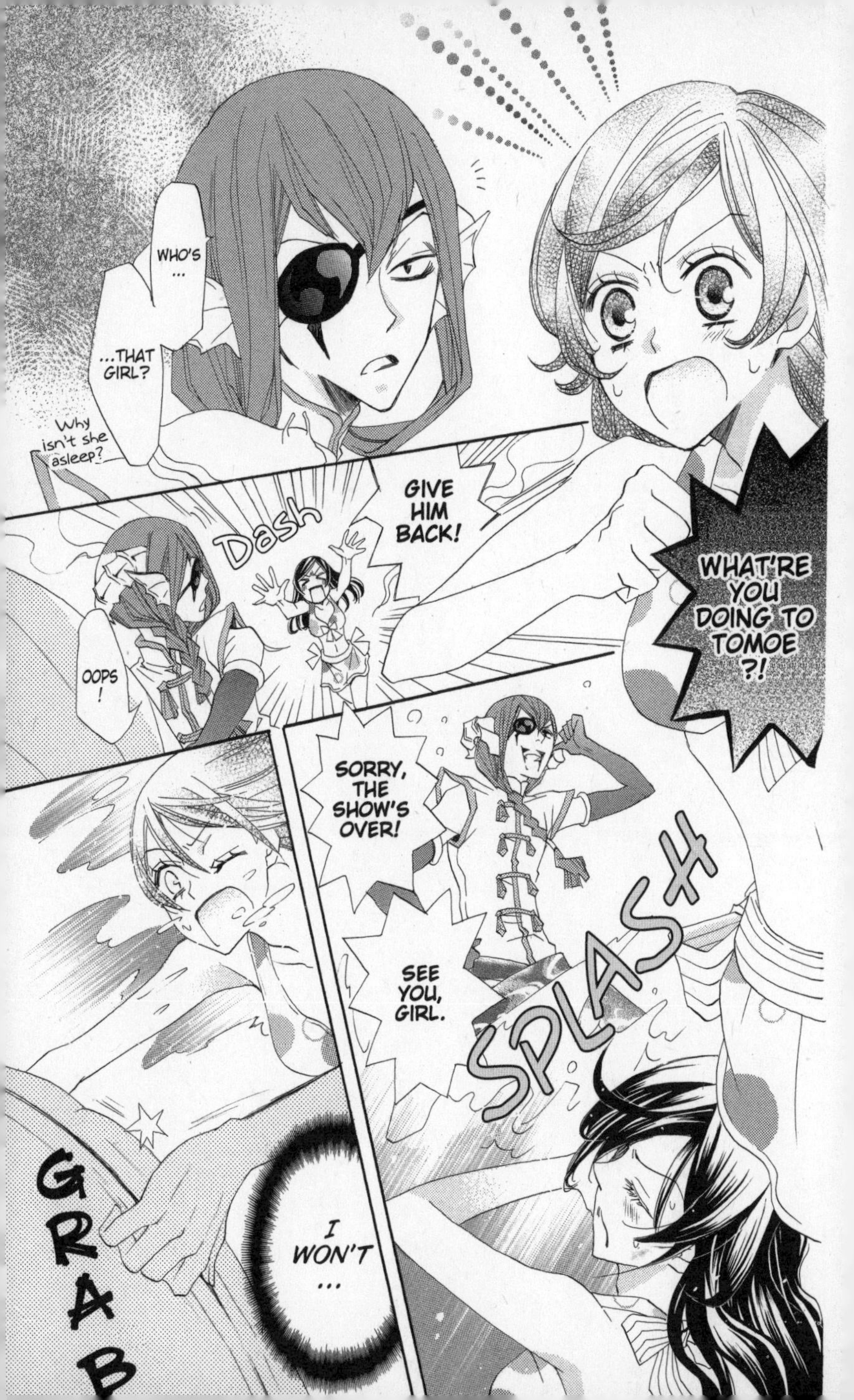
WHO'S ...
...THAT GIRL?
Why isn't she asleep?
WHAT'RE YOU DOING TO TOMOE?!
GIVE HIM BACK!
Dash
OOPS!
SORRY, THE SHOW'S OVER!
SEE YOU, GIRL.
SPLASH
I WON'T ...
GRAB

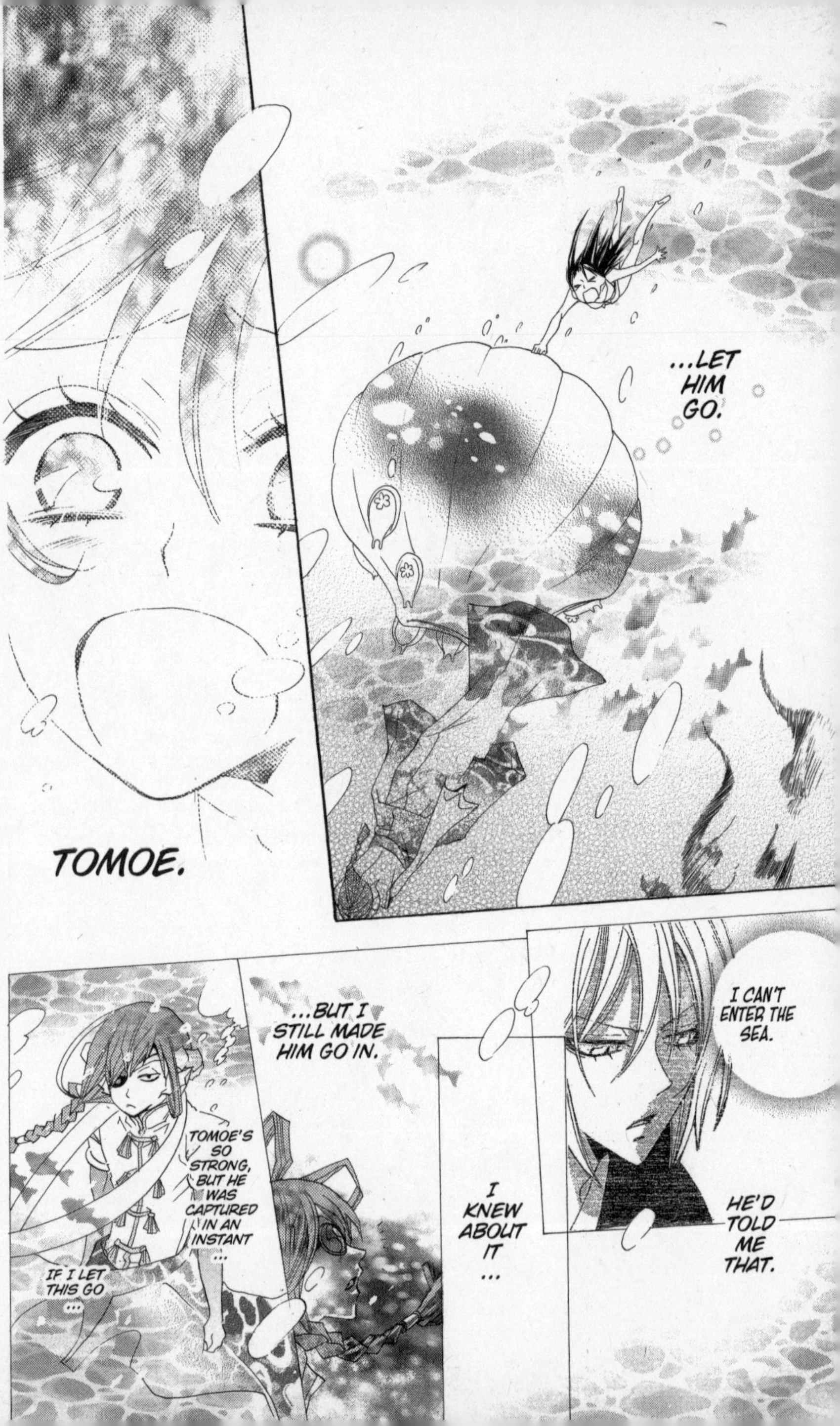
...LET HIM GO.
TOMOE.
I CAN'T ENTER THE SEA.
HE'D TOLD ME THAT.
I KNEW ABOUT IT...
...BUT I STILL MADE HIM GO IN.
TOMOE'S SO STRONG, BUT HE WAS CAPTURED IN AN INSTANT...
IF I LET THIS GO...

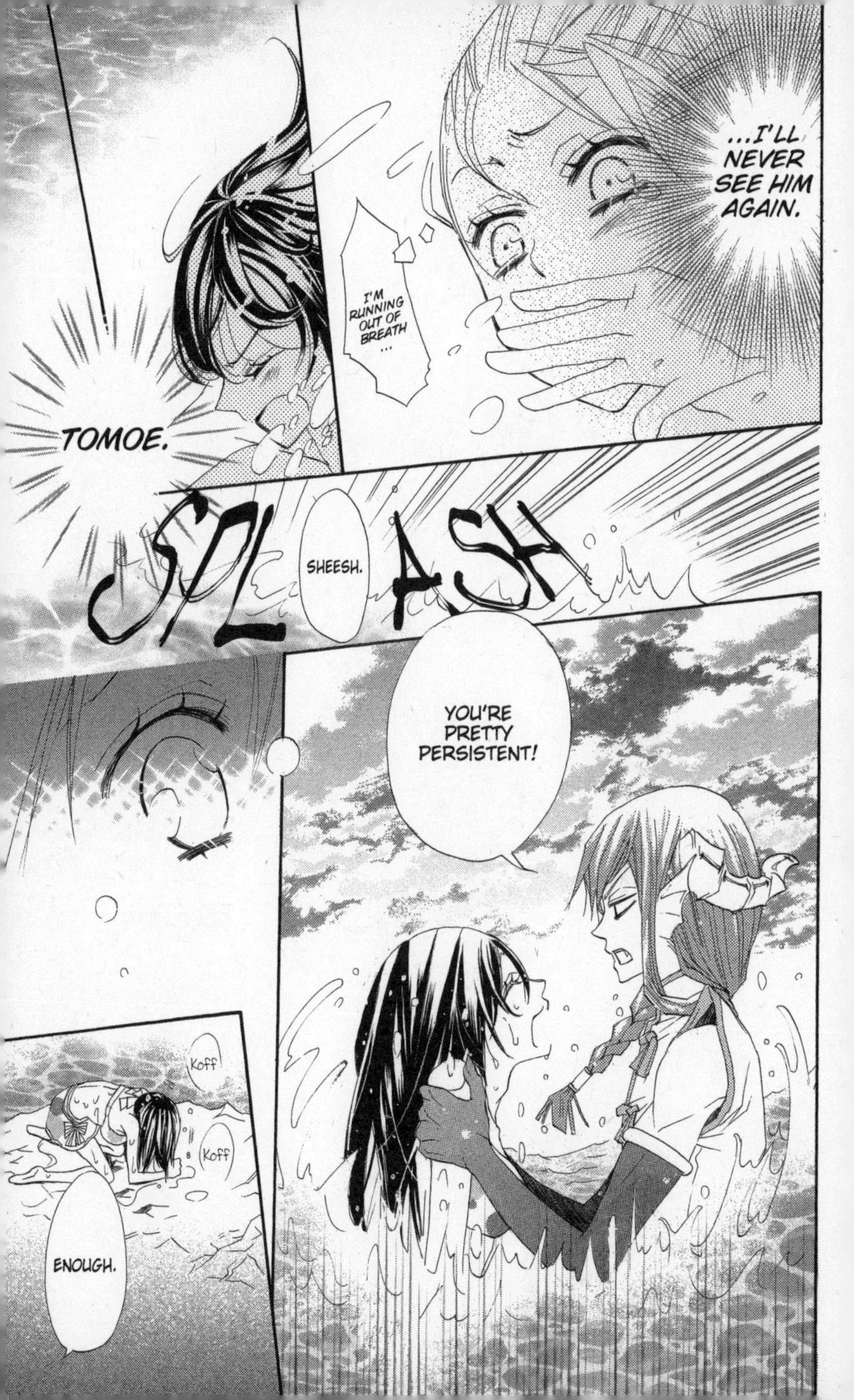
...I'LL NEVER SEE HIM AGAIN.
I'M RUNNING OUT OF BREATH ...
TOMOE.
SPLASH
SHEESH.
YOU'RE PRETTY PERSISTENT!
Koff
Koff
ENOUGH.

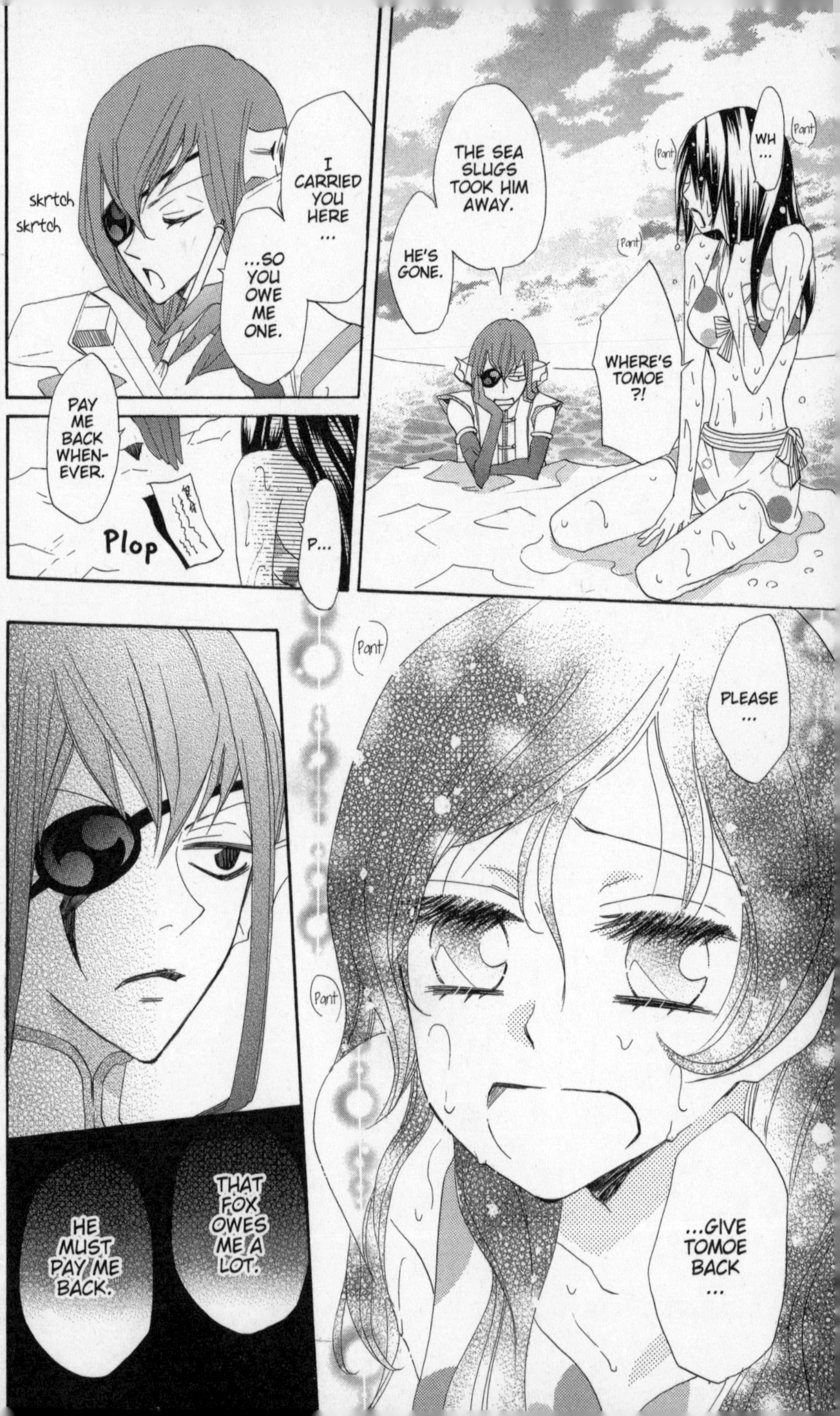
WH...
(Pant)
(Pant)
WHERE'S TOMOE?!
(Pant)
THE SEA SLUGS TOOK HIM AWAY.
HE'S GONE.
I CARRIED YOU HERE...
...SO YOU OWE ME ONE.
skrtch
skrtch
PAY ME BACK WHENEVER.
Plop
P...
(Pant)
PLEASE...
(Pant)
...GIVE TOMOE BACK...
THAT FOX OWES ME A LOT.
HE MUST PAY ME BACK.

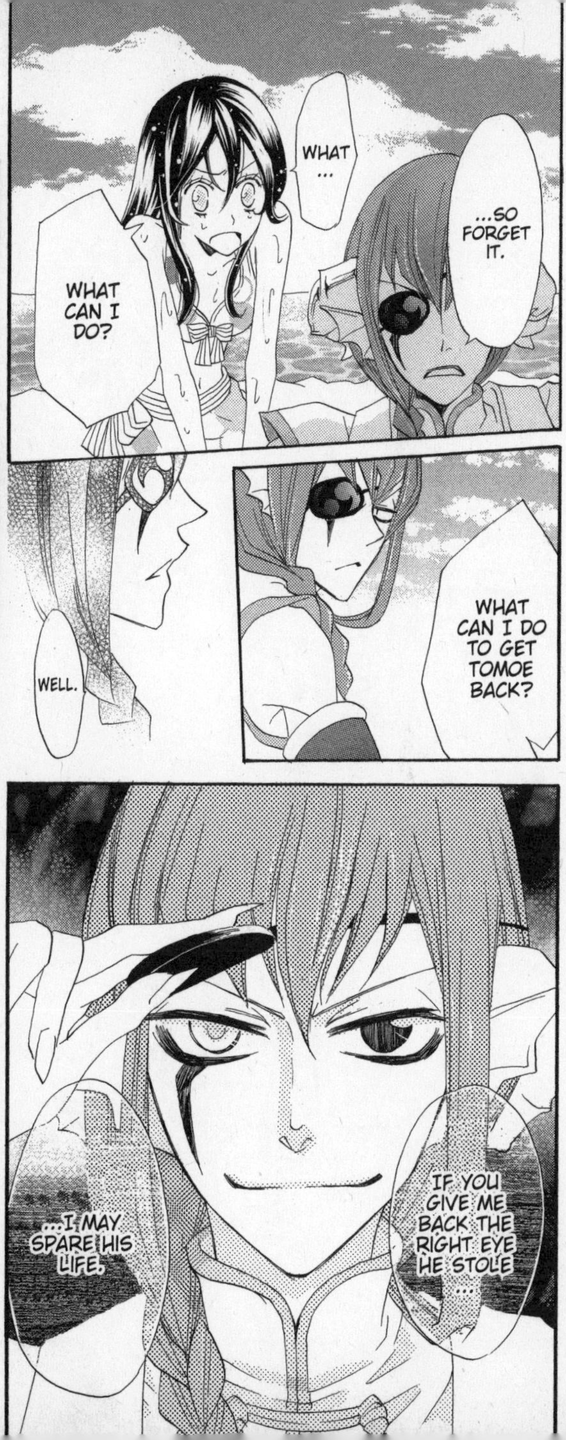
...SO FORGET IT.
WHAT ...
WHAT CAN I DO?
WHAT CAN I DO TO GET TOMOE BACK?
WELL.
IF YOU GIVE ME BACK THE RIGHT EYE HE STOLE ...
...I MAY SPARE HIS LIFE.

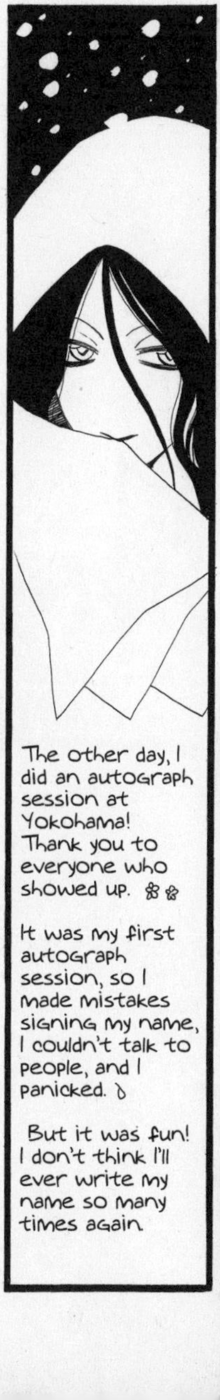

The other day, I did an autograph session at Yokohama! Thank you to everyone who showed up. ✿✿

It was my first autograph session, so I made mistakes signing my name, I couldn't talk to people, and I panicked. ♪

But it was fun! I don't think I'll ever write my name so many times again.

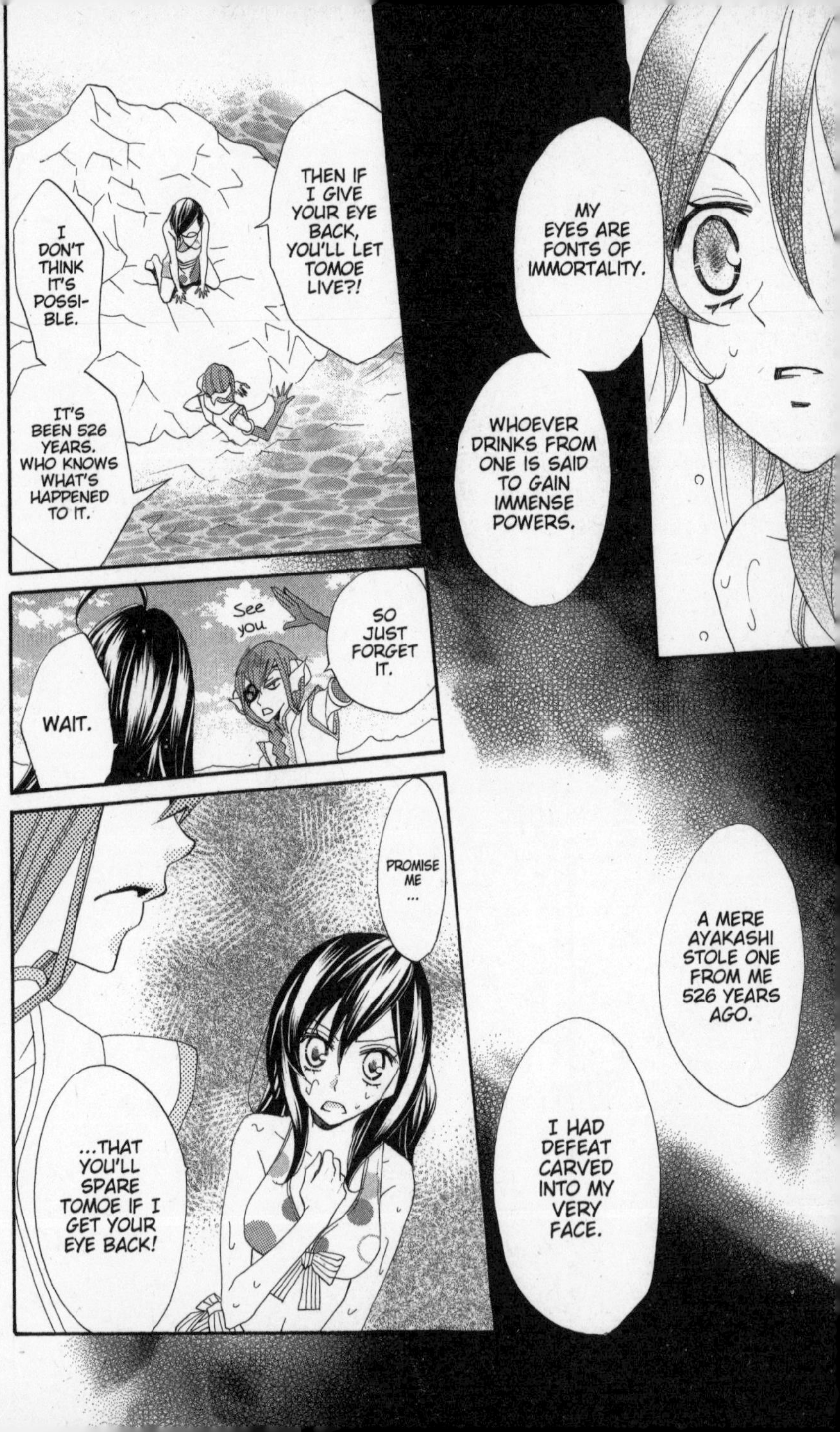
MY EYES ARE FONTS OF IMMORTALITY.
WHOEVER DRINKS FROM ONE IS SAID TO GAIN IMMENSE POWERS.
A MERE AYAKASHI STOLE ONE FROM ME 526 YEARS AGO.
I HAD DEFEAT CARVED INTO MY VERY FACE.
THEN IF I GIVE YOUR EYE BACK, YOU'LL LET TOMOE LIVE?!
I DON'T THINK IT'S POSSI-BLE.
IT'S BEEN 526 YEARS. WHO KNOWS WHAT'S HAPPENED TO IT.
SO JUST FORGET IT.
See you.
WAIT.
PROMISE ME...
...THAT YOU'LL SPARE TOMOE IF I GET YOUR EYE BACK!

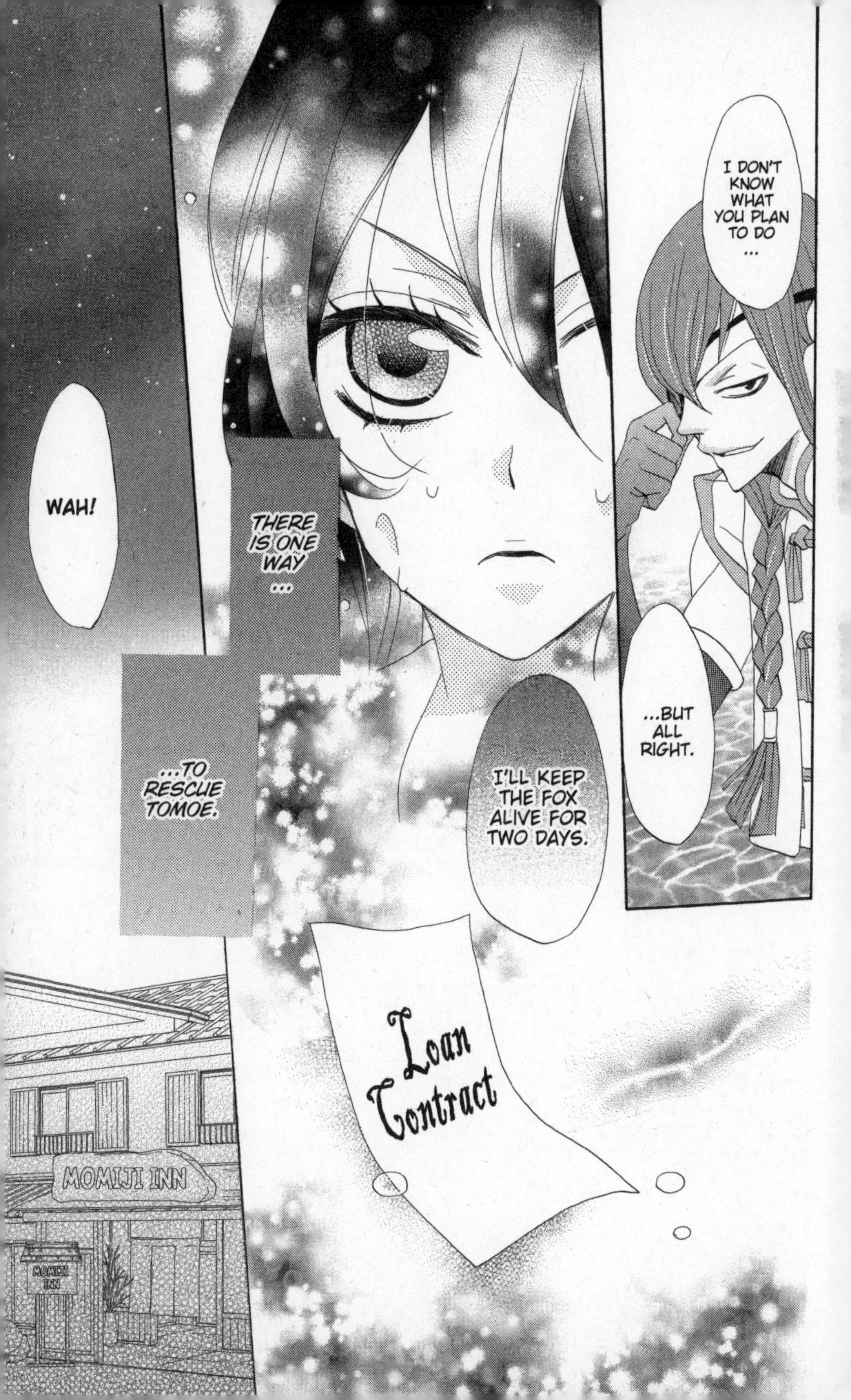
I DON'T KNOW WHAT YOU PLAN TO DO ...
...BUT ALL RIGHT.
I'LL KEEP THE FOX ALIVE FOR TWO DAYS.
THERE IS ONE WAY ...
...TO RESCUE TOMOE.
WAH!
Loan Contract
MOMIJI INN
MOMIJI INN

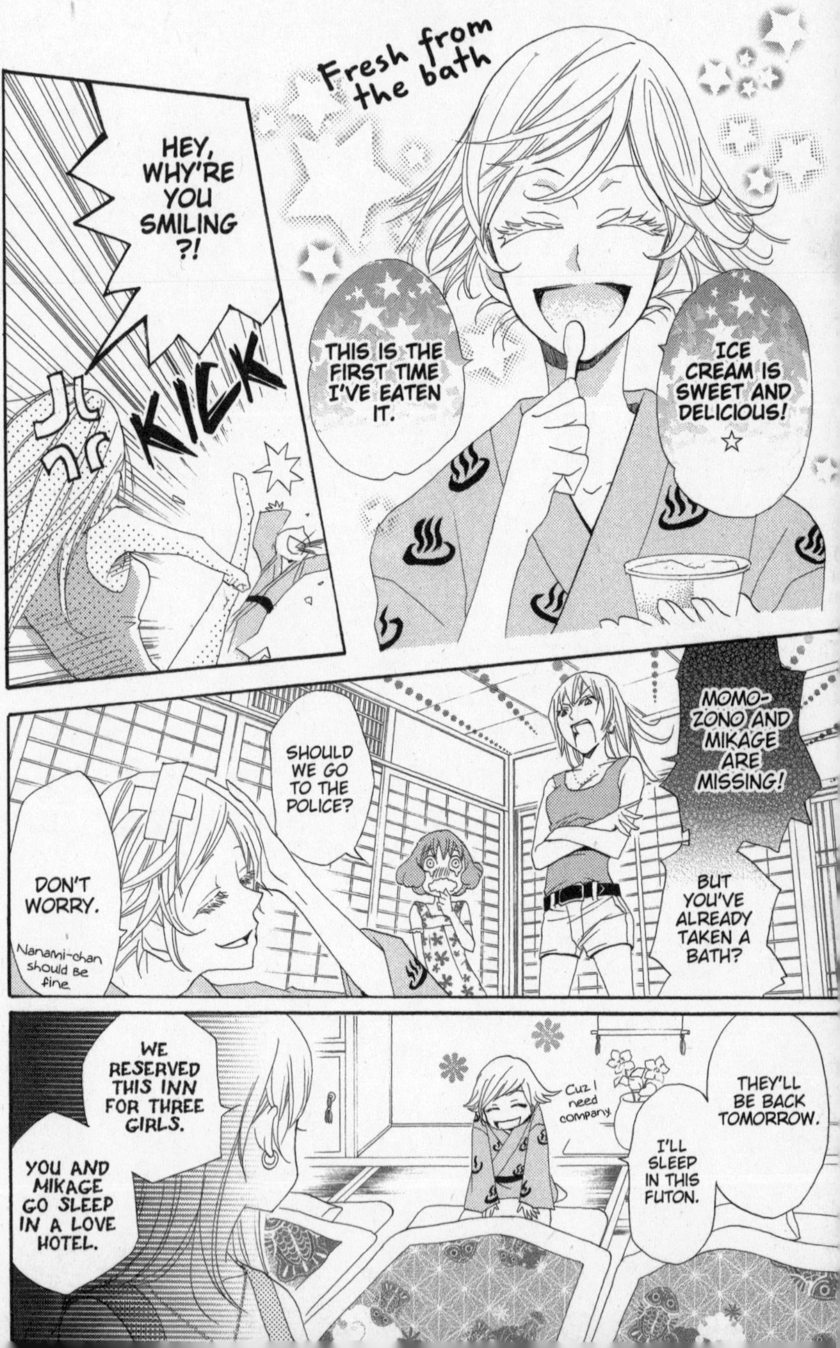
Fresh from the bath
ICE CREAM IS SWEET AND DELICIOUS! ☆
THIS IS THE FIRST TIME I'VE EATEN IT.
HEY, WHY'RE YOU SMILING?!
KICK
MOMO-ZONO AND MIKAGE ARE MISSING!
BUT YOU'VE ALREADY TAKEN A BATH?
SHOULD WE GO TO THE POLICE?
DON'T WORRY.
Nanami-chan should be fine.
THEY'LL BE BACK TOMORROW.
I'LL SLEEP IN THIS FUTON.
Cuz I need company.
WE RESERVED THIS INN FOR THREE GIRLS.
YOU AND MIKAGE GO SLEEP IN A LOVE HOTEL.

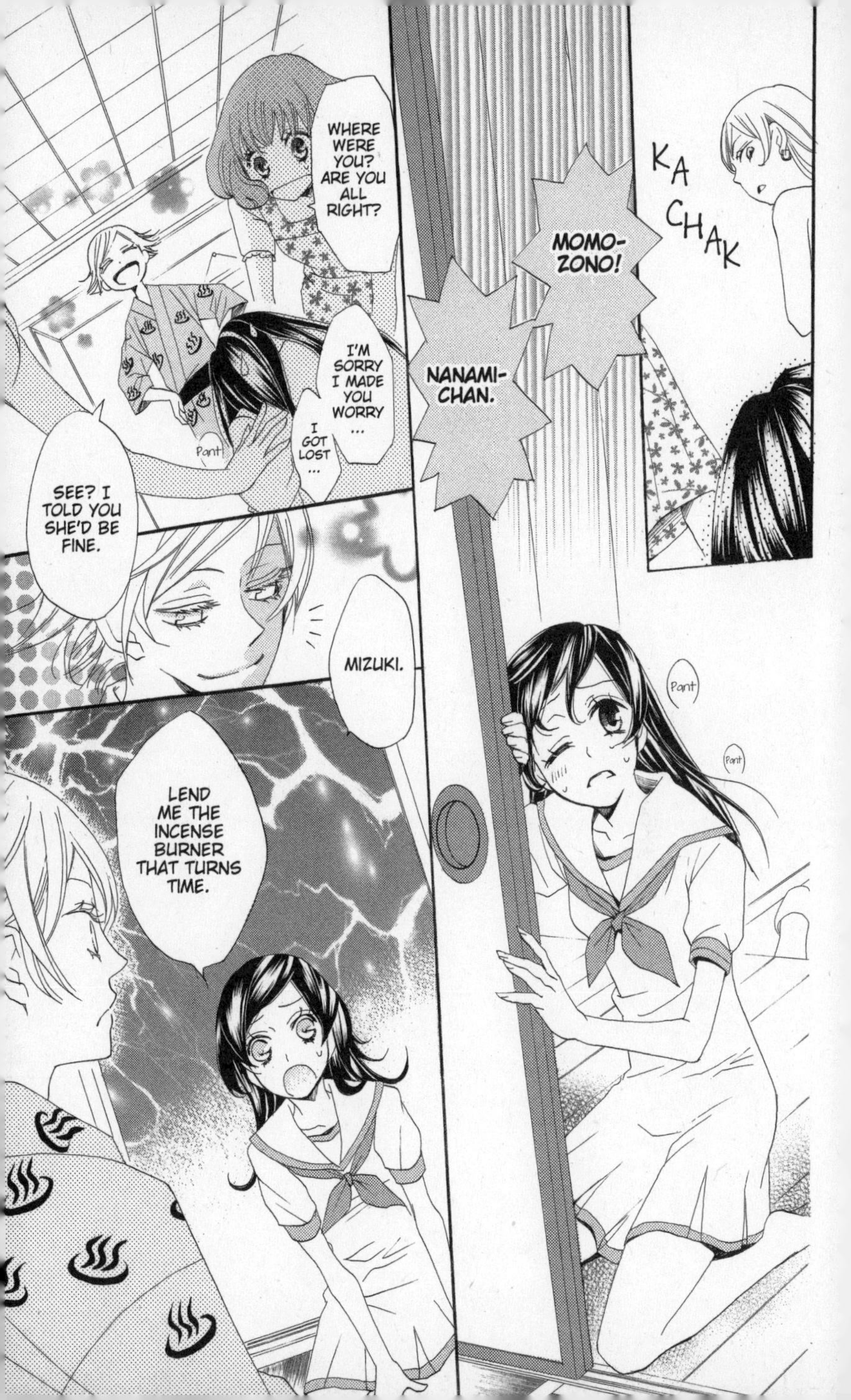
KA CHAK
MOMO-ZONO!
NANAMI-CHAN.
Pant
Pant
WHERE WERE YOU? ARE YOU ALL RIGHT?
I'M SORRY I MADE YOU WORRY ...
I GOT LOST ...
Pant
SEE? I TOLD YOU SHE'D BE FINE.
MIZUKI.
LEND ME THE INCENSE BURNER THAT TURNS TIME.

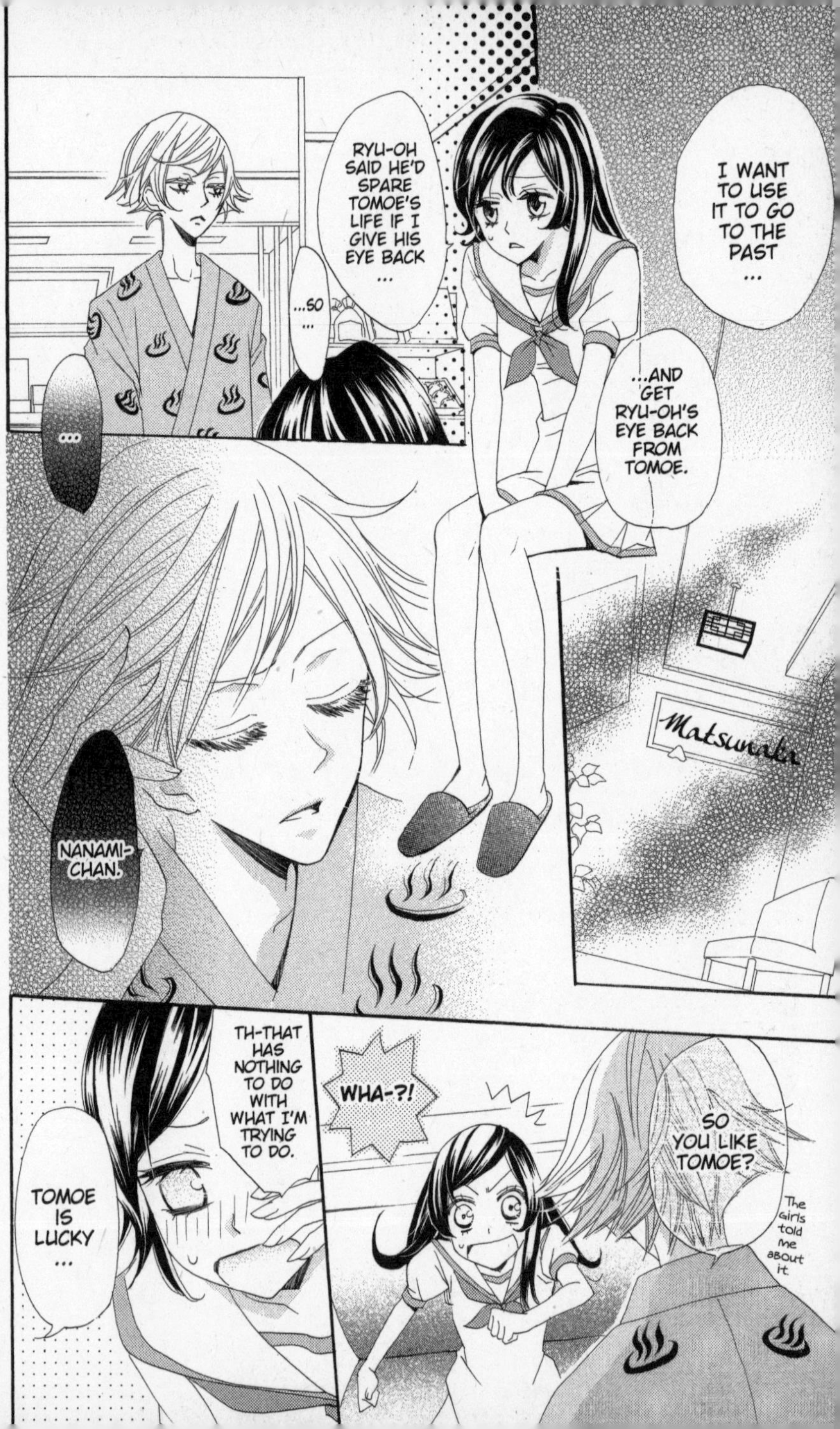
RYU-OH SAID HE'D SPARE TOMOE'S LIFE IF I GIVE HIS EYE BACK ...
...SO ...
I WANT TO USE IT TO GO TO THE PAST ...
...AND GET RYU-OH'S EYE BACK FROM TOMOE.
Matsunaki
...
NANAMI-CHAN.
SO YOU LIKE TOMOE?
The Girls told me about it.
WHA-?!
TH-THAT HAS NOTHING TO DO WITH WHAT I'M TRYING TO DO.
TOMOE IS LUCKY ...

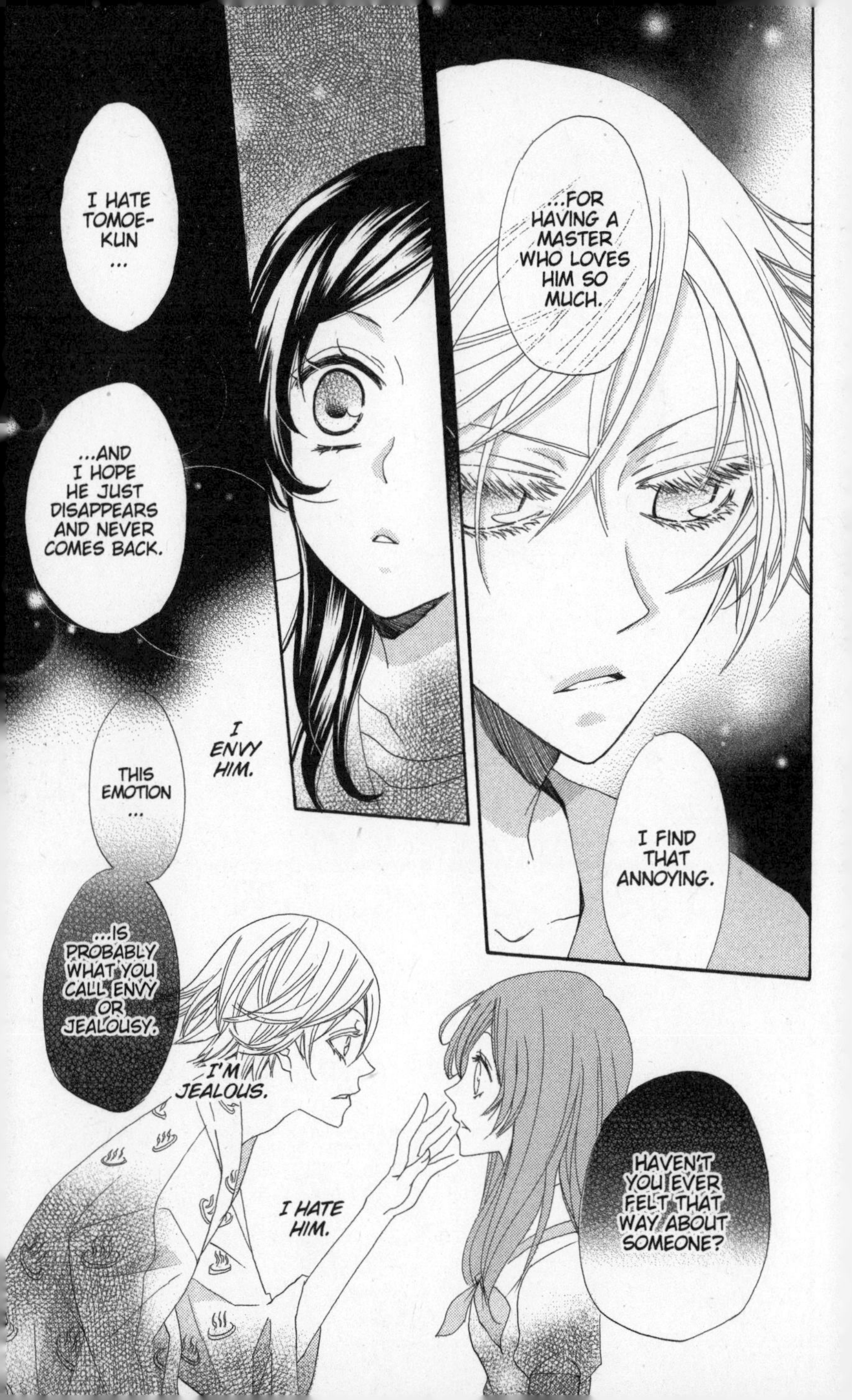

...FOR HAVING A MASTER WHO LOVES HIM SO MUCH.
I FIND THAT ANNOYING.
I HATE TOMOE-KUN ...
...AND I HOPE HE JUST DISAPPEARS AND NEVER COMES BACK.
I ENVY HIM.
THIS EMOTION ...
...IS PROBABLY WHAT YOU CALL ENVY OR JEALOUSY.
HAVEN'T YOU EVER FELT THAT WAY ABOUT SOMEONE?
I'M JEALOUS.
I HATE HIM.

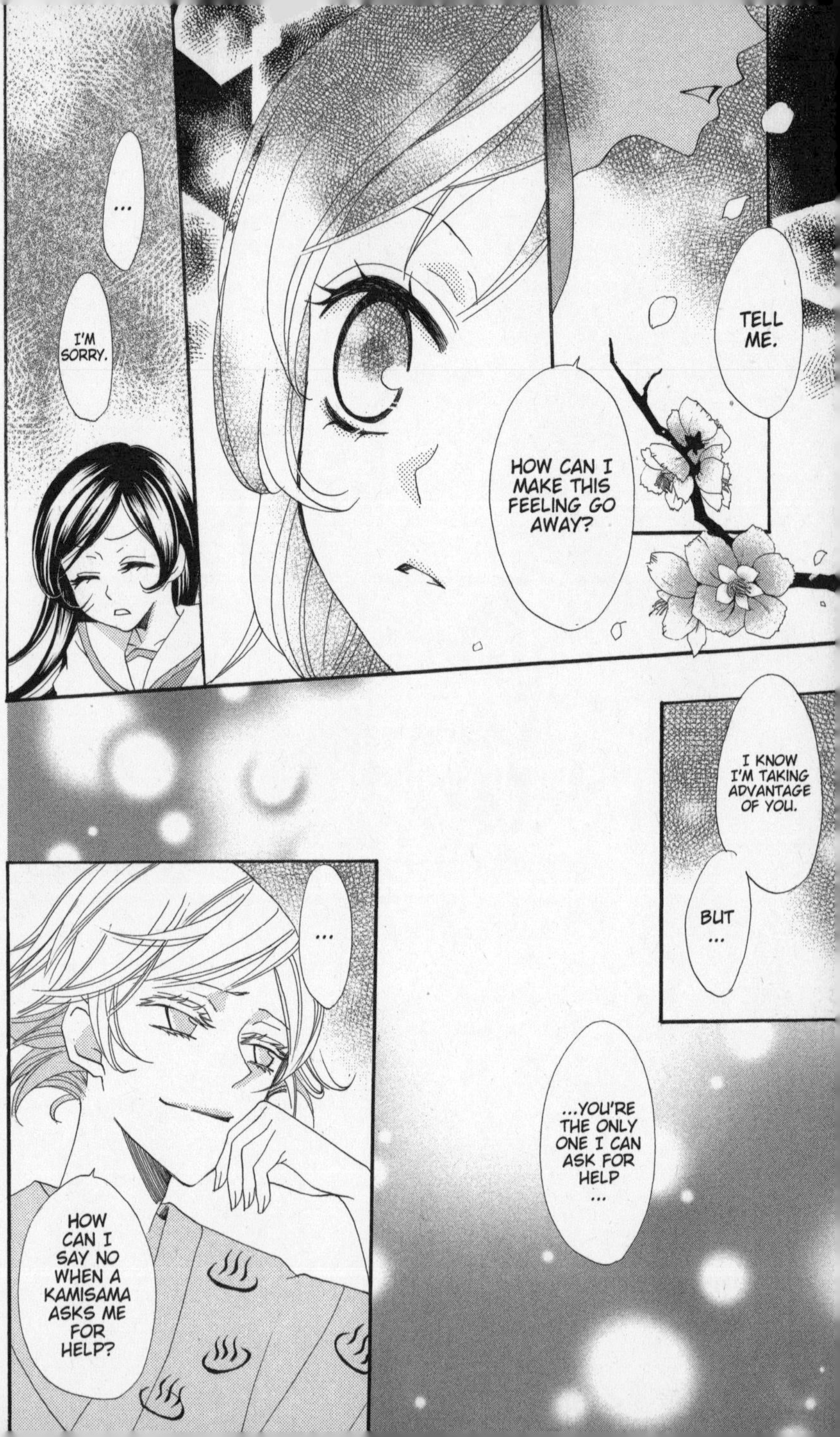
TELL ME.
HOW CAN I MAKE THIS FEELING GO AWAY?
...
I'M SORRY.
I KNOW I'M TAKING ADVANTAGE OF YOU.
BUT ...
...YOU'RE THE ONLY ONE I CAN ASK FOR HELP ...
...
HOW CAN I SAY NO WHEN A KAMISAMA ASKS ME FOR HELP?

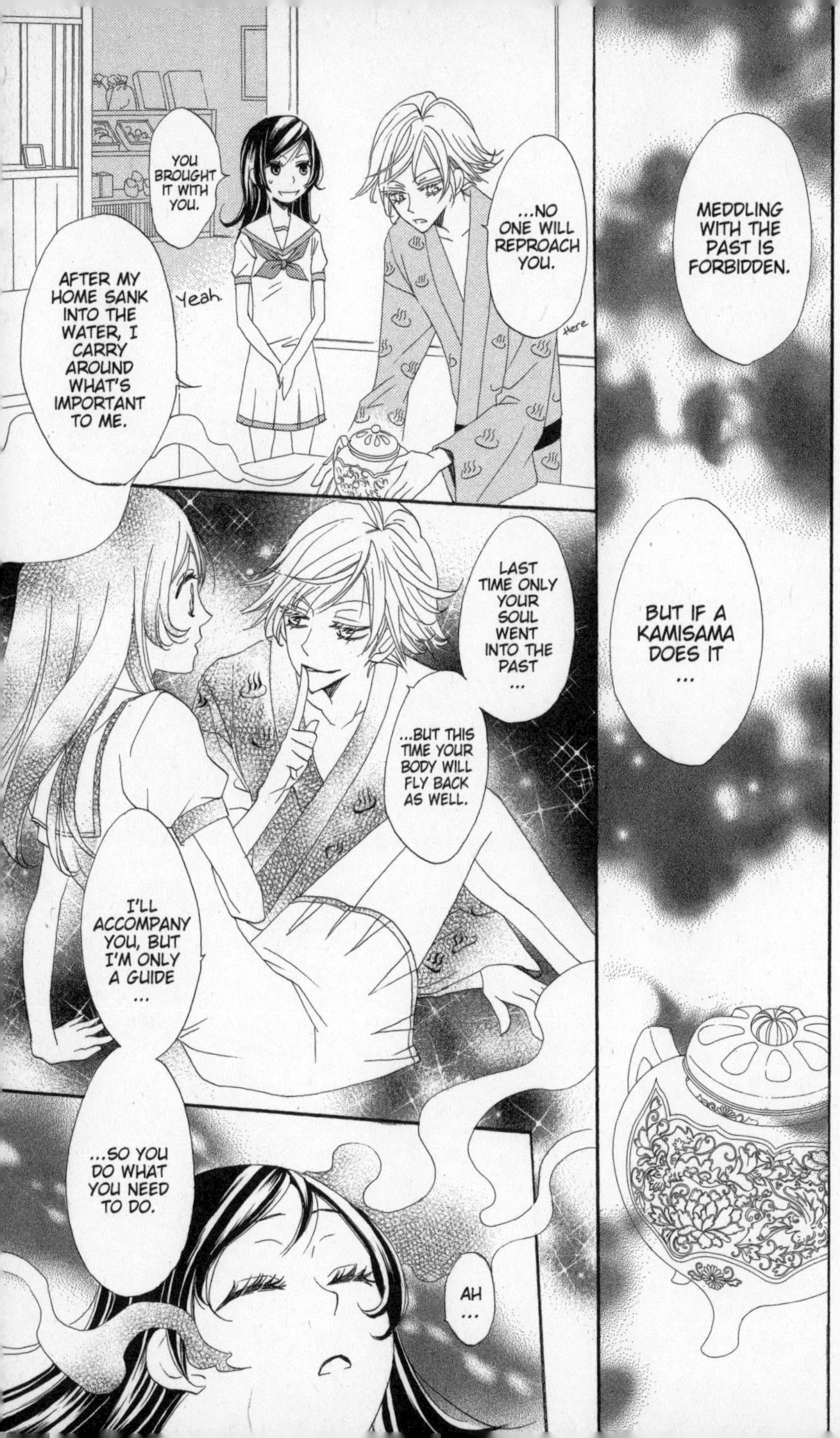
MEDDLING WITH THE PAST IS FORBIDDEN.
BUT IF A KAMISAMA DOES IT ...
...NO ONE WILL REPROACH YOU.
Here
YOU BROUGHT IT WITH YOU.
Yeah.
AFTER MY HOME SANK INTO THE WATER, I CARRY AROUND WHAT'S IMPORTANT TO ME.
LAST TIME ONLY YOUR SOUL WENT INTO THE PAST ...
...BUT THIS TIME YOUR BODY WILL FLY BACK AS WELL.
I'LL ACCOMPANY YOU, BUT I'M ONLY A GUIDE ...
...SO YOU DO WHAT YOU NEED TO DO.
AH ...

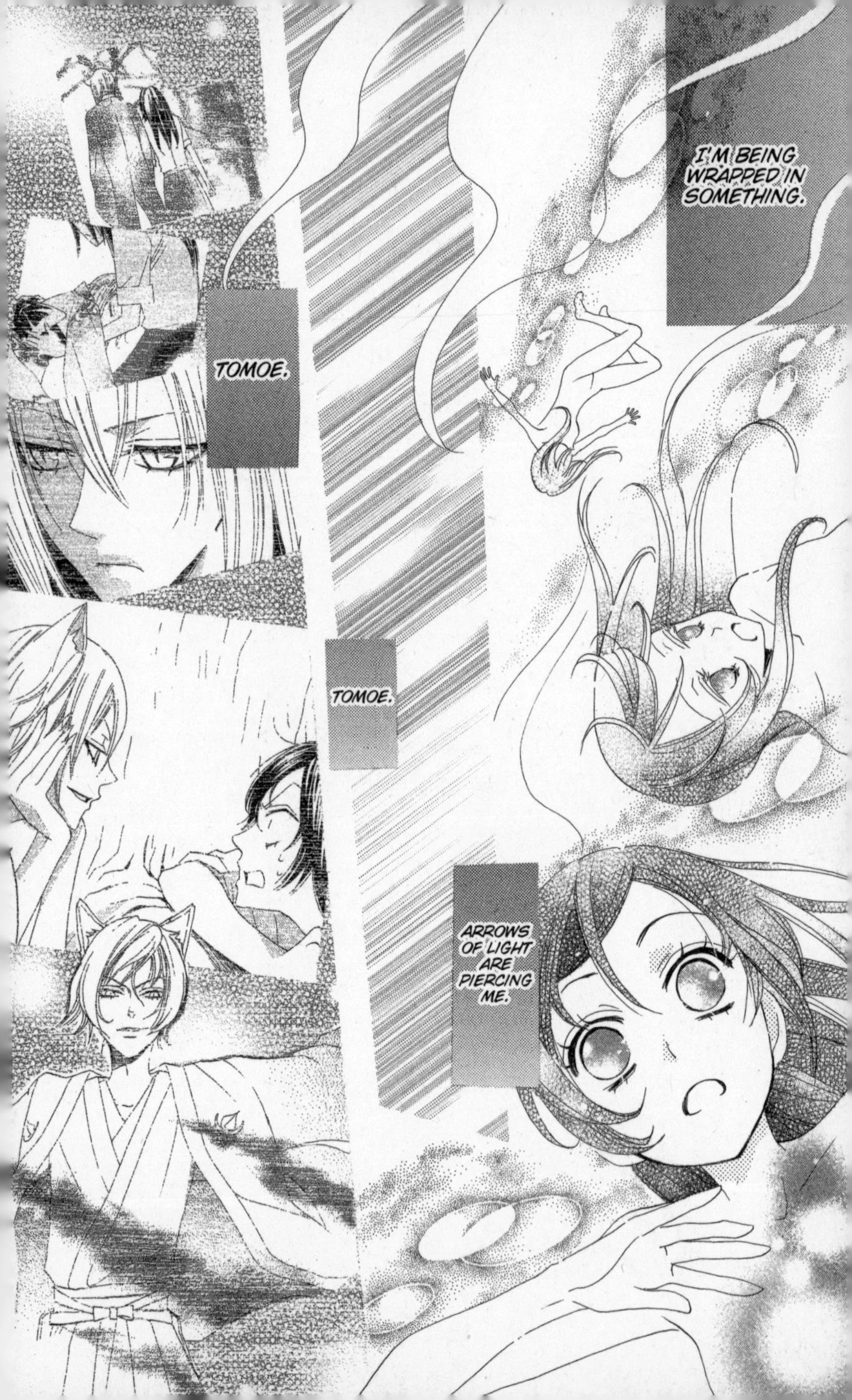
I'M BEING WRAPPED IN SOMETHING.
ARROWS OF LIGHT ARE PIERCING ME.
TOMOE.
TOMOE.

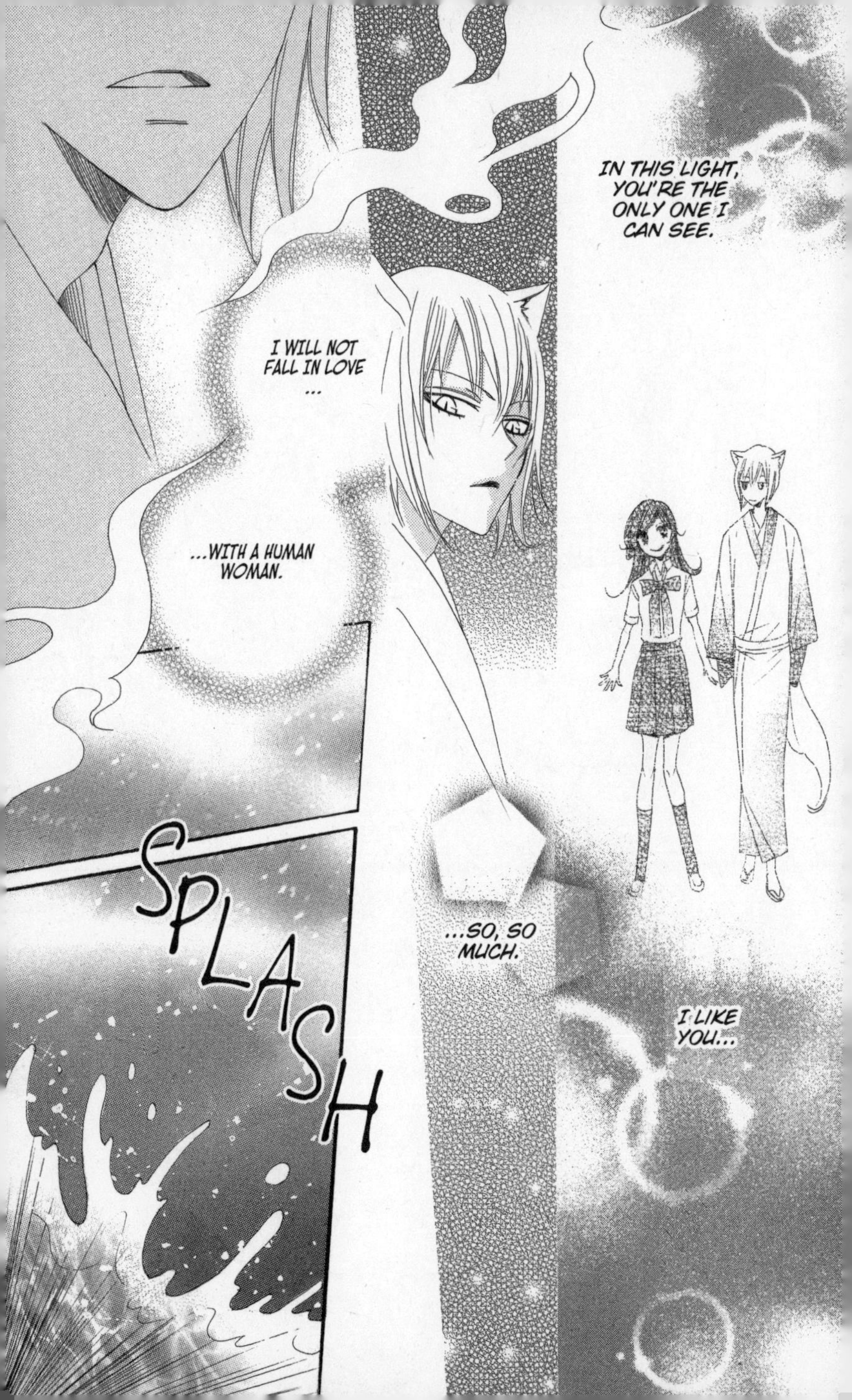
IN THIS LIGHT, YOU'RE THE ONLY ONE I CAN SEE.
I LIKE YOU...
...SO, SO MUCH.
I WILL NOT FALL IN LOVE ...
...WITH A HUMAN WOMAN.
SPLASH

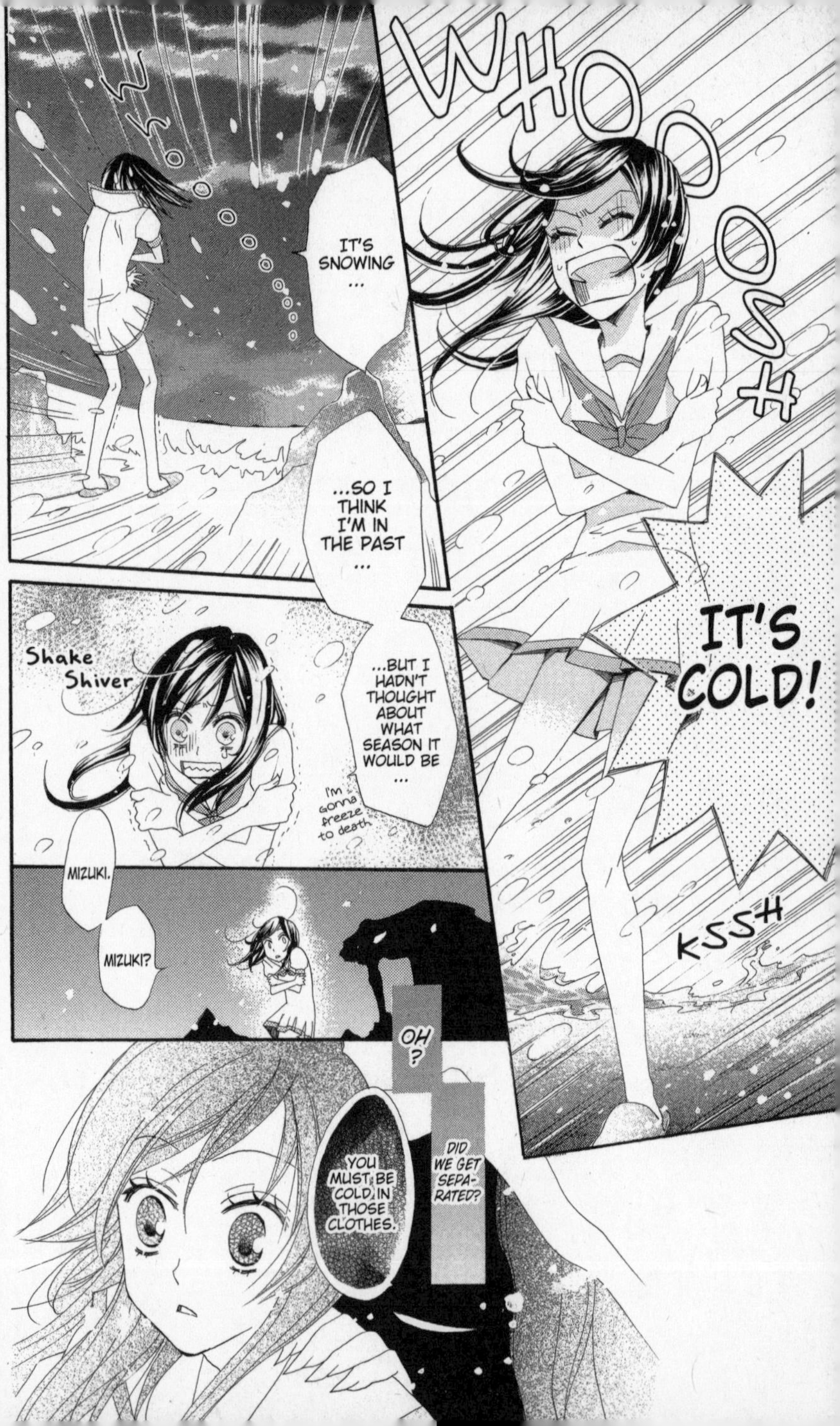
WHOOOOSH
IT'S COLD!
KSSH
IT'S SNOWING...
...SO I THINK I'M IN THE PAST...
...BUT I HADN'T THOUGHT ABOUT WHAT SEASON IT WOULD BE...
Shake Shiver
I'm gonna freeze to death
MIZUKI.
MIZUKI?
OH?
DID WE GET SEPA-RATED?
YOU MUST BE COLD IN THOSE CLOTHES.

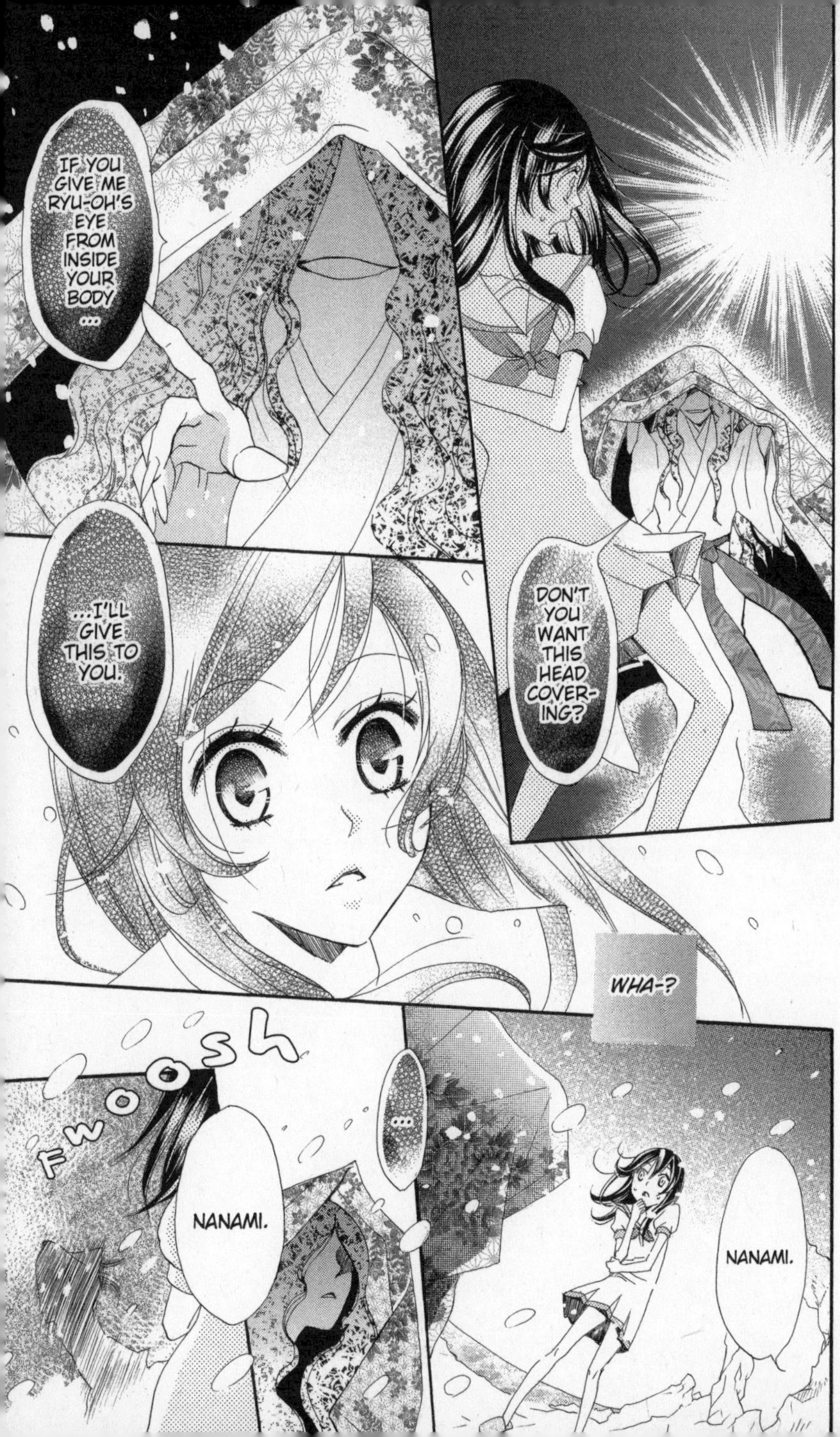
DON'T YOU WANT THIS HEAD COVERING?
IF YOU GIVE ME RYU-OH'S EYE FROM INSIDE YOUR BODY...
...I'LL GIVE THIS TO YOU.
WHA-?
NANAMI.
...
NANAMI.
FWOOSH

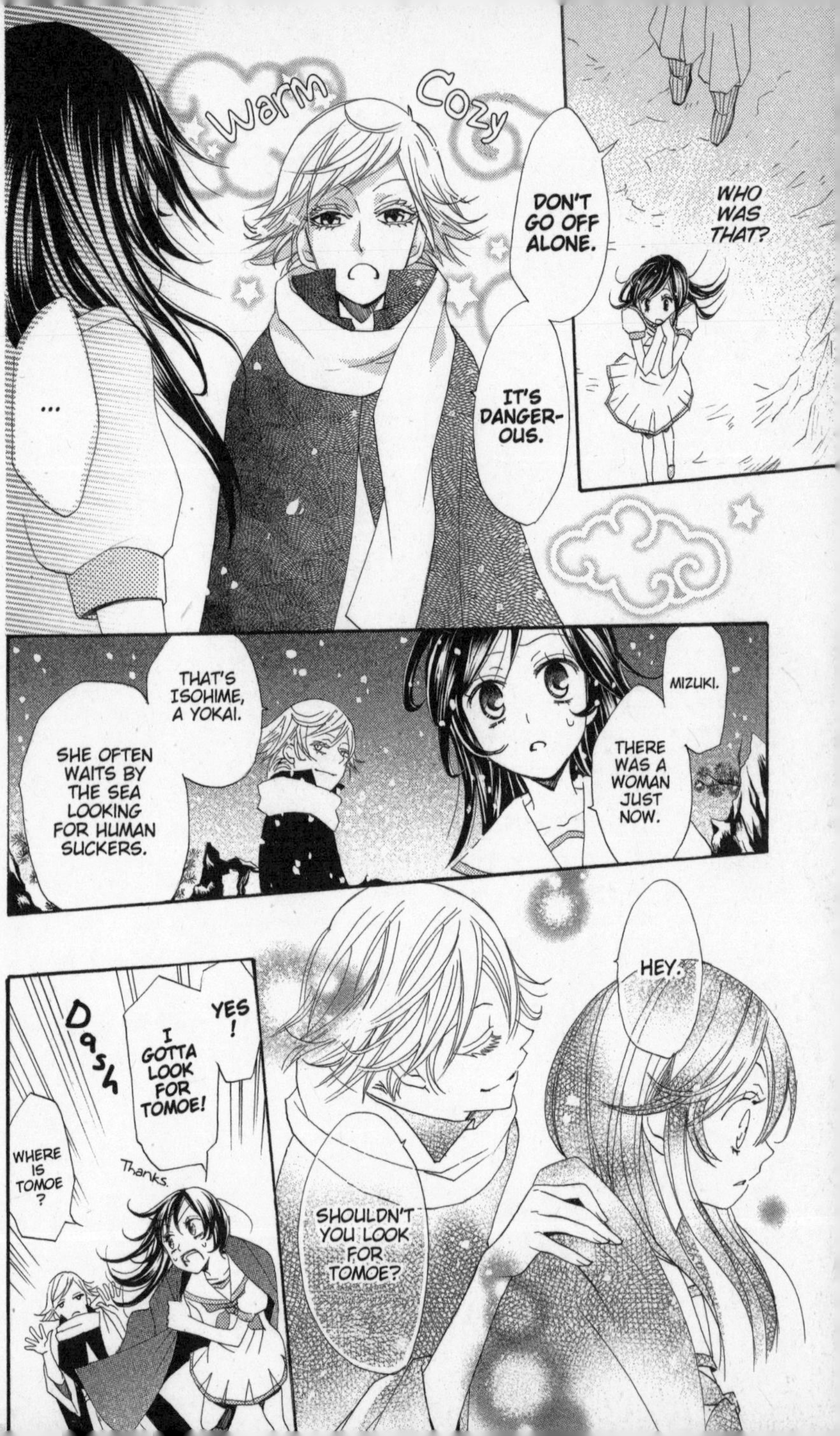
WHO WAS THAT?
Cozy
Warm
DON'T GO OFF ALONE.
IT'S DANGER-OUS.
...
MIZUKI.
THERE WAS A WOMAN JUST NOW.
THAT'S ISOHIME, A YOKAI.
SHE OFTEN WAITS BY THE SEA LOOKING FOR HUMAN SUCKERS.
HEY.
SHOULDN'T YOU LOOK FOR TOMOE?
YES!
I GOTTA LOOK FOR TOMOE!
Dash
WHERE IS TOMOE?
Thanks.

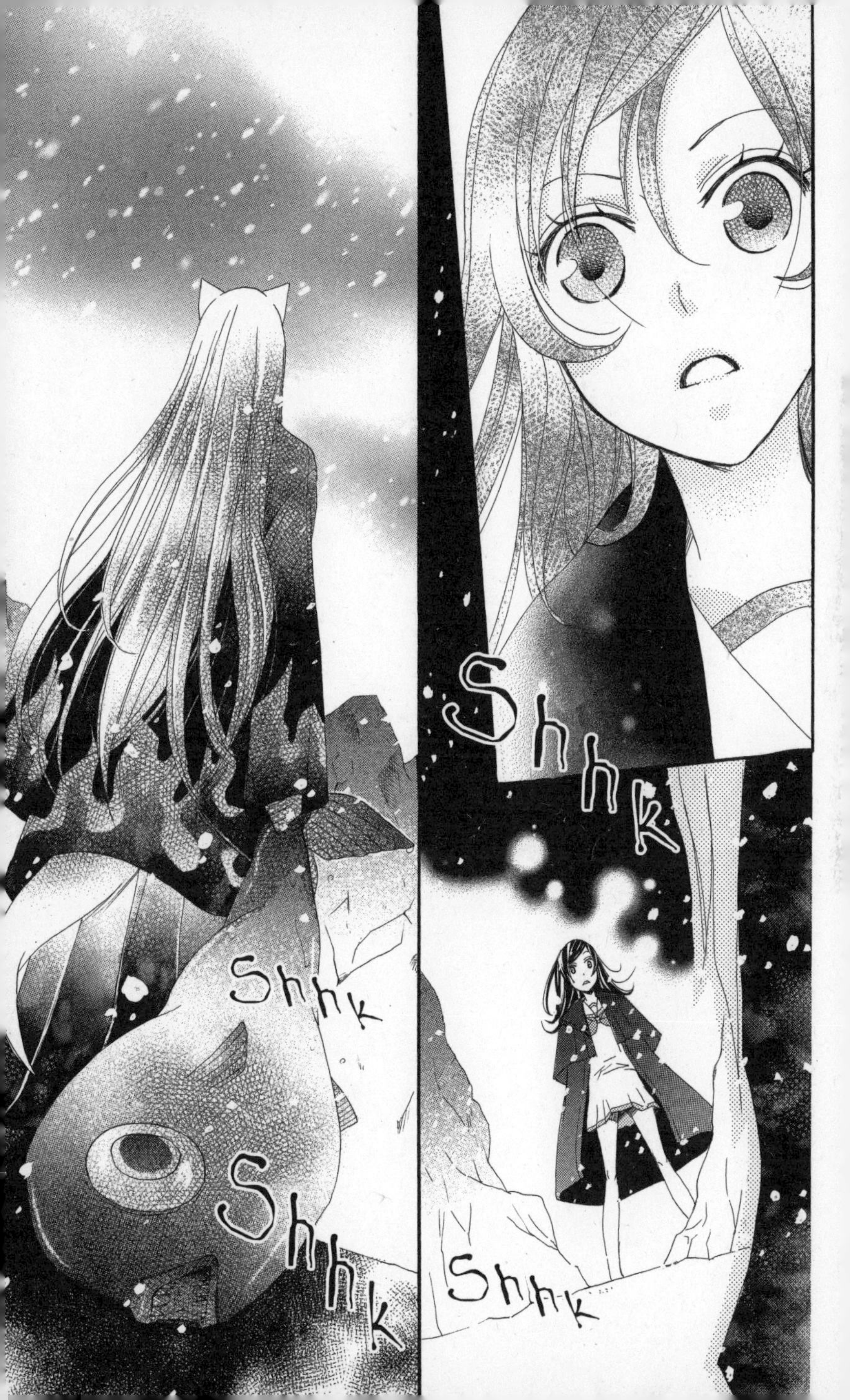
Shhk
Shhk
Shhk
Shhk

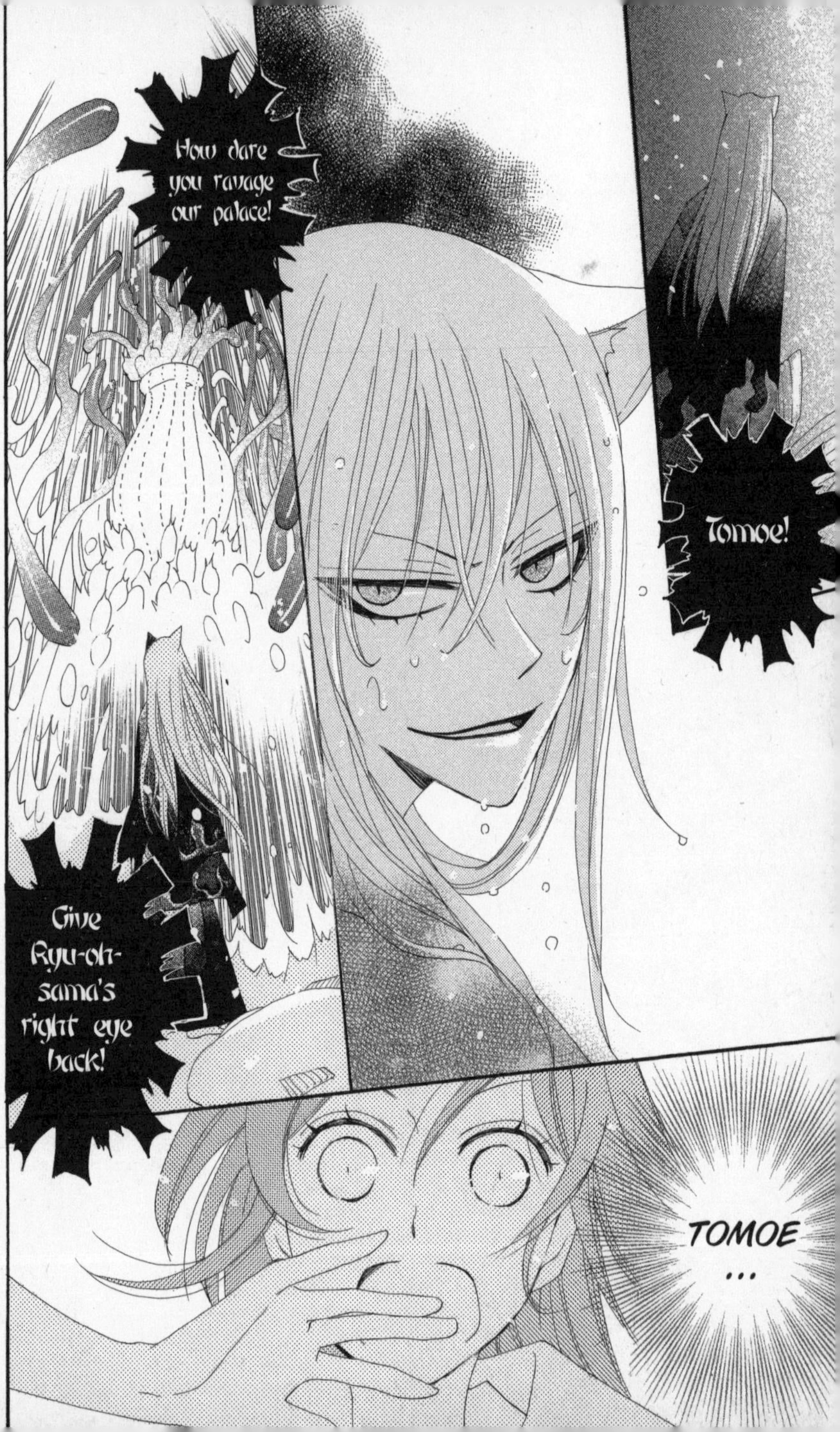
Tomoe!
How dare you ravage our palace!
Give Ryu-oh-sama's right eye back!
TOMOE ...

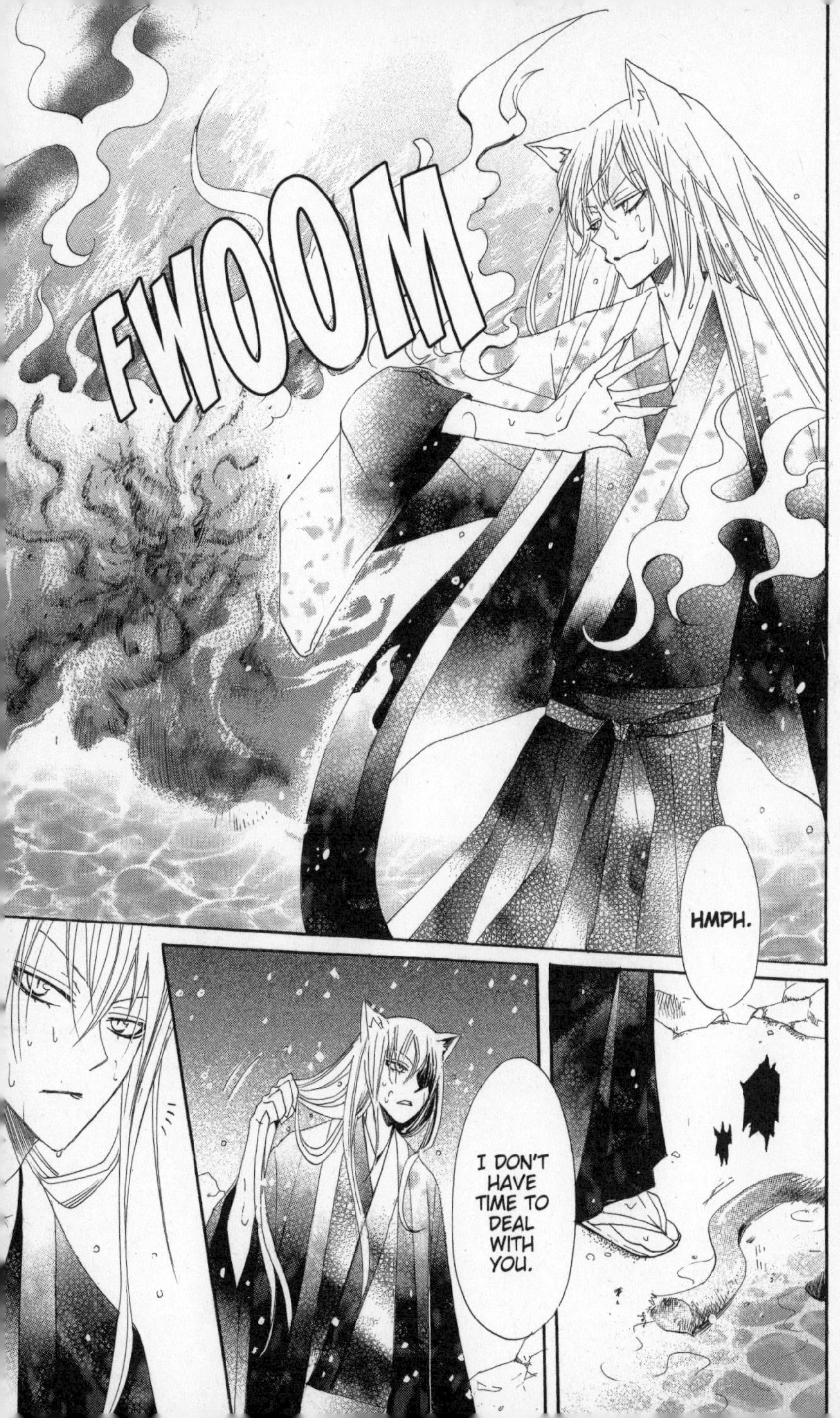
FWOOM
HMPH.
I DON'T HAVE TIME TO DEAL WITH YOU.

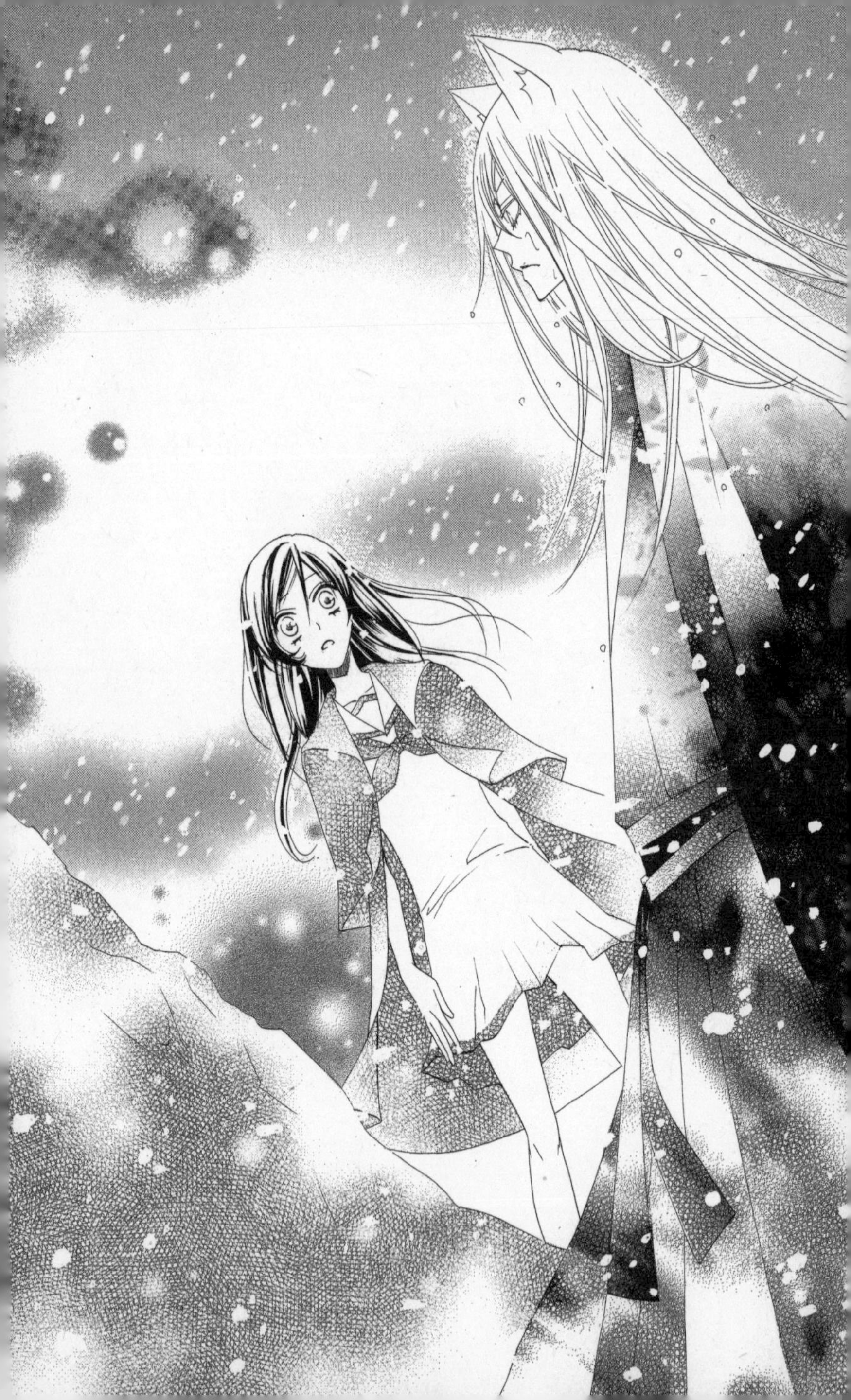

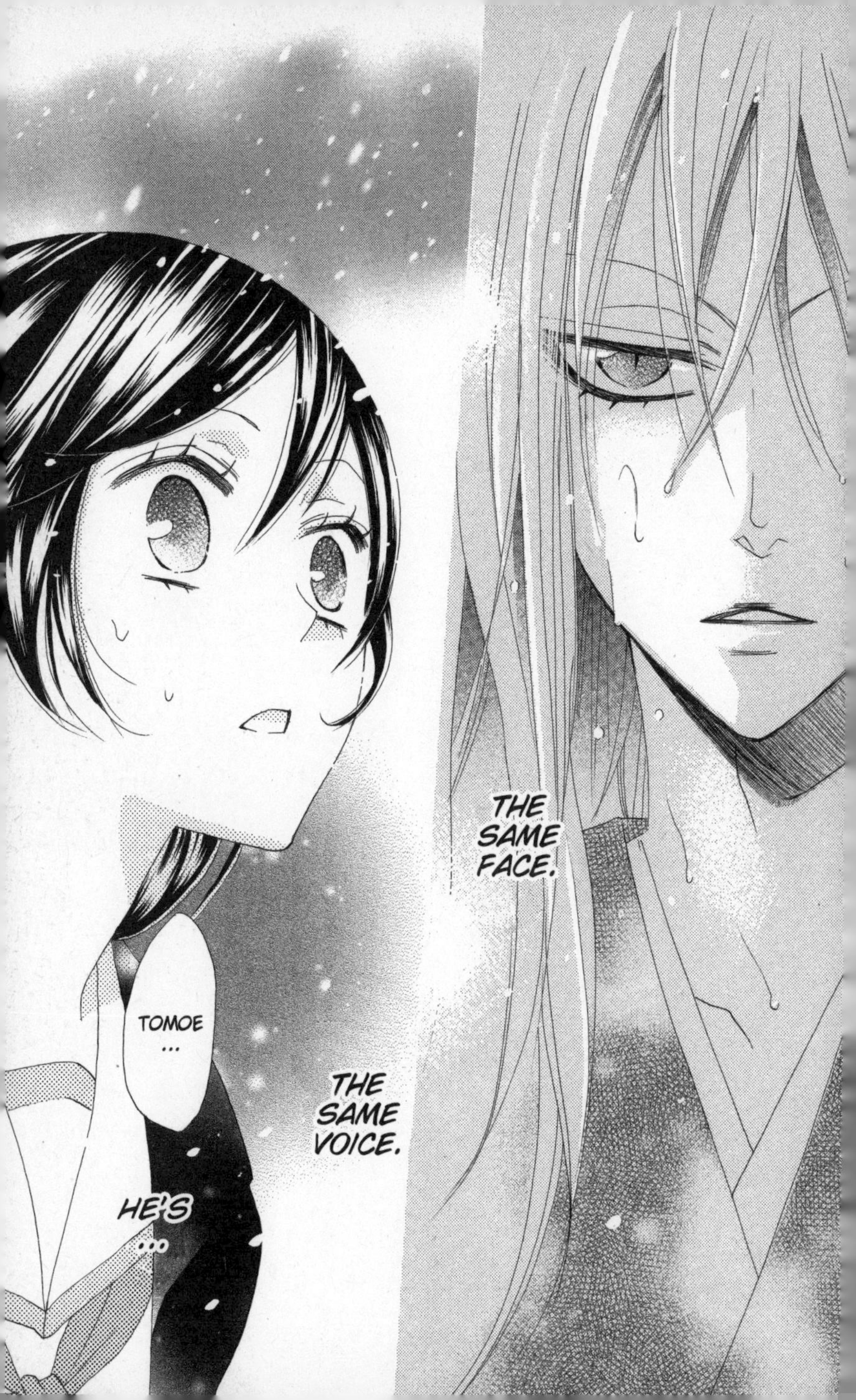
THE SAME FACE.
THE SAME VOICE.
TOMOE ...
HE'S ...

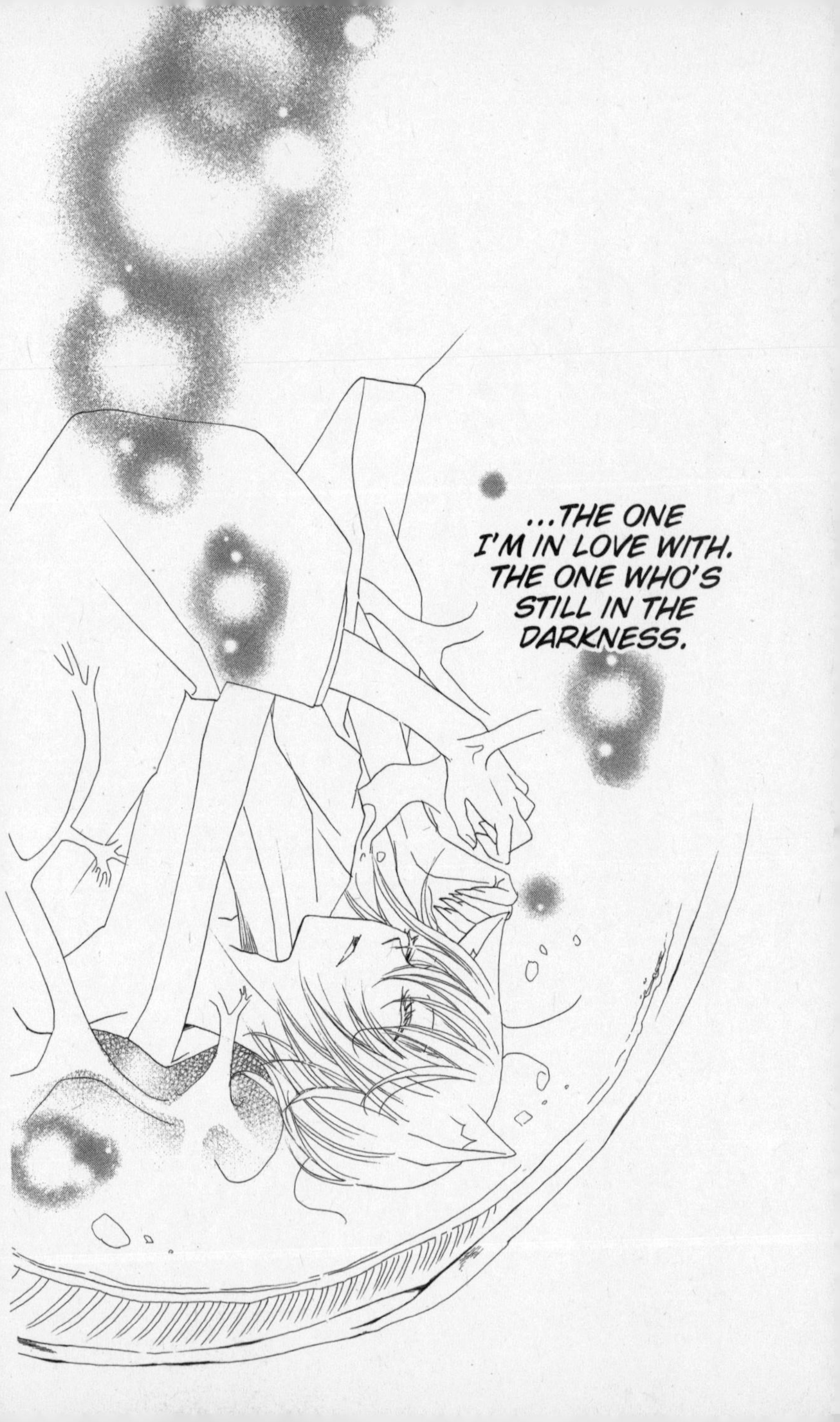
...THE ONE I'M IN LOVE WITH. THE ONE WHO'S STILL IN THE DARKNESS.

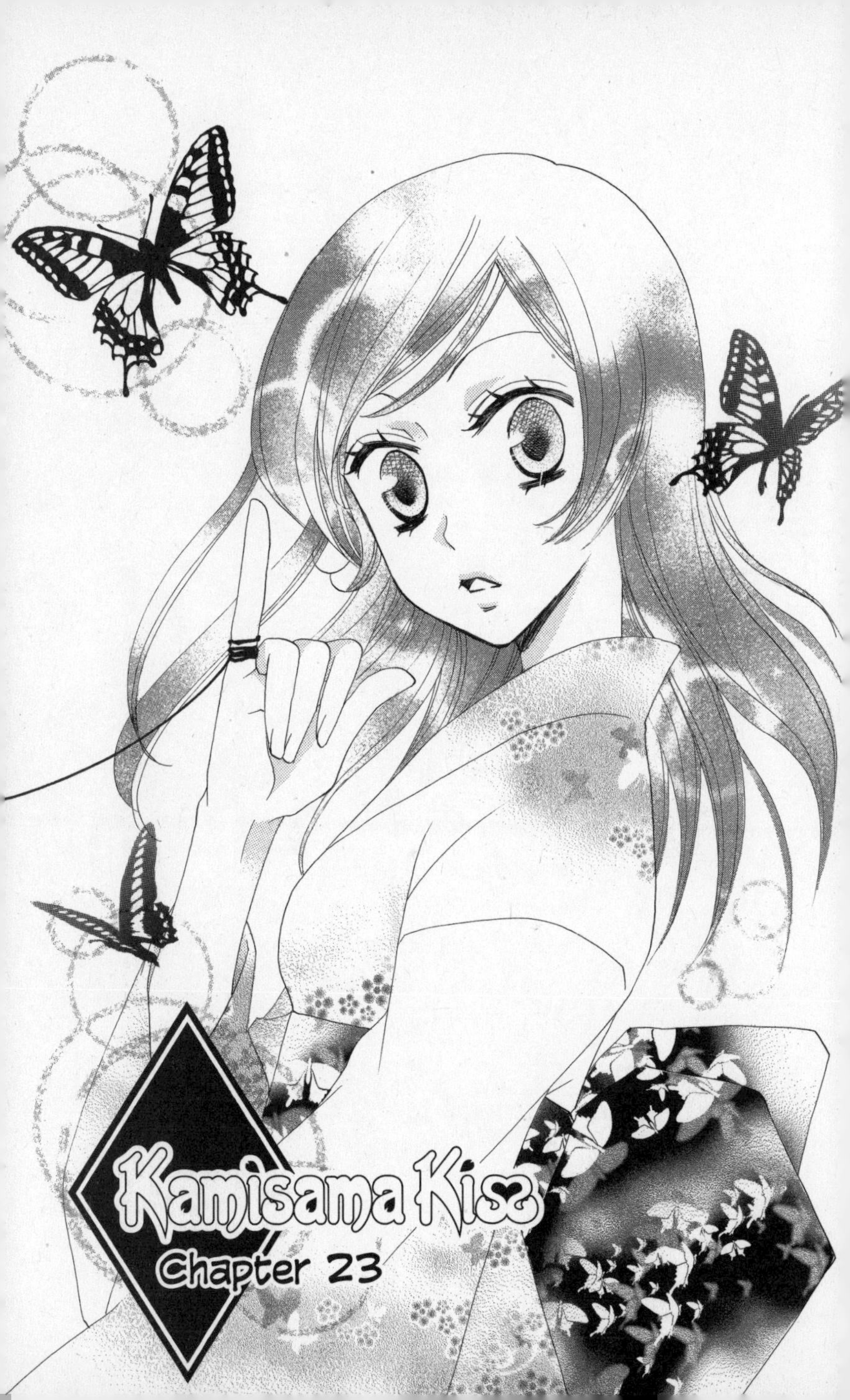
Kamisama Kiss
Chapter 23

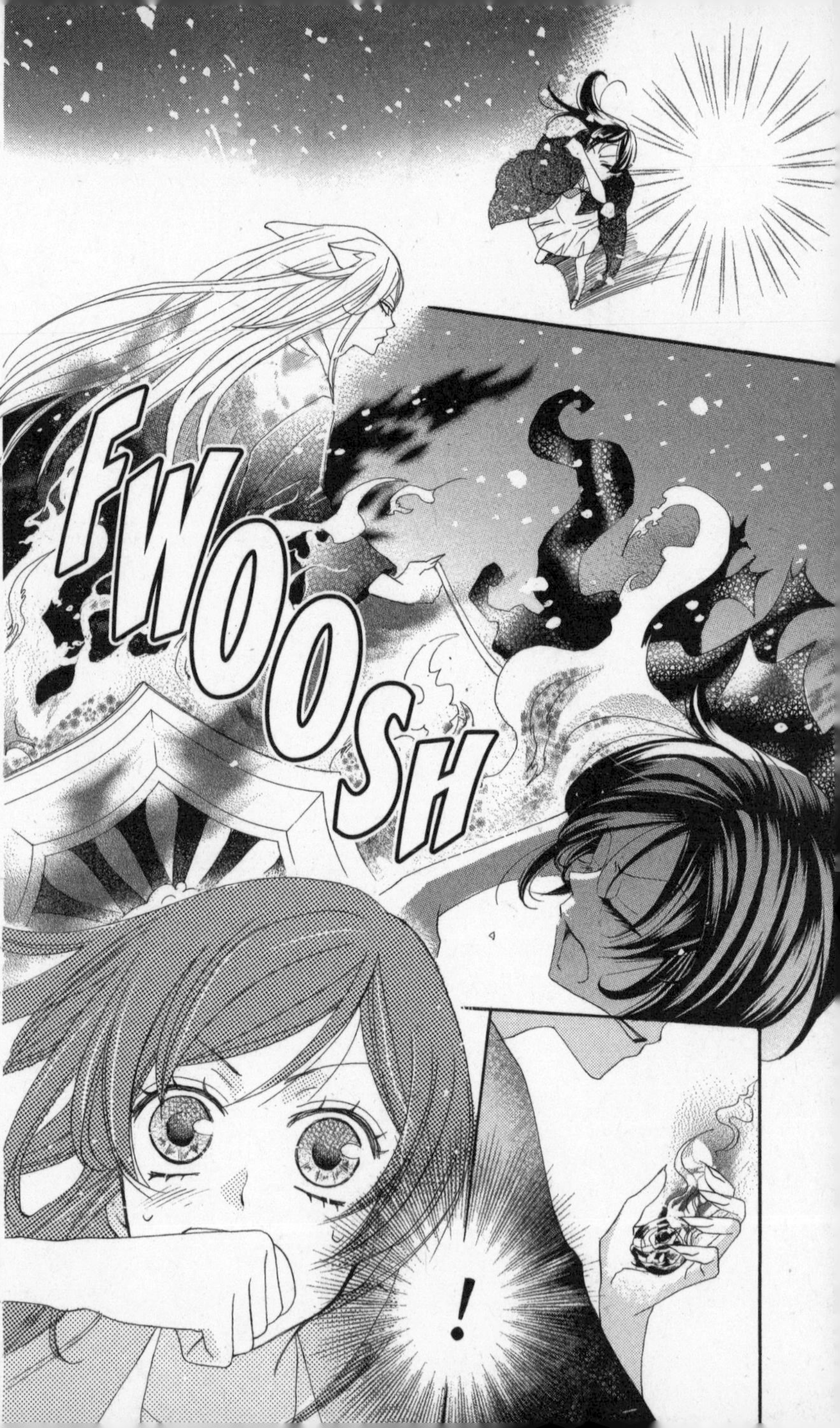
FWOOOSH
!

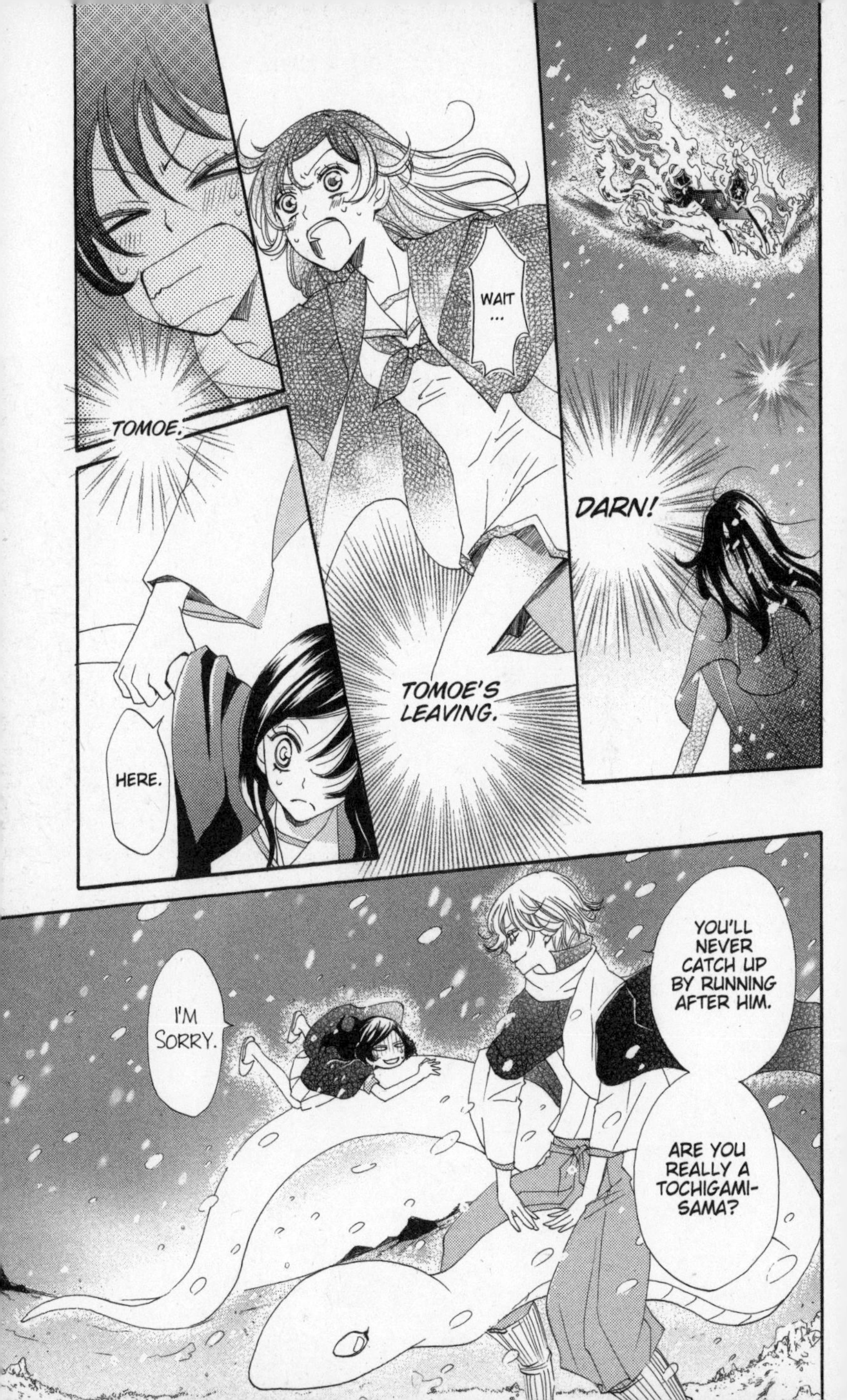
DARN!
WAIT...
TOMOE'S LEAVING.
TOMOE.
HERE.
YOU'LL NEVER CATCH UP BY RUNNING AFTER HIM.
ARE YOU REALLY A TOCHIGAMI-SAMA?
I'M SORRY.

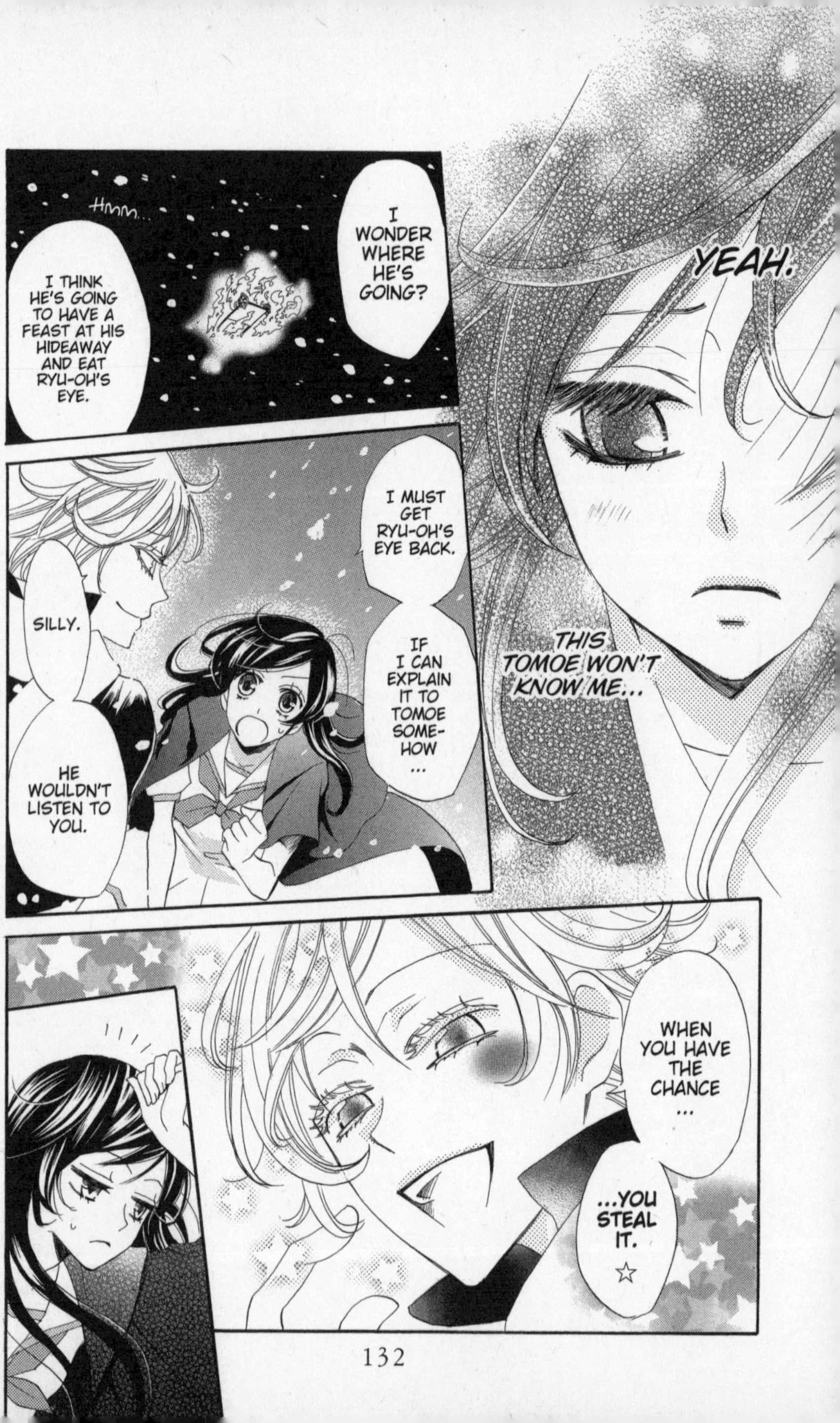
YEAH.
THIS TOMOE WON'T KNOW ME...
I WONDER WHERE HE'S GOING?
Hmm...
I THINK HE'S GOING TO HAVE A FEAST AT HIS HIDEAWAY AND EAT RYU-OH'S EYE.
I MUST GET RYU-OH'S EYE BACK.
IF I CAN EXPLAIN IT TO TOMOE SOME-HOW...
SILLY.
HE WOULDN'T LISTEN TO YOU.
WHEN YOU HAVE THE CHANCE...
...YOU STEAL IT. ☆

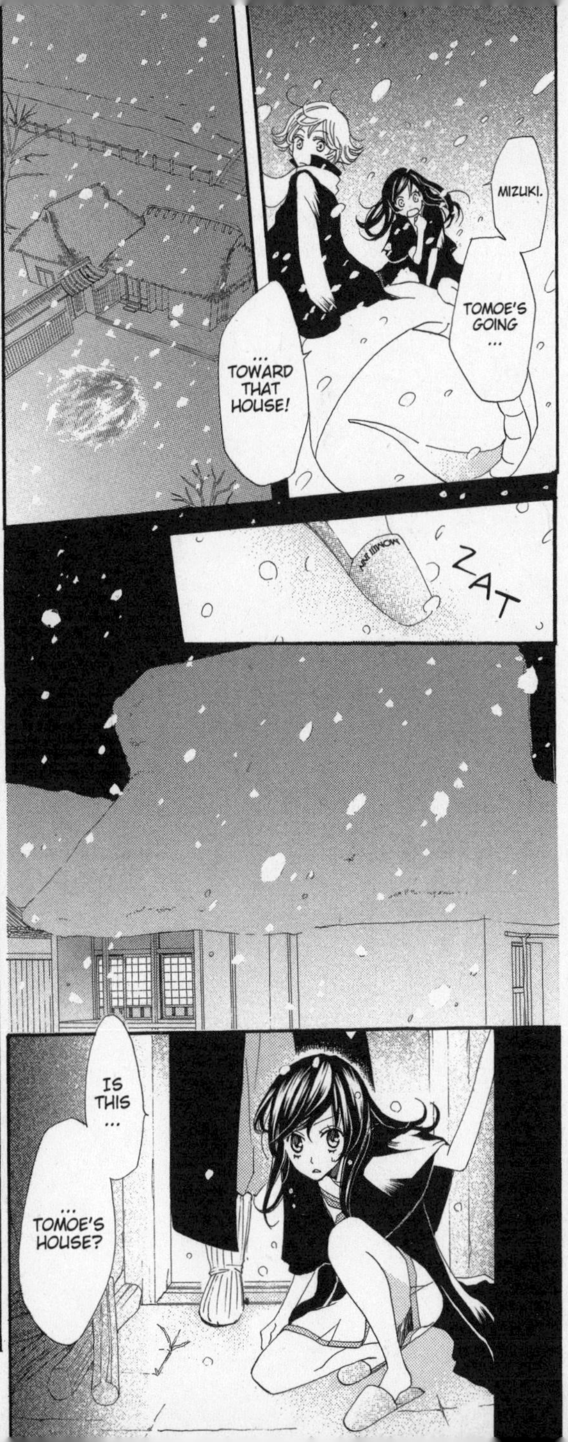
MIZUKI.
TOMOE'S GOING ...
... TOWARD THAT HOUSE!
ZAT
IS THIS ...
... TOMOE'S HOUSE?

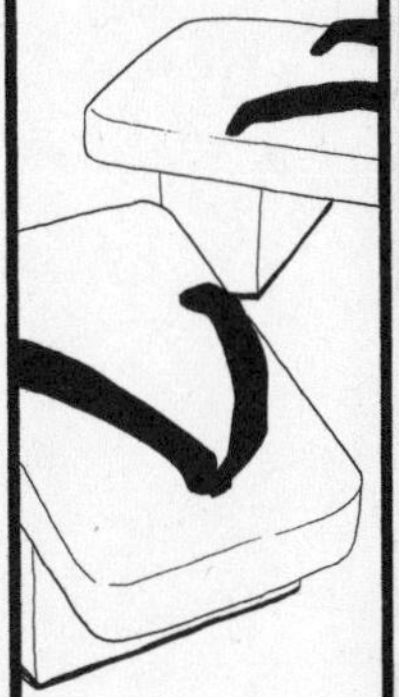

When I'm working on my manuscripts, my assistants come over and things are fun.

I need to work, so I don't have much time to hang out, but I always have fun talking to my assistants. The people who come over are all nice people, and I feel that I'm really blessed.

Thank you so much, everyone. I'm sorry the schedules are always tight. I'll do my best so I can do my work well.

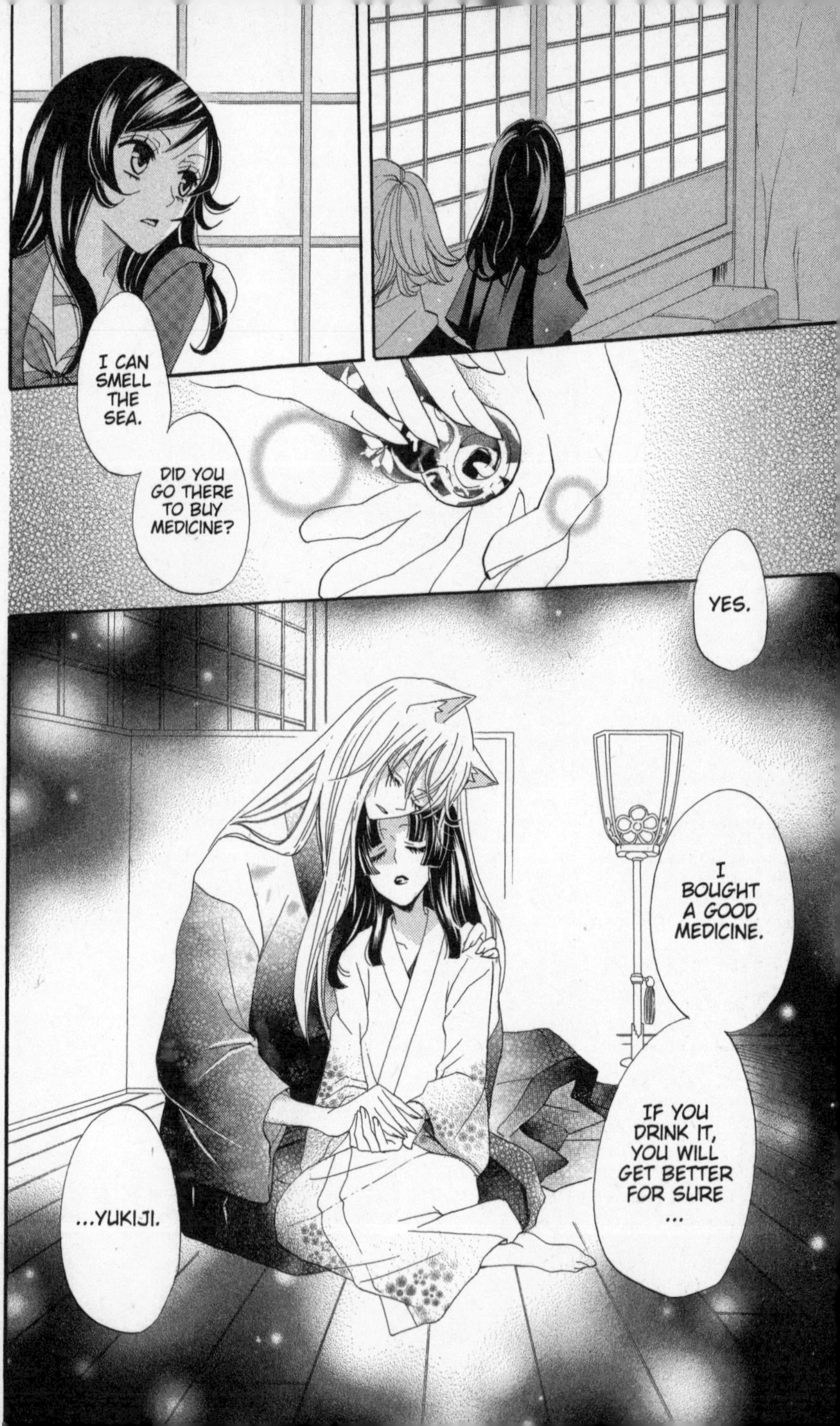
I CAN SMELL THE SEA.
DID YOU GO THERE TO BUY MEDICINE?
YES.
I BOUGHT A GOOD MEDICINE.
IF YOU DRINK IT, YOU WILL GET BETTER FOR SURE ...
...YUKIJI.

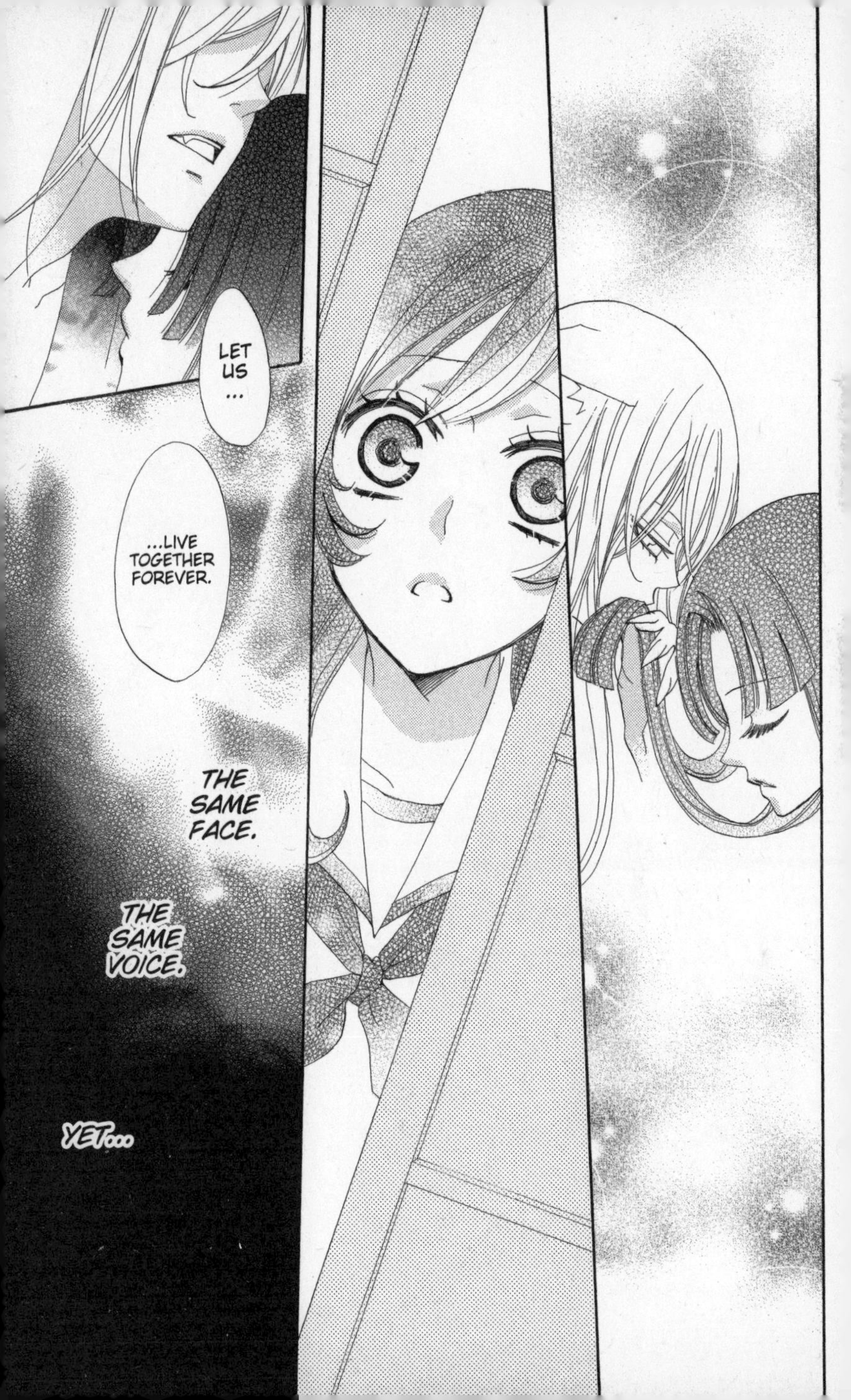
LET US ...
...LIVE TOGETHER FOREVER.
THE SAME FACE.
THE SAME VOICE.
YET...

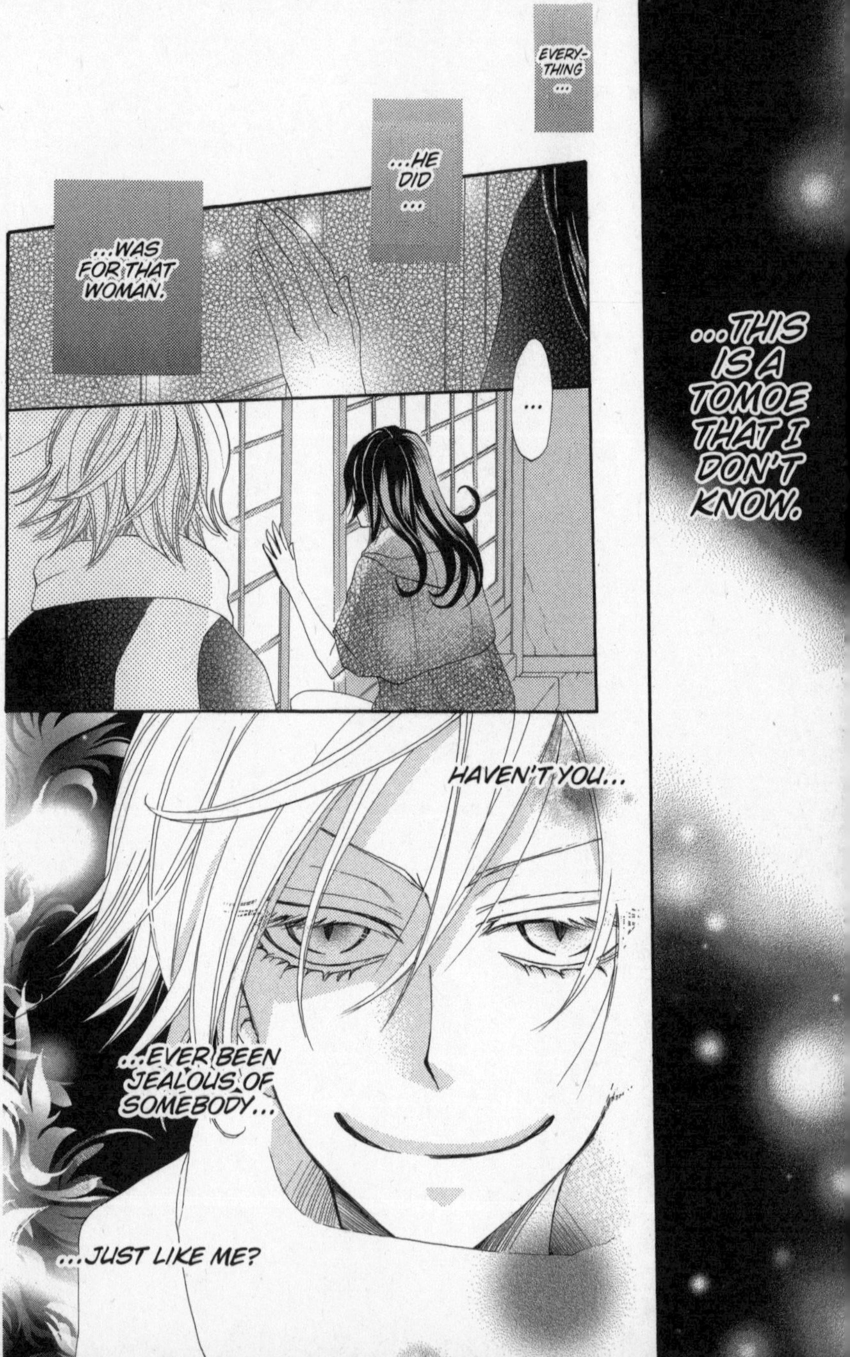
EVERY-THING...
...HE DID...
...WAS FOR THAT WOMAN.
...
...THIS IS A TOMOE THAT I DON'T KNOW.
HAVEN'T YOU...
...EVER BEEN JEALOUS OF SOMEBODY...
...JUST LIKE ME?

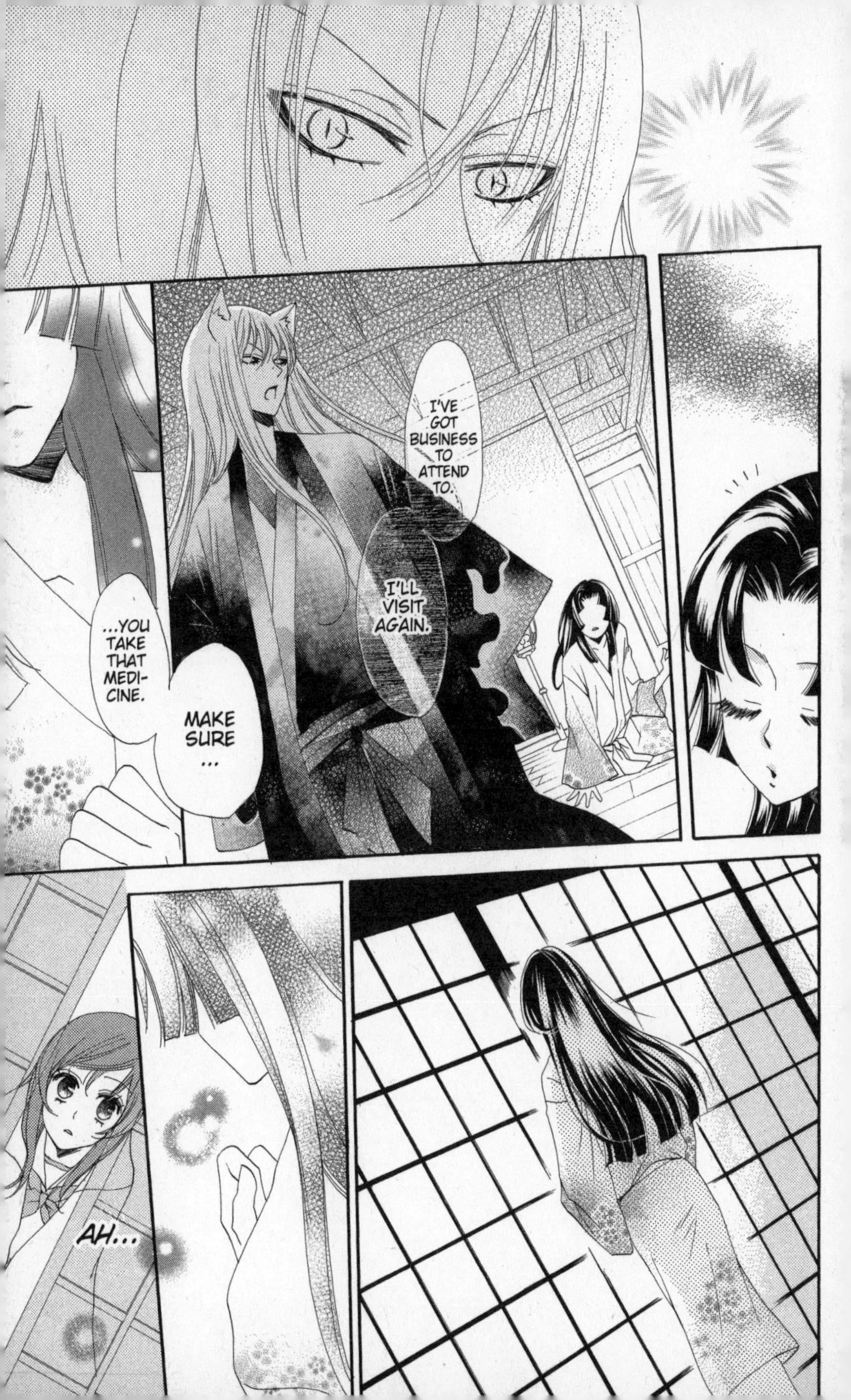
I'VE GOT BUSINESS TO ATTEND TO.
I'LL VISIT AGAIN.
MAKE SURE...
...YOU TAKE THAT MEDICINE.
AH...

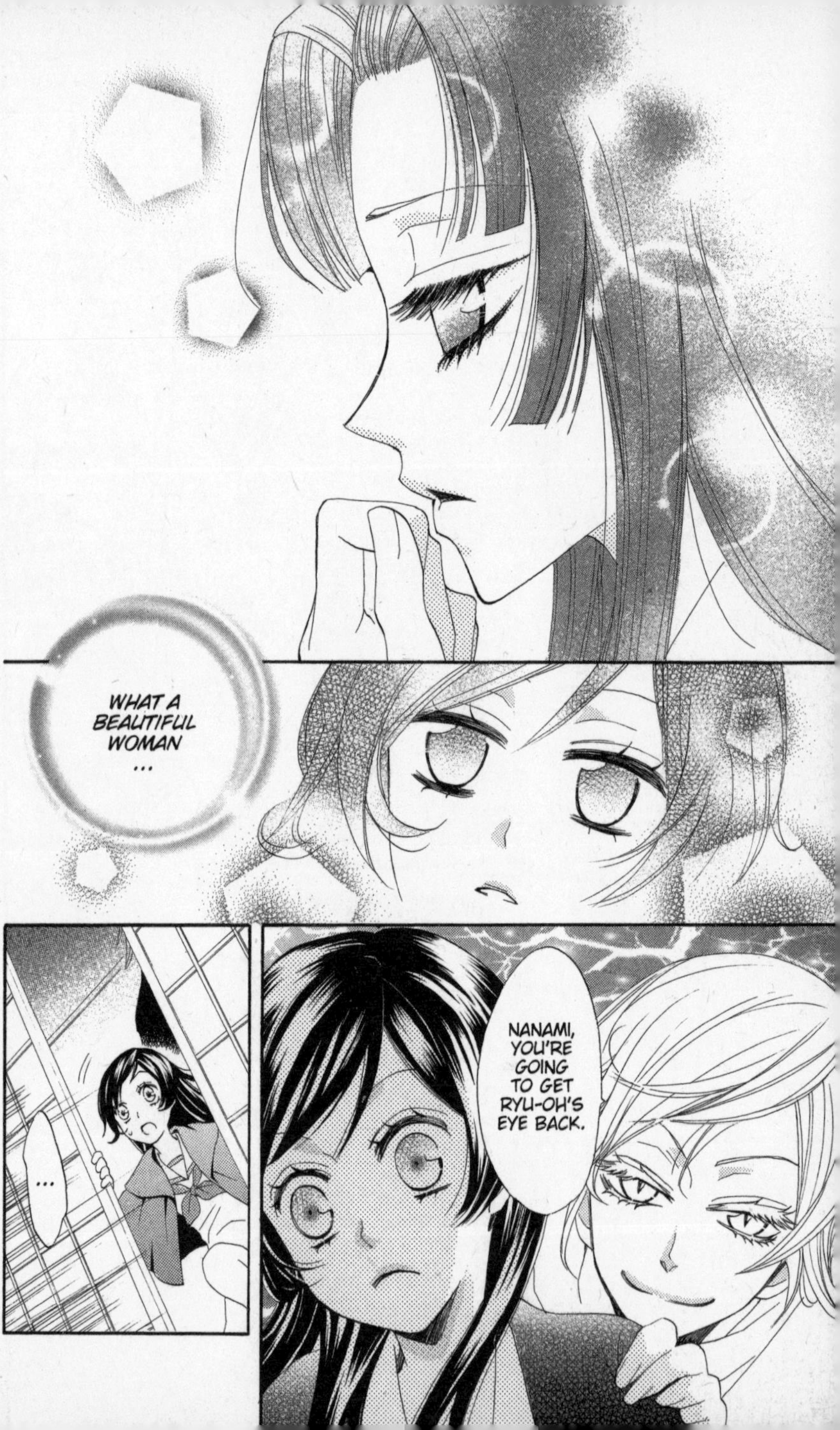
WHAT A BEAUTIFUL WOMAN ...
NANAMI, YOU'RE GOING TO GET RYU-OH'S EYE BACK.
...

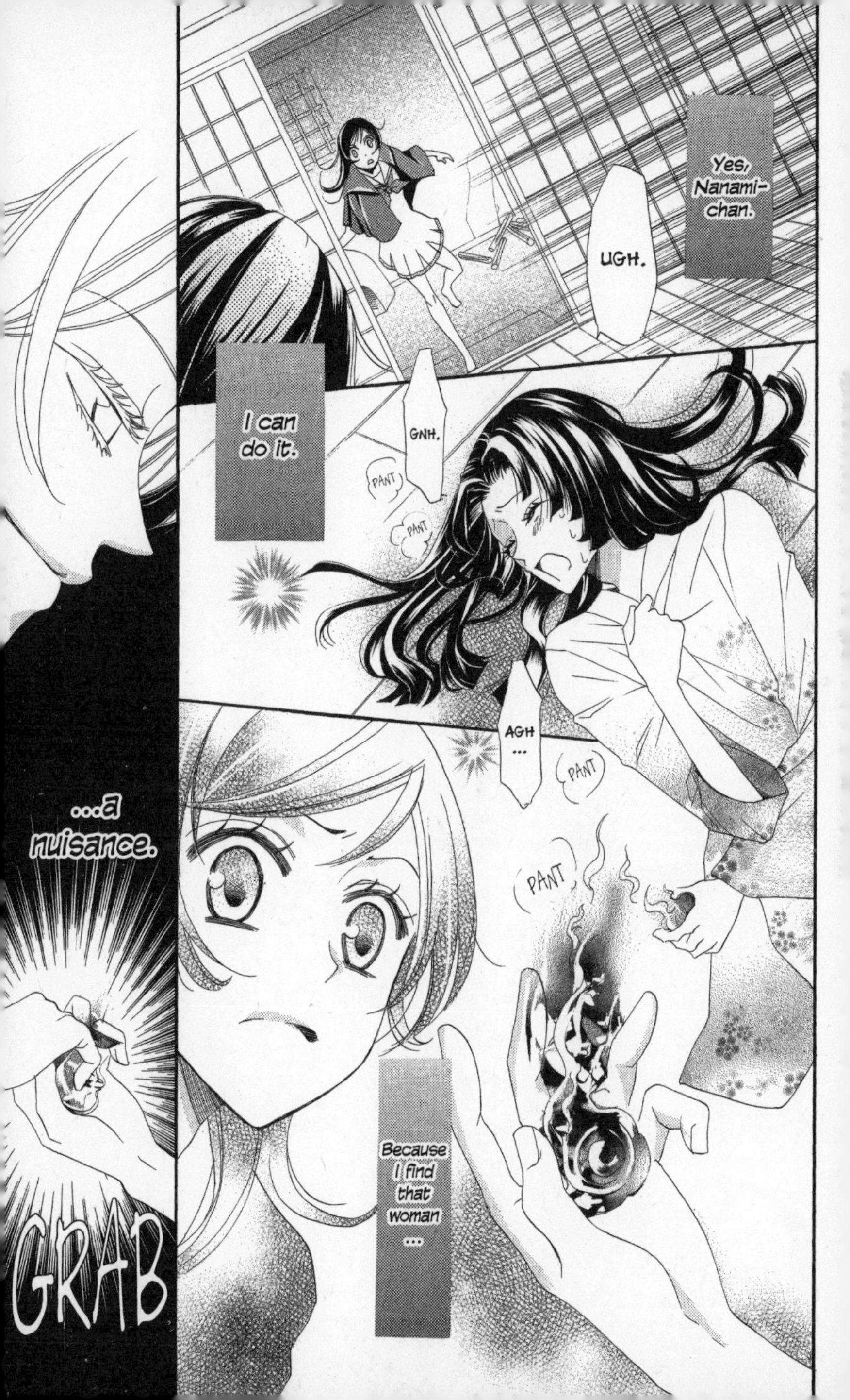
Yes, Nanami-chan.
UGH.
GNH.
PANT
PANT
I can do it.
AGH ...
PANT
PANT
Because I find that woman ...
...a nuisance.
GRAB

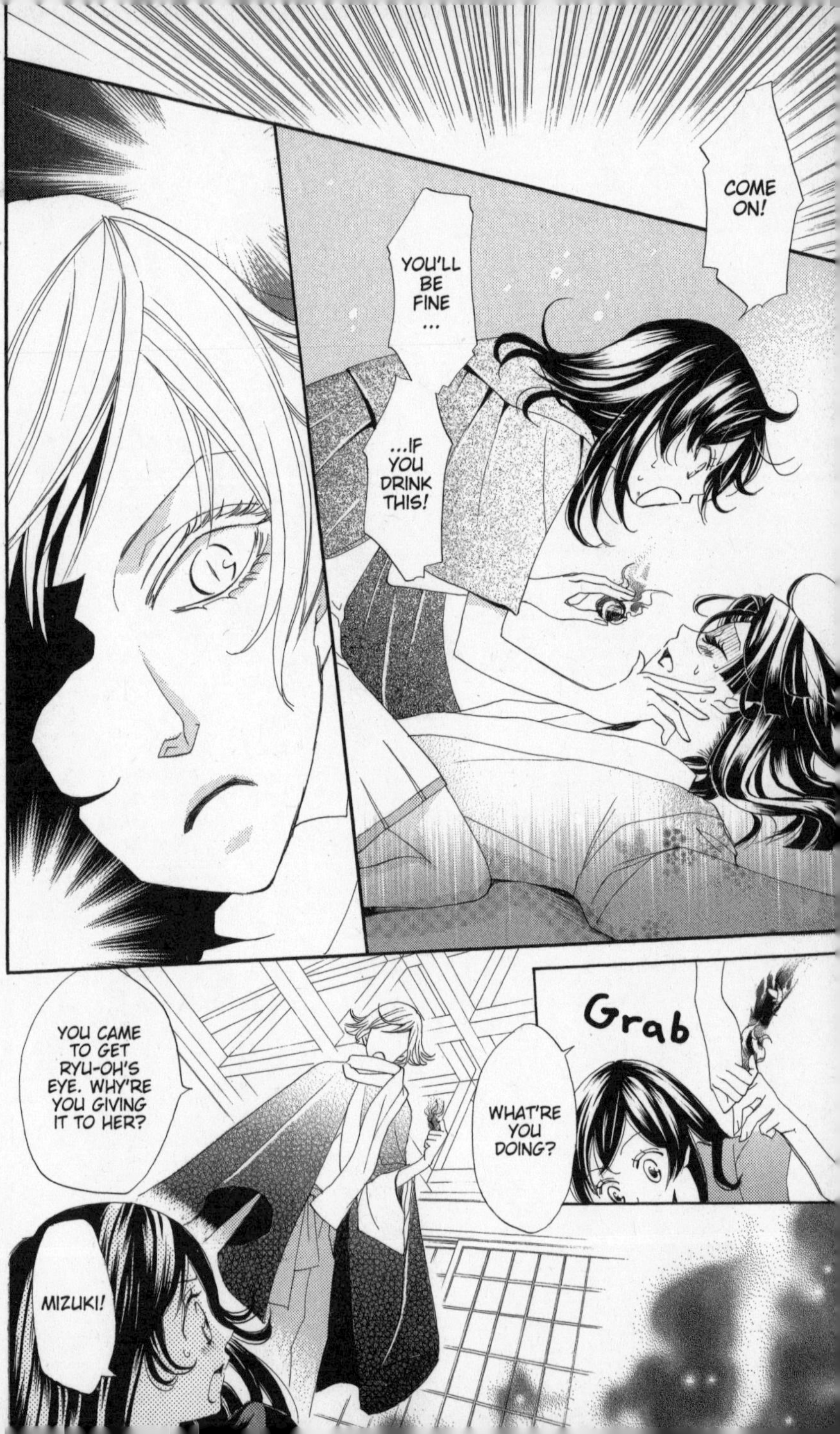
COME ON!
YOU'LL BE FINE ...
...IF YOU DRINK THIS!
Grab
WHAT'RE YOU DOING?
YOU CAME TO GET RYU-OH'S EYE. WHY'RE YOU GIVING IT TO HER?
MIZUKI!

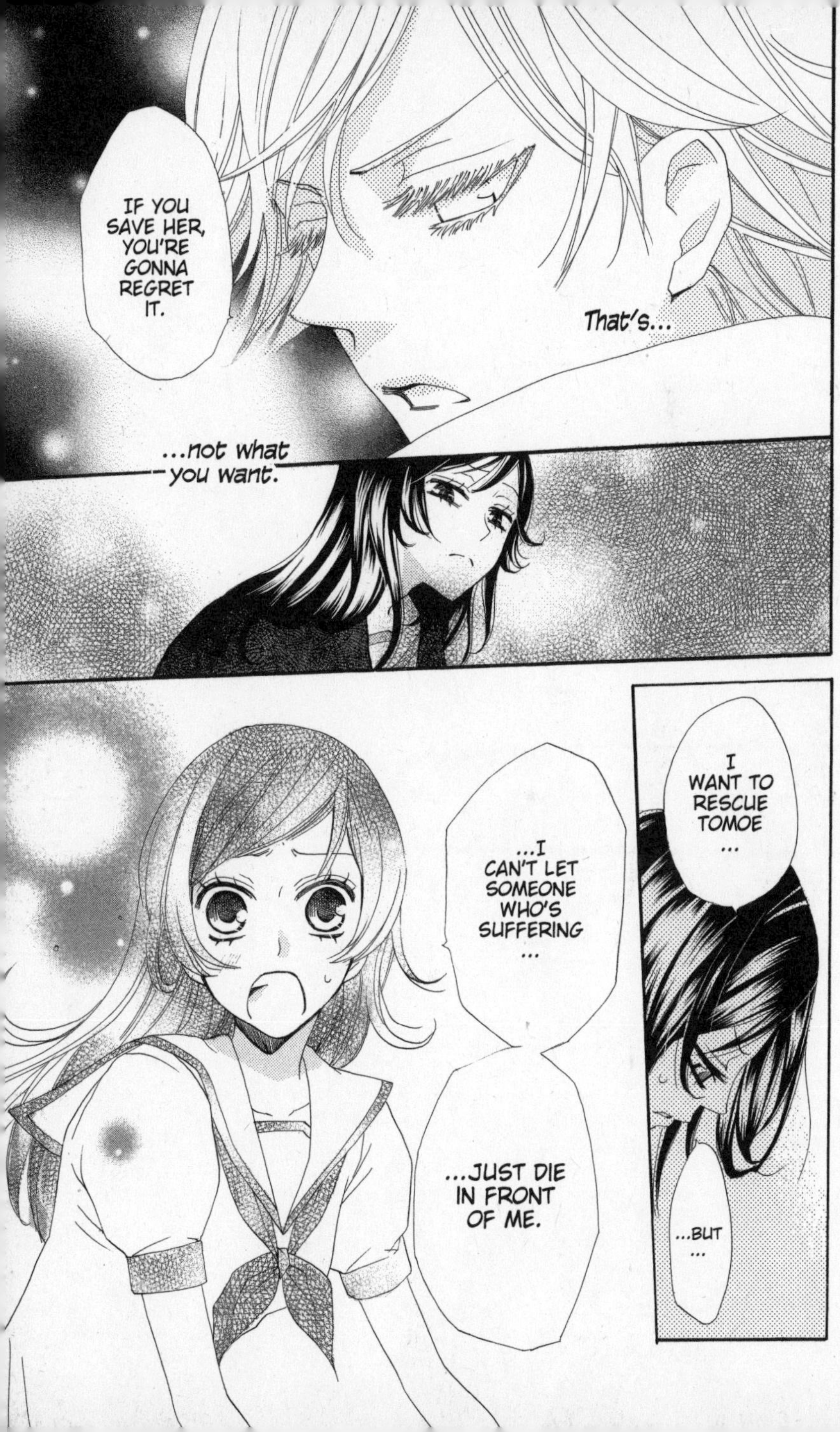
IF YOU SAVE HER, YOU'RE GONNA REGRET IT.
That's...
...not what you want.
I WANT TO RESCUE TOMOE...
...BUT...
...I CAN'T LET SOMEONE WHO'S SUFFERING...
...JUST DIE IN FRONT OF ME.

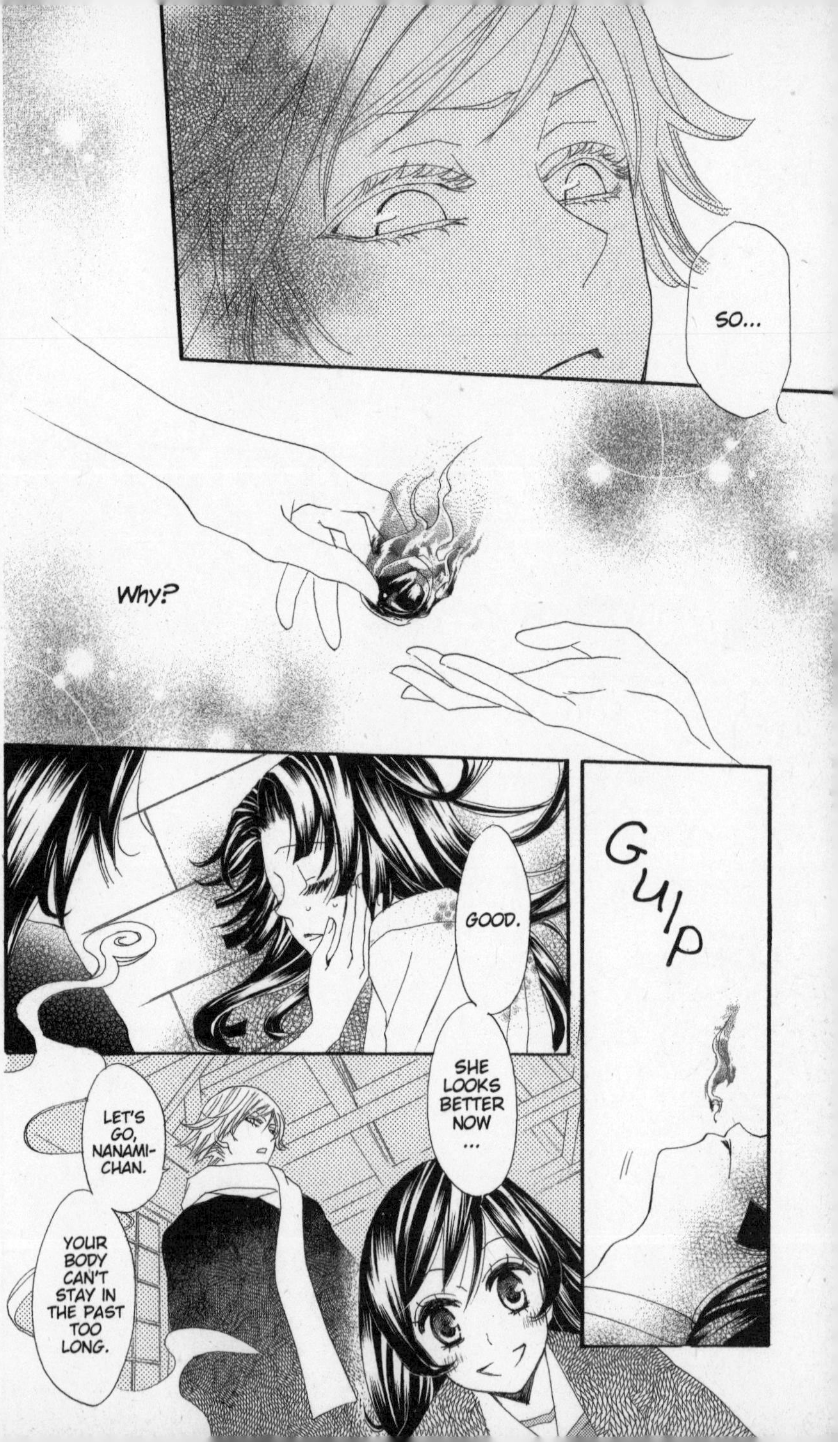
SO...
Why?
Gulp
GOOD.
SHE LOOKS BETTER NOW ...
LET'S GO, NANAMI-CHAN.
YOUR BODY CAN'T STAY IN THE PAST TOO LONG.

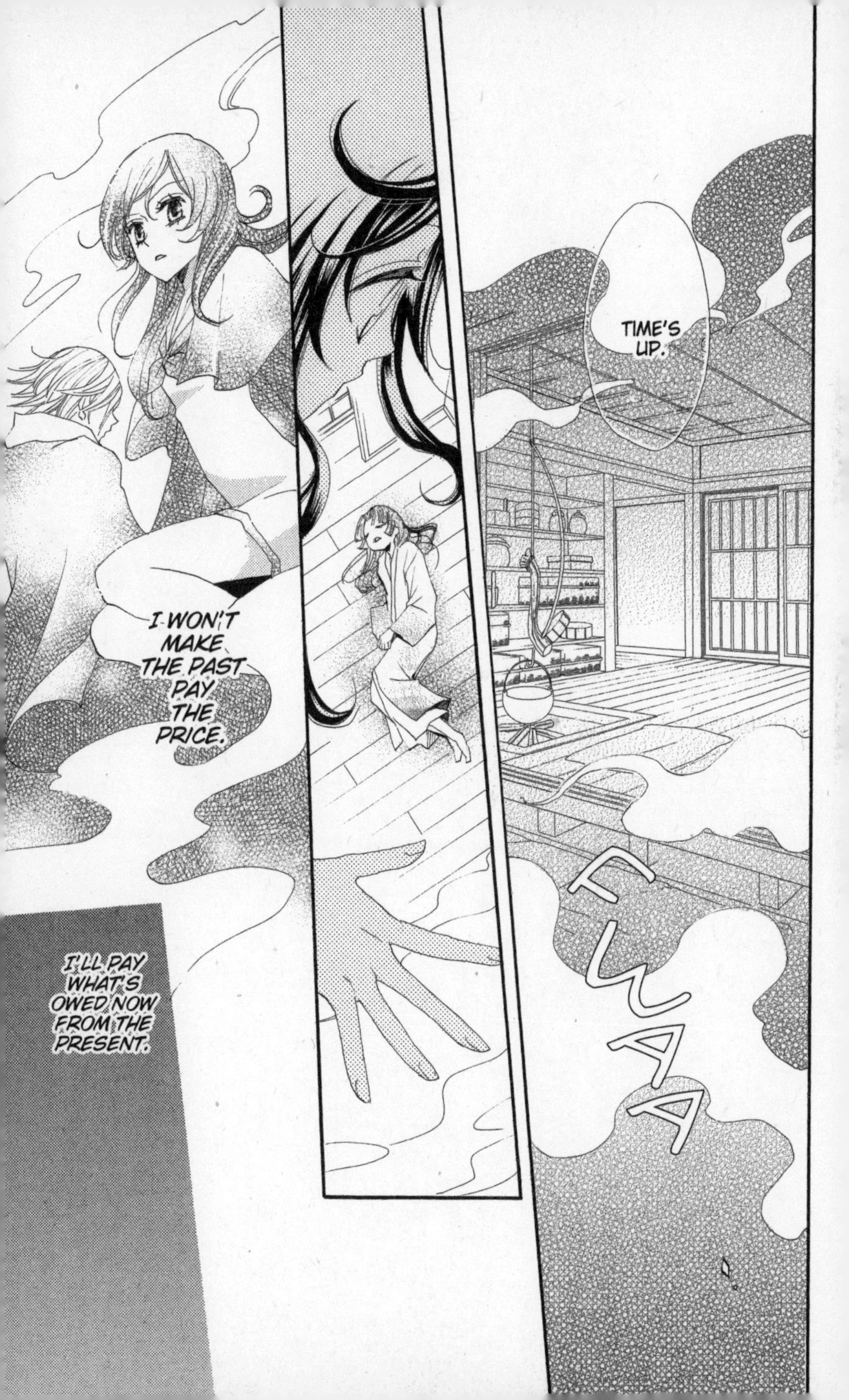
TIME'S UP.
FWAA
I WON'T MAKE THE PAST PAY THE PRICE.
I'LL PAY WHAT'S OWED NOW FROM THE PRESENT.

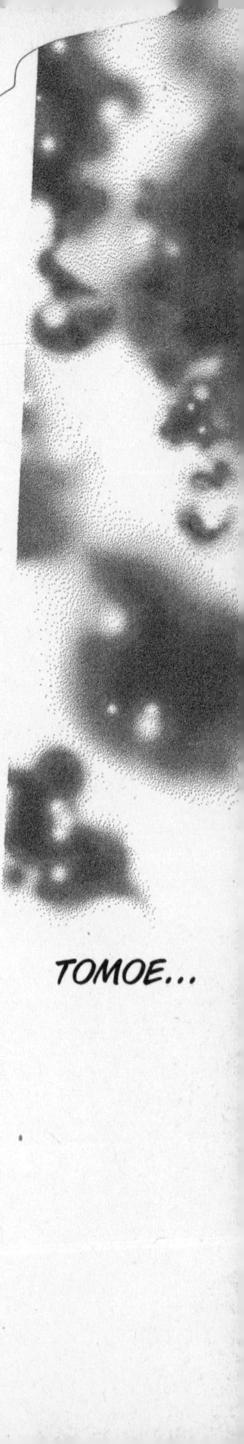
TOMOE...

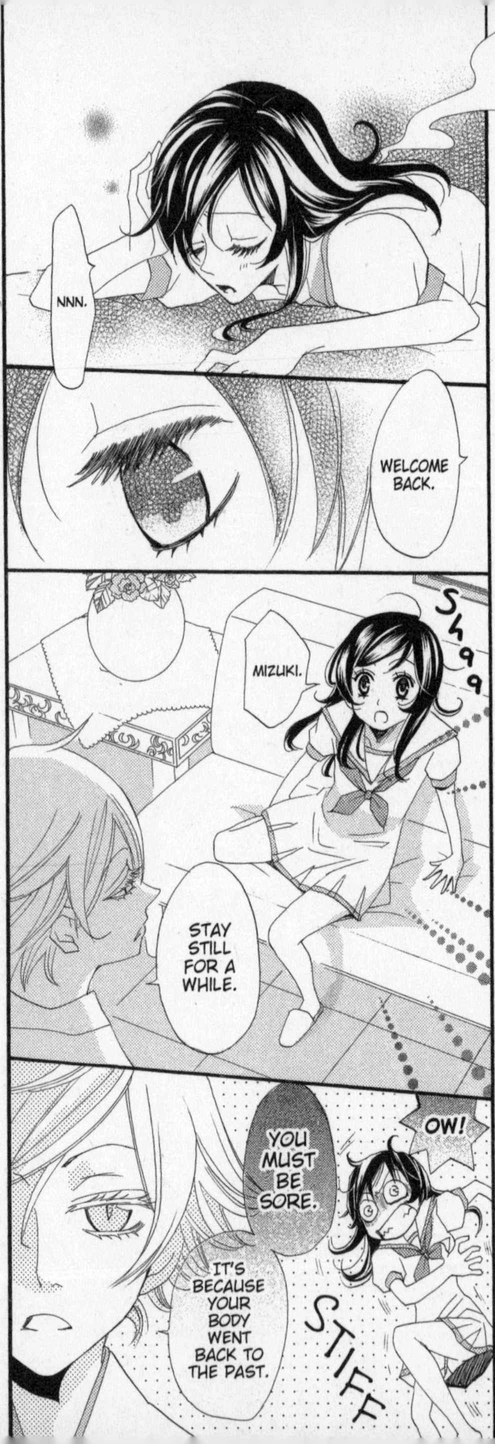
NNN.
WELCOME BACK.
Shaa
MIZUKI.
STAY STILL FOR A WHILE.
OW!
YOU MUST BE SORE.
IT'S BECAUSE YOUR BODY WENT BACK TO THE PAST.
STIFF

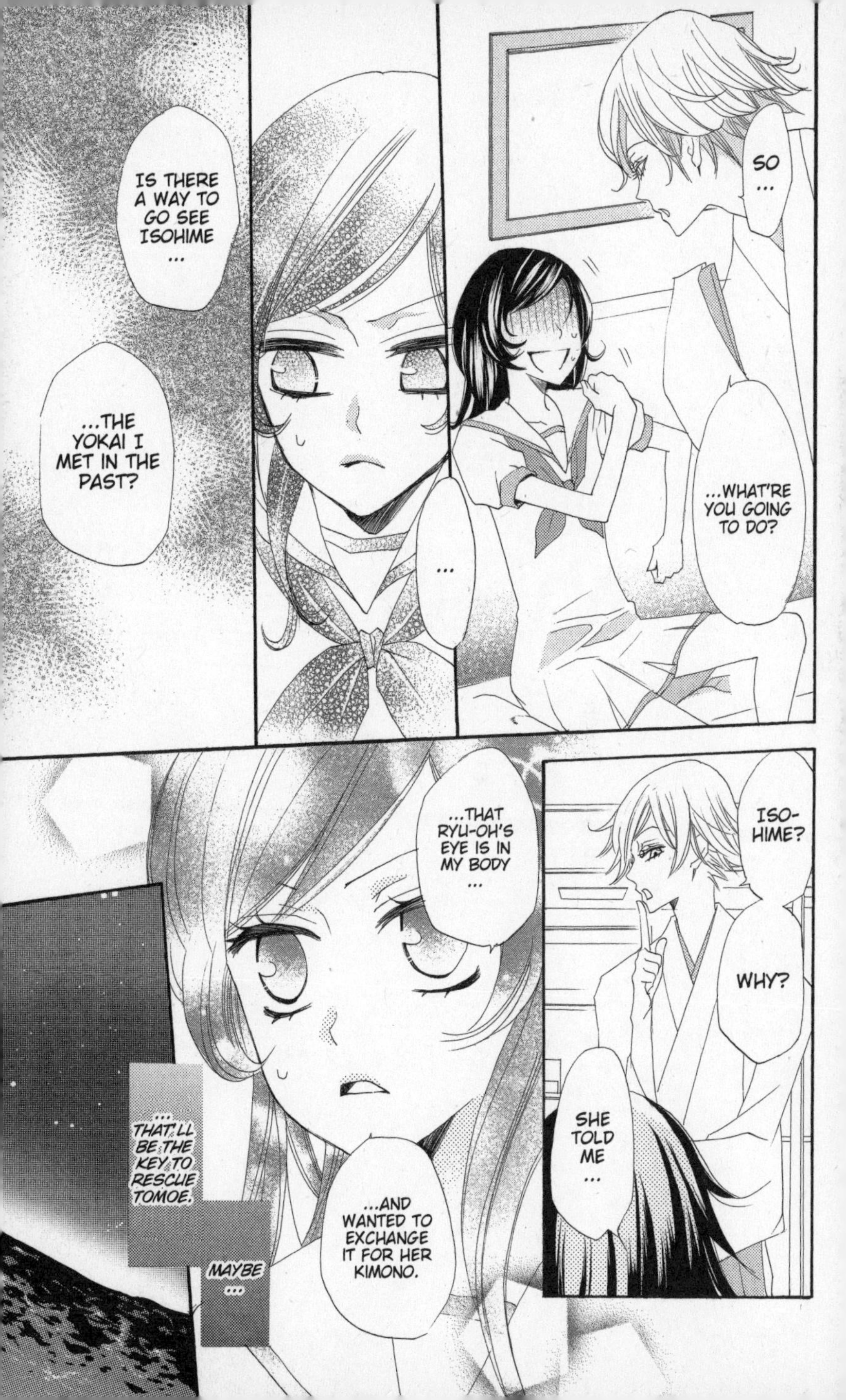
SO ...
...WHAT'RE YOU GOING TO DO?
...
IS THERE A WAY TO GO SEE ISOHIME ...
...THE YOKAI I MET IN THE PAST?
ISO-HIME?
WHY?
SHE TOLD ME ...
...THAT RYU-OH'S EYE IS IN MY BODY ...
...AND WANTED TO EXCHANGE IT FOR HER KIMONO.
...THAT'LL BE THE KEY TO RESCUE TOMOE.
MAYBE ...

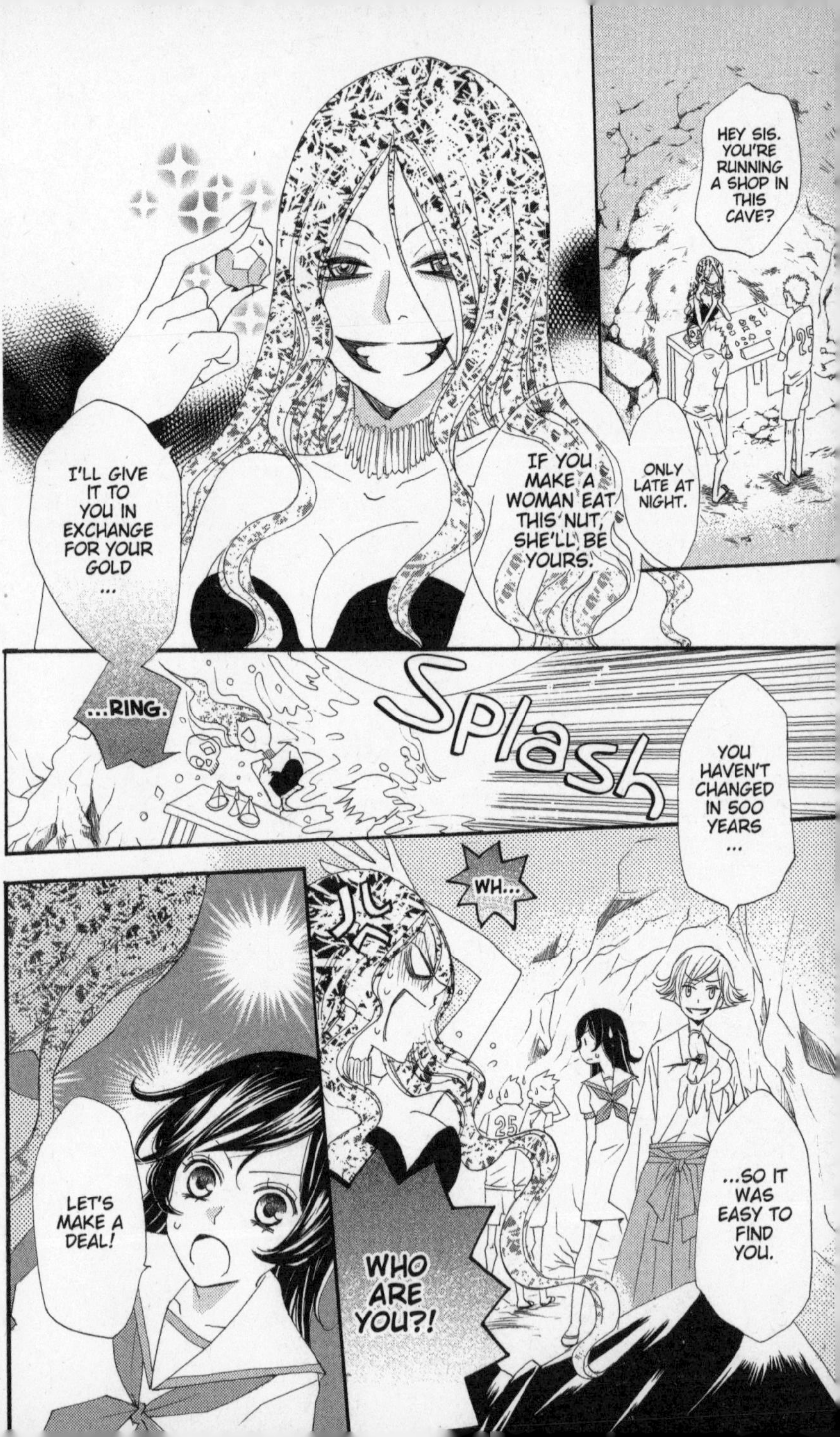
HEY SIS. YOU'RE RUNNING A SHOP IN THIS CAVE?
ONLY LATE AT NIGHT.
IF YOU MAKE A WOMAN EAT THIS NUT, SHE'LL BE YOURS.
I'LL GIVE IT TO YOU IN EXCHANGE FOR YOUR GOLD ...
...RING.
Splash
YOU HAVEN'T CHANGED IN 500 YEARS ...
WH...
...SO IT WAS EASY TO FIND YOU.
WHO ARE YOU?!
LET'S MAKE A DEAL!

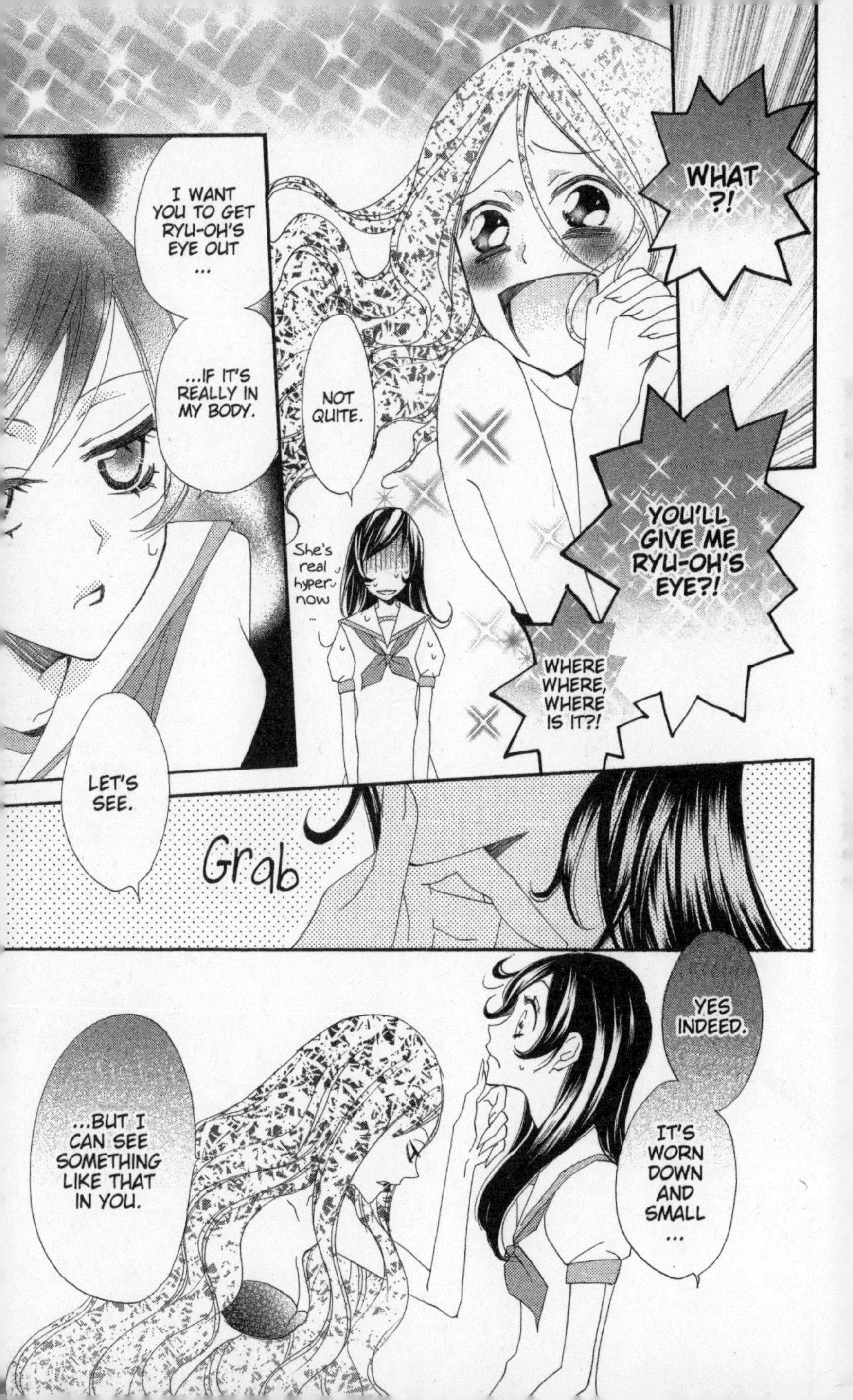
I WANT YOU TO GET RYU-OH'S EYE OUT ...
...IF IT'S REALLY IN MY BODY.
WHAT?!
YOU'LL GIVE ME RYU-OH'S EYE?!
WHERE WHERE, WHERE IS IT?!
NOT QUITE.
She's real hyper now ...
LET'S SEE.
Grab
YES INDEED.
IT'S WORN DOWN AND SMALL ...
...BUT I CAN SEE SOMETHING LIKE THAT IN YOU.

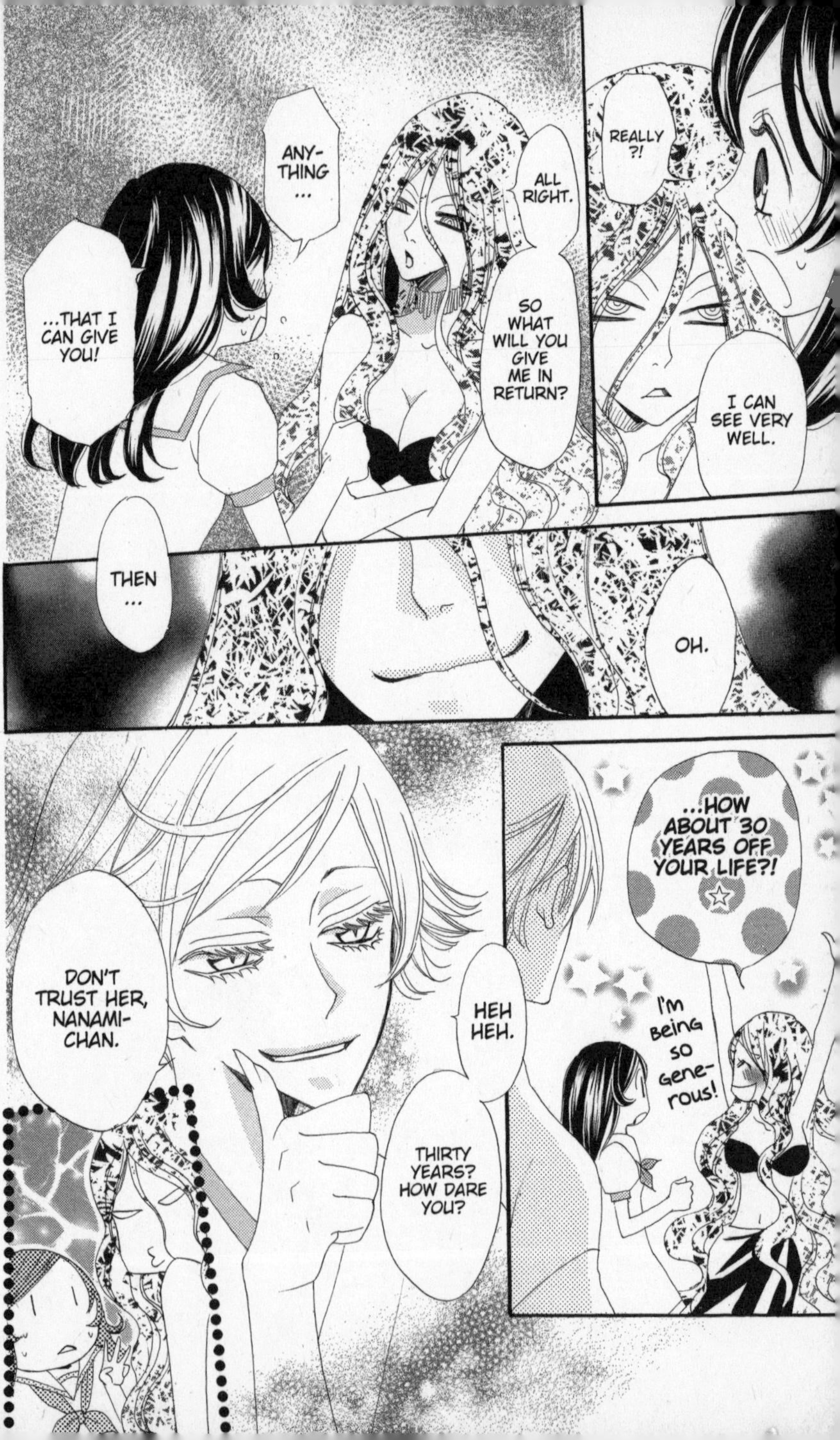
REALLY ?!
I CAN SEE VERY WELL.
ALL RIGHT.
SO WHAT WILL YOU GIVE ME IN RETURN?
ANY-THING ...
...THAT I CAN GIVE YOU!
OH.
THEN ...
...HOW ABOUT 30 YEARS OFF YOUR LIFE?!
I'm being so gene-rous!
HEH HEH.
THIRTY YEARS? HOW DARE YOU?
DON'T TRUST HER, NANAMI-CHAN.

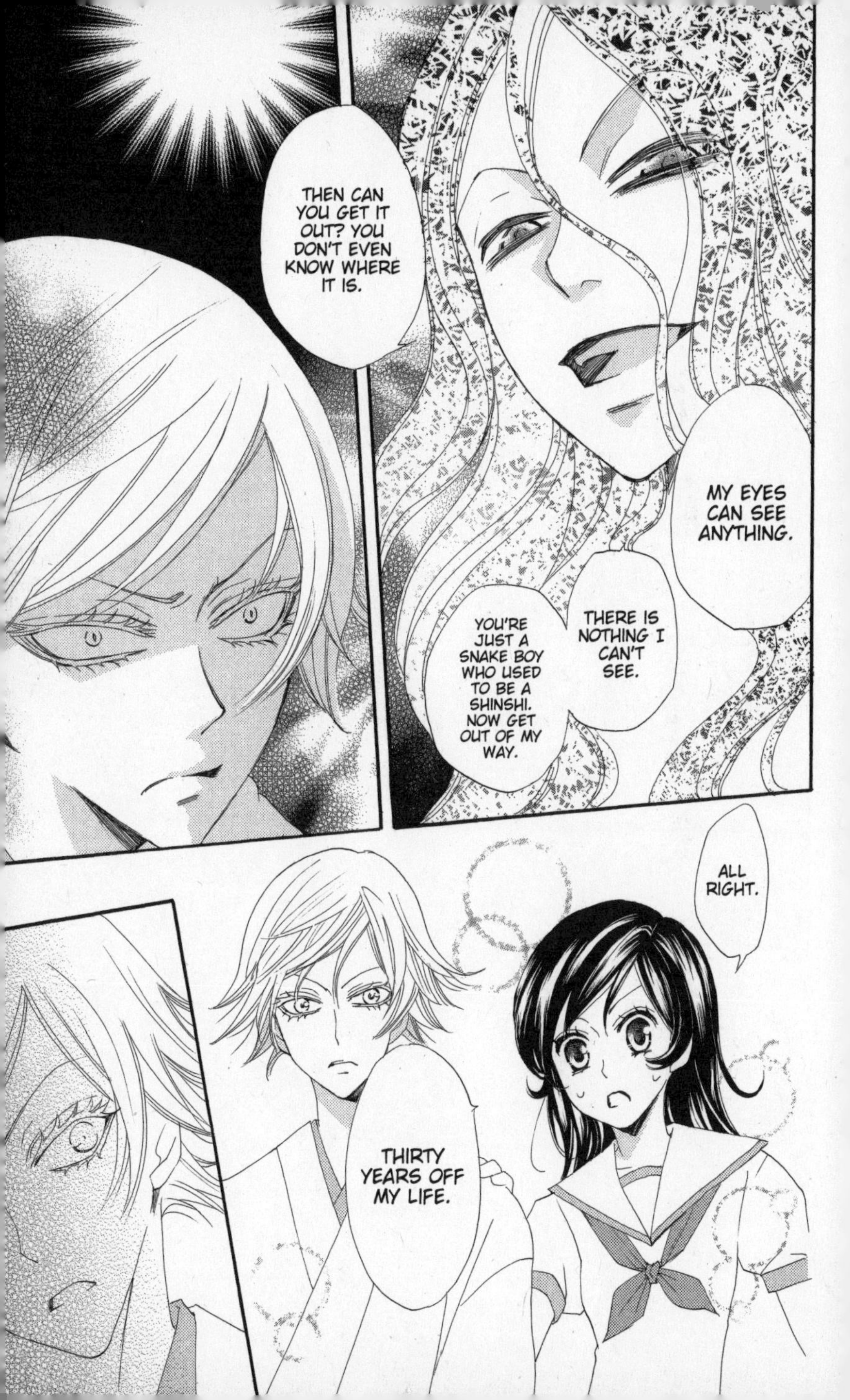
THEN CAN YOU GET IT OUT? YOU DON'T EVEN KNOW WHERE IT IS.
MY EYES CAN SEE ANYTHING.
THERE IS NOTHING I CAN'T SEE.
YOU'RE JUST A SNAKE BOY WHO USED TO BE A SHINSHI. NOW GET OUT OF MY WAY.
ALL RIGHT.
THIRTY YEARS OFF MY LIFE.

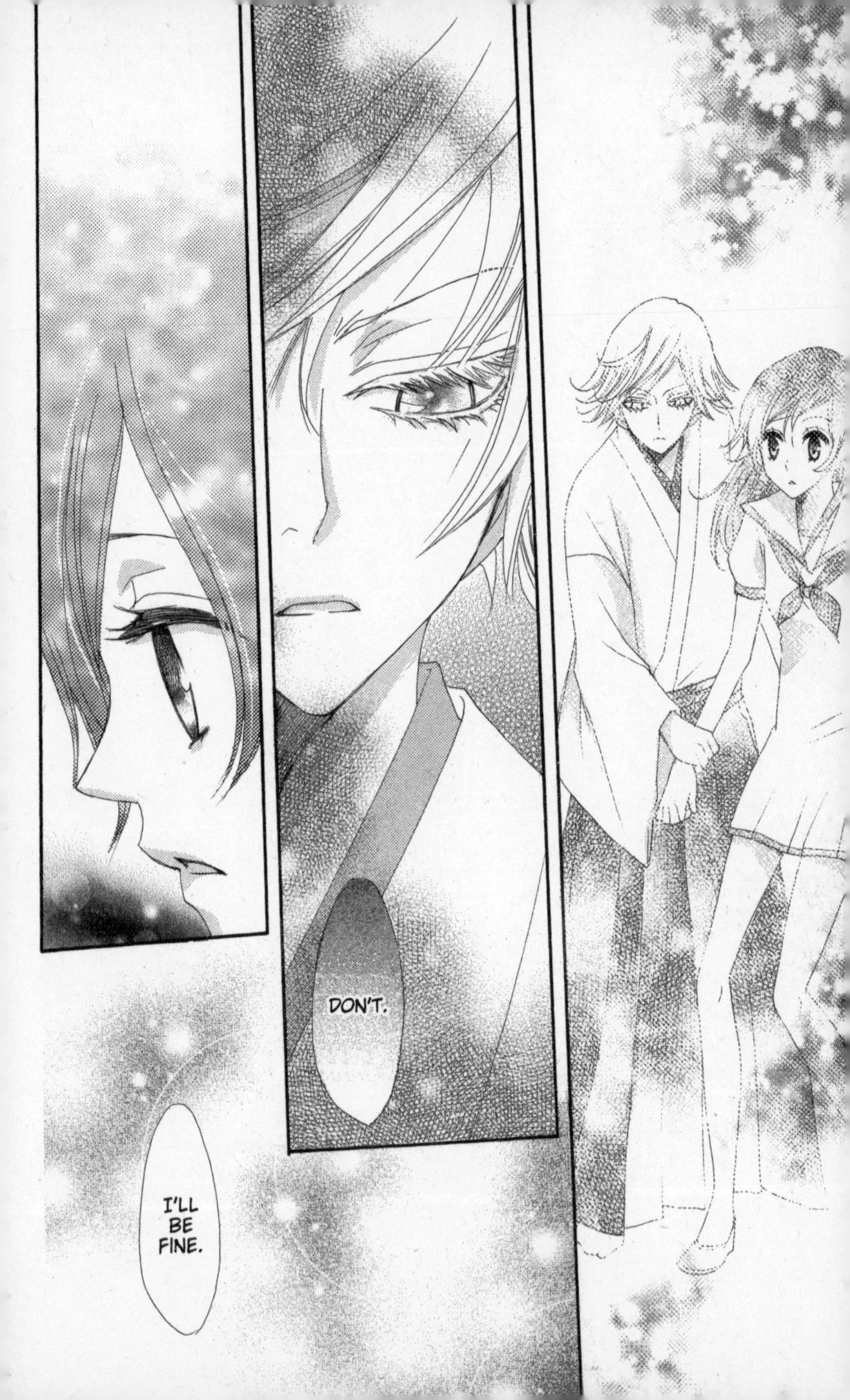
DON'T.
I'LL BE FINE.

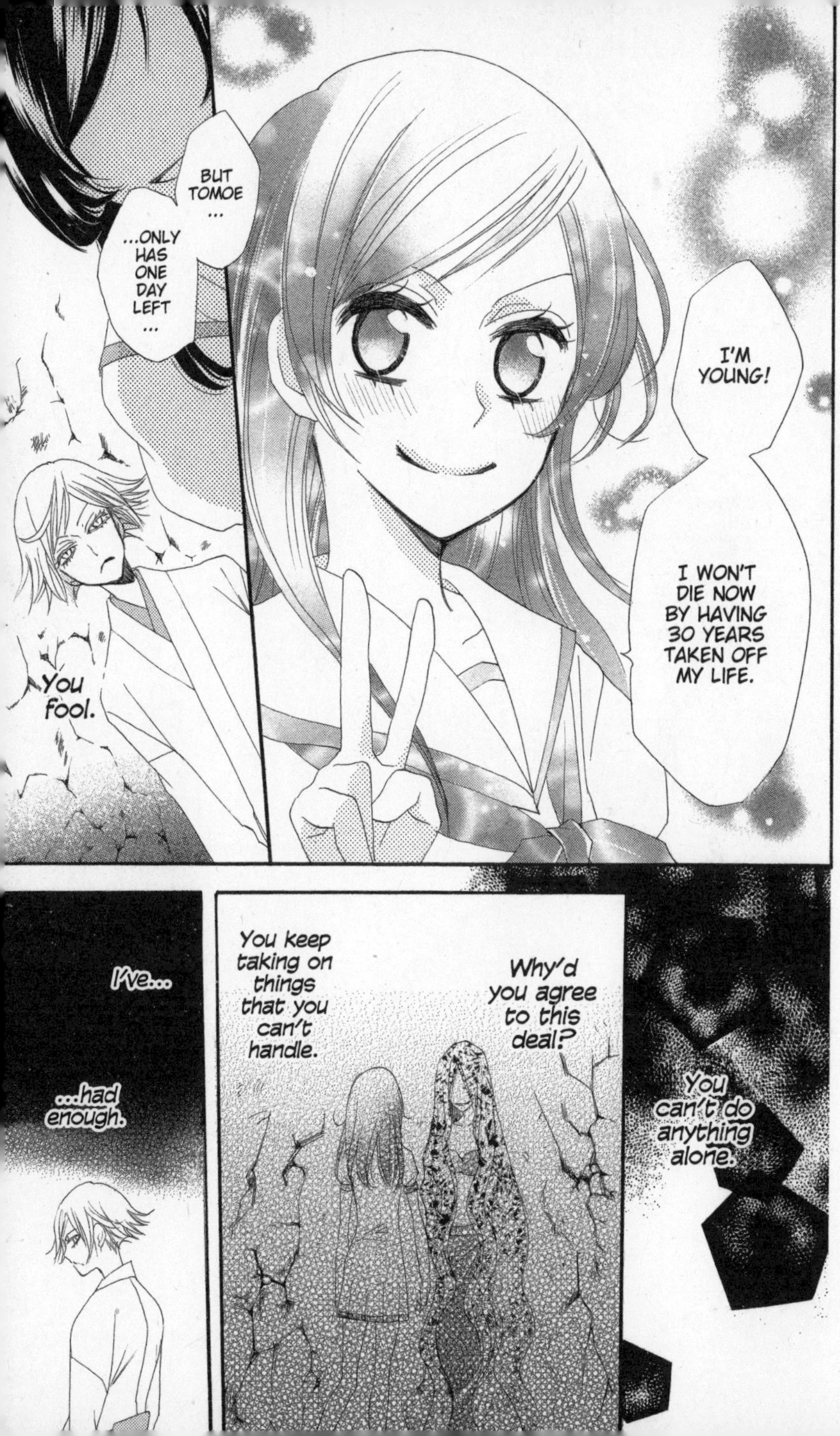
I'M YOUNG!
I WON'T DIE NOW BY HAVING 30 YEARS TAKEN OFF MY LIFE.
BUT TOMOE ...
...ONLY HAS ONE DAY LEFT ...
You fool.
You can't do anything alone.
Why'd you agree to this deal?
You keep taking on things that you can't handle.
I've...
...had enough.

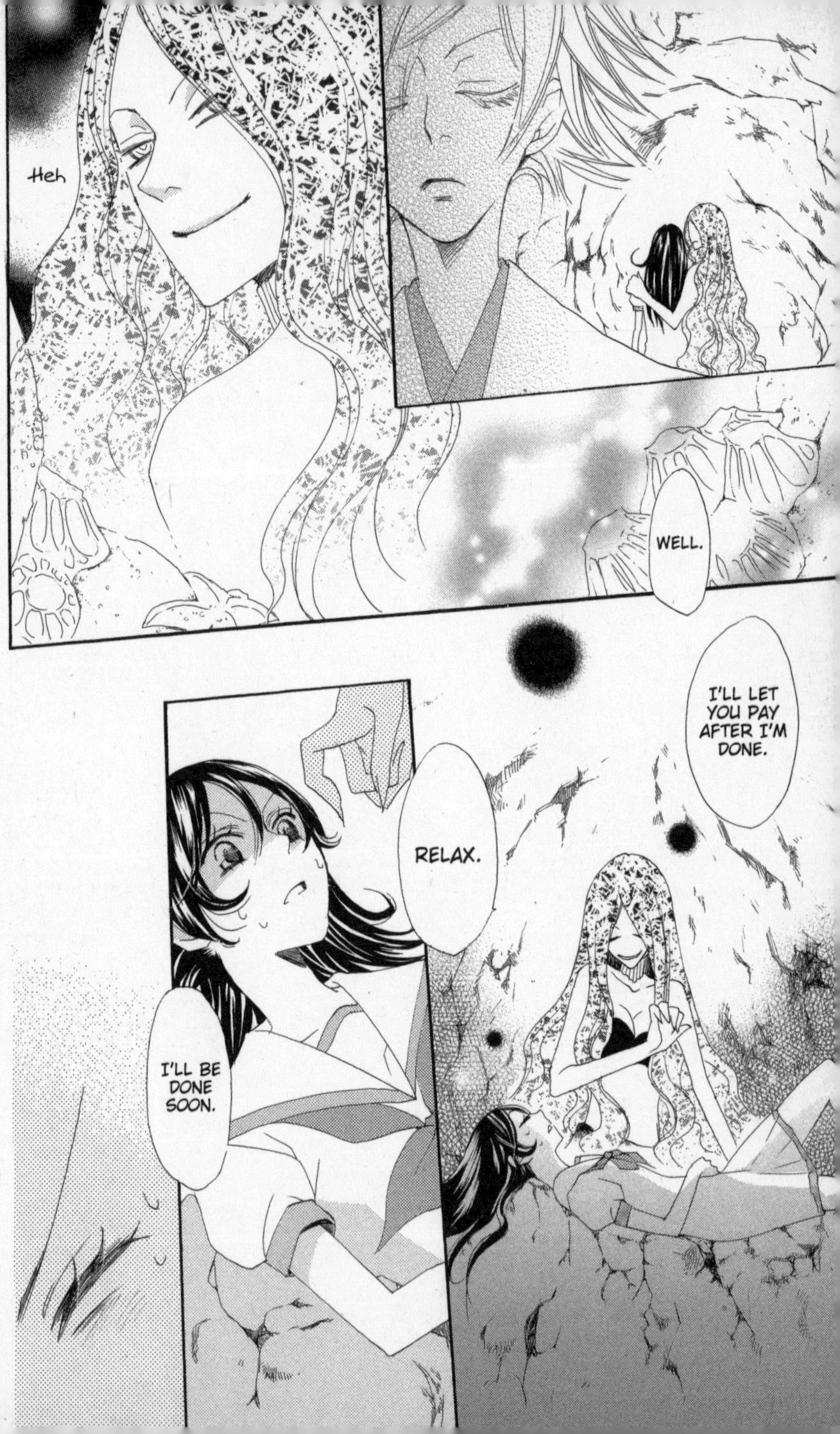
WELL.
Heh
I'LL LET YOU PAY AFTER I'M DONE.
RELAX.
I'LL BE DONE SOON.

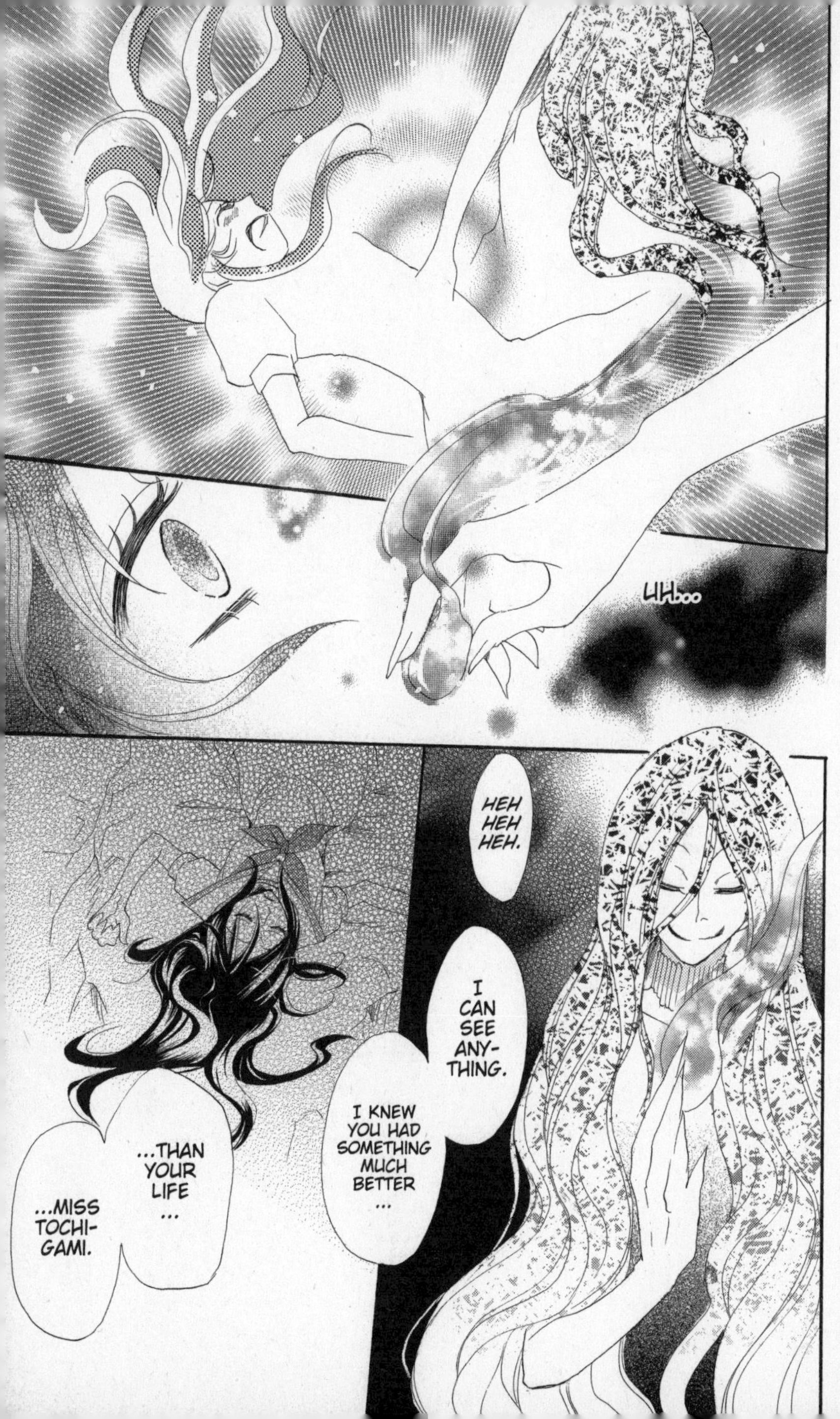
UHboo
HEH HEH HEH.
I CAN SEE ANYTHING.
I KNEW YOU HAD SOMETHING MUCH BETTER ...
...THAN YOUR LIFE ...
...MISS TOCHIGAMI.

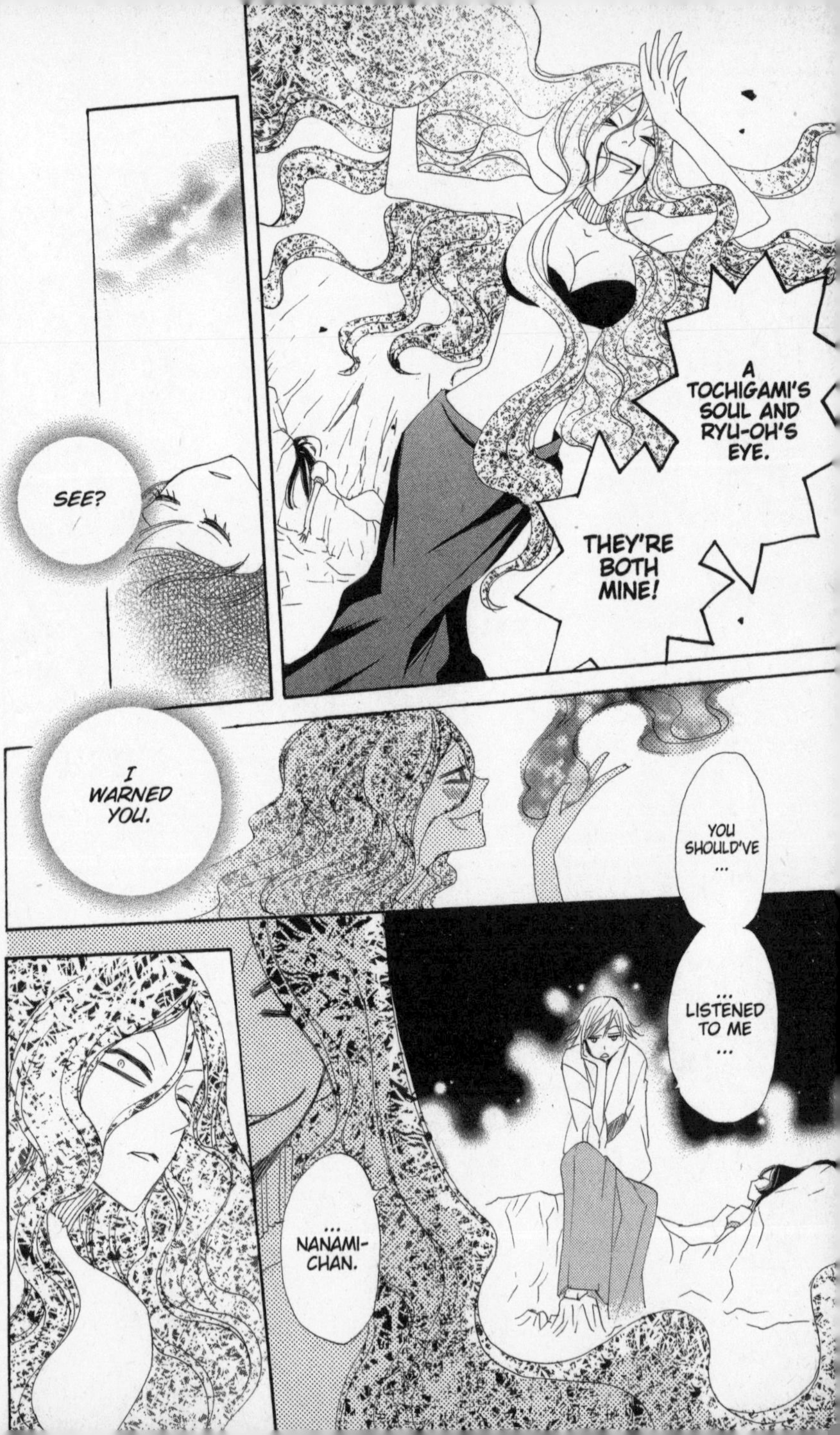
A TOCHIGAMI'S SOUL AND RYU-OH'S EYE.
THEY'RE BOTH MINE!
SEE?
YOU SHOULD'VE ...
I WARNED YOU.
... LISTENED TO ME ...
... NANAMI-CHAN.

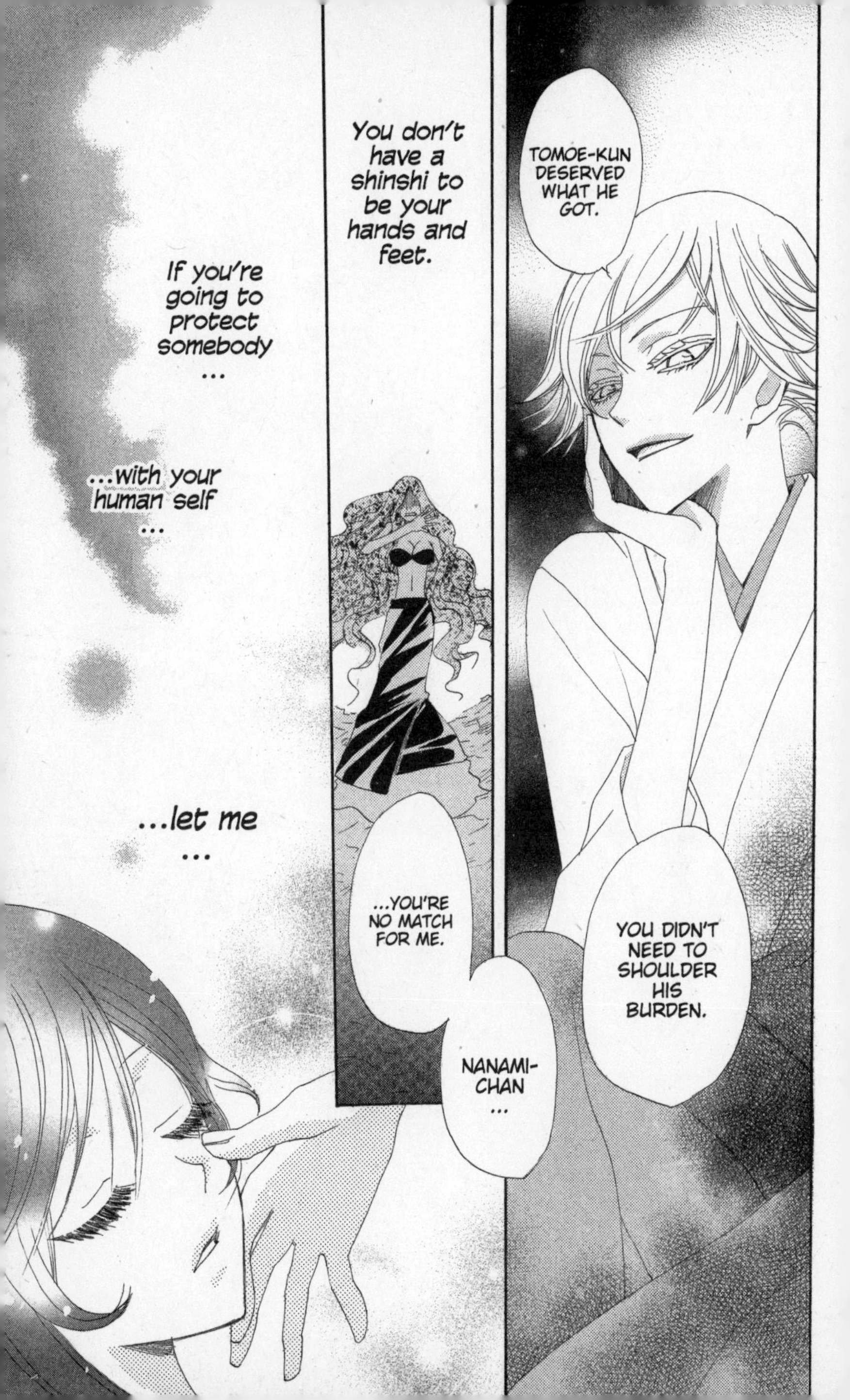
TOMOE-KUN DESERVED WHAT HE GOT.
YOU DIDN'T NEED TO SHOULDER HIS BURDEN.
NANAMI-CHAN ...
You don't have a shinshi to be your hands and feet.
...YOU'RE NO MATCH FOR ME.
If you're going to protect somebody ...
...with your human self ...
...let me ...

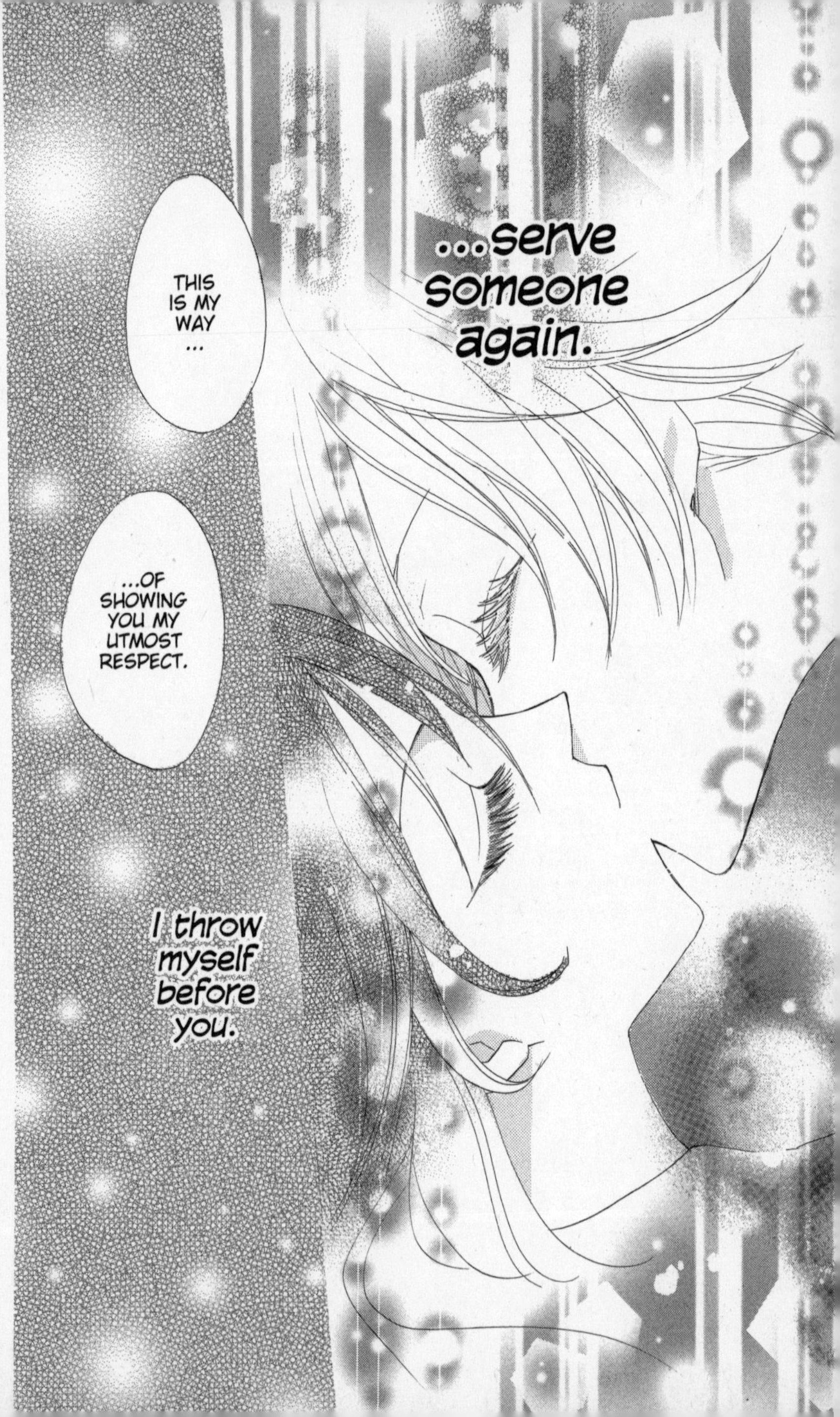
...serve someone again.
THIS IS MY WAY ...
...OF SHOWING YOU MY UTMOST RESPECT.
I throw myself before you.

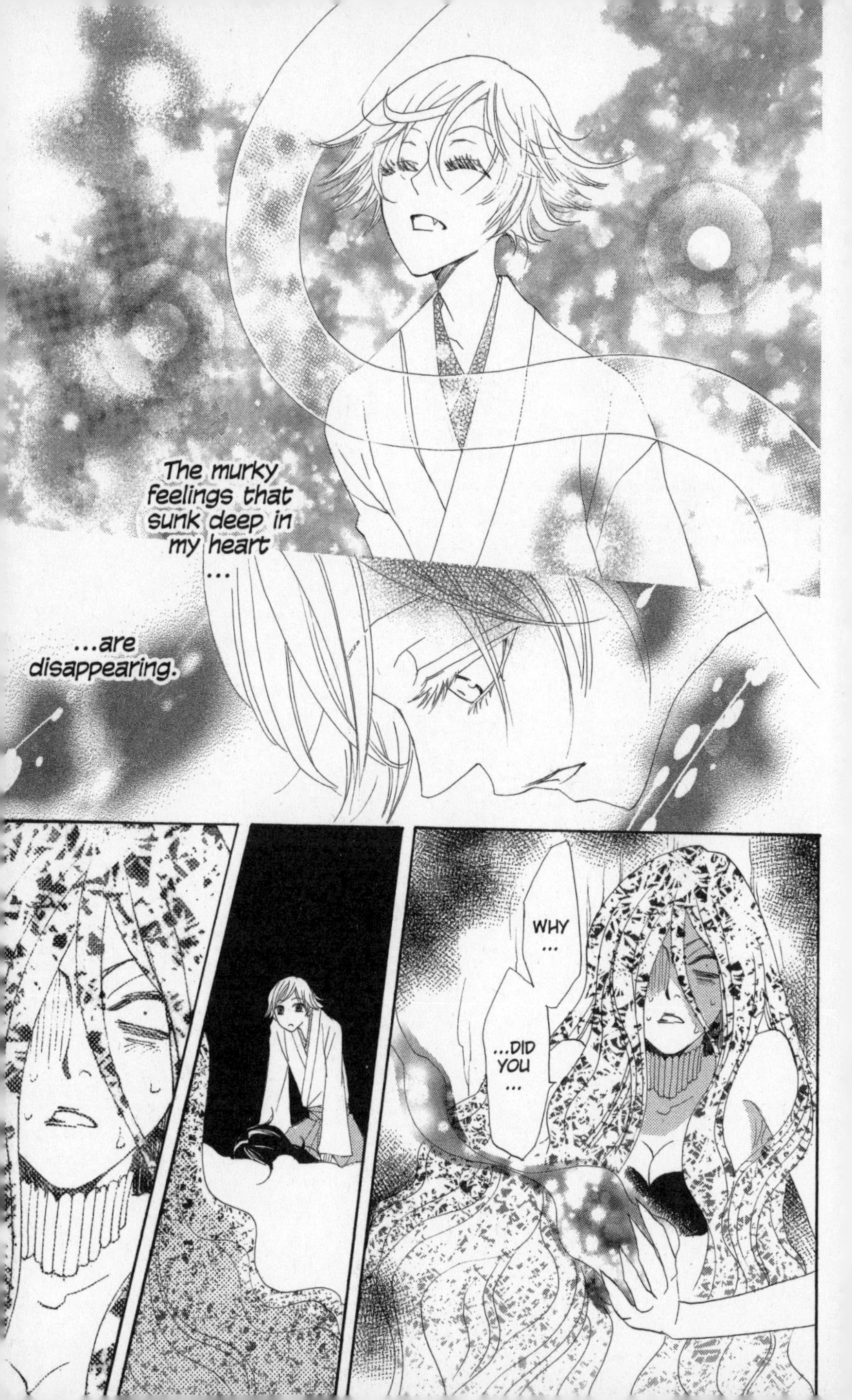
The murky feelings that sunk deep in my heart ...
...are disappearing.
WHY ...
...DID YOU ...

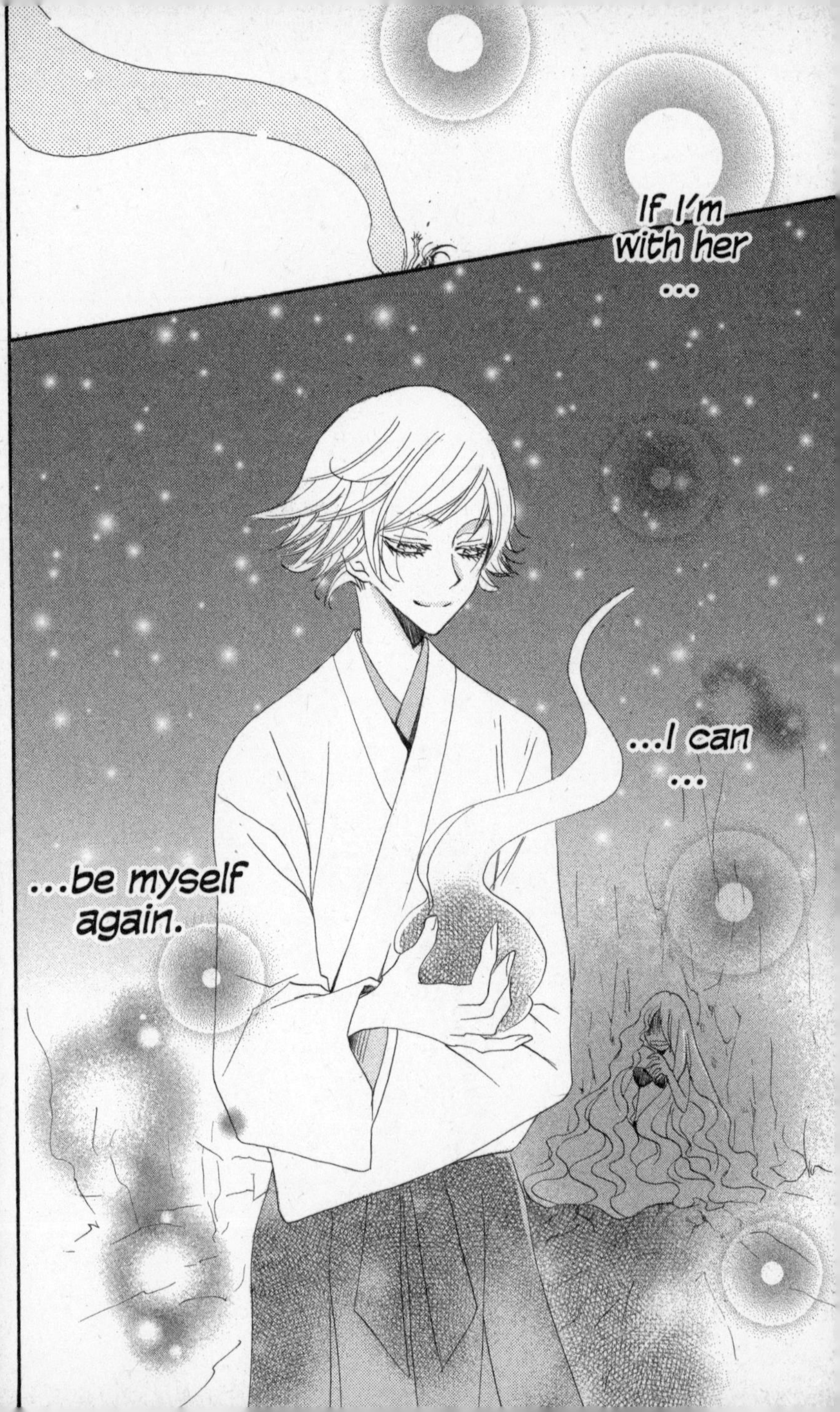
If I'm with her ...
...I can ...
...be myself again.

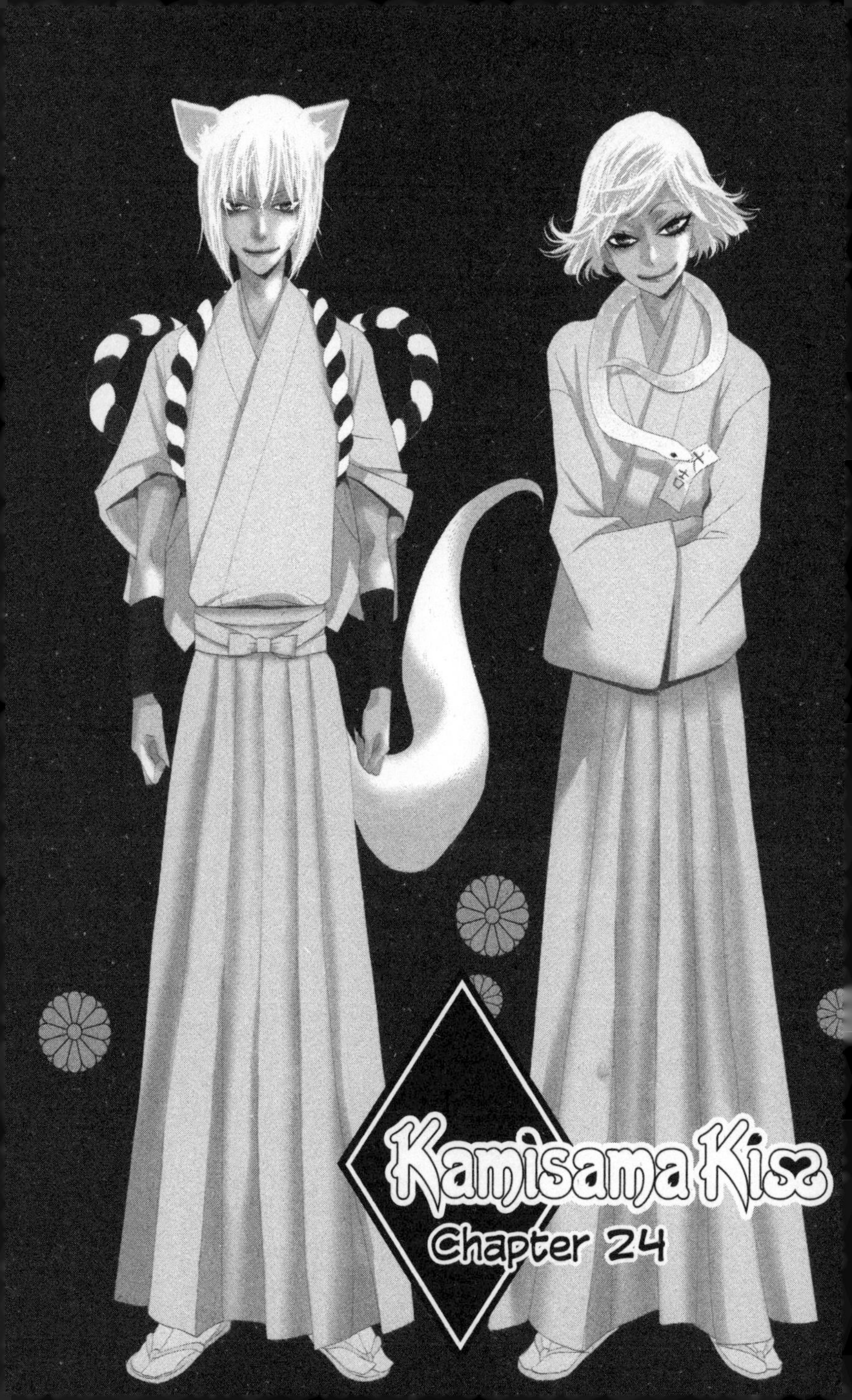
Kamisama Kiss
Chapter 24

Tomoe's
Ennui Blog

Aba!

Food!

I have to go on hiatus for a while.

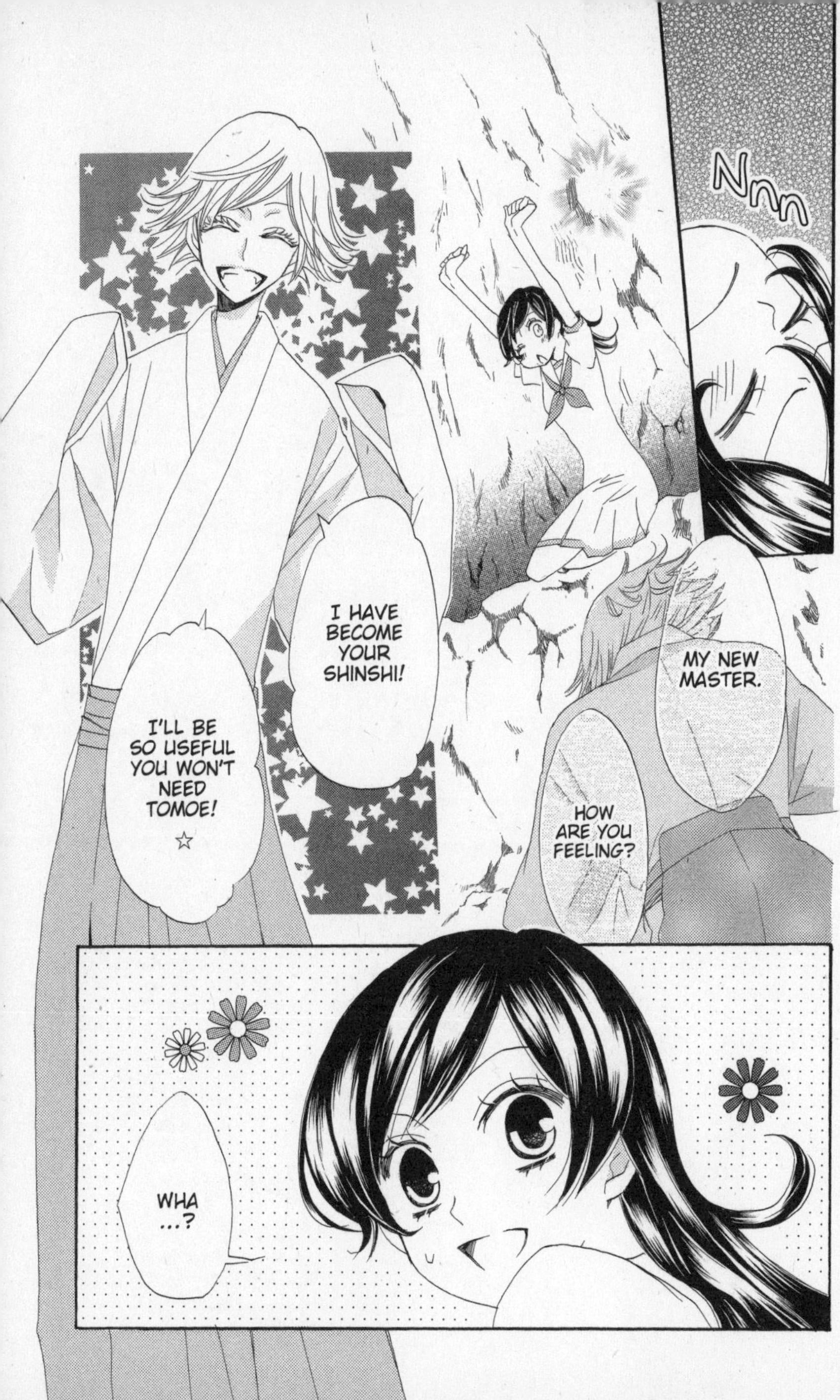
Nnn
MY NEW MASTER.
HOW ARE YOU FEELING?
I HAVE BECOME YOUR SHINSHI!
I'LL BE SO USEFUL YOU WON'T NEED TOMOE! ☆
WHA ...?

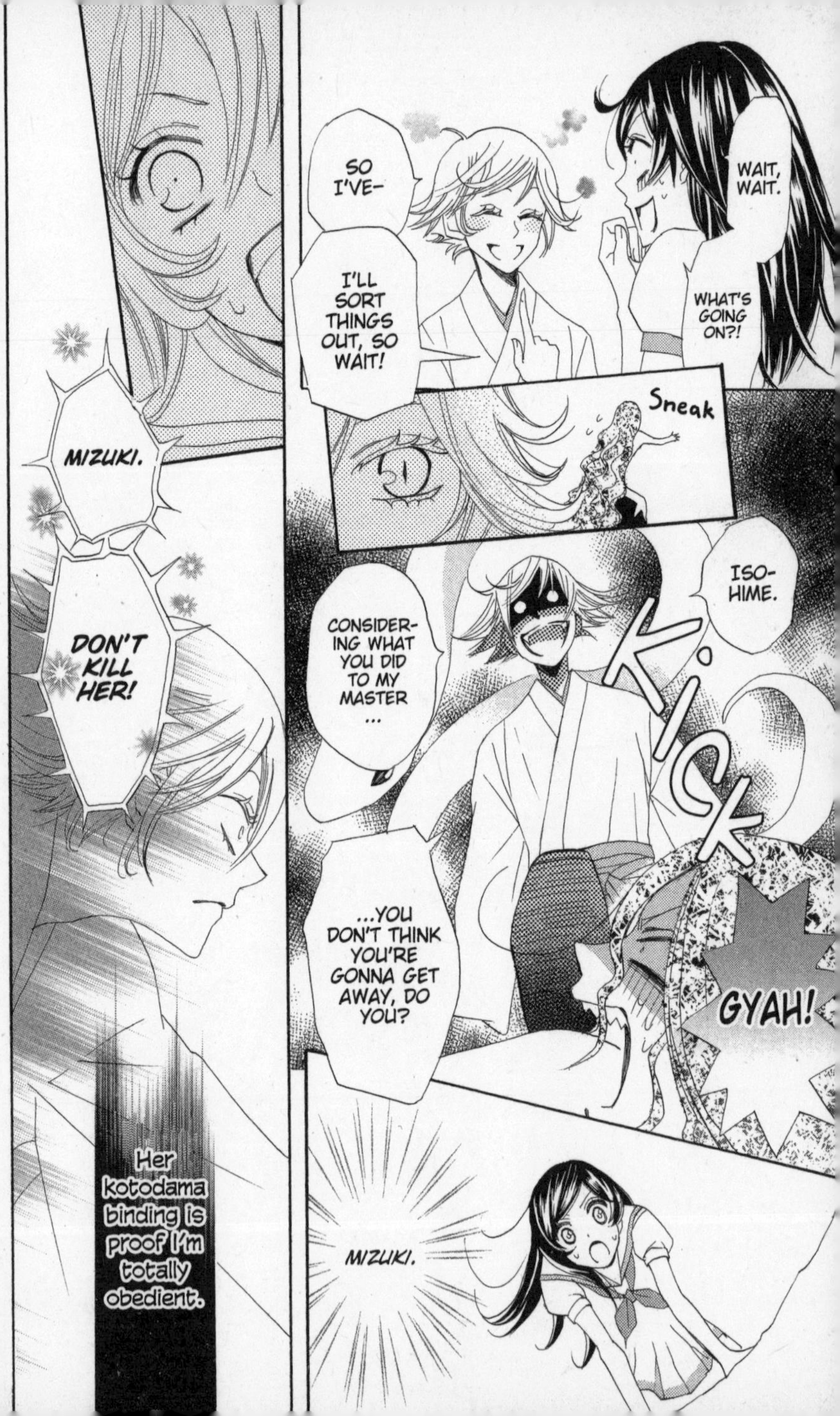
WAIT, WAIT.
WHAT'S GOING ON?!
SO I'VE-
I'LL SORT THINGS OUT, SO WAIT!
Sneak
ISO-HIME.
KICK
CONSIDER-ING WHAT YOU DID TO MY MASTER ...
...YOU DON'T THINK YOU'RE GONNA GET AWAY, DO YOU?
GYAH!
MIZUKI.
MIZUKI.
DON'T KILL HER!
Her kotodama binding is proof I'm totally obedient.

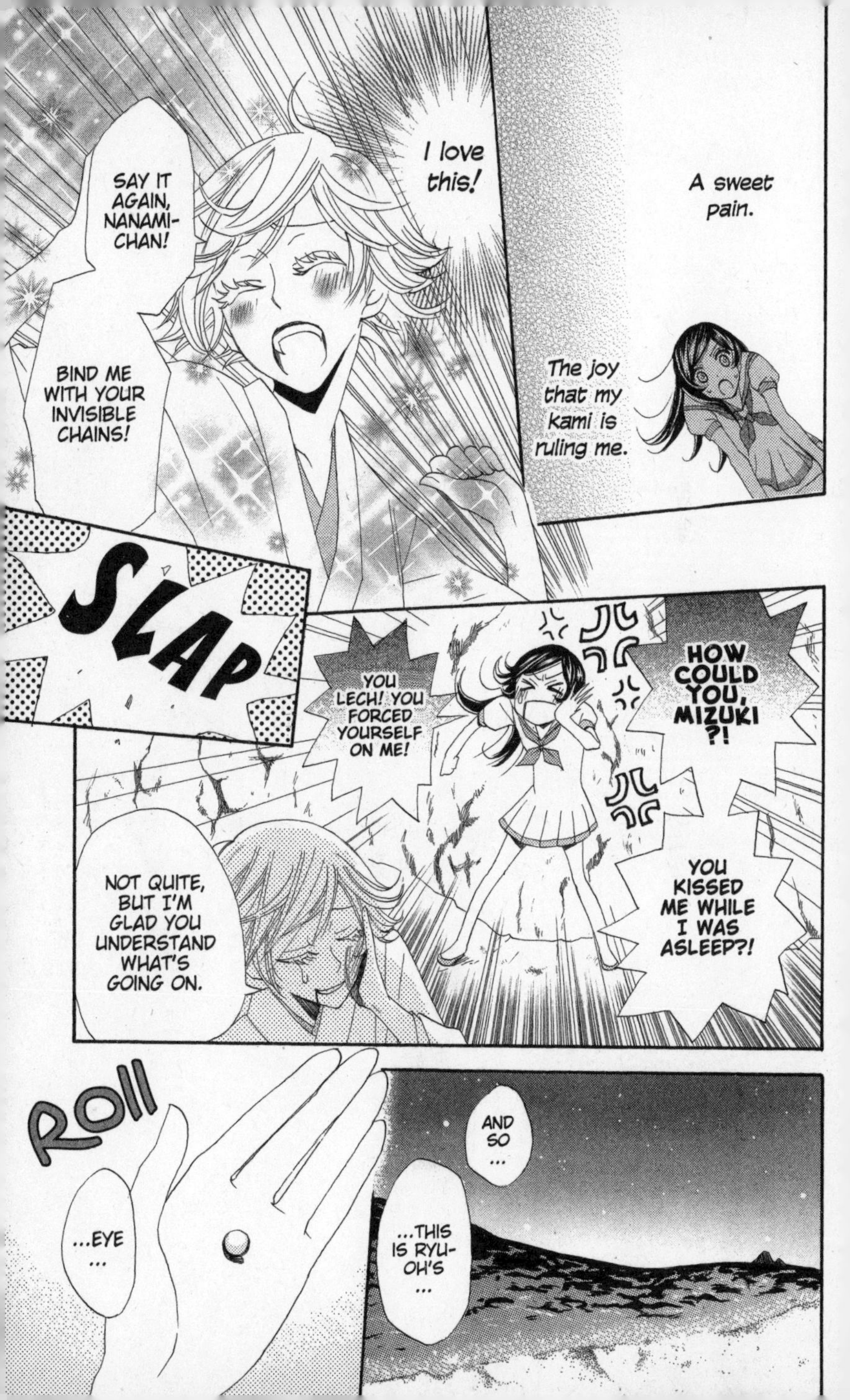
A sweet pain.
The joy that my kami is ruling me.
I love this!
SAY IT AGAIN, NANAMI-CHAN!
BIND ME WITH YOUR INVISIBLE CHAINS!
SLAP
HOW COULD YOU, MIZUKI?!
YOU KISSED ME WHILE I WAS ASLEEP?!
YOU LECH! YOU FORCED YOURSELF ON ME!
NOT QUITE, BUT I'M GLAD YOU UNDERSTAND WHAT'S GOING ON.
AND SO...
...THIS IS RYU-OH'S...
Roll
...EYE...

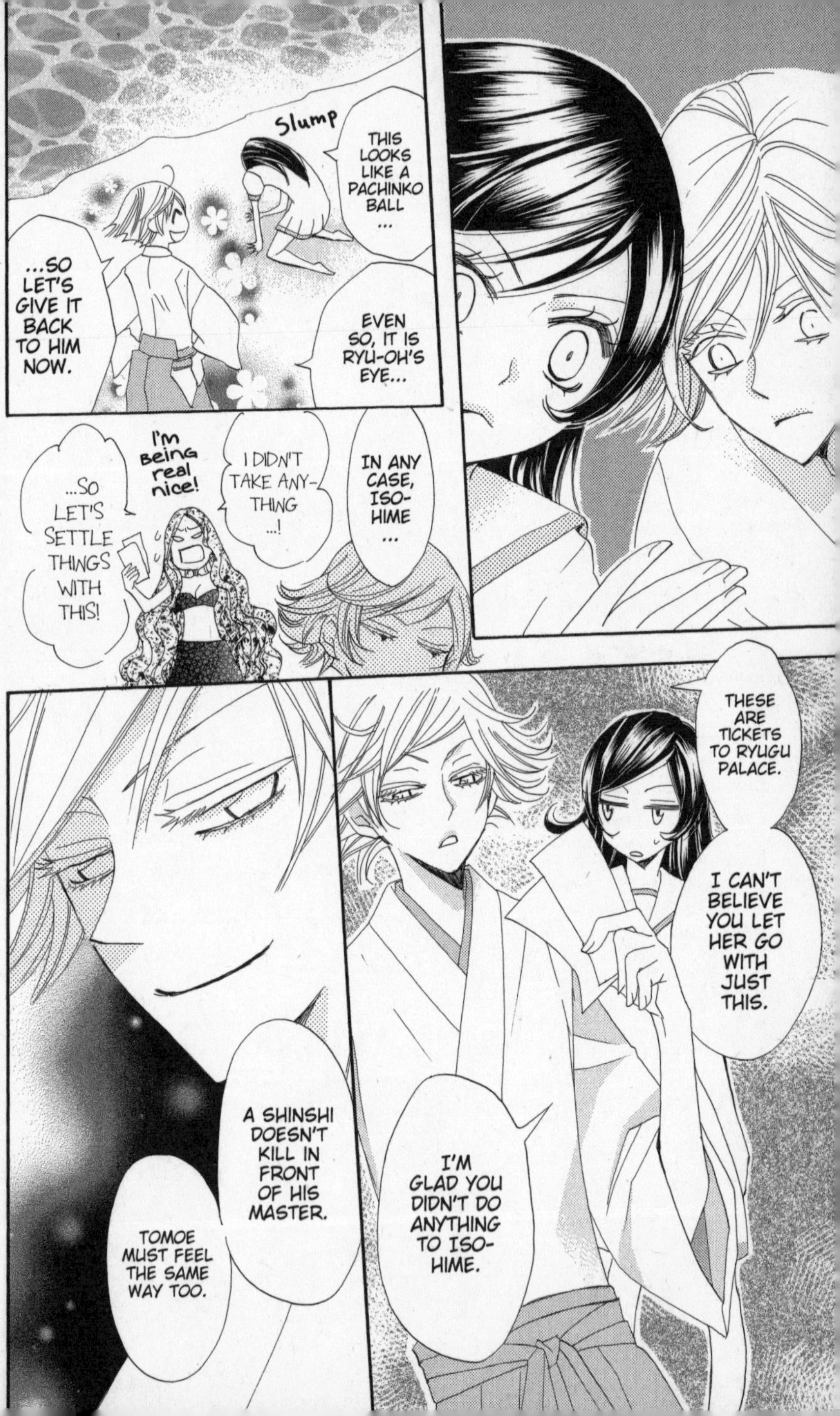
Slump
THIS LOOKS LIKE A PACHINKO BALL...
EVEN SO, IT IS RYU-OH'S EYE...
...SO LET'S GIVE IT BACK TO HIM NOW.
IN ANY CASE, ISO-HIME...
I DIDN'T TAKE ANYTHING...!
I'm being real nice!
...SO LET'S SETTLE THINGS WITH THIS!
THESE ARE TICKETS TO RYUGU PALACE.
I CAN'T BELIEVE YOU LET HER GO WITH JUST THIS.
I'M GLAD YOU DIDN'T DO ANYTHING TO ISO-HIME.
A SHINSHI DOESN'T KILL IN FRONT OF HIS MASTER.
TOMOE MUST FEEL THE SAME WAY TOO.

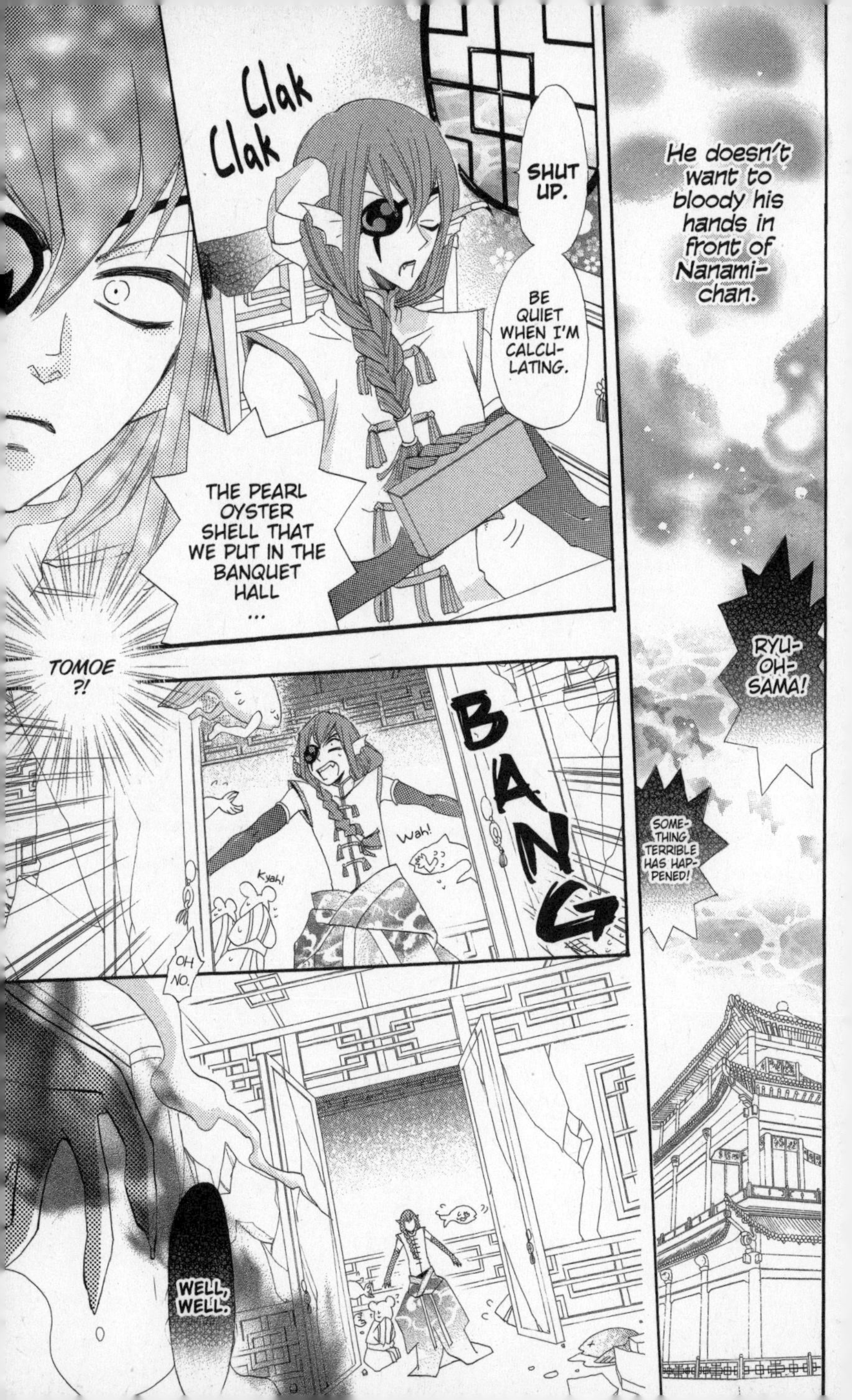

He doesn't want to bloody his hands in front of Nanami-chan.
RYU-OH-SAMA!
SOMETHING TERRIBLE HAS HAPPENED!
Clak Clak
SHUT UP.
BE QUIET WHEN I'M CALCULATING.
THE PEARL OYSTER SHELL THAT WE PUT IN THE BANQUET HALL ...
TOMOE ?!
BANG
Wah!
Kyah!
OH NO.
WELL, WELL.

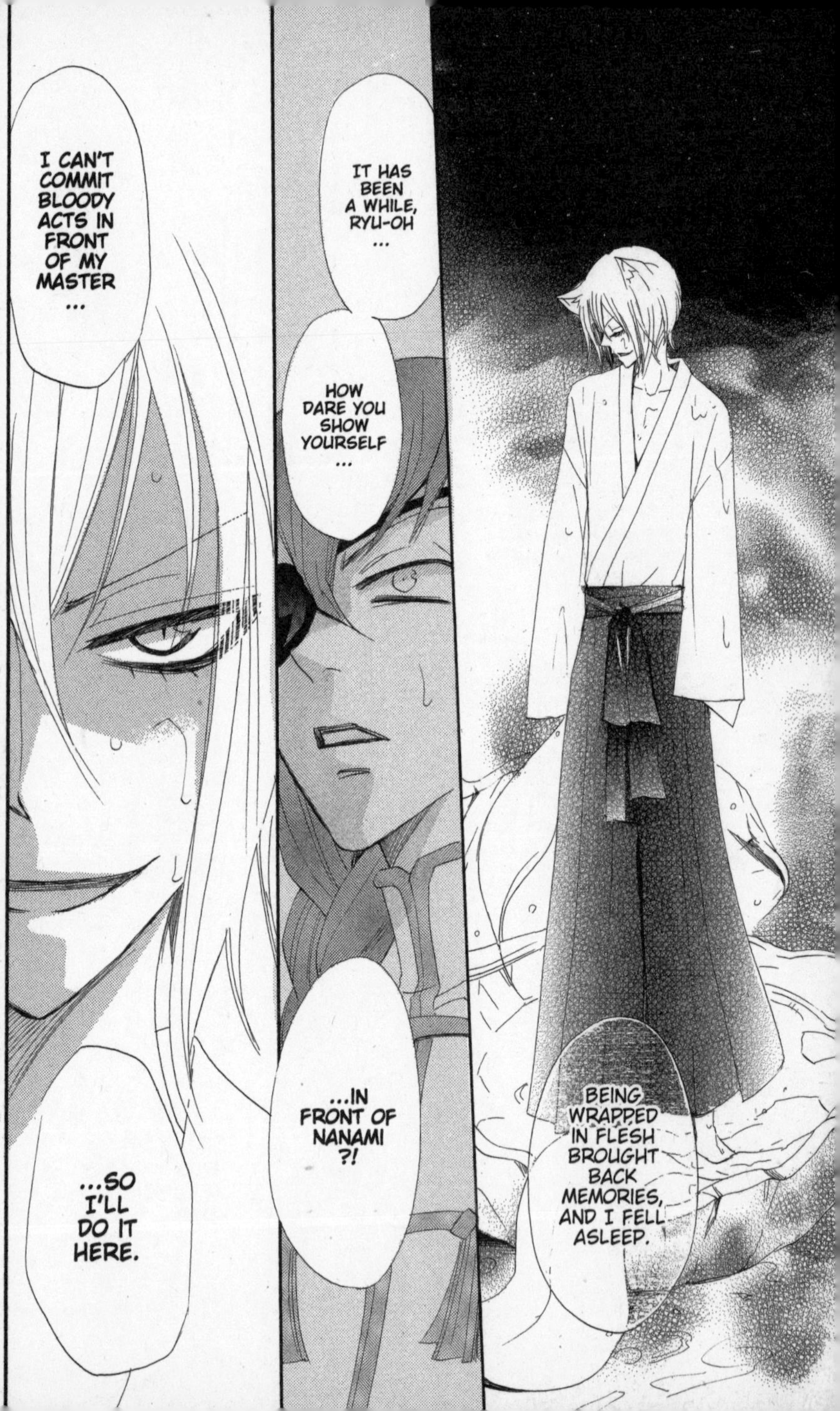
BEING WRAPPED IN FLESH BROUGHT BACK MEMORIES, AND I FELL ASLEEP.
IT HAS BEEN A WHILE, RYU-OH ...
HOW DARE YOU SHOW YOURSELF ...
...IN FRONT OF NANAMI ?!
I CAN'T COMMIT BLOODY ACTS IN FRONT OF MY MASTER ...
...SO I'LL DO IT HERE.

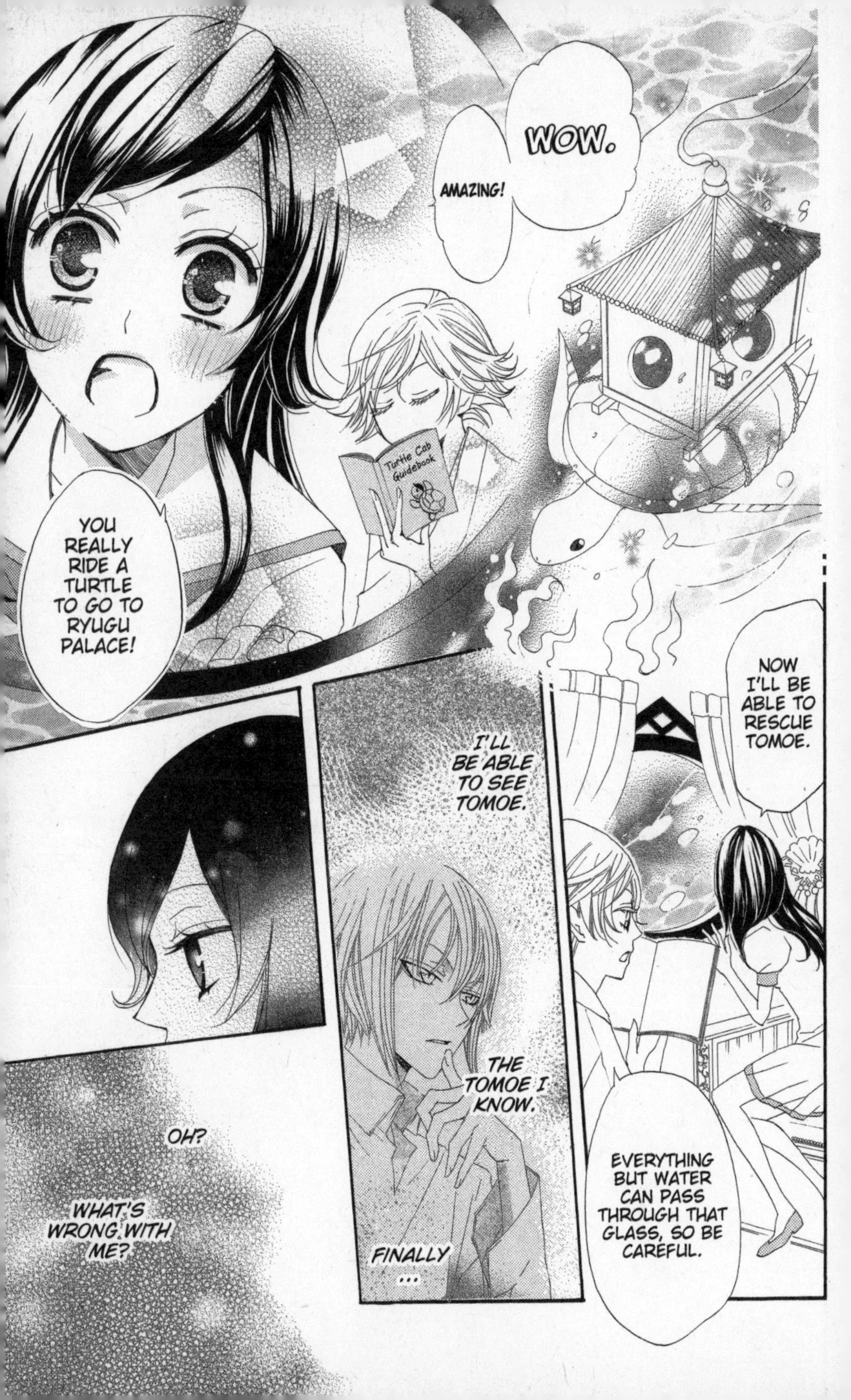
WOW.
AMAZING!
Turtle Cab Guidebook
YOU REALLY RIDE A TURTLE TO GO TO RYUGU PALACE!
NOW I'LL BE ABLE TO RESCUE TOMOE.
EVERYTHING BUT WATER CAN PASS THROUGH THAT GLASS, SO BE CAREFUL.
I'LL BE ABLE TO SEE TOMOE.
THE TOMOE I KNOW.
FINALLY ...
OH?
WHAT'S WRONG WITH ME?

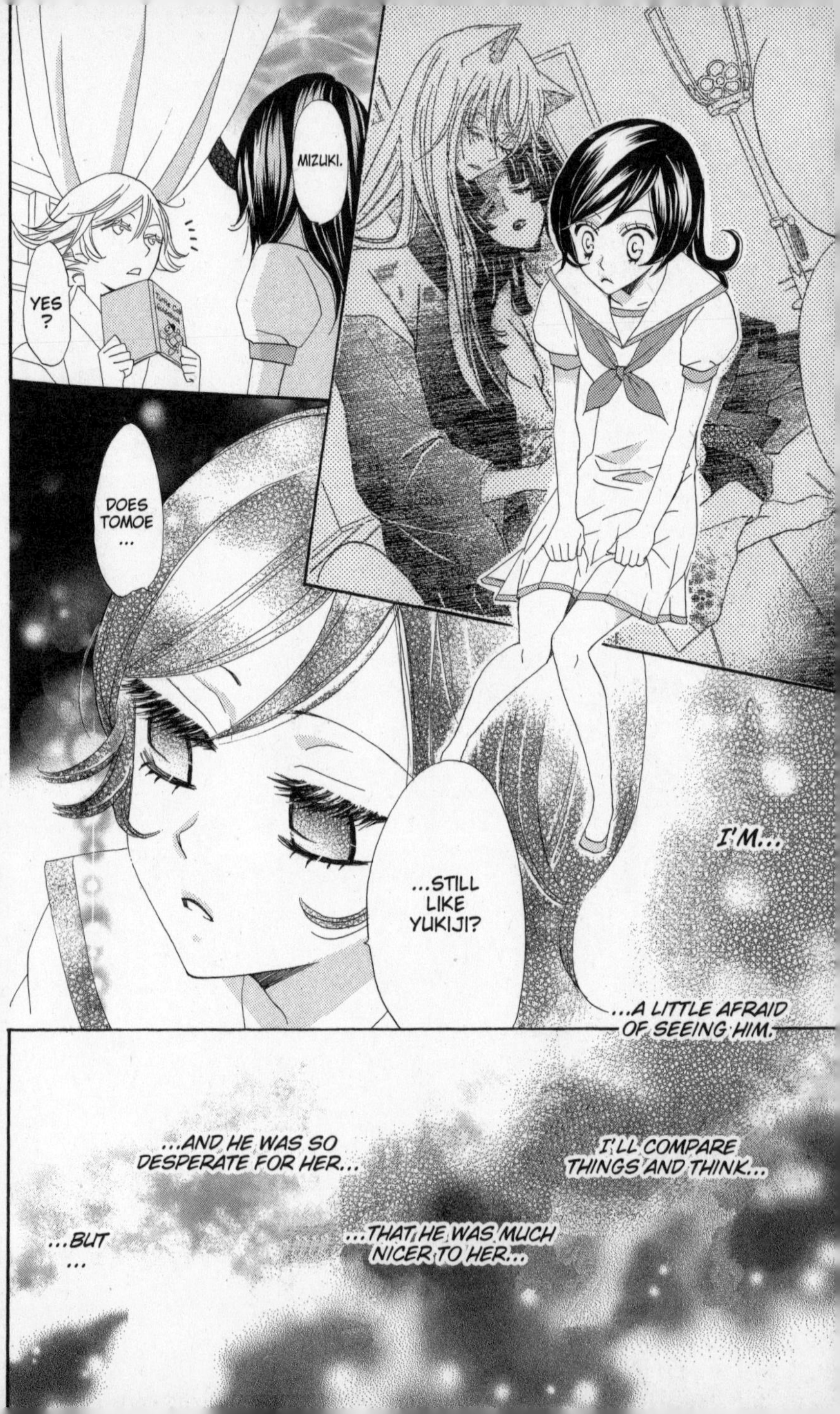
MIZUKI.
YES ?
DOES TOMOE ...
...STILL LIKE YUKIJI?
I'M...
...A LITTLE AFRAID OF SEEING HIM.
I'LL COMPARE THINGS AND THINK...
...THAT HE WAS MUCH NICER TO HER...
...AND HE WAS SO DESPERATE FOR HER...
...BUT ...

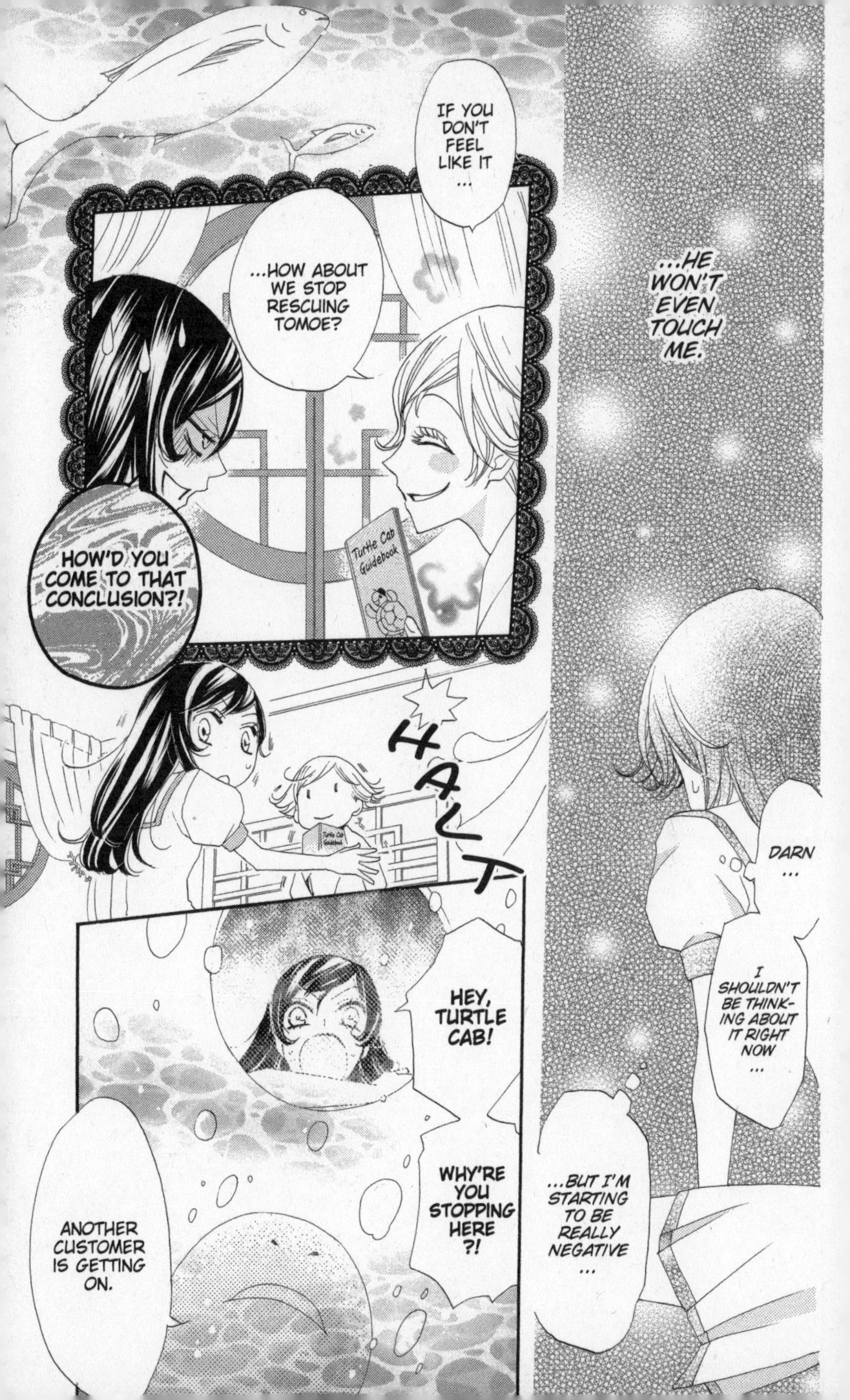
...HE WON'T EVEN TOUCH ME.
DARN...
I SHOULDN'T BE THINKING ABOUT IT RIGHT NOW...
...BUT I'M STARTING TO BE REALLY NEGATIVE...
IF YOU DON'T FEEL LIKE IT...
...HOW ABOUT WE STOP RESCUING TOMOE?
HOW'D YOU COME TO THAT CONCLUSION?!
Turtle Cab Guidebook
HALT
HEY, TURTLE CAB!
WHY'RE YOU STOPPING HERE?!
ANOTHER CUSTOMER IS GETTING ON.

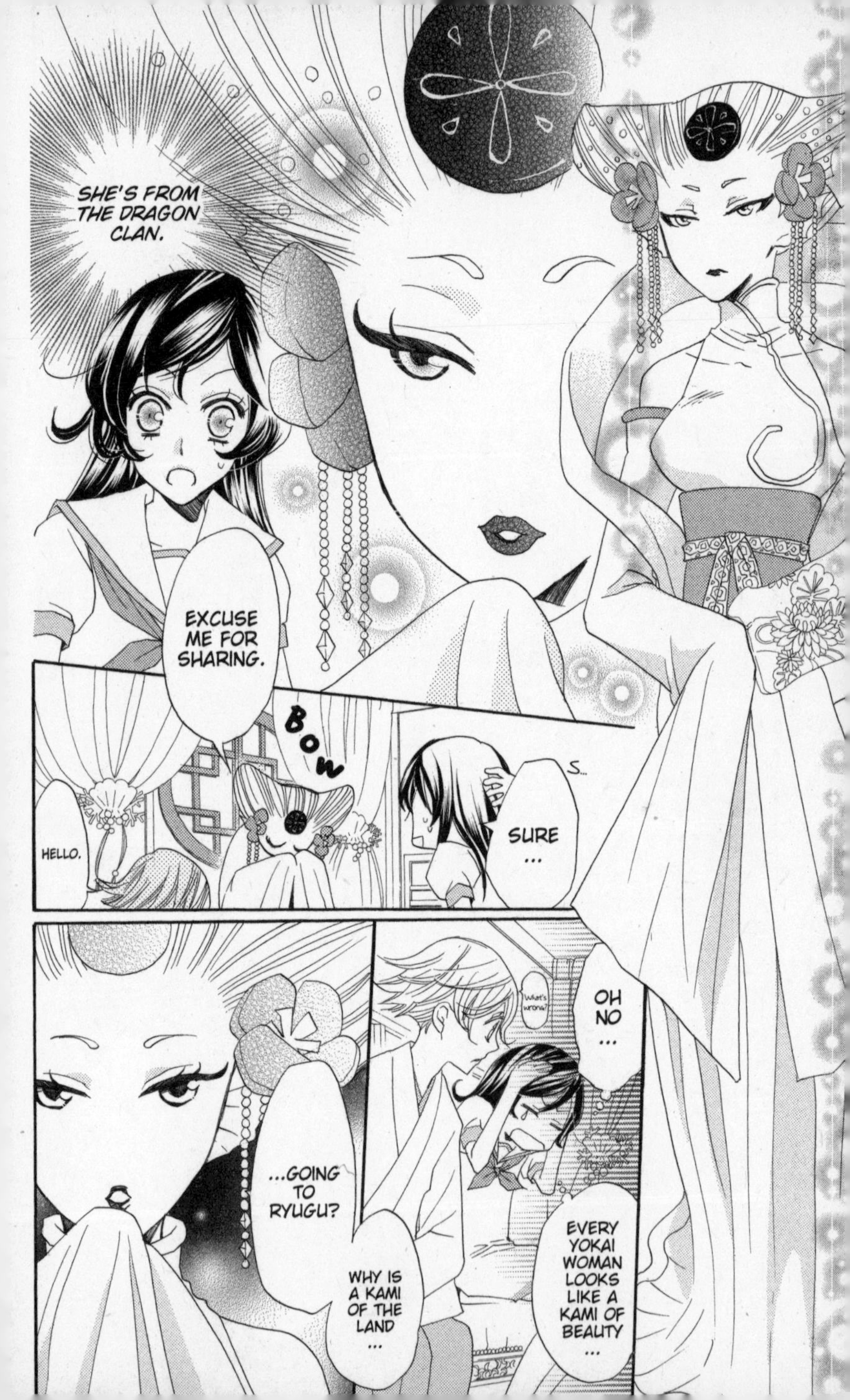
SHE'S FROM THE DRAGON CLAN.
EXCUSE ME FOR SHARING.
S...
SURE ...
BOW
HELLO.
What's wrong?
OH NO ...
EVERY YOKAI WOMAN LOOKS LIKE A KAMI OF BEAUTY ...
WHY IS A KAMI OF THE LAND ...
...GOING TO RYUGU?

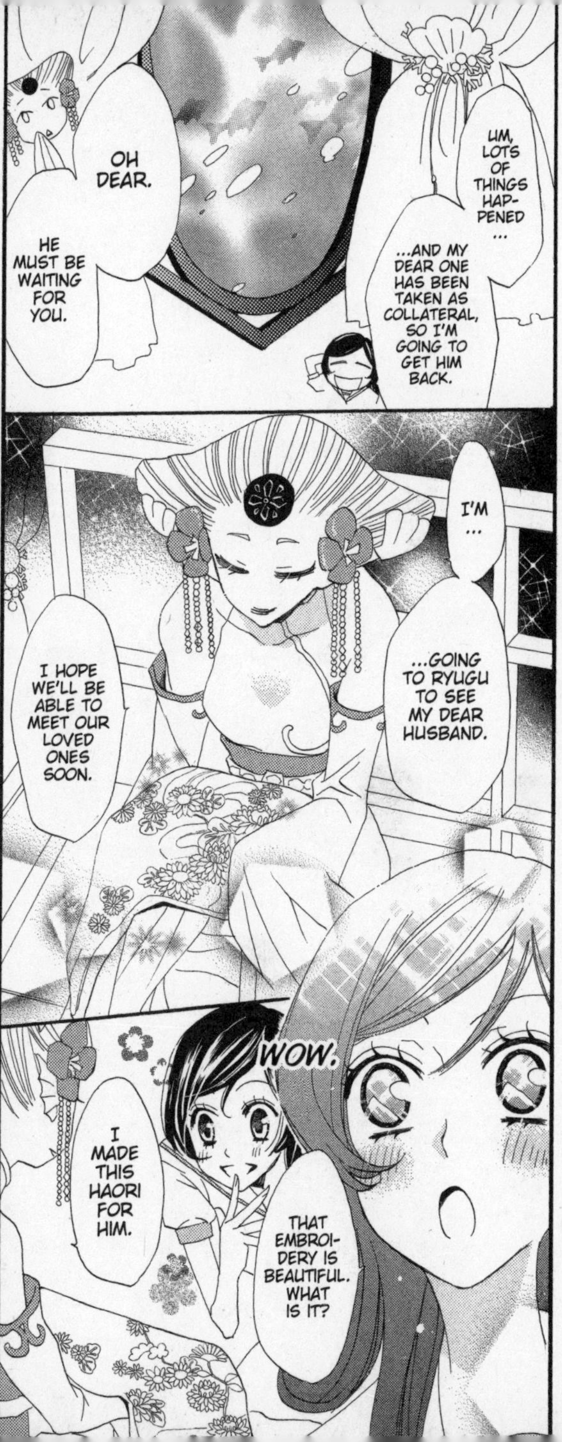
UM, LOTS OF THINGS HAPPENED...
...AND MY DEAR ONE HAS BEEN TAKEN AS COLLATERAL, SO I'M GOING TO GET HIM BACK.
OH DEAR.
HE MUST BE WAITING FOR YOU.
I'M...
...GOING TO RYUGU TO SEE MY DEAR HUSBAND.
I HOPE WE'LL BE ABLE TO MEET OUR LOVED ONES SOON.
WOW.
THAT EMBROIDERY IS BEAUTIFUL. WHAT IS IT?
I MADE THIS HAORI FOR HIM.

Thank you for reading!

I hope we can meet again in Volume 5. Kaga-san, Shun, Okazaki-san, thank you for coming over to help!

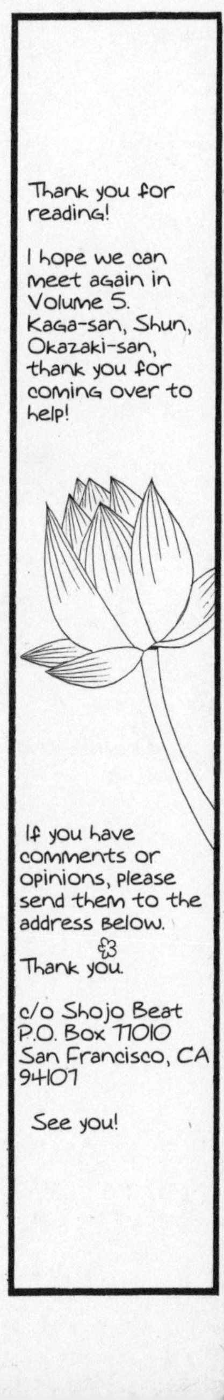

If you have comments or opinions, please send them to the address below.

Thank you.

c/o Shojo Beat
P.O. Box 77010
San Francisco, CA
94107

See you!

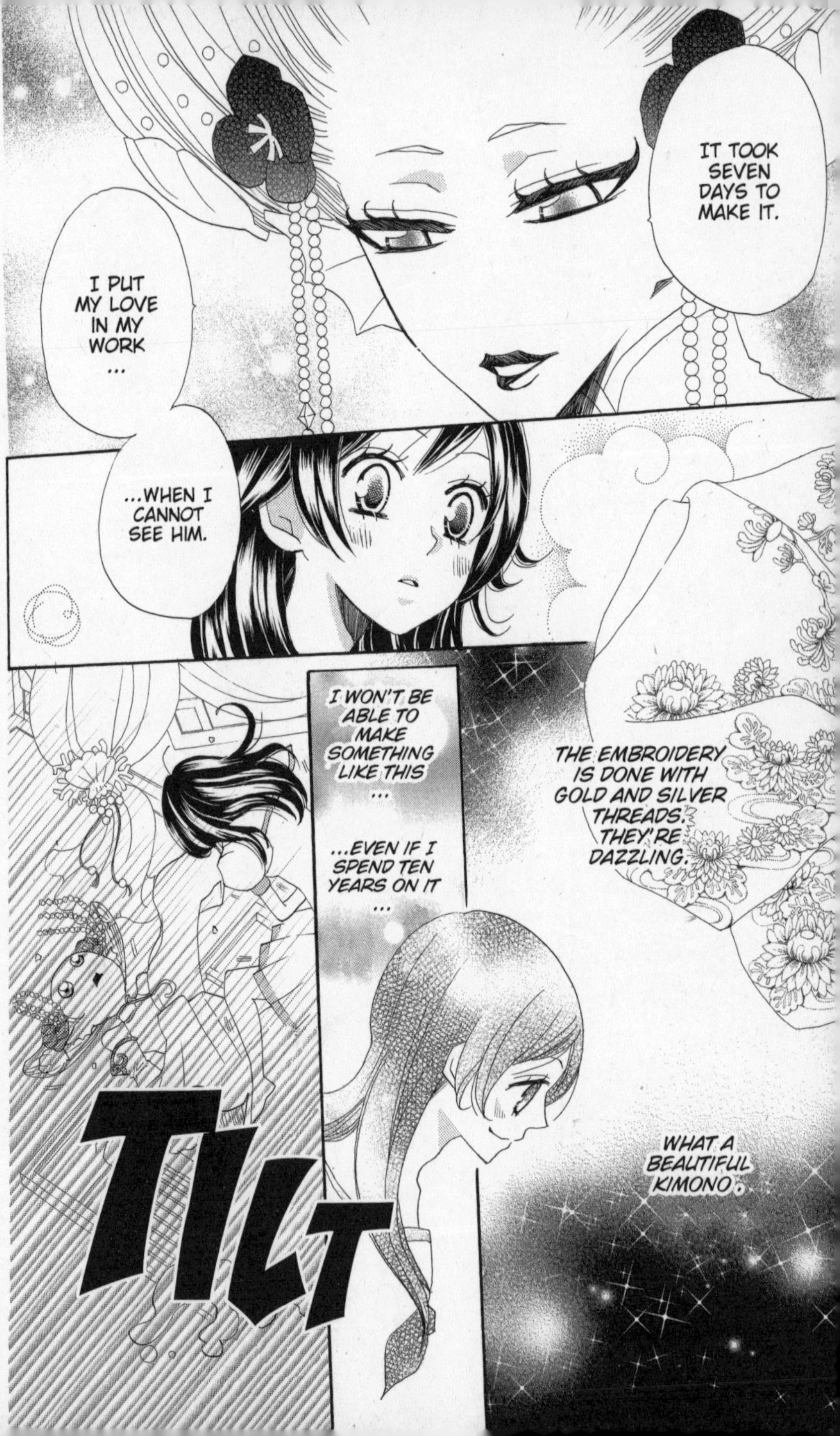

IT TOOK SEVEN DAYS TO MAKE IT.
I PUT MY LOVE IN MY WORK ...
...WHEN I CANNOT SEE HIM.
THE EMBROIDERY IS DONE WITH GOLD AND SILVER THREADS. THEY'RE DAZZLING.
WHAT A BEAUTIFUL KIMONO.
I WON'T BE ABLE TO MAKE SOMETHING LIKE THIS ...
...EVEN IF I SPEND TEN YEARS ON IT ...
TILT

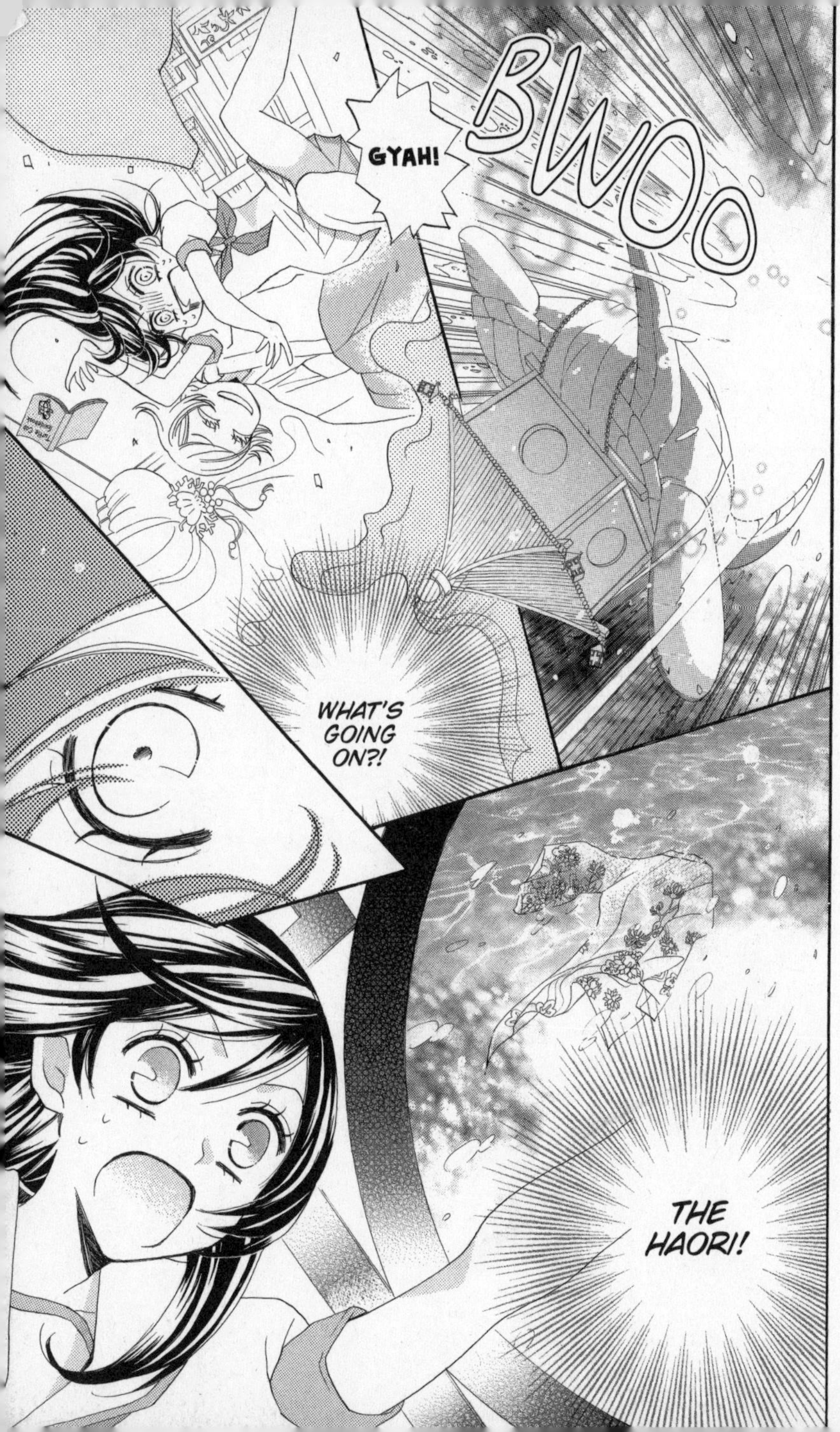
BWOO
GYAH!
WHAT'S GOING ON?!
THE HAORI!

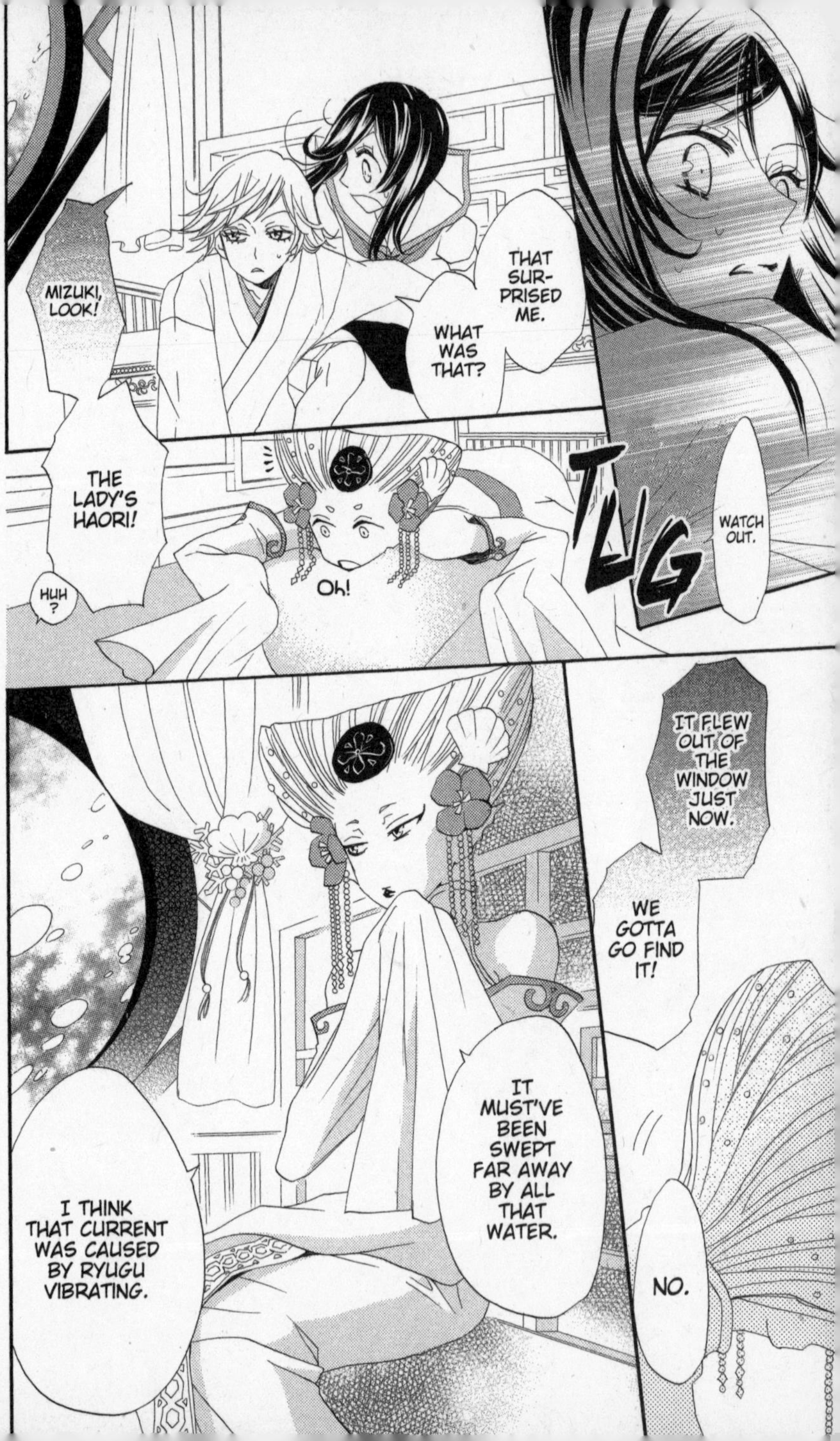

TUG
WATCH OUT.
THAT SURPRISED ME.
WHAT WAS THAT?
MIZUKI, LOOK!
THE LADY'S HAORI!
Oh!
HUH?
IT FLEW OUT OF THE WINDOW JUST NOW.
WE GOTTA GO FIND IT!
NO.
IT MUST'VE BEEN SWEPT FAR AWAY BY ALL THAT WATER.
I THINK THAT CURRENT WAS CAUSED BY RYUGU VIBRATING.

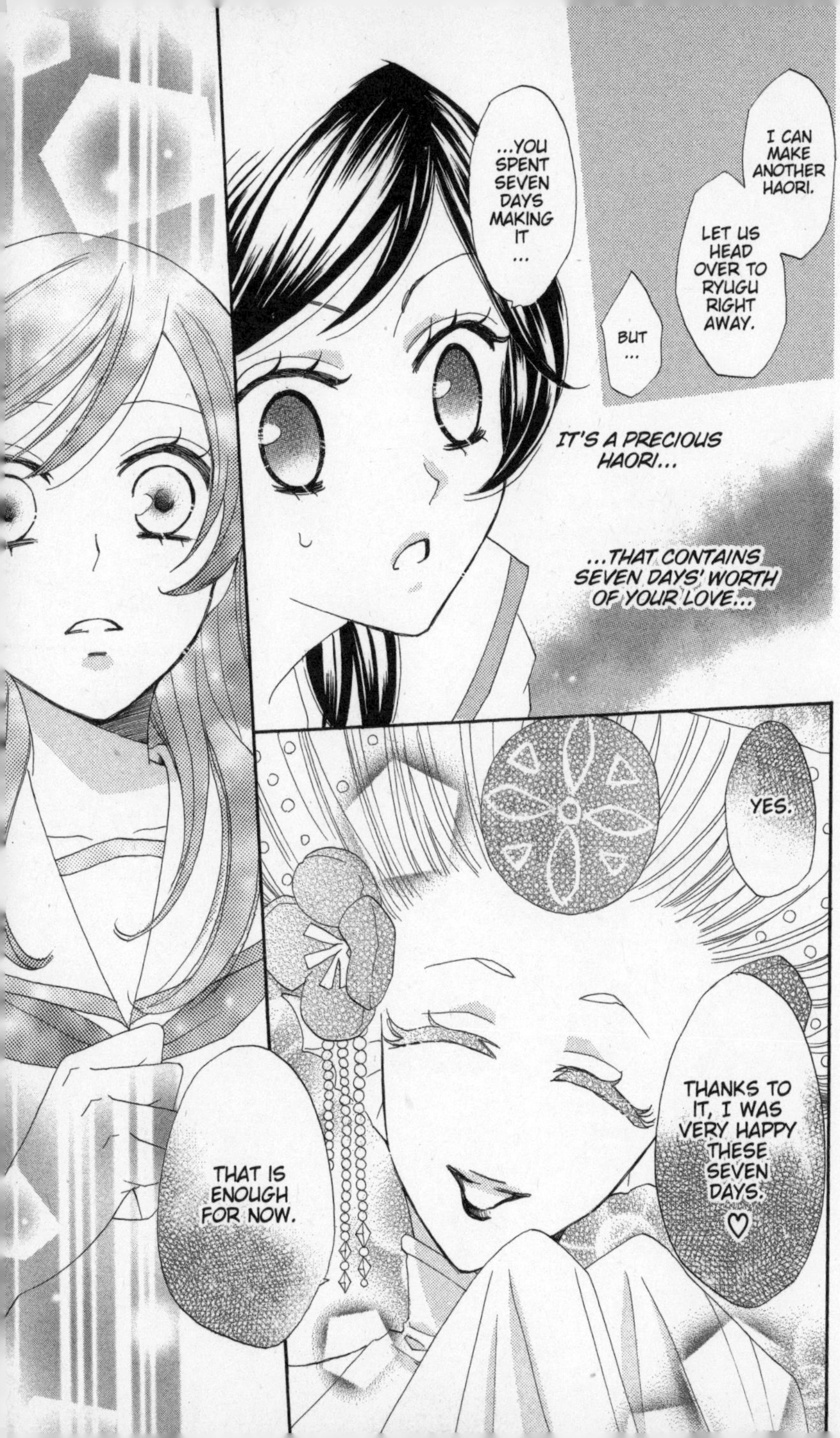
I CAN MAKE ANOTHER HAORI.
LET US HEAD OVER TO RYUGU RIGHT AWAY.
BUT ...
...YOU SPENT SEVEN DAYS MAKING IT ...
IT'S A PRECIOUS HAORI...
...THAT CONTAINS SEVEN DAYS' WORTH OF YOUR LOVE...
YES.
THANKS TO IT, I WAS VERY HAPPY THESE SEVEN DAYS. ♡
THAT IS ENOUGH FOR NOW.

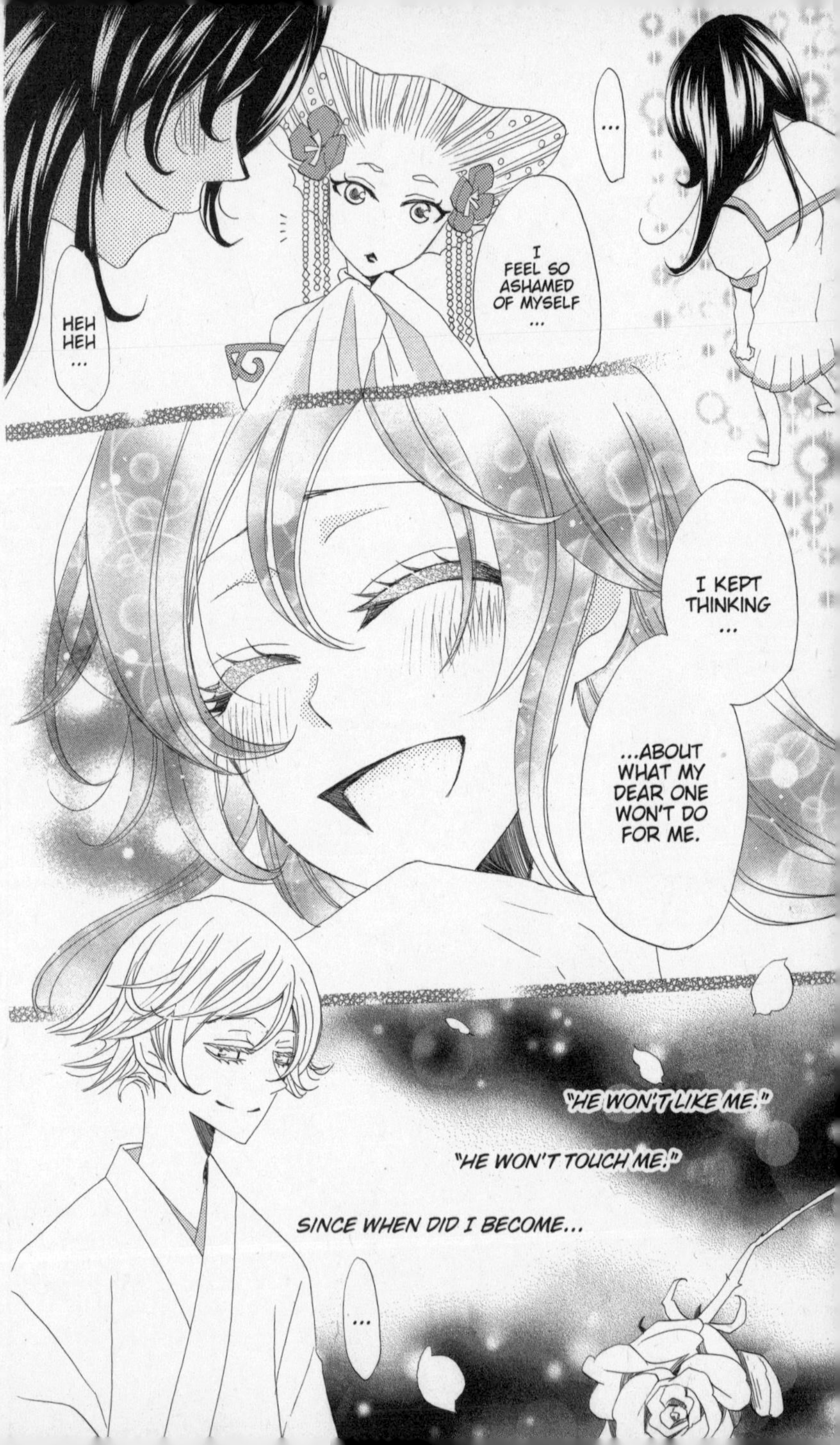
...
I FEEL SO ASHAMED OF MYSELF...
HEH HEH...
I KEPT THINKING...
...ABOUT WHAT MY DEAR ONE WON'T DO FOR ME.
"HE WON'T LIKE ME."
"HE WON'T TOUCH ME."
SINCE WHEN DID I BECOME...
...

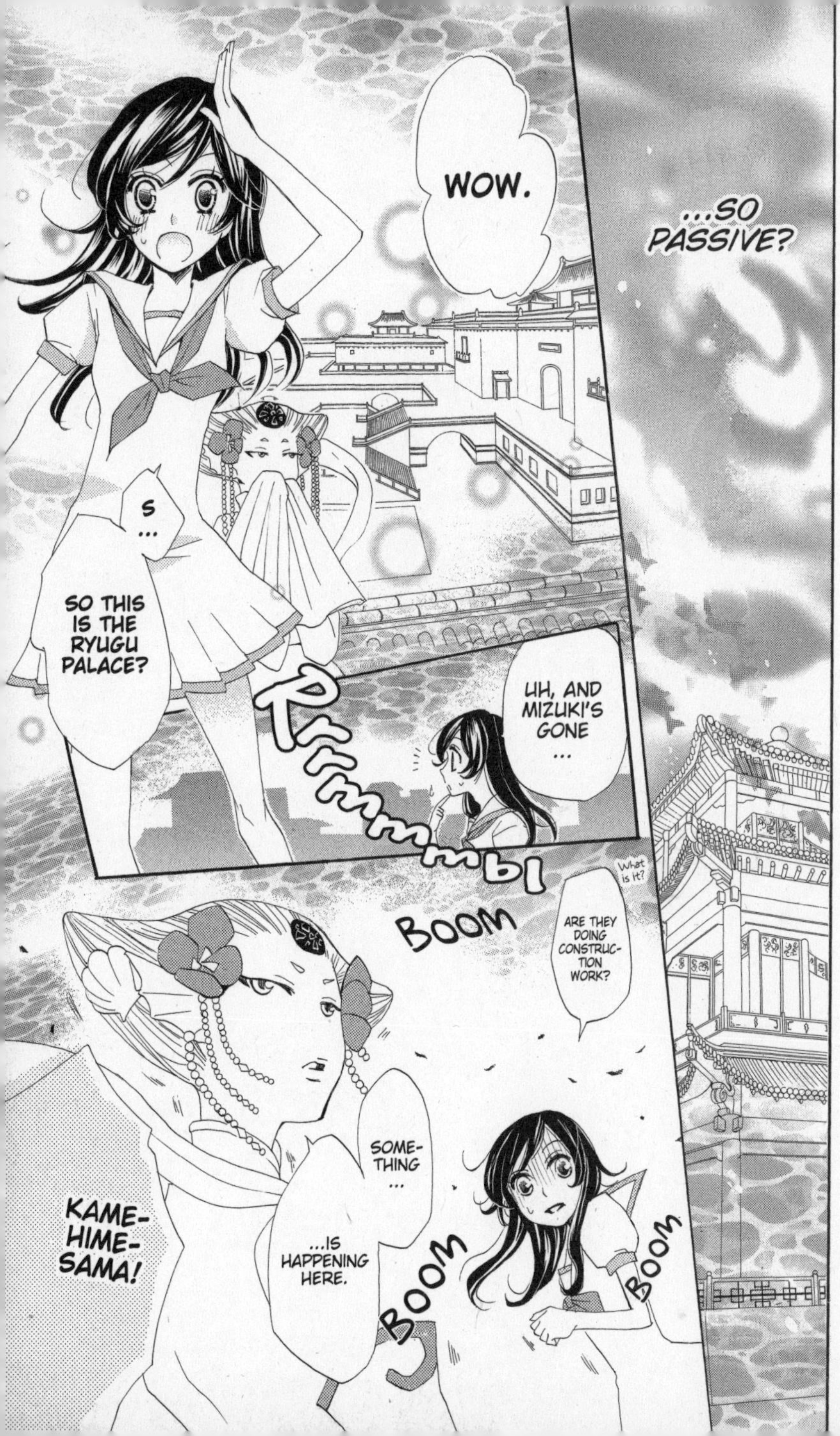
...SO PASSIVE?
WOW.
S...
SO THIS IS THE RYUGU PALACE?
UH, AND MIZUKI'S GONE ...
Prrmmmbl
BOOM
What is it?
ARE THEY DOING CONSTRUCTION WORK?
SOMETHING...
...IS HAPPENING HERE.
KAME-HIME-SAMA!
BOOM
BOOM

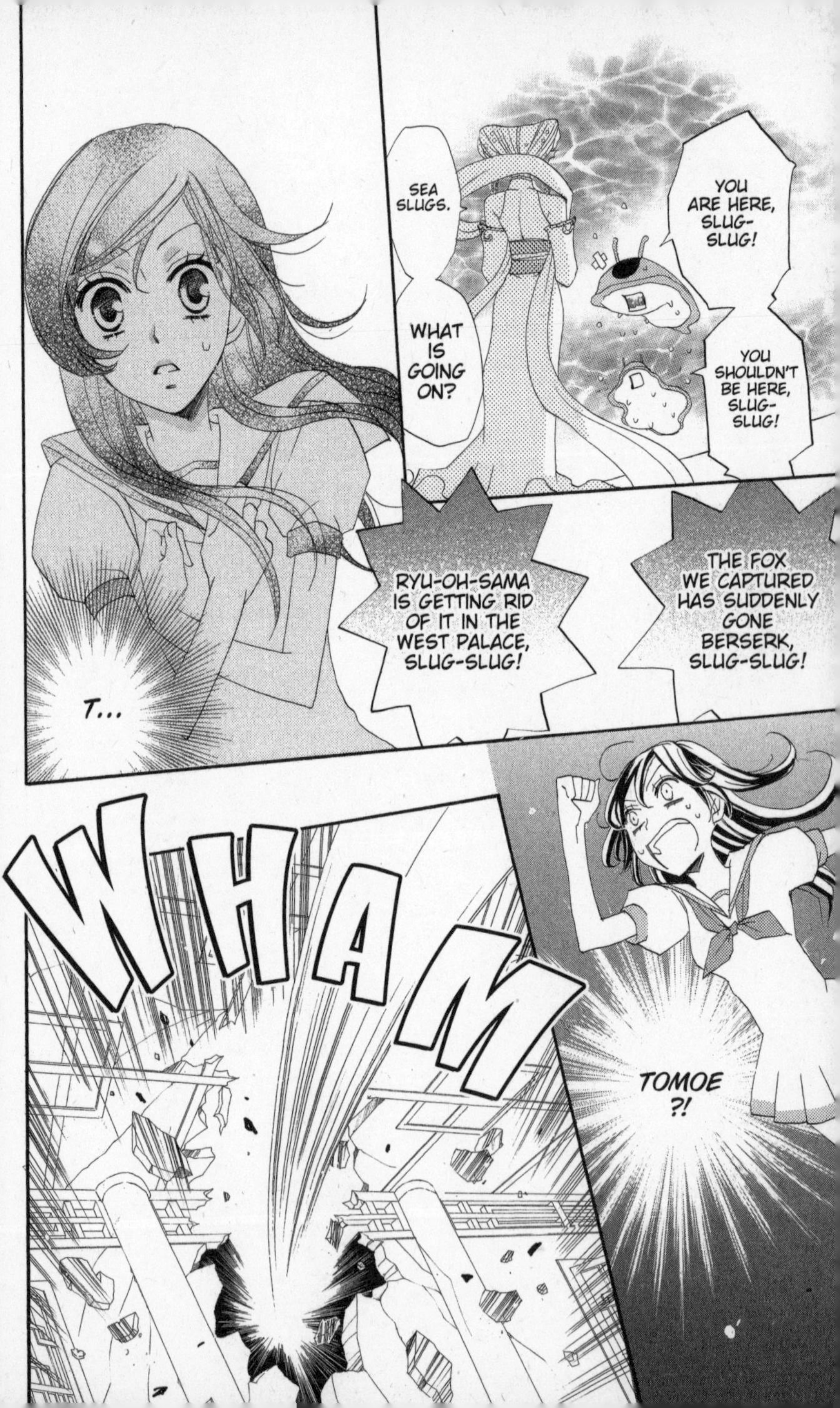
YOU ARE HERE, SLUG-SLUG!
YOU SHOULDN'T BE HERE, SLUG-SLUG!
SEA SLUGS.
WHAT IS GOING ON?
THE FOX WE CAPTURED HAS SUDDENLY GONE BERSERK, SLUG-SLUG!
RYU-OH-SAMA IS GETTING RID OF IT IN THE WEST PALACE, SLUG-SLUG!
T...
TOMOE ?!
WHAM

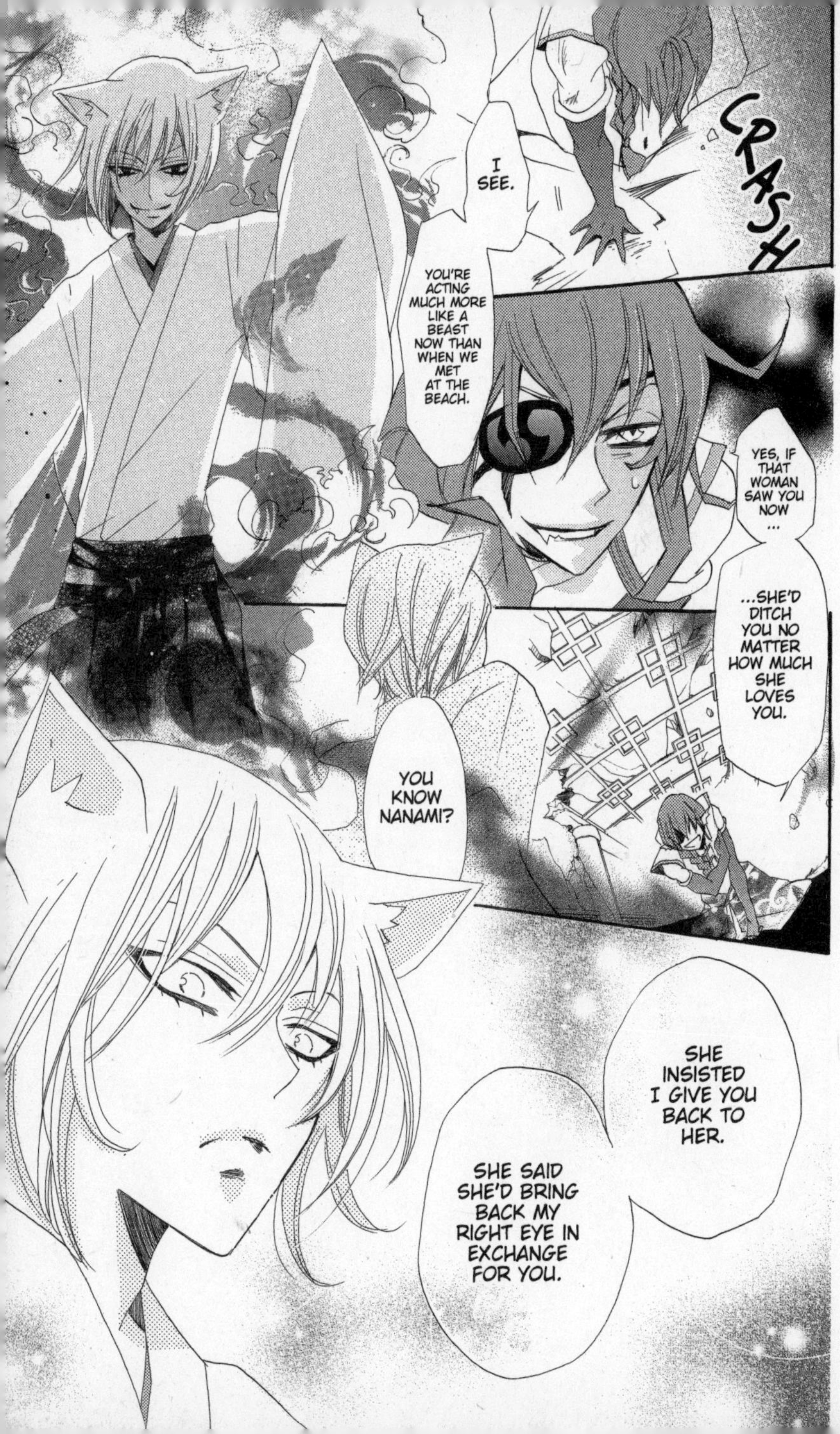
CRASH
I SEE.
YOU'RE ACTING MUCH MORE LIKE A BEAST NOW THAN WHEN WE MET AT THE BEACH.
YES, IF THAT WOMAN SAW YOU NOW ...
...SHE'D DITCH YOU NO MATTER HOW MUCH SHE LOVES YOU.
YOU KNOW NANAMI?
SHE INSISTED I GIVE YOU BACK TO HER.
SHE SAID SHE'D BRING BACK MY RIGHT EYE IN EXCHANGE FOR YOU.

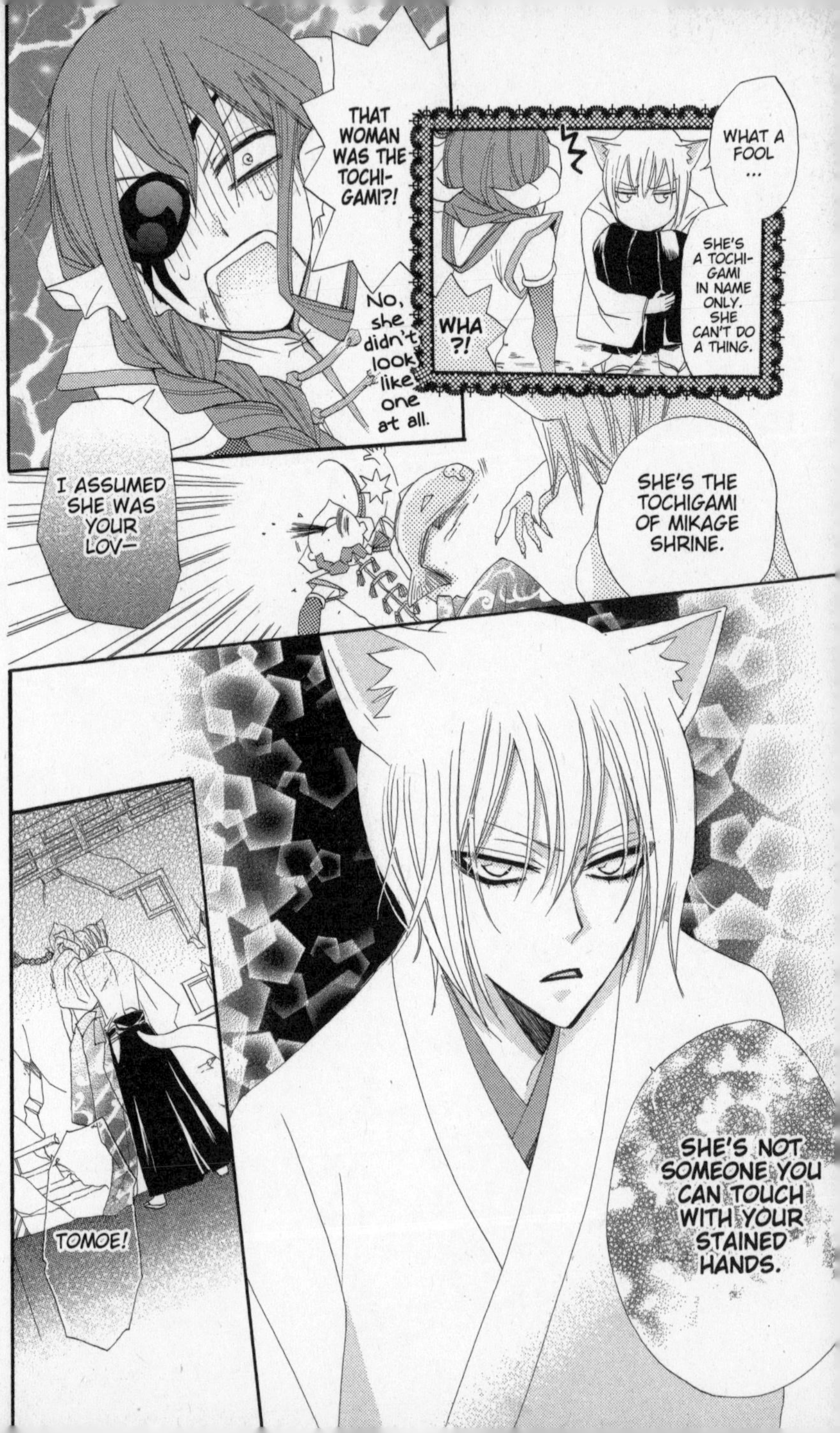
WHAT A FOOL ...
SHE'S A TOCHIGAMI IN NAME ONLY. SHE CAN'T DO A THING.
WHA ?!
THAT WOMAN WAS THE TOCHIGAMI?!
No, she didn't look like one at all.
SHE'S THE TOCHIGAMI OF MIKAGE SHRINE.
I ASSUMED SHE WAS YOUR LOV—
SHE'S NOT SOMEONE YOU CAN TOUCH WITH YOUR STAINED HANDS.
TOMOE!

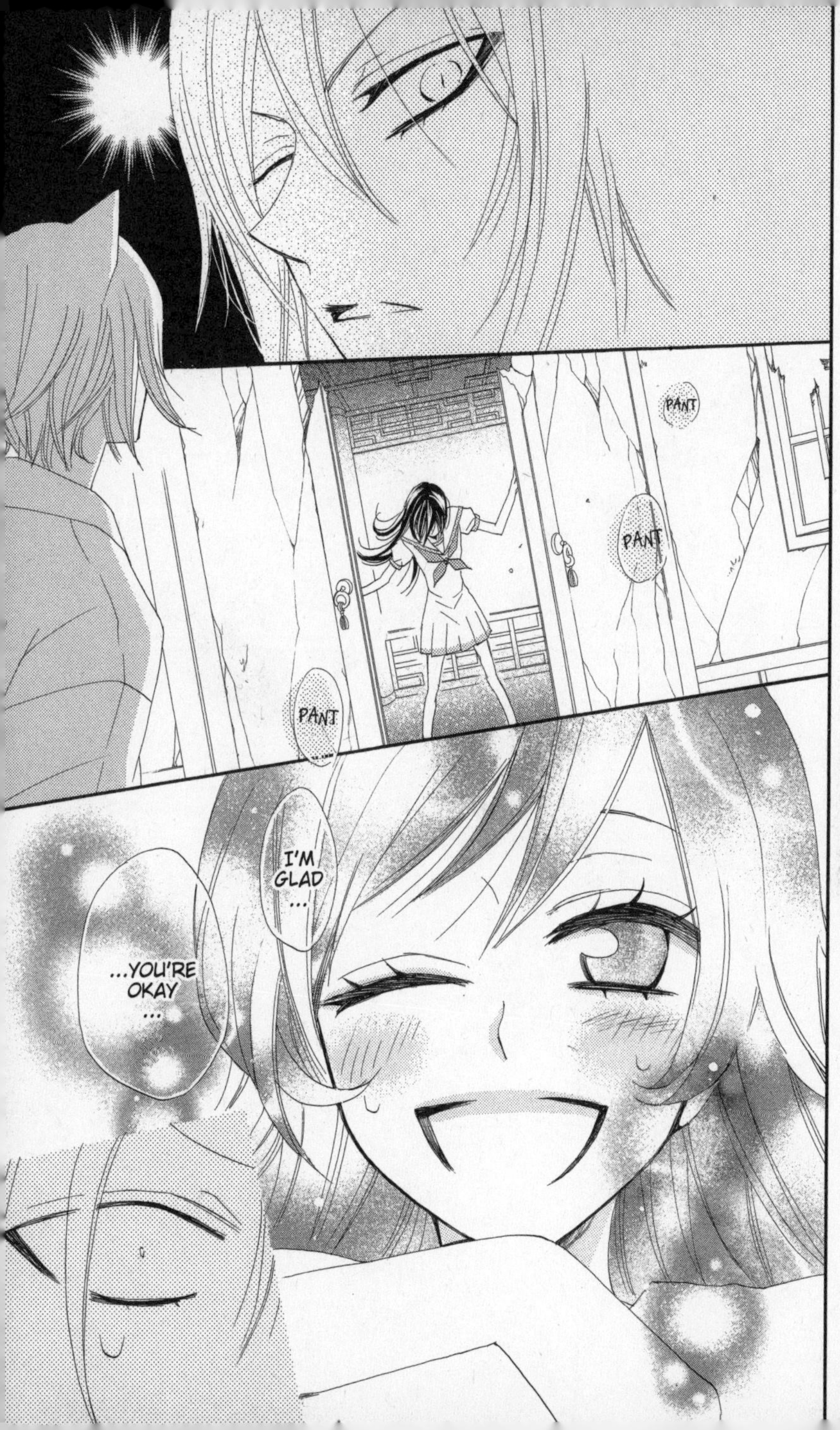
PANT
PANT
PANT
I'M GLAD...
...YOU'RE OKAY...

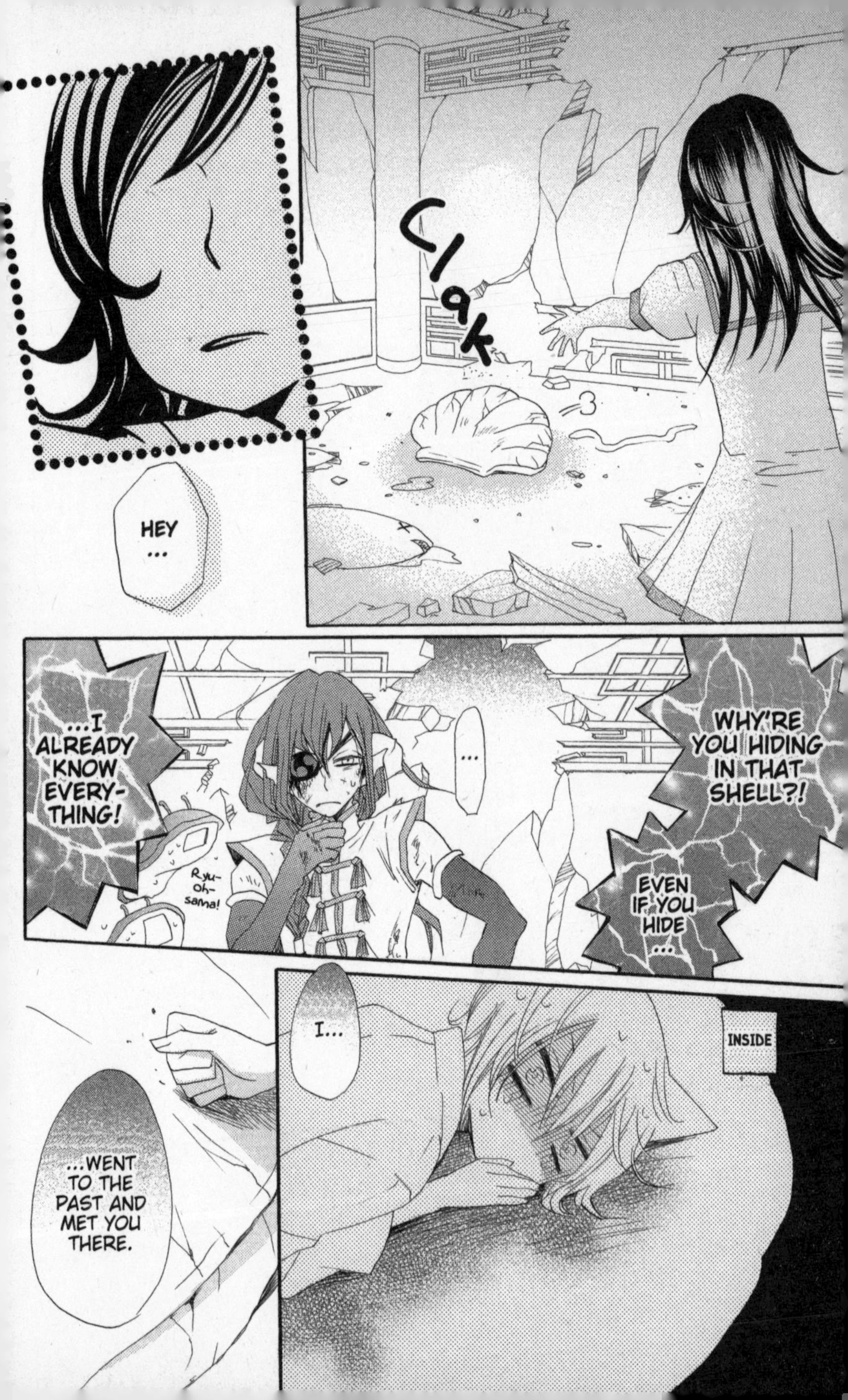
Clak
HEY ...
WHY'RE YOU HIDING IN THAT SHELL?!
EVEN IF YOU HIDE ...
...
Ryu-Oh-sama!
...I ALREADY KNOW EVERY-THING!
INSIDE
I...
...WENT TO THE PAST AND MET YOU THERE.

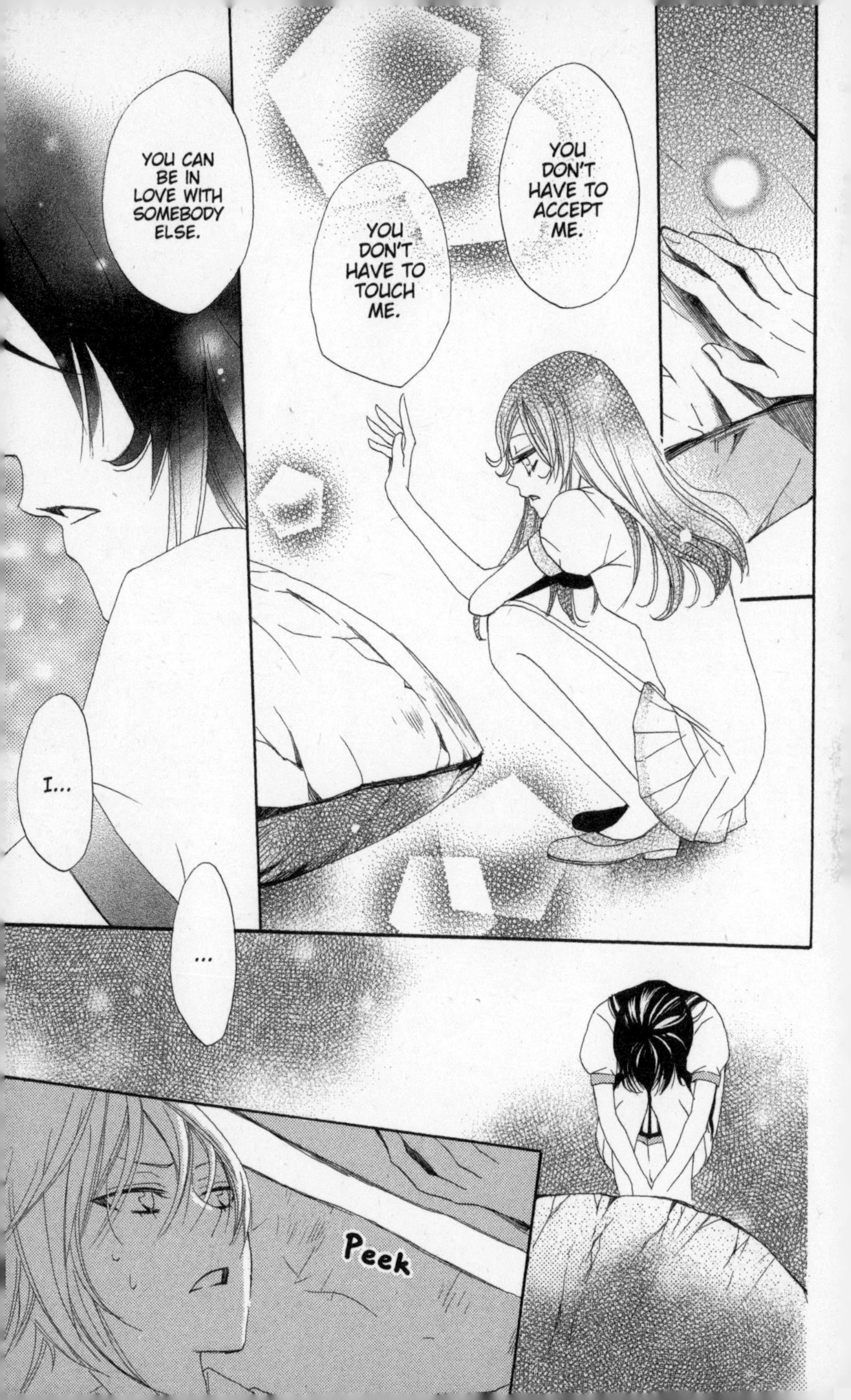
YOU DON'T HAVE TO ACCEPT ME.
YOU DON'T HAVE TO TOUCH ME.
YOU CAN BE IN LOVE WITH SOMEBODY ELSE.
I...
...
Peek

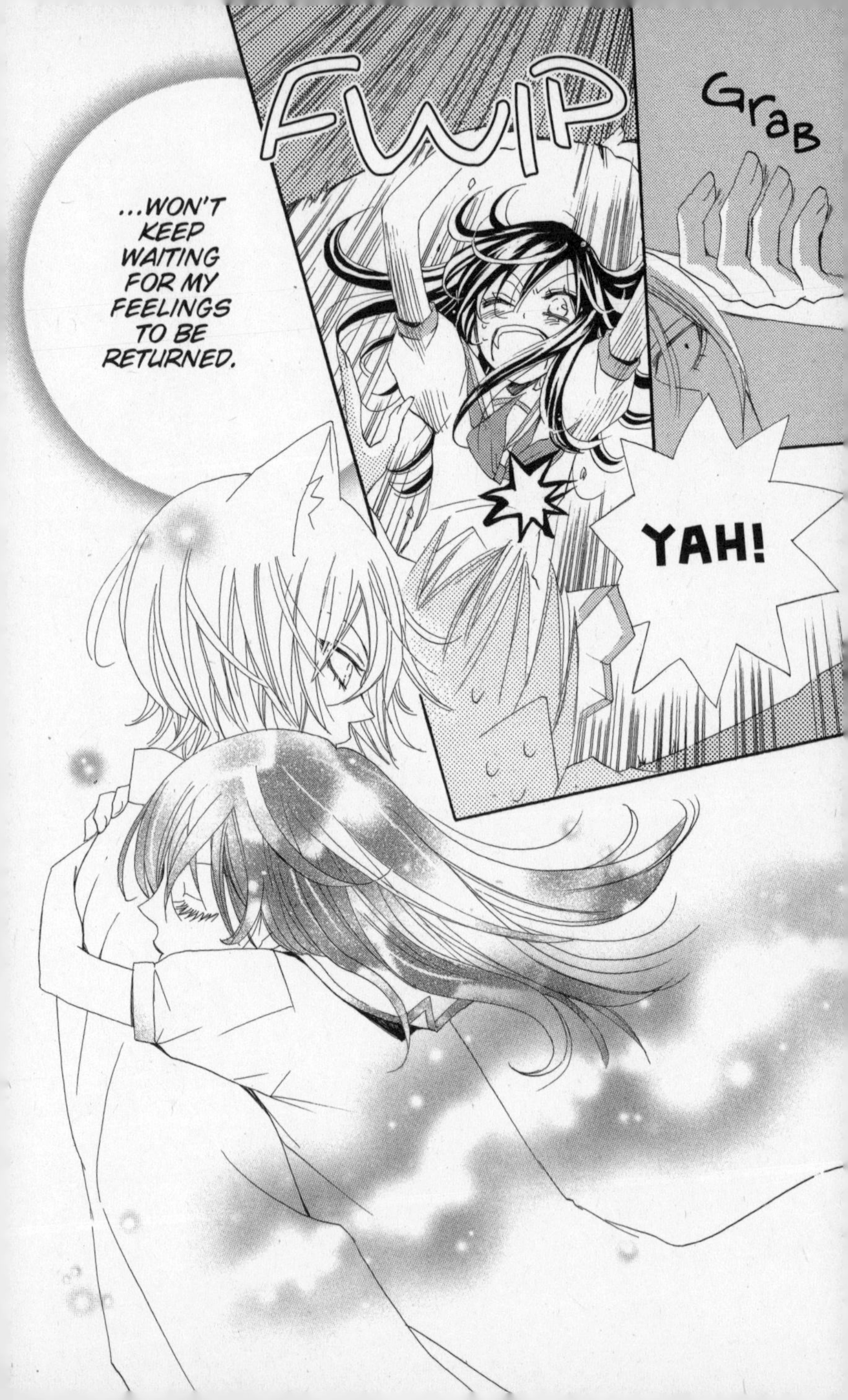
Grab
FWIP
YAH!
...WON'T KEEP WAITING FOR MY FEELINGS TO BE RETURNED.

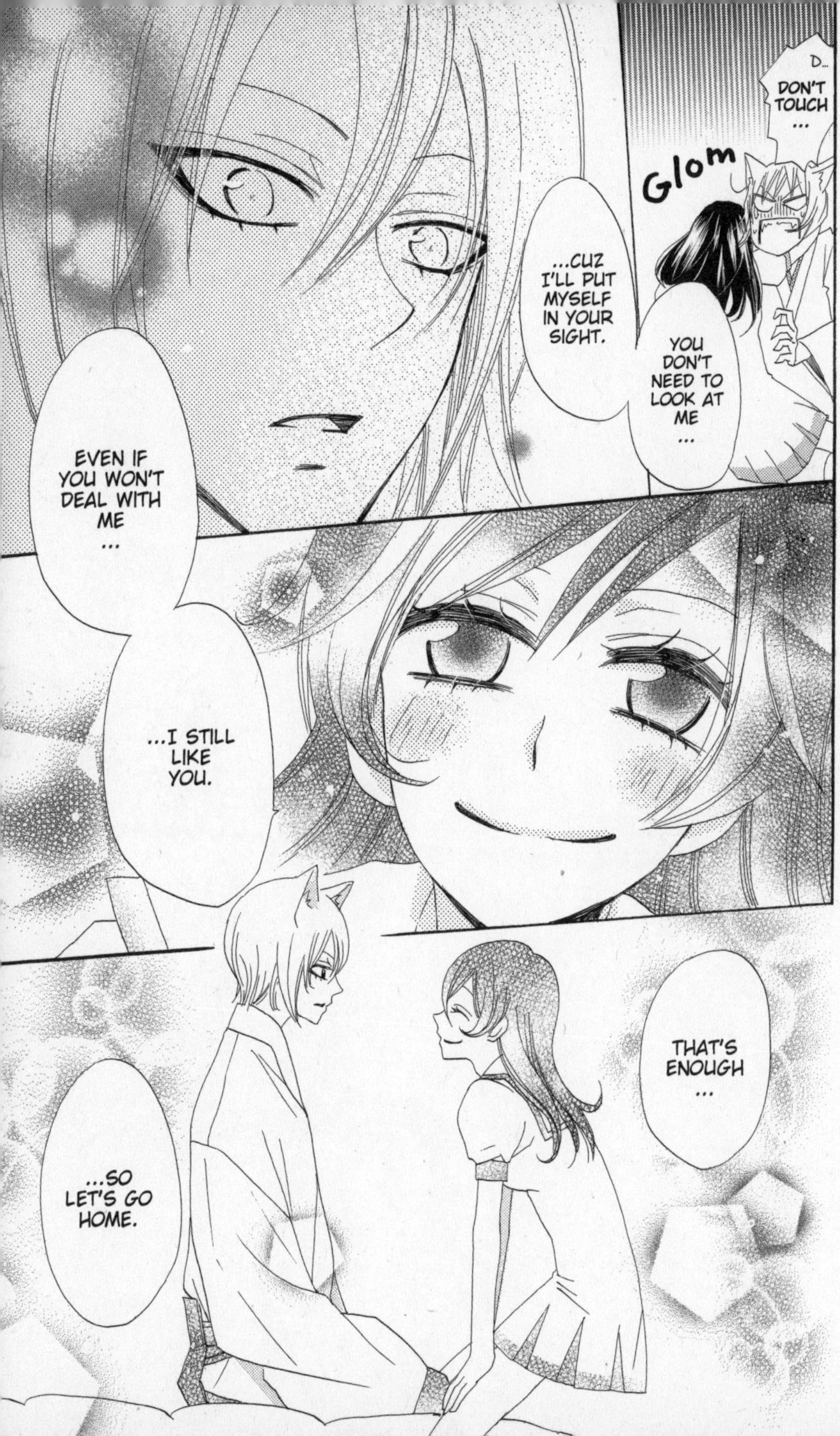
D... DON'T TOUCH ...
Glom
YOU DON'T NEED TO LOOK AT ME ...
...CUZ I'LL PUT MYSELF IN YOUR SIGHT.
EVEN IF YOU WON'T DEAL WITH ME ...
...I STILL LIKE YOU.
THAT'S ENOUGH ...
...SO LET'S GO HOME.

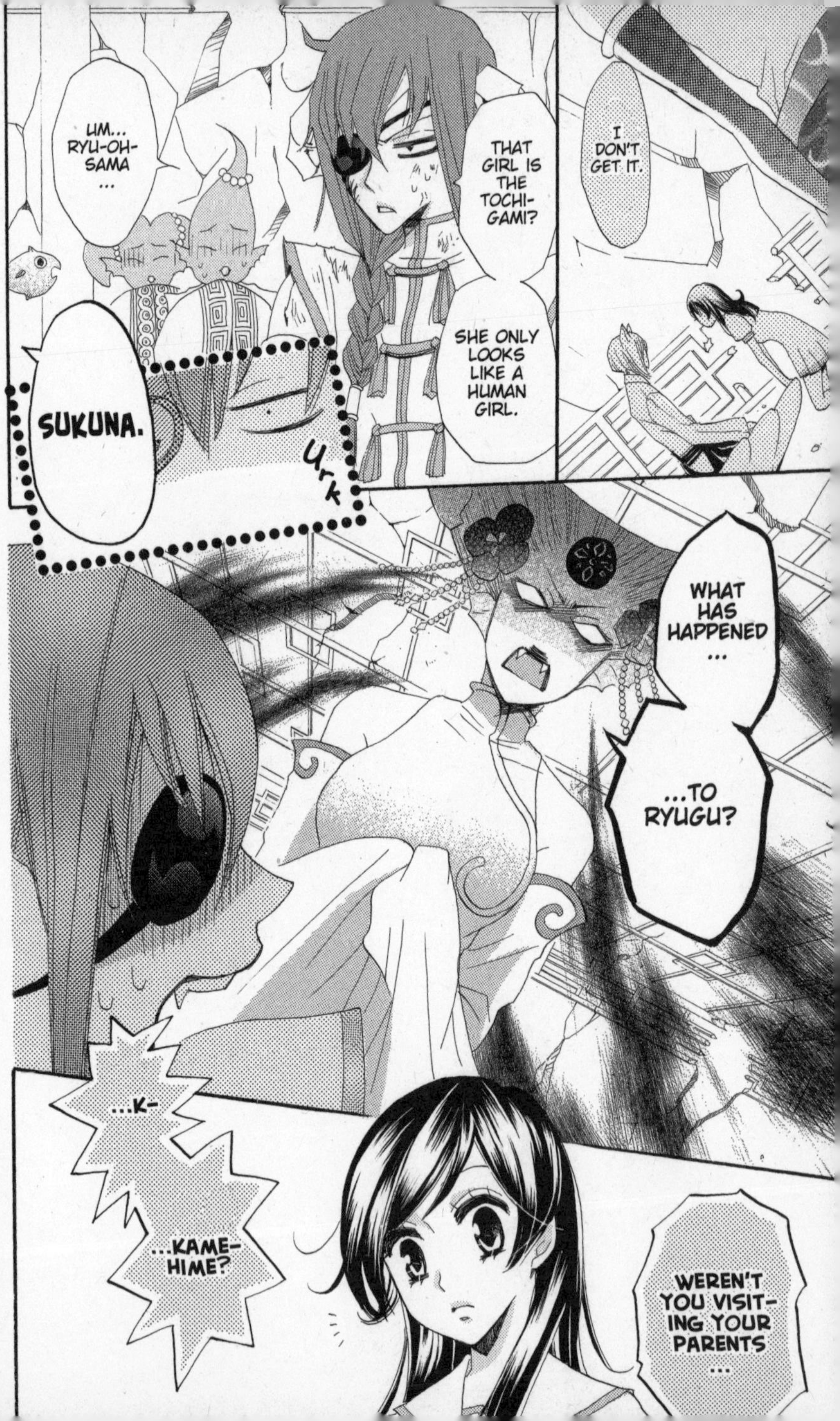
I DON'T GET IT.
THAT GIRL IS THE TOCHI-GAMI?
SHE ONLY LOOKS LIKE A HUMAN GIRL.
UM... RYU-OH-SAMA...
SUKUNA.
Urk
WHAT HAS HAPPENED...
...TO RYUGU?
...K-
...KAME-HIME?
WEREN'T YOU VISITING YOUR PARENTS...

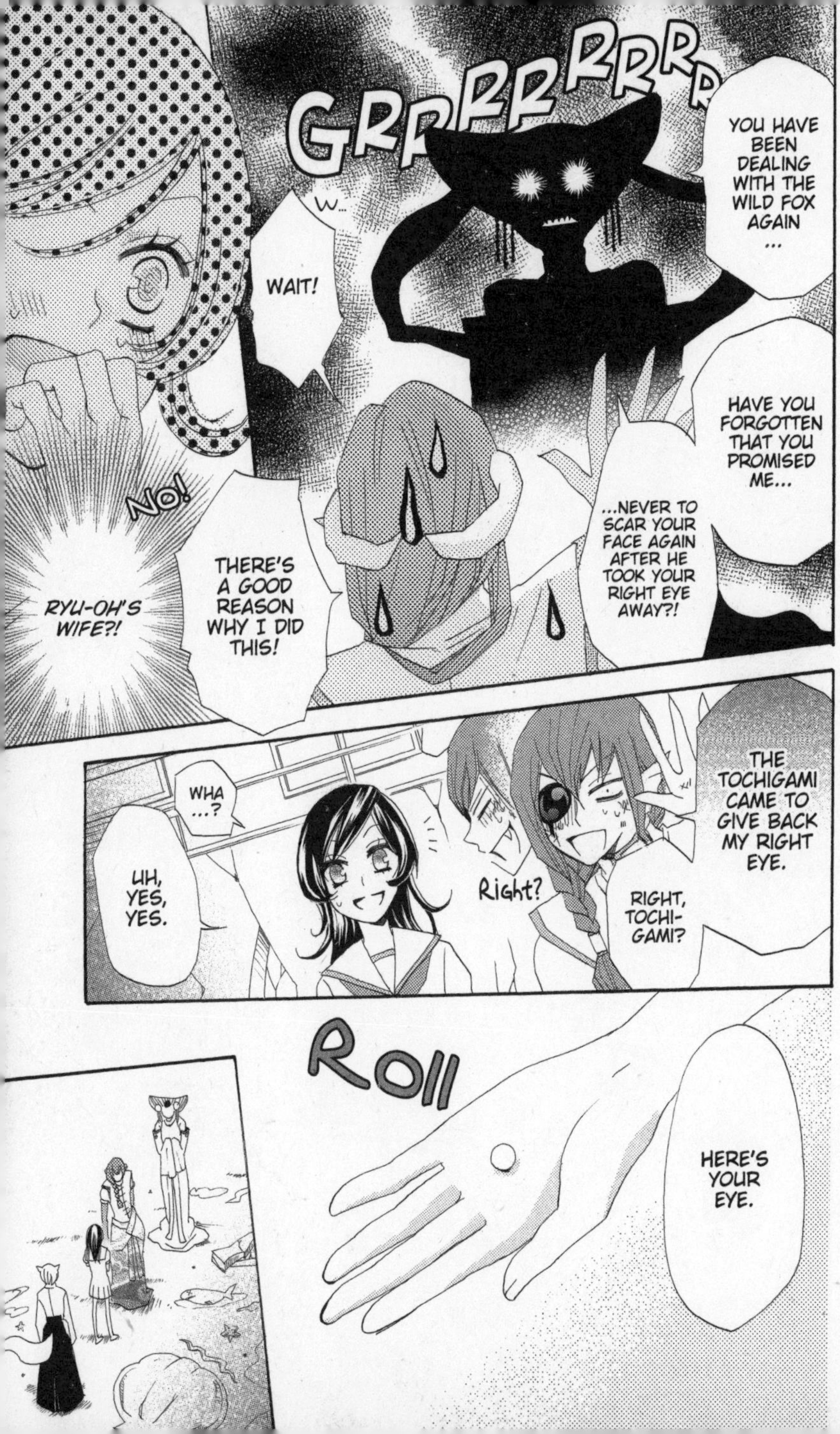
GRRRRRRRRR
YOU HAVE BEEN DEALING WITH THE WILD FOX AGAIN ...
W...
WAIT!
HAVE YOU FORGOTTEN THAT YOU PROMISED ME...
...NEVER TO SCAR YOUR FACE AGAIN AFTER HE TOOK YOUR RIGHT EYE AWAY?!
THERE'S A GOOD REASON WHY I DID THIS!
NO!
RYU-OH'S WIFE?!
THE TOCHIGAMI CAME TO GIVE BACK MY RIGHT EYE.
RIGHT, TOCHIGAMI?
Right?
WHA ...?
UH, YES, YES.
ROll
HERE'S YOUR EYE.

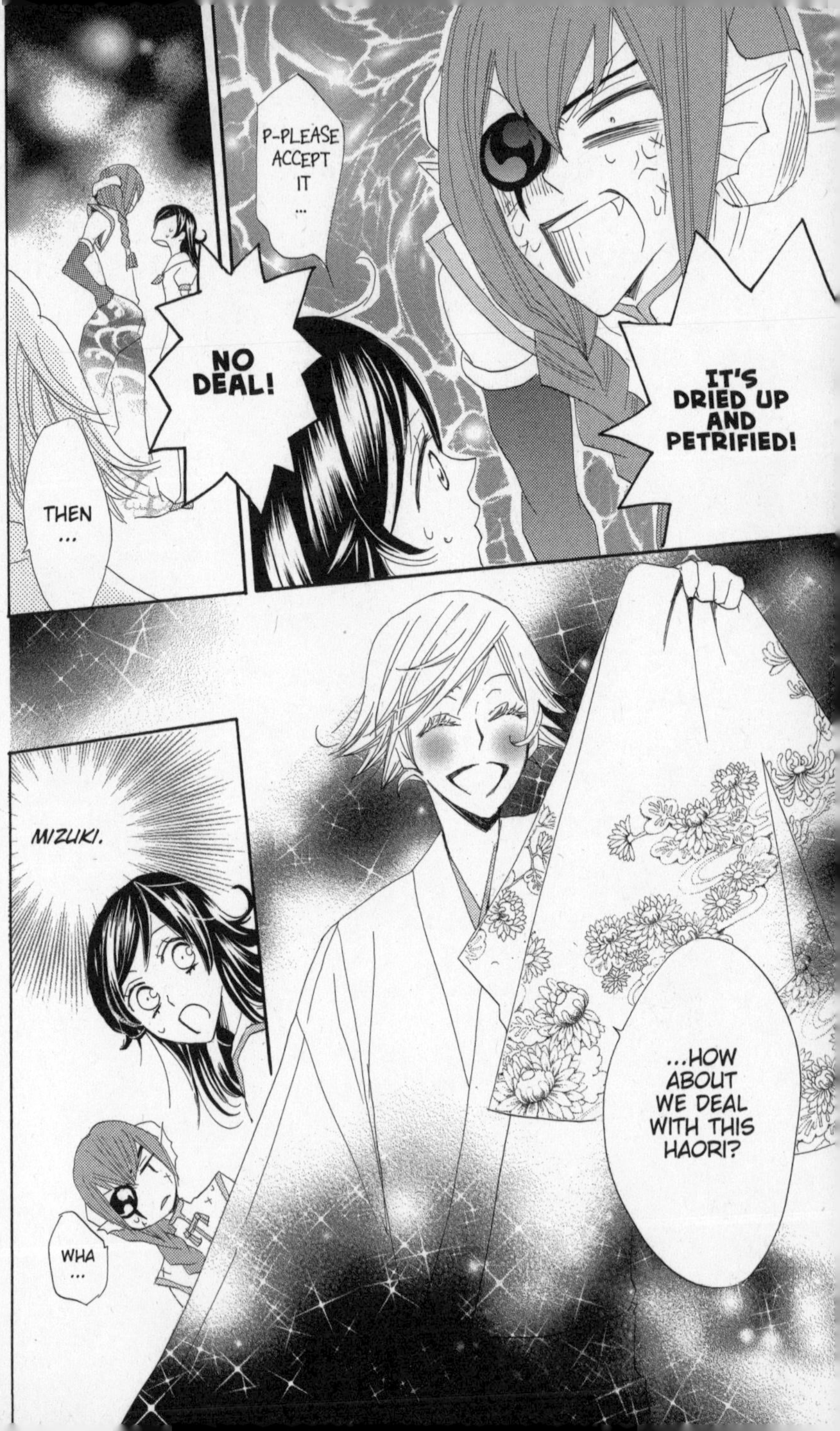
P-PLEASE ACCEPT IT ...
IT'S DRIED UP AND PETRIFIED!
NO DEAL!
THEN ...
...HOW ABOUT WE DEAL WITH THIS HAORI?
MIZUKI.
WHA ...

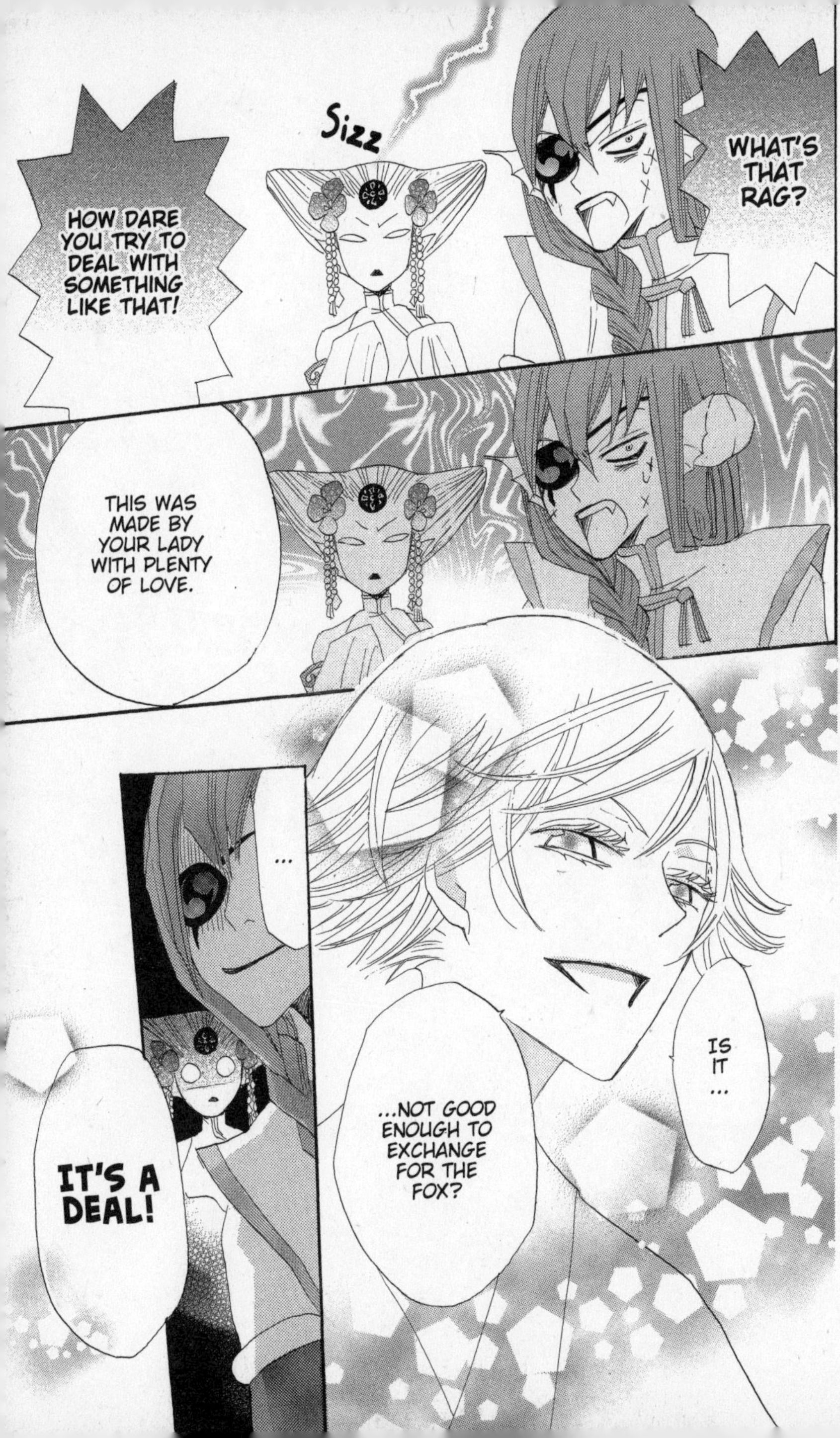
WHAT'S THAT RAG?
Sizz
HOW DARE YOU TRY TO DEAL WITH SOMETHING LIKE THAT!
THIS WAS MADE BY YOUR LADY WITH PLENTY OF LOVE.
IS IT ...
...NOT GOOD ENOUGH TO EXCHANGE FOR THE FOX?
...
IT'S A DEAL!

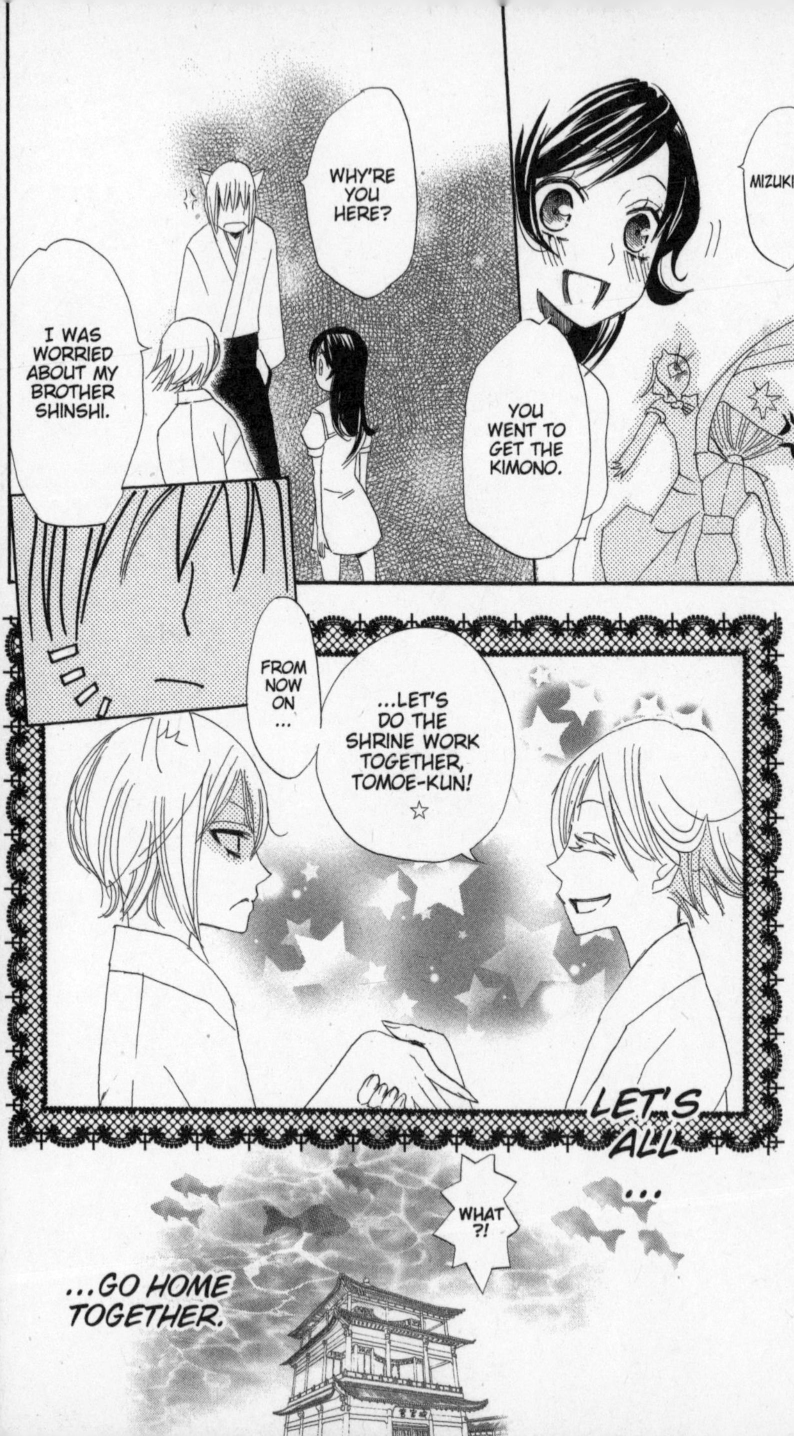
MIZUKI!
YOU WENT TO GET THE KIMONO.
WHY'RE YOU HERE?
I WAS WORRIED ABOUT MY BROTHER SHINSHI.
FROM NOW ON ...
...LET'S DO THE SHRINE WORK TOGETHER, TOMOE-KUN! ☆
LET'S ALL
...
WHAT ?!
...GO HOME TOGETHER.

The Otherworld

Ayakashi is an archaic term for yokai.

Kami are Shinto deities or spirits. The word can be used for a range of creatures, from nature spirits to strong and dangerous gods.

Tengu are a type of yokai. They are sometimes associated with excess pride.

Tsuriki is a kami's power and becomes stronger the more it is used.

Onibi-warashi are like will-o'-the-wisps.

Shinshi are birds, beasts, insects or fish that have a special relationship with a kami.

Yokai are demons, monsters or goblins.

Zashiki-warashi are yokai kami who dwell in the zashiki (tatami room or drawing room) of old houses or the warehouse of a home, and play pranks on the people who live there. It is said that seeing a zashiki-warashi will bring good fortune, and that the house where a zashiki-warashi lives will be blessed with wealth. Zashiki-warashi are said to exist mainly in Iwate Prefecture and the Tohoku area.

Honorifics

-sama is used with people of much higher rank.

Notes

Page 5, panel 3: Nikujaga
Meat, potatoes and other vegetables simmered in soy sauce, sugar and sake.

Page 50, panel 3: Ryugu Palace
The undersea palace of the dragon god Ryujin. In the fairy tale *Urashima Taro*, Taro is taken to Ryugu Palace as a reward for rescuing a turtle that was being bullied by kids. When Taro returns to his village, a few hundred years have passed.

Page 100, panel 1: Ryu-oh
Literally "dragon king."

Page 167, panel 1: Turtle cab
In the fairy tale *Urashima Taro*, the rescued turtle ferries Taro to Ryugu Palace.

Page 171, panel 3: Haori
A lightweight silk jacket that is worn over a kimono. It is traditionally a part of a man's formal outfit.

Julietta Suzuki's debut manga *Hoshi ni Naru Hi* (The Day One Becomes a Star) appeared in the 2004 *Hana to Yume Plus*. Her other books include *Akuma to Dolce* (The Devil and Sweets) and *Karakuri Odette*. Born in December in Fukuoka Prefecture, she enjoys having movies play in the background while she works on her manga.

KAMISAMA KISS
VOL. 4
Shojo Beat Edition

STORY AND ART BY
Julietta Suzuki

English Translation & Adaptation/Tomo Kimura
Touch-up Art & Lettering/Joanna Estep
Cover Design/Hidemi Dunn
Interior Design/Yukiko Whitley
Editor/Pancha Diaz

KAMISAMA HAJIMEMASHITA by Julietta Suzuki
© Julietta Suzuki 2009
All rights reserved.
First published in Japan in 2009 by HAKUSENSHA, Inc., Tokyo.
English language translation rights arranged with
HAKUSENSHA, Inc., Tokyo.

Published by VIZ Media, LLC
P.O. Box 77010
San Francisco, CA 94107

10 9 8 7 6 5 4
First printing, August 2011
Fourth printing, March 2015

www.viz.com

www.shojobeat.com

Ouran High School

Host Club BOX SET

Story and Art by
Bisco Hatori

Escape to the world of the young, rich and sexy

All 18 volumes
in a collector's box
with an Ouran High
School stationery
notepad!

n this screwball romantic
omedy, Haruhi, a poor girl at
rich kids' school, is forced to
epay an $80,000 debt by working
or the school's swankiest, all-
ale club—as a boy! There she
iscovers just how wealthy the six
embers are and how different
e rich are from everybody else...

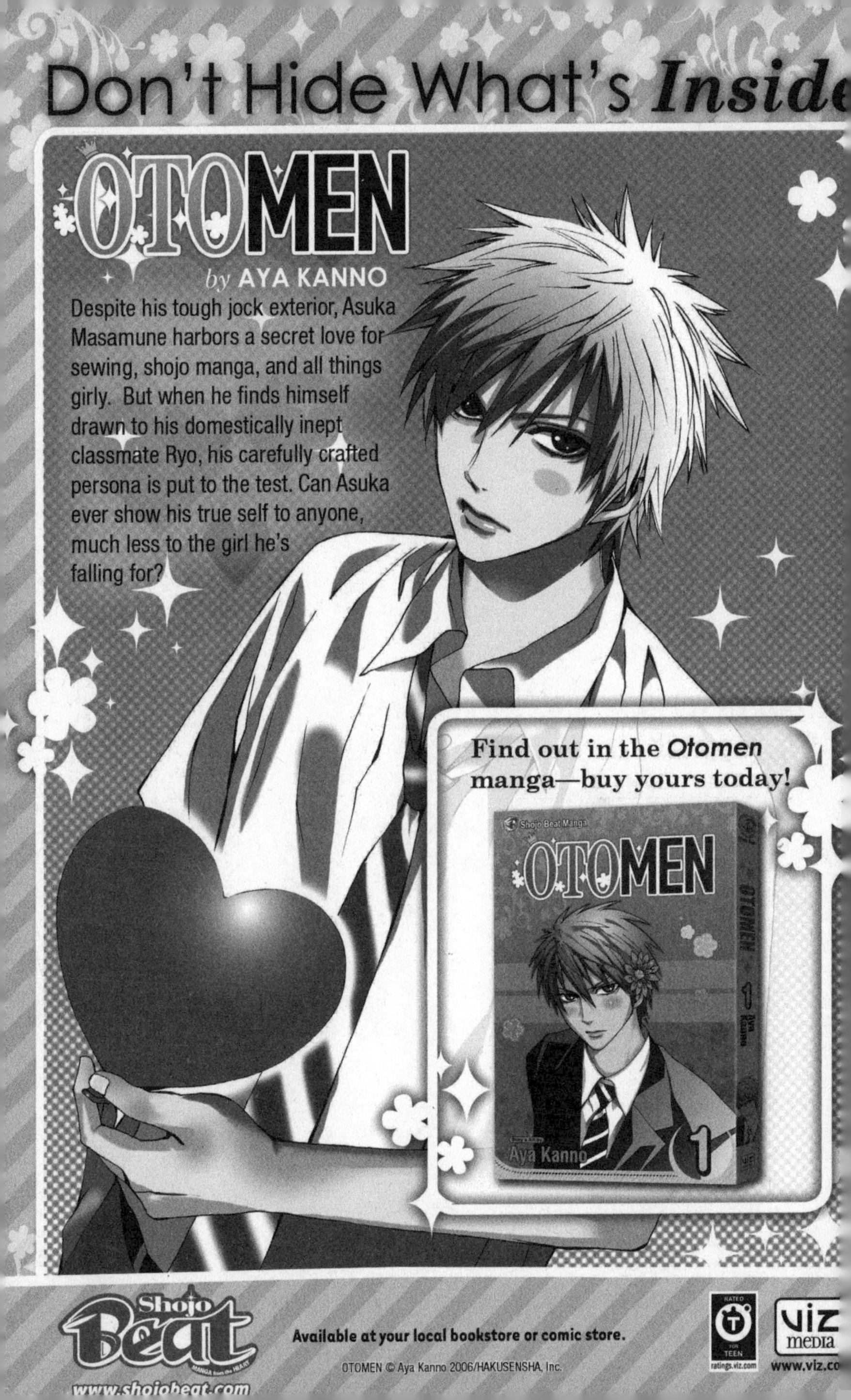

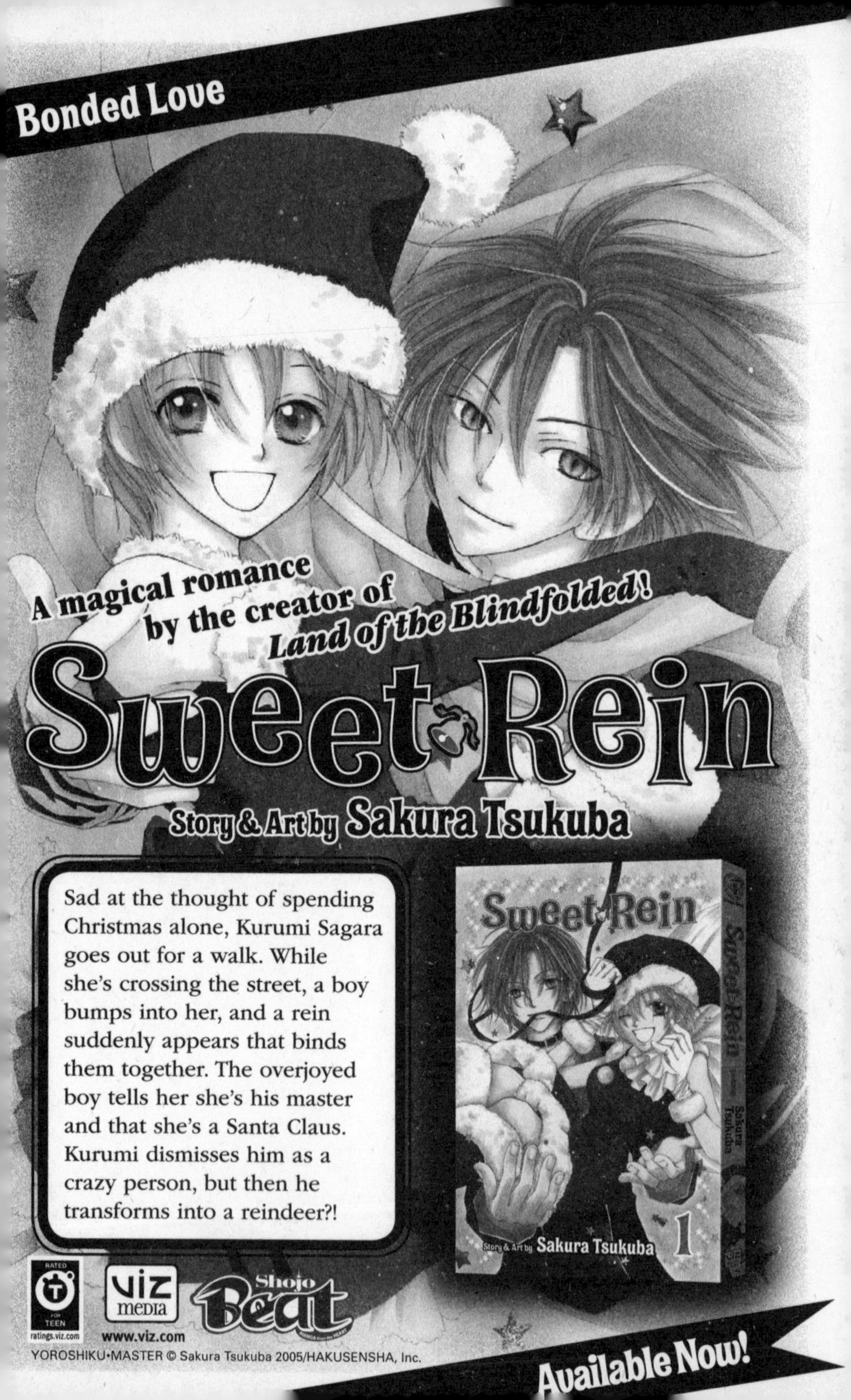
Bonded Love
A magical romance by the creator of Land of the Blindfolded!
Sweet Rein
Story & Art by Sakura Tsukuba
Sad at the thought of spending Christmas alone, Kurumi Sagara goes out for a walk. While she's crossing the street, a boy bumps into her, and a rein suddenly appears that binds them together. The overjoyed boy tells her she's his master and that she's a Santa Claus. Kurumi dismisses him as a crazy person, but then he transforms into a reindeer?!
Sweet Rein
Story & Art by Sakura Tsukuba
1
RATED T FOR TEEN
ratings.viz.com
viz media
Shojo Beat
www.viz.com
YOROSHIKU•MASTER © Sakura Tsukuba 2005/HAKUSENSHA, Inc.
Available Now!

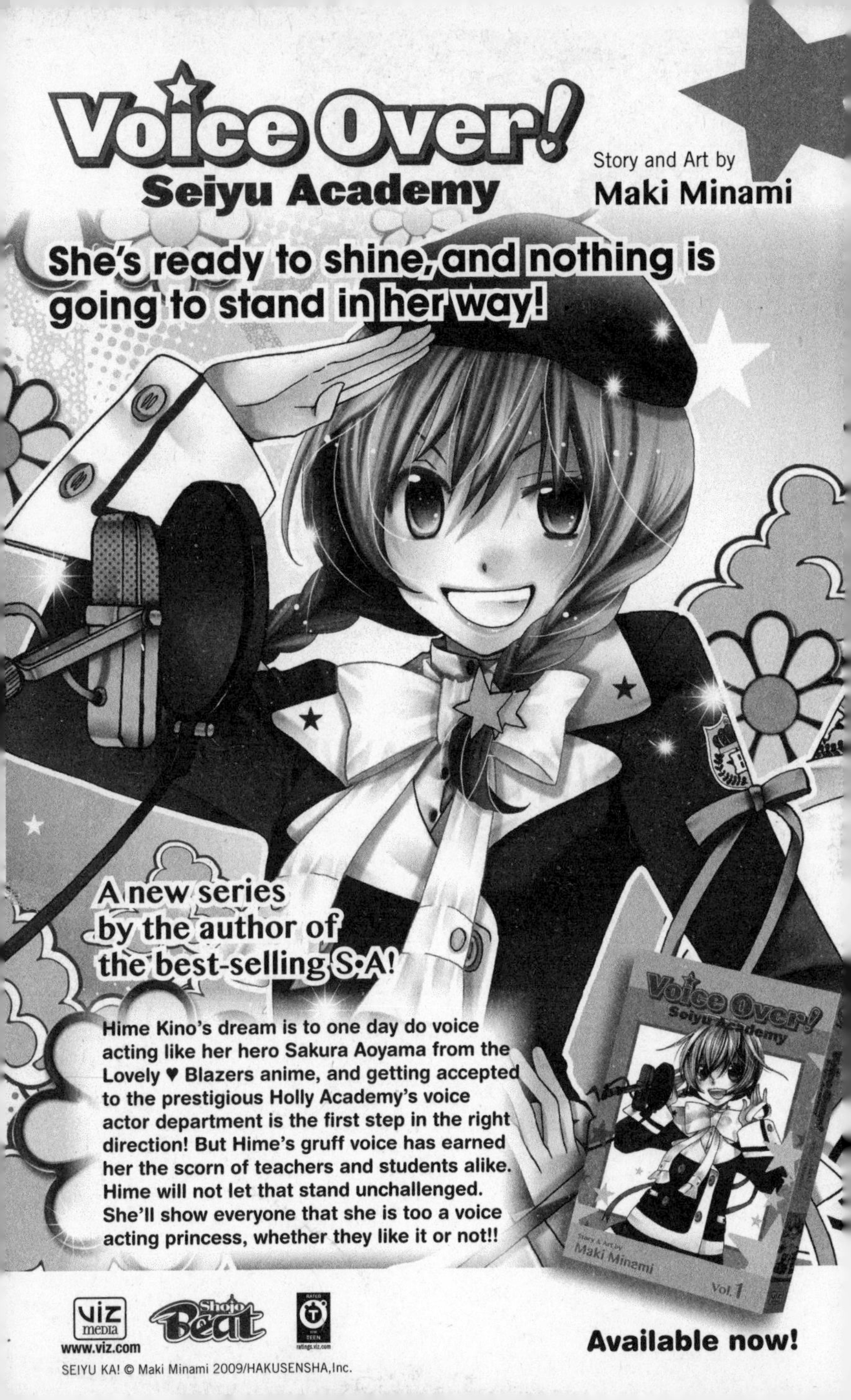

Voice Over!
Seiyu Academy
Story and Art by
Maki Minami
She's ready to shine, and nothing is going to stand in her way!
A new series by the author of the best-selling S•A!
Hime Kino's dream is to one day do voice acting like her hero Sakura Aoyama from the Lovely ♥ Blazers anime, and getting accepted to the prestigious Holly Academy's voice actor department is the first step in the right direction! But Hime's gruff voice has earned her the scorn of teachers and students alike. Hime will not let that stand unchallenged. She'll show everyone that she is too a voice acting princess, whether they like it or not!!
Voice Over! Seiyu Academy
Story & Art by
Maki Minami
Vol. 1
viz media
www.viz.com
Shojo Beat
T TEEN
ratings.viz.com
Available now!
SEIYU KA! © Maki Minami 2009/HAKUSENSHA,Inc.

This is the last page.

In keeping with the original Japanese comic format, this book reads from right to left—so action, sound effects, and word balloons are completely reversed. This preserves the orientation of the original artwork—plus, it's fun! Check out the diagram shown here to get the hang of things, and then turn to the other side of the book to get started!